Voyage to Discovery

VOYAGE TO DISCOVERY

An Activity Guide to the Age of Exploration

Diane P. Ramsay

Illustrated by
Marsha M. Gleason

1992
TEACHER IDEAS PRESS
A Division of
Libraries Unlimited, Inc.
Englewood, Colorado

This book is dedicated with love to my husband John for all his work in keeping the computers operating, our children fed, and me up and running—D.P.R.

To my family, in appreciation for their understanding and patience during this project—M.M.G.

TEACHER IDEAS PRESS
A Division of
Libraries Unlimited, Inc.
P.O. Box 6633
Englewood, CO 80155-6633

Library of Congress Cataloging-in-Publication Data

Ramsay, Diane P.
Voyage to discovery : an activity guide to the age of exploration / Diane P. Ramsay ; illustrated by Marsha M. Gleason.
xiii, 346 p. 22x28 cm.
Includes bibliographical references and index.
ISBN 1-56308-063-X
1. Discoveries in geography. 2. Explorers. 3. Activity programs in education. I. Title.
G81.R36 1992
910.9--dc20 92-27424
CIP

Contents

Preface

Humans have always been restless creatures. From the earliest records we have, we can see that human history has been a series of journeys to new places and new ways of doing things. For better or worse, the concept of progress, of moving from where we are to somewhere else, seems intrinsic to who we are.

Ancient history offers countless examples of this restless spirit. The earliest people were constantly on the move following game animals to new areas of the world, such as the Stone Age nomads who crossed the Bering Strait to the North American continent. The empire building of Alexander the Great and the raids of the Vikings are part of this history. During the centuries immediately before and after the birth of Jesus Christ, new civilizations, new methods of government, new religions, and new ways of life developed. Except for a brief hiatus during the so-called Dark Ages, when the European world seemed frozen, this quest for new ideas and new ways of doing things has continued. Even during the Dark Ages there were always a few restless spirits on the move: knights traveling on Crusades, merchants following trade routes, pilgrims visiting religious shrines, and barbarians insidiously moving into new territory.

At the same time, the peoples of the American continents were also on the move, eventually traveling from present-day Alaska to the tip of South America. Great civilizations rose and fell. Though our information is not as complete for pre-Columbian America as it is for Europe, archaeology has provided tantalizing clues of development during this early age.

In the fifteenth century came the great Age of Exploration when lasting contact was made between the Old World and the New. This meeting of two worlds has given rise to the world we live in today. Though it appears at first glance that the restless searching of the Age of Exploration ended with the mapping of the entire globe in the twentieth century, we are on the move now more than ever. The world truly has become a global village where cultures that once were the stuff of exotic legends are now our next-door neighbors. And the thirst to comprehend the unknown is still with us. We constantly strive to learn more about our world, about our origins, and about what lies under the sea, out in space, and in the future.

Plans to celebrate the 500th anniversary of Columbus's voyage to the New World have met with controversy. Many people have argued that rather than celebrate, we would do better to let these events fade into obscurity because of the frequently disastrous results that befell that indigenous populations. However, if we are to learn anything from the mistakes of the past, we need to look at what our predecessors did, understand their motivations, recognize their shortsightedness, and try to do better. Though we are certainly not perfect, in many ways our treatment of each other has improved over the centuries, perhaps in part by learning from the mistakes of our past.

The great explorers such as Columbus accomplished amazing feats and changed the world forever. They also made some decisions that were to have tragic results, as did indigenous groups involved in these epic events. No one group can hold itself blameless for the course of history. Often a series of actions were taken for immediate gain with no consideration for future consequences. Rather than sit in judgment, it is important to look at the past and to try to avoid repeating the same kinds of mistakes in the future.

It is not necessary to feel a sense of celebration as we approach the 500th anniversary of Columbus's voyage, but we should have a sense of commemoration. Few people in the world today are unaffected by the monumental meeting of the Old and New Worlds. In my immediate family the impact can be seen. My oldest son is a mestizo from Central America, an ethnic product of the mixing of the natives of the West Indies, and the Spanish conquerors (with African influence, sometimes). In Central America today, they celebrate not Columbus Day, but El Día de la Raza, the Day of the People (*raza* means race in terms of people, not competition). My ancestors were Irish who came to this country after the potato blight hit Ireland in the 1840s. However, this migration would not have occurred unless Columbus had traveled to the New World first. One of the consequences of his voyage was the introduction of potatoes, along with a variety of other new foods, to the Old World.

Humans have come a long way, and no one knows how much farther we are going. If the human spirit basically seeks forward movement, it may seem of little worth to look back at our past. But the Age of Exploration has much to teach us that is crucial to our future progress.

HOW TO USE THIS BOOK

Part of the need to explore is the need to know. This is as true for the children we teach today as it was for the Phoenicians or the Vikings. If we can tap children's curiosity, exploit their thirst for knowledge, and present them with the opportunity to explore the unknown, our job as teachers becomes that of navigator.

Preschool children need concrete activities that enable them to understand the experiences of taking a boat on the water, going someplace unknown, and discovering new things. Primary school children need activities that involve them in the thoughts and emotions of the people who lived long ago. These children need to put themselves in the place of an explorer and "experience" these adventures for themselves. Intermediate students are ready to go beyond learning about facts and feelings to analyzing and evaluating the information. They need to confront the various moral dilemmas the explorers faced and decide for themselves what they might have done in a similar situation. These activities will help children develop the ability to think critically so that in learning about history they are able to bring a healthy skepticism to their studies. Through the application of problem-solving and decision-making skills, they will be able to use what they learn to form their own opinions and beliefs.

Children's literature provides the materials to present history as an exciting search. We are not limited today to dry textbooks and the memorization of dates and names. Children's nonfiction collections include many books full of beautiful illustrations and exciting, well-written text. Fiction and picture books also have much to offer in our search for ways to make history live. A book that provides insight into how someone felt in a particular situation can trigger emotional responses in children that are an important part of learning. Though identifying with historical figures as human beings may not help children remember the date of a particular event, it will help them to understand and remember the meaning of that event.

This book is organized chronologically from ancient times through Columbus's voyage and briefly touches on the explorers who came after him. Each chapter includes an introduction to the topic covered to help teachers and librarians in presenting the material. The introduction is followed by a list of resources. A number of books are included because not every library collection is the same. If you cannot find one of the books on a list, you probably can find others. All of the resources are listed separately at the back of the book.

Following each set of resources is a variety of activities including games, songs, creative dramatics, writing projects, crafts, and group discussions. Such activities not only make historical events more meaningful, but they also make the process of learning enjoyable.

The resources and activities are coded for the appropriate age level, but remember that these levels are suggestions only. Many activities can be used with children older or younger than the age stated, depending both on the group and on the way the material is presented. Read through the whole section and then choose the most appealing activities. Your own enthusiasm will provide a spark for your students' interest.

Many of the activities are ideal for classroom settings, and librarians will also find much that they can use. Many books and activities can be used in a story-hour setting. For example, with preschoolers, you could offer a storytime series on the topics of exploration, knights, boats, sea creatures, pirates, and outer space. For older children, combine books, games, songs, and crafts to create an activity program. Use the book lists to help with book displays, and share the lists with teachers. In addition, many libraries offer reading programs, not just in the summer but year-round. The exploration theme is a natural for such a program.

Whether you are a teacher, a librarian, an interested parent, or an adult working with children, mix your creativity and enthusiasm for teaching into your programs and lessons and you and your students will be set for your own "age of exploration."

ACKNOWLEDGMENTS

Several people were especially helpful while I was working on this book. I thank Marsha Gleason for taking a chance with me. I'd like to thank my sister Paula Polk for letting me use the Wilbraham library collection for my research and for reading the manuscript and offering suggestions. Jane Dutton, children's librarian of the Gale Free Library in Holden, Massachusetts, was indispensable. She was constantly on the watch for materials I could use and let me use her collection, as well. The staff of the Auburn Public Library deserve a medal for allowing me to practically move in and ransack their collection. I also used the collections of the Northborough and Shrewsbury Public Libraries extensively. In fact, this book could not have been written and could not be used without libraries.

1

The Spirit of Exploration

Exploration encompasses more than just the examination of a physical place we have never been before. There are many kinds of explorers besides those who explore new lands, such as Marco Polo. There are also inventors, such as Thomas Edison, whose spirit of exploration leads them to create new ways of doing things. There are those who attempt to accomplish things never done before, such as Amelia Earhart and her attempted flight around the world at the equator. And there are discoverers of new ideas, people who change the very way we think about our world, such as Albert Einstein.

What is the source of humanity's drive to explore the world, a drive exemplified by Christopher Columbus? In simple terms, Columbus was curious about the world, he imagined a great enterprise, and he had the determination and creativity to see the effort through. In addition, he was restless, ambitious, and competitive. These qualities are embodied in the spirit of exploration.

All the explorers mentioned here had these qualities. An explorer is an innovator and an inventor with the imagination to think of new ideas and new ways of doing things. Explorers need curiosity, the desire to learn new information. And they need the creativity to make ideas come alive. They must be restless enough to be discontented with where they are and with the way things are. They need a certain amount of ambition and competitiveness to push them to meet their goals. And finally, in our modern age explorers need understanding and tolerance to examine, protect, and nourish the new lands, people, and ideas they find and share. (Such understanding and tolerance were rare during the Age of Exploration.)

EXPLORATION

Exploration is visiting someplace we have never been. Children usually think of exploring this way—as a trip to strange, exotic places. Although we examine other aspects of the spirit of exploration later, we start with the fun of pretending we are bona fide explorers off to investigate the unknown.

Book List

Aitken, Amy. *Kate and Mona in the Jungle*. Bradbury, 1981. (PreK-2)
Two friends visit the zoo and turn the trip into an imaginary exploration of the jungle.

Baker, Leslie. *Third-Story Cat*. Little, Brown, 1987. (PreK-1)
The cat in this story has a day out of the house to explore the world.

Blos, Joan. *Martin's Hats*. Morrow, 1984. (PreK-3)
Martin explores the world wearing a variety of hats.

Bodsworth, Nan. *A Nice Walk in the Jungle*. Viking, 1990. (K-2)
A class of children explore the jungle with their teacher.

Burningham, John. *Where's Julius?* Crown, 1986. (PreK-3)
Julius is unable to come to the dinner table because he is too busy exploring.

Jonas, Ann. *The Trek*. Greenwillow, 1985. (K-3)
A child describes her trip through a jungle and across a desert—all on the way to school.

Lingelbach, Jenepher. *Hands-On Nature: Information and Activities for Exploring the Environment with Children*. Vermont Institute of Natural Science, 1986. (All ages)
A wide variety of ways to explore nature.

Lionni, Leo. *I Want to Stay Here! I Want to Go There!* Pantheon, 1977. (PreK-2)
Two fleas, one who loves to travel and one who prefers to stay home, decide to go their separate ways.

Milord, Susan. *The Kids' Nature Book*. Williamson, 1989. (Gr. 2-up)
A book of indoor and outdoor activities and explorations.

Moerbeek, Kees. *Six Brave Explorers*. Price Stern Sloan, 1988. (PreK-1)
A pop-up book about six mountain explorers.

Moses, Amy. *I Am an Explorer*. Children's Press, 1990. (PreK-2)
A young boy pretends to be an explorer on his way to the park.

Newsham, Ian, and Wendy Newsham. *Lost in the Jungle*. Kaye & Ward, 1984. (PreK-1)
When a young explorer gets lost, he meets animals from all around the world.

Redleaf, Rhoda. *Open the Door, Let's Explore: Neighborhood Field Trips for Young Children*. Toys 'n Things Press, 1983. (Adult)
This is an excellent resource for planning field trips for young children.

Seymour, Peter. *What's in the Jungle?* Henry Holt, 1988. (PreK-2)
A pop-up book about exploring the jungle.

Shaffer, Carolyn, and Erica Fielder. *City Safaris: A Sierra Club Explorer's Guide to Urban Adventures for Grownups and Kids*. Sierra Club, 1987. (Gr. 3-up)
A book on how to explore the environment.

Silverstein, Shel. *Where the Sidewalk Ends*. Harper & Row, 1974. (Gr. 2-up)
This collection includes the poem "The Search."

Smith, Jim. *Nimbus the Explorer*. Little, Brown, 1981. (K-3)
When Nimbus explores the jungle, he finds some surprises.

Smyth, Gwenda. *A Pet for Mrs. Arbuckle*. Crown, 1981. (PreK-2)
Mrs. Arbuckle explores the world before finding the perfect pet.

Steig, William. *The Zabajaba Jungle*. Farrar, Straus & Giroux, 1991. (Gr. 1-4)
A young boy has a variety of adventures in the Zabajaba jungle.

Taylor, Mark. *Henry Explores the Jungle*. Atheneum, 1968. (PreK-2)
Henry sets off on safari to discover jungle animals.

Titherington, Jeanne. *Where Are You Going, Emma?* Greenwillow, 1988. (PreK)
While apple picking with her grandfather, Emma enjoys exploring on her own.

Watanabe, Shigeo. *I Can Take a Walk!* Putnam, 1984. (PreK)
The little bear in this book imaginatively explores his neighborhood but is still glad to see his father.

Related Activities

1. Share the picture books *A Nice Walk in the Jungle* by Nan Bodsworth, *Where's Julius?* by John Burningham, *What's in the Jungle?* by Peter Seymour, and *A Pet for Mrs. Arbuckle* by Gwenda Smyth. Then start an explorers' book club, to be held for the next few weeks. You will need to make a spinner or have slips of paper to draw from a hat, with a variety of topics to explore, such as "Biographies of Real Explorers," "Books about Exploration in Outer Space," "Books about Undersea Exploration," "Books about Inventors and Inventions," "Geography Books Describing Other Countries," and "Books about Searches and Quests." Let the children take turns selecting a reading destination. Then help them find books on the topics they choose. For each book they read, they could receive a clue for the explorer's search (activity 2).
(Primary, intermediate)

2. Read a couple of books about lost explorers, such as *Lost in the Jungle* by Ian and Wendy Newsham and *The Zabajaba Jungle* by William Steig. Hold an explorer's search. Start by creating a lifesize figure of an explorer. You can either borrow a mannequin from a local store and dress it as an explorer or create a figure from cardboard. To make the cardboard figure, have someone lie down, draw around his or her body, and then attach the explorer's face (fig. 1.1) to the cardboard. Hide the explorer somewhere in your school, library, or other public building in town. Next, devise a series of clues to help participants find the explorer. For example, "Explorers are smart, they know their art" could be a clue to lead the searchers to the art department, where they would find the next clue. If possible, purchase a field guide, map, backpack, or binoculars to give as a prize for the student who finds the lost explorer first.
(Primary, intermediate)

Fig. 1.1.

3. Share *Six Brave Explorers* (Kees Moerbeek) and *Henry Explores the Jungle* (Mark Taylor) and ask the children to imagine themselves in a scene from one of the books. Now, make a picture of an explorer on a large piece of cardboard, but cut out an opening where the face should be (see fig. 1.2). Decorate the picture with a pith helmet and an explorer's outfit. The children can take turns standing behind the frame with their faces in the opening, to actually appear as explorers. Take pictures with an instant camera.
(Preschool, primary)

Fig. 1.2.

4. Read Joan Blos's *Martin's Hats*, about a boy who dresses up to explore various occupations. Then have the children dress up as explorers in pith helmets and binoculars. To make binoculars, each child will need two toilet paper rolls, which can either be decorated with markers or covered with construction paper. Black paper would probably look most authentic. Glue the two rolls together. Then thread a string through each tube, as shown in figure 1.3, long enough to go over the child's head.
(Preschool, primary)

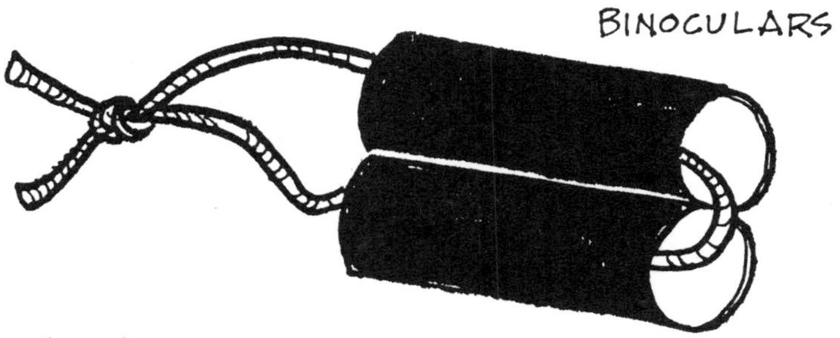

Fig. 1.3.

5. Plan a field trip around the neighborhood to explore a park, woods, or other interesting location. Pretend you will be out in the wilds for at least a week. As a group, decide where you are going, what provisions you will need, what equipment you will take, how and where you will sleep, and how you will protect yourselves. Use the books listed above by Lingelbach, Milord, Redleaf, and Shaffer and Fielder, to help you plan your trip.
(Primary, intermediate)

6. Read the book *I Am an Explorer* by Amy Moses. Then give the children copies of the explorer finger puppets (fig. 1.4) to color and cut out. They can use these puppets to act out explorations. (Preschool, primary)

Fig. 1.4.

7. Read Leslie Baker's *Third-Story Cat*, about a cat that finally gets out into the world. Then ask the children to each tell about a place they want to explore someday but that they have not been to yet. These destinations could be places such as Disneyworld, kindergarten, the park by themselves, or another exciting location. Have them draw pictures of the places they would like to explore. (Preschool, primary)

8. Read Jeanne Titherington's book *Where Are You Going, Emma?* about a little girl who explores the orchard on her own. Ask the children to describe someplace new that they have recently visited. If possible, have them bring in an object from this exploration for "show-and-tell." (Preschool)

9. Read Shigeo Watanabe's book *I Can Take a Walk*, about a little bear and the exciting walk through his neighborhood that he creates in his imagination. Then act out the following action story with the children. Feel free to add your own actions.
(Preschool, primary)

Exploring

We're going exploring! This is a new land that no one has visited before. We need our maps, our binoculars, a camera to record what we find, and a backpack of food. *(Pretend to gather these items.)* Here we go! *(Pretend to walk by slapping your palms on your thighs.)* I'm not afraid! Are you? Noooo! Whew! It's hot! *(Wipe forehead.)* Oh, no, we're coming to a swamp! We can't go over it, we can't go under it, so we'll have to go through it. I hope there are no snakes! Squish, squish, squish. *(Pretend to be struggling through thick mud.)* Oh, good! Here's dry land again. Let's go through this tall grass. Swish, swish, swish. *(Pretend to be pushing through tall grass.)* I wonder if there's a river near here. Let's climb this tree to look. *(Pretend to climb tree.)* Hold up your binoculars. *(Make circles with your hands and hold them up to your eyes.)* Yes! I see a river. Let's climb down and run to it. *(Pretend to climb down the tree and run.)* Now that we're here by the river, let's stop and have lunch. *(Sit down.)* Open your packs. I have tuna fish. What do you have? *(Pretend to eat.)* I'm thirsty! Glug, glug, glug. *(Pretend to drink.)* Ouch! A mosquito! *(Slap cheek.)* I think it's time to go. How will we cross the river? Oh, here's a canoe. *(Pretend to climb into a canoe.)* Let's paddle. *(Pretend to paddle the canoe.)* Okay, let's tie up the canoe in case we need it again. *(Pretend to tie up canoe.)* It's getting hilly. Look up there! *(Shield eyes from sun with hand.)* What a big mountain! Shall we climb it? *(Pretend to climb.)* Okay. *(Catch your breath.)* Now that we're up here, let's take a picture! *(Pretend to take a picture.)* What a beautiful spot! *(Gasp.)* Oh, dear, here comes a bear! We'd better run! Let's climb down the mountain. *(Pretend to climb down.)* Grab the canoe! *(Pretend to untie and climb into the canoe.)* Paddle as fast as you can! *(Pretend to paddle rapidly.)* Here we go through the tall grass. Swish, swish, swish. Now we go back through the swamp! We're almost home! *(Pretend to run.)* Home! Whew, it's good to be back! Is everyone here? *(Count the group.)* Do you have your packs, binoculars, and cameras? *(Check for gear.)* Great! Let's rest. *(Lean back and close eyes.)*

10. Read *Nimbus the Explorer* by Jim Smith, and play the game Explorer. Tape a piece of paper with the name of a different country to each child's back. On a signal, all the children go around the room trying to write down the names of the countries on the other players' backs. The children twist and turn to prevent the other players from "discovering" their countries. After ten minutes the group sits down. Each player takes off the piece of paper and announces his or her country to the group. The player who has discovered the most countries is the winner.
(Primary, intermediate)

11. Read Shel Silverstein's poem "The Search." Have a group discussion about what the poem means.
(Primary, intermediate)

12. Read Leo Lionni's book *I Want to Stay Here! I Want to Go There!* Then use enlargements of the patterns in figure 1.5 for the children to create "Armchair Explorers," who explore only in their imaginations as they sit in comfort. Let the children color the living room scene and cut out the picture window. Then, on the second sheet, have children draw four scenes of places they would like to explore. Cut around the outline of the travel scenes, and place this sheet behind the living room page so that the exploration pictures appear in the picture window. Attach the two sheets with a paper brad, so the children can change the scene by turning the back page.
(Preschool, primary)

13. Read Amy Aitken's *Kate and Mona in the Jungle* and Ann Jonas's *The Trek*, in which the characters turn ordinary trips into adventurous explorations. Ask the children in your group to create the same kind of treks in their imaginations on their next walk home and then to write about their trips. Encourage children to include drawings and make picture books to share with the group.
(Primary, intermediate)

14. Set up a modern travel agency for explorers. Ask the group to create a list of current issues and events that need to be explored, such as issues on outer space, the environment, or medicine. Then let each child pick a "destination" from the list and "explore" it. Have them report back to the group about what they learned on their "trip."
(Intermediate)

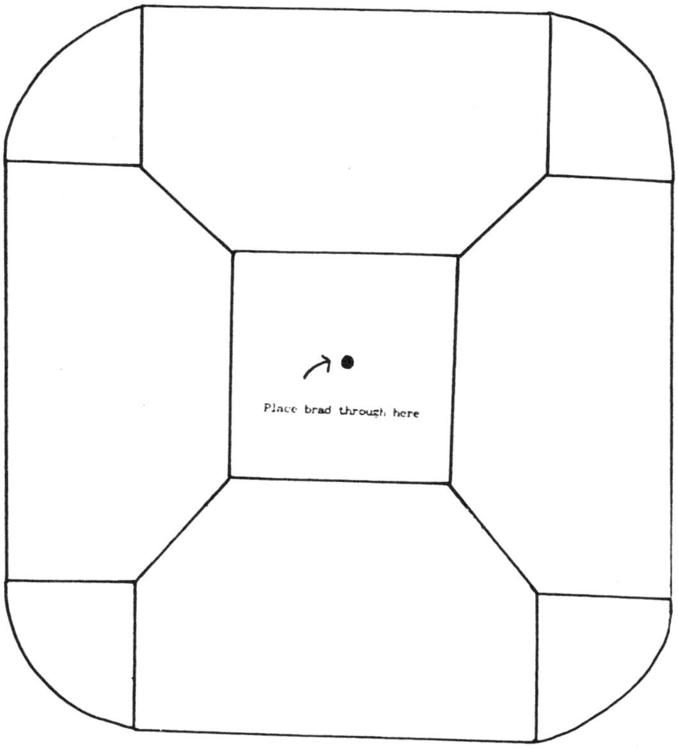

Fig. 1.5.

IMAGINATION

Imagination allows us to dream of things that have never existed. Imagination means thinking of new ideas and new ways of doing things. It is the ability we have to create something in our minds that has never existed in reality. Sometimes imagination is used for invention; Eli Whitney imagined an easier way of processing cotton. Sometimes imagination is used to create a world that lives and breathes only between the covers of a book. Sometimes we use our imaginations to pretend things are the way we want them to be. And sometimes we use imagination just for fun!

Book List

Anderson, Joan. *Harry's Helicopter*. Morrow, 1990. (PreK-2)
When Harry's father makes him a helicopter from a cardboard box, Harry's imagination makes the helicopter fly.

Ballard, Robin. *Cat and Alex and the Magic Flying Carpet*. HarperCollins, 1991. (PreK-2)
Cat has a magic carpet to share with Alex.

Buckingham, Simon. *Alec and His Flying Bed*. Lothrop, Lee & Shepard, 1990. (PreK-2)
When Alec finds an old bed at the dump, he is off for magical adventures.

Burningham, John. *Time to Get Out of the Bath, Shirley*. Crowell, 1978. (PreK-1)
Shirley has many adventures exploring in her bathtub.

Drescher, Henrik. *Simon's Book*. Lothrop, Lee & Shepard, 1983. (K-4)
After Simon goes to sleep, the pen and ink come alive and continue the story he was writing.

Felix, Monique. *The Further Adventures of the Little Mouse Trapped in a Book*. Green Tiger Press, 1983. (PreK-3)
This wordless story is about a mouse trapped in the pages of a book. The mouse starts to gnaw his way out, but when he realizes an ocean is on the other side of the page, he uses the page to build a paper boat to sail away in.

Haus, Felice. *Beep! Beep! I'm a Jeep!* Random House, 1986. (PreK)
The child in this book turns boxes, chairs, and everyday materials into a variety of vehicles.

Keats, Ezra Jack. *The Trip*. Greenwillow, 1978. (PreK-2)
Although lonely at first after moving to a new town, the boy in this story uses his imagination to get things going.

Lillegard, Dee. *Sitting in My Box*. Dutton, 1989. (PreK-1)
This boy has some strange adventures while sitting in his cardboard box.

Lund, Doris Herold. *Did You Ever Dream?* Parents Magazine Press, 1969. (PreK-2)
Situations to stretch the imagination.

McLerran, Alice. *Roxaboxen*. Lothrop, Lee & Shepard, 1991. (K-3)
This picture book describes an imaginary world created in an empty lot.

McPhail, David. *Andrew's Bath*. Little, Brown, 1984. (PreK-K)
Andrew has a variety of adventures with visitors in his bath.

______. *Dream Child*. Dutton, 1985. (PreK-2)
A child sails through a dream world with her tame bear.

Matsuoka, Kyoko. *There's a Hippo in My Bath!* Doubleday, 1982. (PreK-K)
A little boy discovers that he is not alone in his bath.

Paterson, Diane. *The Bathtub Ocean*. Dial, 1979. (PreK-1)
This little girl has adventures in her tub and shower.

Roche, P. K. *Webster and Arnold and the Giant Box*. Dial, 1980. (PreK-3)
Webster and Arnold have a number of adventures with an empty cardboard box.

Sendak, Maurice. *Where the Wild Things Are*. Harper & Row, 1963. (PreK-2)
When Max is naughty, he is sent to bed without his supper. In his imagination, he sails off on an adventure to the land "where the wild things are."

Silverstein, Shel. *A Light in the Attic*. Harper & Row, 1974. (Gr. 2-up)
This collection of poems includes several on imagination.

Stevenson, James. *"Could Be Worse!"* Greenwillow, 1977. (PreK-4)
Grandpa conjures up a strange and frightening trip in his imagination.

Stevenson, Robert Louis. *Block City*. Dutton, 1988. (PreK-K)
In this illustrated poem, a boy's imagination turns his blocks into a world.

Tafuri, Nancy. *Junglewalk*. Greenwillow, 1988. (PreK-K)
A child takes off on an imaginary nighttime exploration.

Van Allsburg, Chris. *Ben's Dream*. Houghton Mifflin, 1982. (Gr. 2-6)
Ben falls asleep while studying for a geography test and has a fantastic dream.

______. *The Mysteries of Harris Burdick*. Houghton Mifflin, 1984. (Gr. 3-up)
Illustrations are presented and the reader must supply the story.

Wade, Alan. *I'm Flying*. Knopf, 1990. (PreK-3)
A boy flies away with balloons to his own private island.

Wiesner, David. *Hurricane*. Clarion, 1990. (PreK-3)
The morning after a hurricane, two brothers find an uprooted tree that becomes a magical place, transporting them on imaginary adventures to the jungle, over the sea, and into outer space.

Related Activities

1. Read aloud the picture books *Cat and Alex and the Magic Flying Carpet* by Robin Ballard and *Where the Wild Things Are* by Maurice Sendak. Then give each child a small carpet square or a bath towel to use as a magic carpet or a boat. Encourage children to enact different situations they might experience on their flying carpets. You can let the children make up individual voyages or have the group go exploring as a "fleet."
(Preschool, primary)

2. Read Shel Silverstein's poem "Magic Carpet" from *A Light in the Attic, Alec and the Flying Bed* by Simon Buckingham, and *I'm Flying* by Alan Wade. Ask the children to write and draw about where they would go if they could take off on a magic carpet ride. Tell them they can go anywhere, in any time period.
(Primary, intermediate)

3. Everyone likes to play imagination games in the bathtub. Read John Burningham's *Time to Get Out of the Bath, Shirley*, David McPhail's *Andrew's Bath*, Kyoko Matsuoka's *There's a Hippo in My Bath*, and Diane Paterson's *The Bathtub Ocean*. Next, ask the children in the group to share their favorite bathtime fantasies. Give each child an enlargement of the bathtub in figure 1.6 to decorate as a boat. They can add themselves as sailors or make up other scenes.
(Preschool)

Fig. 1.6.

4. Boxes can spark imagination. If you have several large boxes, decorate them as vehicles for the children to use for make-believe exploring trips. If you prefer, leave the boxes plain, and let the children use their imaginations to turn the boxes into whatever they want. Read the books *Harry's*

Helicopter by Joan Anderson, *Beep! Beep! I'm a Jeep* by Felice Haus, *The Trip* by Ezra Jack Keats, *Sitting in My Box* by Dee Lillegard, and *Webster and Arnold and the Giant Box* by P. K. Roche. Share the poem "Two Boxes" from Shel Silverstein's *Where the Sidewalk Ends*. Finally, give each child a small box and markers, and encourage children to create something with their box, such as a car, a boat, or an animal.
(Preschool, primary)

5. Talk about the difference between daydreams that you make up with your imagination and the kind of dreams you have at night when you are asleep. Share Doris Lund's *Did You Ever Dream?*, David McPhail's *Dream Child*, Nancy Tafuri's *Junglewalk*, and Chris Van Allsburg's *Ben's Dream*. Then make pictures of dreams or daydreams. Give each child a piece of construction paper. They can either draw a picture of their dreams or make a collage using pictures cut from old magazines. For preschoolers, write a short description on the pictures, dictated to you by the children. Older children can write their own descriptions of their dreams. Then show children how to pull apart cotton balls to glue around the edges of the paper as a frame for their pictures.
(Preschool, primary, intermediate)

6. In Robert Louis Stevenson's *Block City*, the boy uses his toy blocks to create an imaginary world. Share the book, and then have a show-and-tell time, with each child showing his or her favorite toy and describing what he or she pretends with it.
(Preschool)

7. Read James Stevenson's book *"Could Be Worse!"* or any of his other stories about Grandpa. Then stretch the children's imaginations with a similar wild story told as a troup. Pick a player to start, and ask him or her to tell a couple of sentences and then stop. For example, the first child might start, "I had a very odd adventure the other day. I was walking down the street when suddenly it grew dark and...." Then the next person picks up the storyline and adds to it. This is even more fun if you tape it so the group can listen to the whole story later.
(Primary, intermediate)

8. Talk about the book *The Further Adventures of the Little Mouse Trapped in a Book* by Monique Felix. The mouse in the book finds an imaginative way to escape from the book's dilemma. Then ask each child to read a different story but to stop at the climax and find his or her own imaginative way to end the story. As an alternative, use the book *The Mysteries of Harris Burdick* by Chris Van Allsburg, which presents situations for readers to complete.
(Primary, intermediate)

9. Read *Simon's Book* by Henrik Drescher. Stretch imaginations by asking the children to describe what it would be like to be an inanimate object such as a pen, an inkwell, a chair, a shoe, a car, or a telephone.
(Primary, intermediate)

10. Almost everyone has a magical place where they can let their imagination run wild. Read the books *Roxaboxen* by Alice McLerran and *Hurricane* by David Wiesner, and share the poem "Tree House" from Shel Silverstein's *Where the Sidewalk Ends*. Then ask the children to describe their own special places. These might include a bed to read adventure stories on, a playhouse, a treehouse, an empty lot, a playground, or anywhere else they feel free to make-believe.
(Primary, intermediate)

11. Read the poem "This Bridge" by Shel Silverstein, from *A Light in the Attic*, and then ask the children to write an essay addressing the question, "What is creativity?" (Intermediate)

CURIOSITY

Curiosity is the driving force behind inventiveness. Curiosity goes hand in hand with discontent. It is the desire to know more about something, sometimes even if gaining that knowledge is not good for us. Curiosity pushes us to find out what is going on, and it accounts in large part for our drive for progress.

Book List

Bender, Lionel. *Invention*. Knopf, 1991. (Gr. 3-up)
Part of the Eyewitness series, this looks at the history of inventions.

Caney, Steven. *Steven Caney's Invention Book*. Workman, 1985. (Gr. 4-up)
Includes both true stories of inventions and information on how to be an inventor, with projects.

Cole, Joanna. *The Magic School Bus Lost in the Solar System*. Scholastic, 1990. (Gr. 1-4)
This title and the author's other two books about the Magic School Bus (*Inside the Human Body* and *At the Waterworks*) present the acquisition of knowledge of any kind as a voyage of discovery.

Dalmais, Anne-Marie. *The Elephant's Airplane and Other Machines*. Golden Books, 1984. (K-2)
This story describes Raccoon's various inventions.

Ekker, Ernst A. *What Is beyond the Hill?* Lippincott, 1985. (K-3)
This is about an imaginary journey beyond the next hill to find out what is on the other side.

Endacott, Geoff. *Inventions and Discoveries*. Viking, 1991. (Gr. 3-up)
An overview of discoveries and inventions throughout history.

Flack, Marjorie. *Angus and the Cat*. Doubleday, 1931. (PreK-K)
When a new cat comes to stay, Angus is very curious. You can also use *Angus and the Ducks*.

Gackenbach, Dick. *Dog for a Day*. Clarion, 1987. (PreK-2)
The boy in this story invents a way to turn himself into a dog for a day.

Giff, Patricia Reilly. *Snaggle Doodles*. Delacorte, 1985. (Gr. 3-6)
The kids at the Polk Street School are working on inventions.

Kipling, Rudyard. *The Elephant's Child*. Harcourt Brace Jovanovich, 1983. (Gr. 1-4)
The elephant's child discovers that curiosity can have its drawbacks.

McCormack, Alan J. *Inventors Workshop*. Pitman Learning, 1981. (Gr. 3-up)
This title includes activities and projects on invention.

Meyers, Bernice. *The Extraordinary Invention*. Macmillan, 1984. (PreK-2)
A couple of inventors come up with a new machine, but the outcome is unpredictable.

Murphy, Jim. *Weird and Wacky Inventions*. Crown, 1978. (Gr. 4-8)
This is a collection of strange inventions, with clues to their uses, for children to guess about. Also use the author's *Guess Again: More Weird and Wacky Inventions* (Bradbury, 1986).

Rey, H. A. *Curious George Takes a Job*. Houghton Mifflin, 1947. (PreK-2)
When Curious George, the monkey, starts working, his curiosity leads him into trouble.

Taylor, Barbara. *Be an Inventor*. Harcourt Brace Jovanovich, 1987. (Gr. 3-6)
A book of projects and ideas for inventive thinking.

Thaler, Mike. *How Far Will a Rubber Band Stretch?* Parents Magazine Press, 1974. (PreK-K)
A little boy travels the world to find out how far a rubber band will stretch.

Weil, Lisl. *Pandora's Box*. Atheneum, 1986. (PreK-3)
This tells the legend of how Pandora's curiosity let trouble out into the world.

Weiss, Harvey. *How to Be an Inventor*. Crowell, 1980. (Gr. 3-6)
This illustrated title gives advice on becoming an inventor.

Westwood, Jennifer. *Going to Squintum's*. Dial, 1985. (PreK-1)
Fox uses his victims' curiosity to make his fortune.

Wulffson, Don L. *The Invention of Ordinary Things*. Lothrop, Lee & Shepard, 1981. (Gr. 2-6)
This book introduces a number of inventions we use everyday.

Related Activities

1. For very young children, read Marjorie Flack's *Angus and the Cat* and explain that being curious means that you want to know more about something. Go around the group and ask each child to tell about something he or she wants to know more about.
(Preschool, primary)

2. In the book *How Far Will a Rubber Band Stretch?* the little boy goes and looks for the answer to what he is curious about. Another way of finding information is through books. If you are in a classroom, take a field trip to the library and help the children find books on topics they are curious about that can be read aloud to them or that they can read themselves.
(Preschool, primary)

3. Show older children the books about the Magic School Bus by Joanna Cole. Then ask them to come up with topics of their own that they would like to explore, such as how a power plant operates or what makes a car run. As a group, turn your research into an adventure story with a lively description of your group as explorers investigating a subject. Add illustrations showing the group on your explorations.
(Primary, intermediate)

4. Sometimes curiosity can lead to trouble. Share the books *Curious George Takes a Job* by H. A. Rey and *Going to Squintum's* by Jennifer Westwood as examples. Then give the children situations similar to those in these books and ask what they think might happen. For instance, "What if you were curious about the inside of a lion's cage?" "What if you were curious about whether you could fly?" "What if you were curious about taking your father's watch apart?"
(Preschool, primary)

5. For older children, share the books *The Elephant's Child* by Rudyard Kipling and *Pandora's Box* by Lisl Weil and ask the children to describe a time when curiosity got them into trouble.
(Primary, intermediate)

6. Tell the children that sometimes curiosity can lead to an invention. Read Anne-Marie Dalmais's *The Elephant's Airplane and Other Machines*, Dick Gackenbach's *Dog for a Day*, and Bernice Meyers's *The Extraordinary Invention*. Then ask the children to list inventions they use every day, such as cars, toasters, electric lights, and more. Ask them to come up with a list of inventions that have had the biggest effect on their lives and reasons for each invention's impact.
(Primary, intermediate)

7. Older children can each choose an inventor to read about, such as Alexander Graham Bell, George Washington Carver, Marie Curie, George Eastman, Thomas Edison, Albert Einstein, Henry Ford, Benjamin Franklin, Robert Goddard, Jan Matzeliger, Samuel Morse, and the Wright brothers. Ask each child to share with the group the information he or she discovers.
(Primary, intermediate)

8. Share the book *Snaggle Doodles* by Patricia Reilly Giff, and read Shel Silverstein's poem "Invention" from *Where the Sidewalk Ends*. (You can also use nonfiction books about invention.) Ask the children to think of a problem and come up with an invention to solve the problem. The problem can be a serious one, such as how to encourage people to quit smoking, or a silly one, such as an invention to keep the butter from dripping off a piece of corn-on-the cob.
(Primary, intermediate)

9. The books by Jim Murphy are fun to use as a game. Show the children the inventions and let them guess what each one is for.
(Primary, intermediate)

10. Read *What Is beyond the Hill?* by Ernst Ekker. Then ask the children to pretend they are millionaires and can spend an unlimited amount of money to find the answer to some question they are curious about. What would their question be?
(Primary, intermediate)

11. Read Shel Silverstein's poem "Never." Ask the children to think of some things they have never done but are curious to try. Make a list.
(Primary, intermediate)

AMBITION AND COMPETITION

Ambition and competitiveness drive us to be first and best. It is ambition that drives an explorer to try to achieve a feat such as reaching the North Pole or finding the source of the Nile River before anyone else. But ambition and competition are like two-edged swords: They can drive us on to some of our best work; they can also act as divisive forces between people. We must try to find a balance between wanting to be first and hurting others in our drive to be the best.

Book List

Burleigh, Robert. *Flight*. Philomel, 1991. (Gr. 2-5)
This picture book recounts Charles Lindbergh's flight in the *Spirit of St. Louis*.

Burnett, Carol. *What I Want to Be When I Grow Up*. Simon & Schuster, 1975. (PreK-3)
This title offers a humorous look at careers children might choose.

Florian, Douglas. *People Working*. Crowell, 1983. (PreK-1)
This picture book shows people working at various jobs.

Gramatky, Hardie. *Little Toot*. Putnam, 1939. (PreK-3)
Little Toot is a tugboat who has no ambition until he rescues a ship in a fierce storm.

Hall, Carol. *Super-Vroomer!* Doubleday, 1978. (PreK-3)
The boy in this story learns that winning is not necessarily as important as feeling good about yourself.

Hoban, Russell. *How Tom Beat Captain Najork and His Hired Sportsmen*. Atheneum, 1974. (K-3)
When Captain Najork tries to teach Tom a lesson about not fooling around, Tom wins the competition. Also use *A Near Thing for Captain Najork*.

Neuhaus, David. *His Finest Hour*. Viking, 1984. (Gr. 1-3)
This picture book describes the unusual outcome of a bicycle race, when one of the contestants is overly competitive.

Seuss, Dr. *Yertle the Turtle and Other Stories*. Random House, 1958. (PreK-3)
This collection has three stories on the folly of being too ambitious and boastful.

Related Activities

1. Ask the children to describe their ambitions of what they want to be when they grow up. Read Carol Burnett's *What I Want to Be When I Grow Up* and Douglas Florian's *People Working* to give children some ideas. Then recite this fingerplay together:

When I Grow Up

When I grow up I'll sail away
(Make sailing motion with hands)
On a giant ship—or, no, I'll play
(Open hands wide to show a large ship)
The game of baseball, or again
(Pretend to swing a bat)
I'll learn ballet, to dance and spin.
(Put hands above head and spin like a dancer)
But maybe I would find it better
(Look thoughtful)
To sew a coat or knit a sweater.
(Make sewing motions)
I might decide to act in plays,
(Put one hand on chest, and the other outflung)
Or better yet, I'll spend my days
In making all the sick folks well
(Pretend to pour medicine into a spoon)
Or be a runner. At the bell
(Crouch like a runner at the starting line)
The coach will holler, "Ready, set!"
(Pretend to take off running)
Yes, that might be the best one yet.
(Nod head)
But whatever I decide to do,
(Shrug shoulders)
I'll be the best before I'm through,
(Clasp hands over head in victor's gesture)
'Cause whatever I will choose to be
I'll always be the very best ME!
(Pat self on chest)

(Preschool)

2. For young children, read *Little Toot* and explain that ambition is wanting to do something well. Ask the children to tell you about things they want to do well and that they have to work at, such as learning to ride a bicycle or learning to button their buttons. Then talk about how good it feels when you succeed.
(Preschool, primary)

3. With an older group, read *Flight* by Robert Burleigh and then have each child describe his or her future ambition. What would he or she like to be famous for? Ask children to write about their answers and draw a picture.
(Primary, intermediate)

4. Read Carol Hall's book *Super-Vroomer!* and explain that there are two winners in this book, each for a different reason. Ask the children to come up with a definition of a winner and as a group list the personal qualities such a person would have.
(Primary, intermediate)

5. Have a group discussion on the question, "How do you measure success?" Read David Neuhaus's *His Finest Hour* to get started, in which the real winner is not the one who makes it to the finish line first.
(Primary, intermediate)

6. Explain that sometimes wanting to be the best can be carried too far. Read the stories in *Yertle the Turtle and Other Stories* by Dr. Seuss as examples. Then, to emphasize how wanting to be the best got Yertle and Gertrude in trouble, let the children create examples of these troubles. They can either make a picture of Yertle (fig. 1.7) on his turtle throne, by gluing together a big pile of turtles, or draw a picture of Gertrude with a tail too heavy to fly. For this activity, give children various scrap materials to glue onto Gertrude's tail.
(Preschool, primary)

Fig. 1.7.

7. Read Russell Hoban's books about Tom and Captain Najork. Then have a discussion about whether competition is a good thing or a bad thing. Do you have to take winning seriously in order to succeed? What is the role of fun in a competition? How does the winner feel? How about the loser? Does competition promote friendship? Is it inevitable that people compete? What is serendipity?
(Intermediate)

TOLERANCE

Tolerance helps us develop compassion and understanding. We get the best from what we find when we can share our discoveries with others. We learn that no one can always be first or best and that no one is always last or worst.

Book List

Friedman, Ina R. *How My Parents Learned to Eat*. Houghton Mifflin, 1984. (K-4)
A young girl describes how her Japanese mother and her American father learned to share their eating customs.

Lennon, John. *Imagine*. Birch Lane Press, 1990. (PreK-6)
This is a visual presentation of John Lennon's song about tolerance.

Lionni, Leo. *Nicholas, Where Have You Been?* Knopf, 1987. (PreK-2)
When the other mice find out from Nicholas that the birds have eaten the best berries, the mice want to fight the birds, until Nicholas convinces them to get along.

Morris, Ann. *Bread, Bread, Bread*. Lothrop, Lee & Shepard, 1989. (PreK-2)
In this book, Morris shows how people all over the world eat bread. Other titles by this author to use are *Hats, Hats, Hats; Loving;* and *On the Go*.

Pinkwater, Daniel. *The Big Orange Splot*. Hastings House, 1977. (K-4)
This story of a nonconforming neighbor emphasizes how valuable our differences are.

Spier, Peter. *People*. Doubleday, 1980. (PreK-3)
Spier shows the differences among people all over the world.

Related Activities

1. Talk about differences. Read *Nicholas, Where Have You Been?* and discuss whether being different necessarily means we cannot get along. You can also share Peter Spier's *People*. Give the children the picture in figure 1.8 to color, and suggest that they make each person different.
(Preschool, primary)

2. Read Ina Friedman's book *How My Parents Learned to Eat*. Then ask the children to describe something they do at home differently from their friends that is drawn from their family's ethnic background. For instance, a family from Central America might celebrate El Día de la Raza (Day of the People) instead of Columbus Day.
(Primary, intermediate)

3. Demonstrate how different people do things differently by reading Ann Morris's books. Then let the children try a variety of breads from different cultures. Discuss what it would be like if all bread were the same.
(Preschool, primary)

4. For older children, read Daniel Pinkwater's *The Big Orange Splot*. Then have a discussion about what the world would be like if everyone did things just alike. To make the issue of differences clearer, ask the children to come to school the next day all dressed exactly alike, in white shirts and dark pants. How do they feel about this "uniform"? Do they believe uniforms are used to try to make everyone the same? If not, why are uniforms used?
(Primary, intermediate)

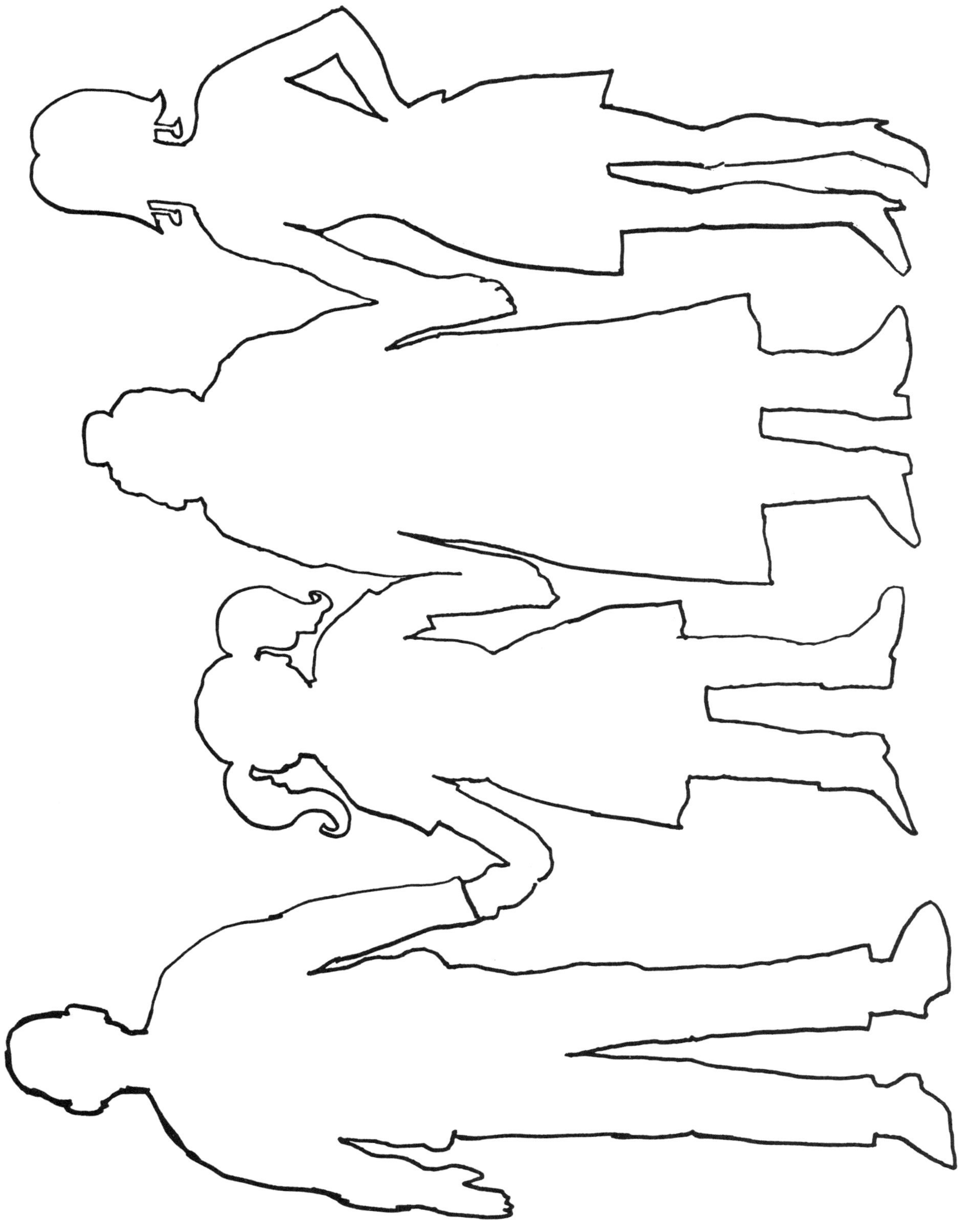

Fig. 1.8.

5. Look at another side of the difference/sameness picture by reading John Lennon's *Imagine*, in which he suggests that our differences keep us apart. Have a discussion about how to reconcile the need for individuality with the need for understanding each other based on our similarities. Play a tape of the John Lennon song of the same name.
(Intermediate)

2

What Is History?

Children (and, indeed, many adults) often think of history as a series of known facts and believe that the author of a history book merely writes down these facts in the proper order. However, history is a continuing process of discovery and interpretation. Often using limited information, historians try to re-create the events they write about while filtering those events through their own perspectives.

The methods historians use in finding out about the past depend on when the events being studied took place. The beginning of the story of the exploration of the world falls into the period of prehistory, before written records were available. In this case, historians depend on the science of archaeology, which is the study of ancient artifacts, for clues about how people lived in the past.

When studying events for which written records exist, historians frequently use original documents to find out what happened. These primary sources about the discovery of America include sagas written by the Vikings, documents written by Christopher Columbus and other explorers, and other records of various kinds from the period.

In studying these documents, historians often must use sources that were originally written in foreign languages; therefore, historians are dependent on the accuracy of the translations they use. Most original documents about Columbus were written in Spanish. An example of how a translation can affect the way an event is reported can be seen in the early story that Queen Isabella pawned her jewels to pay for Columbus's voyage. Retranslation of the original source for this story has revealed that the queen actually said she would sponsor the voyage *even if* she had to sell her jewels but that in the end other sources of income were found.

Sometimes only limited written documentation has survived through the centuries, and historians must use their knowledge about the period and the context of an event to make their best guess about what might have happened. Then, as new information is revealed, these guesses must be revised. History is not static. It changes as our sources of information change. For instance, the belief that Columbus was the first European to discover the New World is a historical interpretation that has undergone much change. Study has revealed that there also were a number of other possible discoverers, such as the Vikings. When new discoveries are made, history must be re-written to reflect the new facts.

The historian's personal point of view is important. Point of view is influenced by culture and the historical period in which a person lives. For example, most accounts we have of Columbus's voyages are written from the European point of view because the first historians to recount these events were European and because we have no original written record of the other side of things. The story would be very different if written by the native inhabitants of the islands and continents Columbus discovered.

Historical facts can become distorted by emotion—the feelings evoked in response to events. Columbus himself is an excellent example. During the forming of the United States, Americans were looking for a hero to exemplify the spirit of the new country. Columbus became that symbol, and in the process he was idealized, was made larger than life, and was credited with a number of traits that may or may not have been present in the real man.

Much of what we read in history books is based on what information is available at the time and on the individual author's beliefs and interpretations, rather than on hard, cold facts. The following books and activities help children understand what history is, what the historian's job is like, and why it is important to try to obtain more than one view when learning about historical events and periods such as the Age of Exploration.

BOOK LIST

Anholt, Catherine. *When I Was a Baby*. Little, Brown, 1989. (PreK-1)
A child goes over her past history.

Brown, Laurene Krasny, and Marc Brown. *Visiting the Art Museum*. Dutton, 1986. (K-3)
This picture book offers a humorous introduction to a museum and the historical artifacts that can be found there.

Cooke, Jean. *Archaeology*. Warwick Press, 1981. (Gr. 3-6)
This book offers a clear, well-illustrated description of the methods used in archaeology, as well as an examination of a number of famous digs.

Fradin, Dennis B. *Archaeology*. Children's Press, 1983. (Gr. 2-6)
For younger children, this title describes the methods archaeologists use and highlights some major archaeological finds.

Hautzig, Esther. *At Home: A Visit in Four Languages*. Macmillan, 1968. (PreK-3)
The English text for this picture book is supplemented by the French, Spanish, and Russian names of everyday items.

Havill, Juanita. *Jamaica's Find*. Houghton Mifflin, 1986. (PreK-2)
This story about a little girl who finds a lost toy can help young children understand that the meaning of any event depends on your point of view.

Hoopes, Lyn Littlefield. *Half-a-Button*. Harper & Row, 1989. (PreK)
A young boy and his grandfather explore the beach and find a sea-smoothed half-button as a treasure.

James, Carolyn. *Digging Up the Past: The Story of an Archaeological Adventure*. Franklin Watts, 1990. (Gr. 4-6)

In this fiction title, two boys use archaeological methods to discover more about their town in the past.

Keats, Ezra Jack. *My Dog Is Lost*. Crowell, 1960. (K-2)

This picture book about a young Puerto Rican boy who has lost his dog will introduce Spanish to very young children in a situation they can sympathize with.

Koehler, Phoebe. *The Day We Met You*. Bradbury, 1990. (PreK-K)

This brief family account of the arrival of a new baby can serve as an example of history—the story of what happened in the past.

Livingston, Myra Cohn, ed. *O Frabjous Day*. Atheneum, 1977. (Gr. 4-up)

This collection includes the poem "The Discovery" by John Collings Squire.

Lowe, Steve, comp. *The Log of Christopher Columbus*. Philomel Books, 1992. (Gr. 2-up)

This book includes selected excerpts from Columbus's log of his first voyage, illustrated as a picture book by Robert Sabuda.

Meredith, Robert, and E. Brooks Smith, eds. *The Quest of Columbus*. Little, Brown, 1966. (Gr. 4-up)

This account of Columbus's voyage was written by his son, Ferdinand Columbus.

Oakley, Graham. *The Diary of a Church Mouse*. Atheneum, 1987. (PreK-3)

A mouse named Humphrey decides to keep a record of his life.

Pelta, Kathy. *Discovering Christopher Columbus: How History Is Invented*. Lerner, 1991. (Gr. 3-6)

This author not only tells the story of Columbus but also describes how this history has been revised as our information has changed.

Pickering, Robert B. *I Can Be an Archaeologist*. Children's Press, 1987. (Gr. 1-3)

This simple text with photographs introduces the job of the archaeologist.

Porell, Bruce. *Digging the Past: Archaeology in Your Own Backyard*. Addison-Wesley, 1979. (Gr. 4-6)

The techniques of archaeology are introduced through explanations, activities, and experiments.

Quackenbush, Robert. *Holiday Song Book*. Lothrop, Lee & Shepard, 1977. (Gr. 3-6)

Includes the song "It's All Wrong," about Columbus's country of origin.

Roop, Peter, and Connie Roop, eds. *I, Columbus: My Journal—1492-3*. Walker, 1990. (Gr. 3-up)

This title offers excerpts from the journal Columbus kept of his first voyage.

Scieszka, Jon. *The True Story of the Three Little Pigs by A. Wolf*. Viking Kestrel, 1989. (K-5)

This presents the traditional story of the three pigs from a new point of view—the wolf's.

Sechrist, Elizabeth Hough, comp. *Poems for Red Letter Days*. Macrae Smith, 1951. (Gr. 4-up)
This collection includes several poems about Columbus.

Syme, Ronald. *Columbus: Finder of the New World*. Morrow, 1952. (Gr. 2-5)
Nowhere in this book does Syme mention that Columbus was not looking for the New World but for the Far East.

Udry, Janice May. *Let's Be Enemies*. Harper & Row, 1961. (PreK-2)
When John and James fight, John believes it is all James's fault. But children can use this story to help them understand that there is always more than one point of view.

Walsh, Jill Paton. *Lost and Found*. Andre Deutsch, 1984. (Gr. 1-4)
In this picture book, the losing and finding of a number of artifacts throughout history is recounted, beginning with a young boy who loses an arrowhead in prehistoric times.

Weil, Lisl. *Let's Go to the Museum*. Holiday House, 1989. (Gr. 1-5)
This book introduces various kinds of museums and what can be found in them.

West, Delno C., and Jean M. West. *Christopher Columbus: The Great Adventure and How We Know about It*. Atheneum, 1991. (Gr. 4-up)
This biography of Columbus also looks at how historians learn about his life.

RELATED ACTIVITIES

1. Young children need help understanding history as a recounting of events that happened in the past. Demonstrate this concept by asking your students to describe themselves as babies. Give them large (12" x 18") pieces of construction paper to fold in half to make simple books. Have children open their books and write their stories on the right-hand side (very young students may need help writing their accounts). On the cover, they can write their name and the title for their book, such as "When I Was a Baby." Ask them to decorate the covers and the inside left-hand page with illustrations showing the events described (see fig. 2.1). Explain that they have each created a personal history. To help children get started thinking about their past, read *When I Was a Baby* by Catherine Anholt or *The Day We Met You* by Phoebe Koehler.
(Preschool, primary)

Fig. 2.1.

2. Children can experience Columbus's voyage as real, as historians try to do, with this craft project, in which they make a book "come alive." A cigar box or similar box with a lid that opens is ideal, but if not available, use a shoebox or similar box and tape a cover that can be opened and shut to one side of the opening. To turn the box into a book, stand it on end and cover three of the four sides (but not the lid or back) with white paper. Draw horizontal lines on the paper so it resembles the pages of a closed book (see fig. 2.2). Decorate the outside of the box with construction paper and markers so it looks like a book cover. Add the title and author. Inside the "book," children can put the characters or objects they want to "bring to life" and create a three-dimensional scene. For example, you might want to create a scene of the *Santa Maria* on the Atlantic Ocean. Use a toy boat for the *Santa Maria* and make small sailors from pipe cleaners. Waves can be cut from blue construction paper folded along the bottom and glued in place to stand up. Then, when the "book" is opened, the story "comes to life."
(Primary)

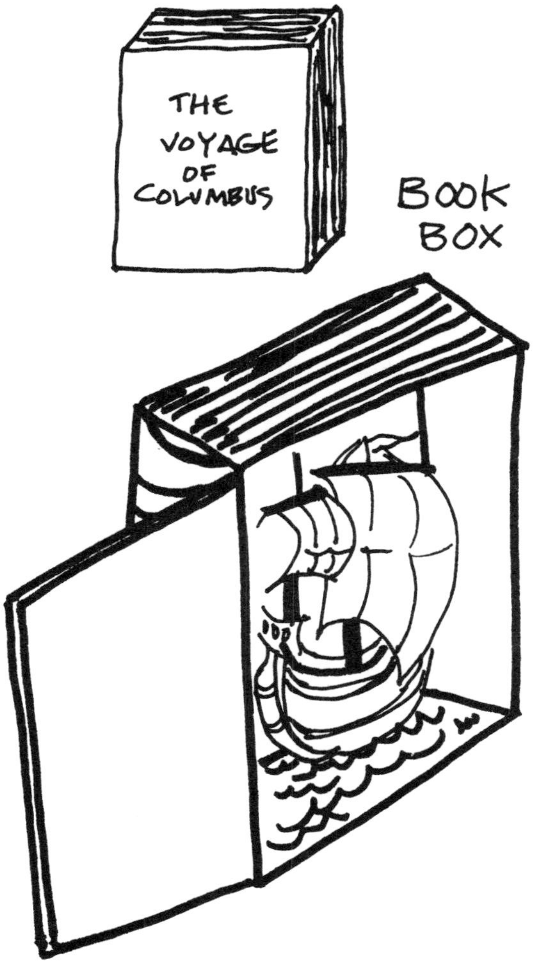

Fig. 2.2.

3. To help young children understand that there can be more than one point of view regarding an event, use the picture book *Jamaica's Find* by Juanita Havill. In this story, a little girl finds a toy dog at the playground. At first she decides to keep the dog for her own, but her mother explains that some other child is probably missing the dog and wondering what happened to it. When Jamaica tries to understand the missing owner's point of view, she decides to take the dog back to the lost-and-found at the playground.

Another picture book to use to help illustrate the concept of another person's point of view is *Let's Be Enemies* by Janice May Udry. This is a story of a fight between two friends, John and James. The story is told from John's point of view, and he describes the things James does that make him angry. After reading the story, explain to the children that James probably would not see these events in the same way. Ask them to imagine what James's version of the story might be. (Preschool, primary)

4. Children can experience how historical accounts are affected by the point of view of the historian through the following activity. Read the poem "The Discovery" by John Collings Squire, from Myra Cohn Livingston's collection *O Frabjous Day*. This poem presents what might have been an islander's first look at Columbus's arrival in the Caribbean. You can also use the reverse fairy tale *The True Story of the Three Little Pigs by A. Wolf* by Jon Scieszka.

Next, let the children pick out nursery rhymes, and ask them to briefly retell the stories from a different point of view. For example, the nursery rhyme "Little Miss Muffet" gives Miss Muffet's point of view of being frightened away by the arrival of a spider. Told from the spider's point of view, the story would be different. The spider might have been returning to her web and come across a huge creature who screamed, caused an earthquake, and then disappeared.
(Primary, intermediate)

5. To illustrate how different historians create different accounts of the same events due to their individual interpretations, have the children read different biographies of Christopher Columbus and compare them. For example, the biography by Columbus's son, Ferdinand, edited by Robert Meredith and E. Brooks Smith, is probably less than objective, and Ronald Syme's biography *Columbus: Finder of the New World* has some serious flaws. Ask the children to answer some of these questions to determine what the differences between the biographies are:

- What is the author's view of Columbus: brave hero and great mariner or greedy, ambitious man?
- What does the author believe were Columbus's greatest accomplishments?
- Does the author portray the mistakes Columbus made, such as mistreating the native peoples he met or his inability to govern a new colony?
- Does the author make it clear that Columbus himself never realized that he had not found the Indies but instead had discovered a "new" continent?
- Does the author give much background about the period when Columbus lived?
- Does the author mention the results of Columbus's voyages, such as the arrival of the conquistadors and the destruction of the Aztec and Inca empires?

(Primary, intermediate)

6. To show how a historical figure can also become a symbol for certain values or feelings, read several poems about Columbus, such as "Immortal Morn" by Hezekiah Butterworth, "Columbian Ode" by Paul Laurence Dunbar, and "Columbus" by Joaquin Miller, all from Elizabeth Sechrist's

collection *Poems for Red Letter Days*. All of these glorify Columbus and his accomplishments. Discuss how these poets have idealized Columbus and for what possible purposes they did so.

Then have the children make a poster about Columbus. Have one of the kids lie down on a sheet of newsprint and draw around his or her body to create an outline of Columbus. Use this outline as a poster, and ask the children to fill the outline with written descriptions such as, "Columbus was a man who dared to challenge the unknown," or, "Christopher Columbus was a slave master." Decide which are descriptions of Columbus as a symbol and which describe him as a real historical figure. You might try this same activity with another idealized symbol such as the Statue of Liberty. Your students might be interested in reading Kathy Pelta's *Discovering Christopher Columbus: How History Is Invented* and Delno and Jean West's *Christopher Columbus: The Great Adventure and How We Know about It*.
(Primary, intermediate)

7. This activity helps children to understand that what they read in a history book frequently depends on how the author filled in the blanks of unknown information. Give each child a copy of the handout in figure 2.3 (see page 30), which is a list of details about an imaginary explorer, and ask the children to write a brief biography that includes these facts. As long as they do not contradict the given facts, the children can add any details that they deduce from the information. After the stories are written, read them aloud so everyone can see how different each interpretation is.
(Intermediate)

8. Explain the study of archaeology by using nonfiction books. *Archaeology* by Dennis Fradin and *I Can Be an Archaeologist* by Robert B. Pickering are good for primary children, and *Archaeology* by Jean Cooke and *Digging the Past* by Bruce Porell are appropriate for older children. Read aloud the picture books *Half-a-Button* by Lyn Littlefield Hoopes and *Lost and Found* by Jill Paton Walsh to show how artifacts are found.

Let older children imagine that they are digging in their backyards and find an ancient artifact of some kind. Give them copies of the activity sheet in figure 2.4 (see page 31), and ask them to draw a picture of the artifact (such as a cup, an arrowhead, a piece of jewelry, or a tool of some kind). Then ask them to write about the item, how it might have been used, when it might have been made, the person who may have left it, how it came to be in their backyard, and other details they can imagine about it.

After completing this exercise, children might also enjoy reversing it by imagining that they themselves have lost something that will be discovered 500 years from now. Using copies of the activity sheet in figure 2.5 (see page 32), let them decide what they have lost (a favorite toy, a tool, a piece of jewelry, etc.), and then let them write about what they imagine this artifact would tell a future society about life in the 1990s.
(Intermediate)

9. To introduce children to historical artifacts, read *Visiting the Art Museum* by Laurene Brown and Marc Brown or *Let's Go to the Museum* by Lisl Weil. These titles introduce various kinds of museums and the items that can be found in them. If possible, take the children on a field trip to a nearby history museum so they can actually see some historical artifacts. If a field trip is not possible, find out whether any museums near you loan exhibits for use in classrooms or libraries.
(Primary, intermediate)

(Text continues on page 33.)

Facts Known about the Explorer Miguel Manton

- Born in 1498, sometime around Easter, in Spain.
- Father was a merchant.
- Believed to have had at least one sister and two brothers.
- One record says he had brown hair, another says black.
- Spoke English, Spanish, and French.
- Sailed for France.
- In 1528, he discovered the island of Pommedore in the middle of the Pacific Ocean.
- Someone with the name Miguel Manton was recorded as being in an Italian prison in 1518.
- Married an English woman.
- A portrait of him was painted that includes two children.
- There is a gravestone with the name Miguel Manton and the date 1538 in a cemetery in England; there is also a tablet on the wall of a church in Pommedore stating his death occurred there in 1535. In addition, an American millionaire claims to have a box of Manton's ashes.

Write a brief biography of the imaginary explorer Miguel Manton. Include the information given above, and add any details of his life you imagine might have happened.

Fig. 2.3.

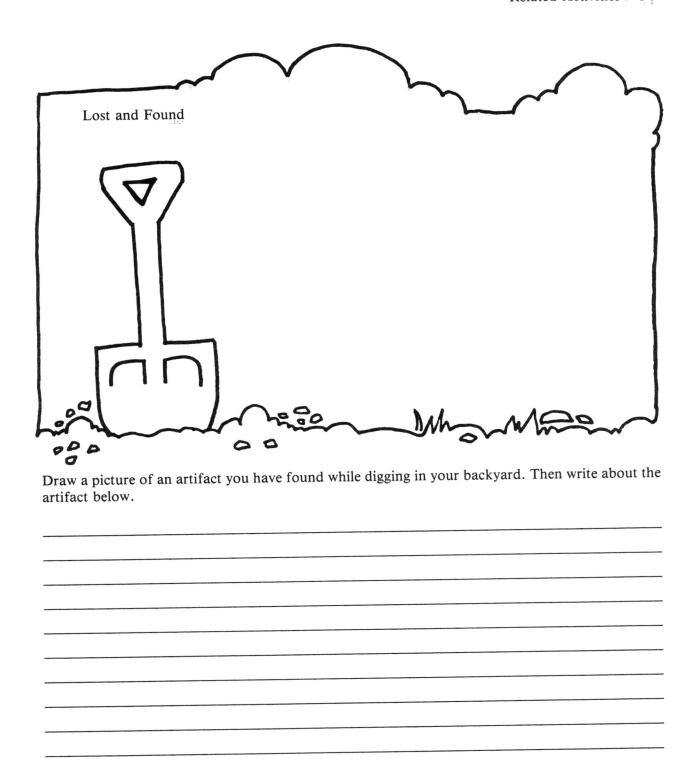

Lost and Found

Draw a picture of an artifact you have found while digging in your backyard. Then write about the artifact below.

Fig. 2.4.

Draw a picture of an item you have lost. Then imagine what that item would tell someone who found it 500 years from now, and write about what you imagine below.

Fig. 2.5.

10. This activity helps young children to understand the idea of learning historical facts from documents written in another language. First, familiarize children with the ideas that various languages are spoken by various people and that words that sound different, because they are in different languages, can have similar meanings. Let young children experience the difference between two languages by reading them a story that includes some words from another language, such as *My Dog Is Lost* by Ezra Jack Keats. Another choice is Esther Hautzig's *At Home: A Visit in Four Languages*, which introduces the words for everyday objects in French, Spanish, and Russian.

Then teach the children a few simple words in another language and play a simplified game of "Simon Says." For example, teach the children that in Spanish the word for head is *la cabeza* and the word for face is *la cara*. Say to the children, "Touch your *cabeza*." Each child who responds correctly stays in the game, and each child who touches the wrong body part is "out." Keep going with other body parts, teaching one new word each round, until you have a winner.
(Preschool, primary)

11. To help the children to understand what it is like to use sources from another language, give each child a copy of the handout in figure 2.6. Ask them to rewrite the paragraph in English. Then compare the translations to see whether different children's versions are identical. Chances are they will not be, and this will demonstrate why differences exist among various translations of historical documents. A translation of the Spanish appears at the bottom of the handout.
(Intermediate)

12. Give children a taste of the original documents that historians use as sources by reading part of Columbus's own journal of his first voyage. Several translations are available. Good ones for children are *The Log of Christopher Columbus* by Steve Lowe and *I, Columbus* edited by Peter Roop and Connie Roop.

Ask the children to keep a diary or journal for a week, in which they write down all the occurrences that would help a future historian interpret life in our time. Tell them to include the kinds of clothes they wear, the food they eat, a description of their homes, what they do in school, recreational activities, and anything else they consider important. Graham Oakley's *Diary of a Church Mouse* might help them get started.
(Primary, intermediate)

13. Historians from a number of different countries have tried to make a case for claiming Columbus as a native son, in order to share in his glory. This is an example of how a historian's own background can color his or her interpretation of history. Though the best evidence indicates that Columbus was born in Genoa, Italy, children will enjoy the song "It's All Wrong" from Robert Quackenbush's *Holiday Song Book*, about a claim that Columbus was an Irishman.
(Primary, intermediate)

La Ciudad de Madrid

Juana visita la ciudad grande de Madrid. Su primo, Miguel, es de esta ciudad. Ella es de la pequeña aldea de Miraflores y desea ver todas las cosas importantes en Madrid. Miguel y Juana visitan los teatros, los restaurantes, los museos, y los parques. Los primos van por muchas calles y avenidas y miran los edificios altos y las tiendas grandes. Para Juana, esta experiencia es interesante y nueva pero es extraña también.

Nouns

la aldea — the town
las avenidas — the avenues
las calles — the streets
la ciudad — the city
las cosas — the things
los edificios — the buildings
la experiencia — the experience
las flores — the flowers
los museos — the museums
los parques — the parks
primo — cousin
los restaurantes — the restaurants
los teatros — the theaters
las tiendas — the stores

Adjectives

alto — tall, high
extraña — strange
grande — big, large
importantes — important
interesante — interesting
muchas — many
nueva — new
pequeña — small, little
su — her
todas — every, all

Pronouns

ella — she

Verbs

desea — (she) wishes, wants
es — is
miran — (they) look at, watch
van — (they) go, walk
visita — (she) visits
visitan — (they) visit

Other words

de — of
en — in
esta — this
la, los, las — the
para — for, in order to
pero — but
por — along, through
también — also
y — and

Fig. 2.6.

Translation of paragraph in figure 2.6: Juana visits the large city of Madrid. Her cousin, Miguel, is from this city. She is from the small town of Flowerview and wants to see all the important things in Madrid. Miguel and Juana visit the theaters, the restaurants, the museums, and the parks. The cousins walk along many streets and avenues and look at the tall buildings and the large stores. For Juana, this is a new and interesting experience, but it is also very strange.

3

Exploration of the Ancient World

During the period of what we now call "ancient history," humans were busy developing new civilizations, new methods of government, new religions, and new ways of life. Lands were explored and peoples were conquered. The area of the Mediterranean Sea (which literally means "sea in the middle of the earth") is the area where our knowledge of voyages of exploration begins.

Not much information has come down to us, but we do know the Egyptians were some of the earliest people to begin to travel beyond their own borders. In 2400 B.C.E., an Egyptian named Hannu traveled to the Land of Punt, believed to be somewhere on the eastern coast of Africa. Around 2200 B.C.E., the Minoans from the island of Crete, with its legendary Minotaur, were voyaging across the Mediterranean for trading purposes.

Around 600 B.C.E., according to the Greek historian Herodotus, the Egyptian King Necho sent an expedition completely around the African continent. This expedition took more than three years to complete, with the explorers periodically landing, growing crops to replenish their supplies, and then continuing on. They were probably traveling in galleys, called biremes if they were propelled by two banks of oars and triremes if they had three oar banks. Each oar may have been as much as 40 feet long and took six men to work. These ships were long and narrow, with a single sail and a covered deck.

The next great group of explorers we know of were the Phoenicians. Around 500 B.C.E., they sent expeditions out through the Pillars of Hercules guarding the passage through the Strait of Gibraltar into the Atlantic to explore both the European and African coasts. The Phoenicians were very secretive about their travels, however, in order to maintain their trading supremacy. They frightened other merchants away from their trade routes with stories of sea serpents in the ocean and lands full of giants and dragons. These tales of monsters were to linger up to the time Columbus set out on his voyage.

Much exploration in ancient times took place as a result of conquest. Around 331 B.C.E., the Macedonian king Alexander the Great conquered and explored most of the then known world, from Greece to India. To collect knowledge of the lands he conquered, Alexander hired surveyors, botanists, biologists, and scribes to accompany him and keep a record of his travels. With his combination of vision and conceit, Alexander foreshadowed many later explorers.

Pytheas was a Greek whose travels in the third century B.C.E. foreshadowed those of Marco Polo in the twelfth century. In Pytheas's day, the Carthaginians had essentially closed the Strait of Gilbraltar to protect their trade routes from Greek traders and others. But Pytheas managed to sneak through. He followed the European coast to Britain and perhaps beyond. He observed many new things, but also like Marco Polo, much of his story was not believed.

The first section below includes books and activities on ancient explorers. Next, some tales about ancient sea monsters are considered. The last section covers myths that have arisen about exploration.

DISCOVERERS AND DISCOVERIES BEFORE COLUMBUS

For the ancient explorers, the new discoveries they made were even more daring and amazing than those made during the Age of Exploration. Though today the feats they accomplished may not seem very significant, in their own times their exploits were as exciting and revolutionary as Columbus's voyage was in 1492.

Book List

Ash, Maureen. *Alexander the Great: Ancient Empire Builder*. Children's Press, 1991. (Gr. 4-up)
A look at this early traveler.

Chadefaud, Catherine. *First Empires*. Silver Burdett, 1988. (Gr. 5-8)
Includes histories of the empires of the Egyptians, Assyrians, Hittites, and Persians.

Foreman, Michael. *Panda's Puzzle and His Voyage of Discovery*. Bradbury, 1977. (PreK-3)
In this picture book Panda travels the world and discovers many civilizations.

Fradin, Dennis B. *Explorers*. Children's Press, 1984. (Gr. 2-4)
Includes exploration from the time of the Egyptians in 2400 B.C.E. up to the present.

Grant, Neil. *The Explorers*. Silver Burdett, 1979. (Gr. 4-up)
Includes an account of Pytheas, who traveled from the Mediterranean to Britain in 320 B.C.E.

Krensky, Stephen. *Conqueror and Hero: The Search for Alexander*. Little, Brown, 1981. (Gr. 4-up)
Describes the life, conquests, and motivations of Alexander the Great.

Lasker, Joe. *Alexander the Great*. Viking, 1983. (Gr. 1-4)
A brief illustrated biography of this conqueror of new lands.

Manson, Christopher. *Two Travelers*. Henry Holt, 1990. (Gr. 1-5)
Charlemagne's messenger, Isaac, is sent to Baghdad with a peace message and must return bringing a gift—an elephant.

Matthews, Rupert. *Explorers*. Knopf, 1991. (Gr. 3-up)
Covers explorers from the Phoenicians to modern times.

Odijk, Pamela. *The Phoenicians*. Silver Burdett, 1989. (Gr. 4-up)
Sketchy history of these early traders and explorers.

Scott, Geoffrey. *Egyptian Boats*. Carolrhoda, 1981. (Gr. 2-4)
This title uses a beginning reader picture-book format to describe the boats used by ancient Egyptians.

Simon, Charnan. *Explorers of the Ancient World*. Children's Press, 1990. (Gr. 4-up)
Excellent coverage of the history of ancient exploration from the Egyptians in 2600 B.C.E. to the Greeks in 100 C.E.

Windrow, Martin. *The Invaders*. Marshall Cavendish, 1979. (Gr. 4-up)
Includes invaders and empire builders from the Roman Empire through Charlemagne, founder of the Holy Roman Empire.

Related Activities

1. Explain to small children that long ago, people started traveling around looking for new things. Read aloud *Panda's Puzzle and His Voyage of Discovery* by Michael Foreman. Tell the children that as people traveled around, they saw many strange things they had never seen before, such as elephants. Read aloud *Two Travelers* by Christopher Manson.
(Preschool, primary)

2. To introduce the early Egyptian and Phoenician explorers, share Pamela Odijk's *The Phoenicians* and Geoffrey Scott's *Egyptian Boats*. Children can make Phoenician galleys from paper cups (see fig. 3.1). Two cups make the hull of the ship. A small piece is cut away from each cup, and the cups are glued together rim to rim. The mast is a drinking straw. Stick one end of the straw in a wad of clay. Then flatten the bottom of the clay and stick it to the inside of the hull. Next, cut a sail from a piece of decorative paper. Curl the paper sufficiently to suggest a sail billowing in the wind and glue the paper to the drinking-straw mast.
(Primary, intermediate)

3. Use the books by Dennis Fradin, Neil Grant, Rupert Matthews, and Charnan Simon to introduce ancient explorers. Then tell the children that when early travelers such as Hanno came across strange animals they had never seen before, they tried to describe those animals using the names of creatures they were familiar with. For example, Hanno's expedition returned with a description of a "horse-fish" (a hippopotamus). They also arrived at an island filled with what they described as a great number of women with hairy bodies, who attacked them. These were probably chimpanzees or gorillas. The Mongols described a giraffe as a "celestial unicorn." Marco Polo described a huge serpent 10 feet long; with two short legs near the head, each with three claws like a tiger's; and with very large eyes, sharp teeth, and jaws large enough to swallow a man. This was a crocodile. One of the early explorers of Africa claimed to have seen men with dog's heads. These were almost certainly baboons.

Fig. 3.1.

Give the children these descriptions without telling them what animals are being referred to. Ask them to draw a picture of what they imagine these "new" animals must look like. Then, after they have shown their pictures, tell the children what each animal really is.
(Primary, intermediate)

4. Because much early exploration took place as part of the conquest of empires, introduce Alexander the Great and other empire builders with the books by Catherine Chadefaud, Stephen Krensky, Joe Lasker, and Martin Windrow. Then have the children imagine that they are a group being taken over by an invasion from a powerful foreign empire. Discuss what their feelings might be as a conquered people. How would they relate to their conquerors? What would be the principal disadvantages of being taken over by another empire? What might be the advantages?
(Intermediate)

5. To illustrate for children the dilemma of early explorers such as Pytheas, ask each child to read about the customs of a different country. Tell them to list any customs that are very different from those in the United States. Next, they should add to their list some more customs that they have made up. Have each child report to the group her or his list of customs and see whether the other children can distinguish between the true and the make-believe customs.
(Primary, intermediate)

TALES OF SEA MONSTERS

Mariners have always tried to fill in the blanks in their information about the unknown depths of the oceans. Any unexplained phenomena were usually credited to the presence of sea monsters. Add to this tendency the stories of sea monsters that were made up by the Phoenician mariners to frighten other merchants away from their trade routes, and we have the beginnings of a legacy of myth and legend about these creatures stretching throughout human history, right into the present day.

Book List

Abels, Harriette. *The Loch Ness Monster*. Crestwood House, 1987. (Gr. 4-6)
Suggests theories about the large creature living in Loch Ness in Scotland.

Armour, Richard. *Strange Monsters of the Sea*. McGraw-Hill, 1979. (Gr. 2-4)
A collection of poetry about real and imaginary sea monsters.

Bendick, Jeanne. *The Mystery of the Loch Ness Monster*. McGraw-Hill, 1976. (Gr. 4-up)
Reviews the history and geography of Loch Ness as well as theories about the monster.

Buehr, Walter. *Sea Monsters*. W. W. Norton, 1966. (Gr. 3-6)
This nonfiction title introduces a number of sea monsters people have believed existed from early times to the present.

Kellogg, Steven. *The Mysterious Tadpole*. Dial, 1977. (PreK-3)
Louis receives what he thinks is a tadpole from his uncle for his birthday. But is it?

Peet, Bill. *Cyrus the Unsinkable Sea Serpent*. Houghton Mifflin, 1975. (PreK-3)
Cyrus the sea serpent aids ships crossing the Atlantic for the New World, saving them from storms and pirates.

Rabinowich, Ellen. *The Loch Ness Monster*. Franklin Watts, 1979. (Gr. 3-6)
This is a heavily illustrated overview of the case for the existence of the Loch Ness monster of Scotland.

San Souci, Robert D. *The Loch Ness Monster*. Greenhaven Press, 1989. (Gr. 5-up)
This title from the Great Mysteries series examines the case for the Loch Ness monster.

Snyder, Gerald. *Is There a Loch Ness Monster?* Messner, 1977. (Gr. 4-up)
Another look at the case for the creature of Loch Ness.

Sweeney, James R. *Sea Monsters*. David McKay, 1977. (Gr. 4-6)
This title is similar to the title by Buehr, above. Sweeney examines both mythical and actual sea monsters.

Wilson, Sarah. *Beware the Dragons!* Harper & Row, 1985. (PreK-2)
When the young heroine is caught by sea dragons on her trip across the bay, she discovers they only want to play.

Related Activities

1. With very young children, tell them that long ago, people believed there were monsters in the sea. Explain that even though we now know this is not true, it is sometimes fun to pretend that there are monsters. Read *The Mysterious Tadpole* by Steven Kellogg, *Cyrus the Unsinkable Sea Serpent* by Bill Peet, and *Beware the Dragons!* by Sarah Wilson. Share some poems from Richard Armour's *Strange Monsters of the Sea*. Then let the children make sea monsters. Give each child a copy of the sea monster in figure 3.2. Have them color it and cut it out. Then curl the tab around to form a ring and tape the ring to make the sea monster into a finger puppet.
(Preschool, primary)

Fig. 3.2.

2. Draw a sea monster for the children (see fig. 3.3) as you tell the following story.

The Little Sea Monster

First I'll draw the body
With a couple of humps.

Then I'll cover the back
And the tail with bumps.

I'll put a pointed triangle
At the end.

And add a long neck
So the head can bend.

I'll add four flippers
So he can swim.

And a head with horns
And a happy grin

I'll add some eyes
So he can see.

Now what do you think
This creature might be?

(Preschool, primary)

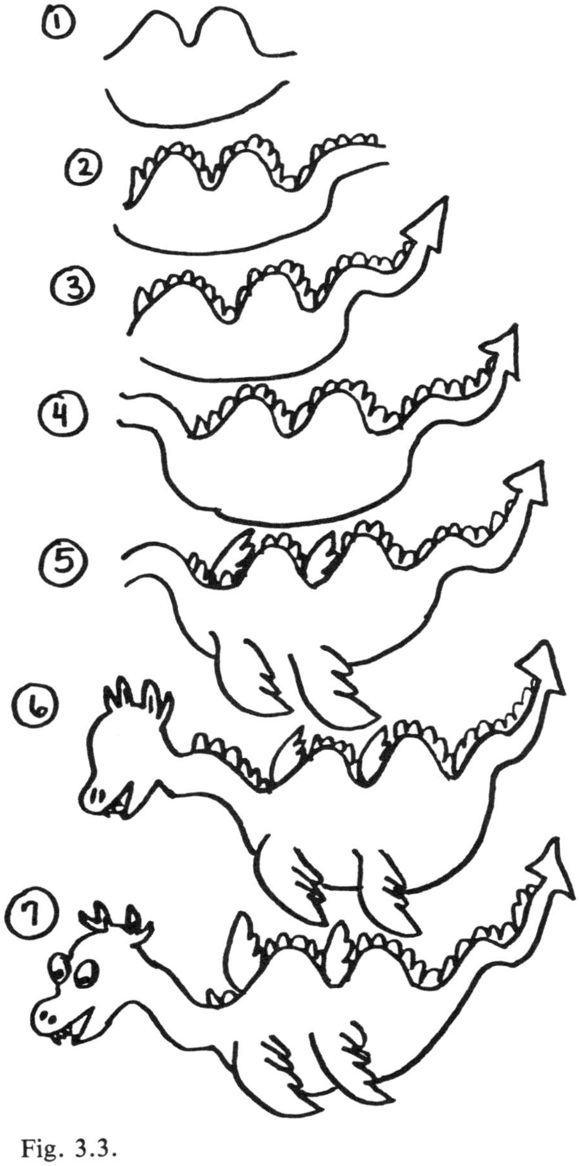

Fig. 3.3.

3. Play the game "Catch the Sea Serpent's Tail." The children form a sea serpent by standing in a line with their hands on the waist of the person in front of them. The line begins to run, twisting and turning, and as it does, the sea serpent's head, which is the first person in line, tries to catch the sea serpent's tail, which is the last person in line. If the head catches the tail, the first player goes to the end of the line and becomes the tail, and the next person in line becomes the new head. Keep playing until every one has had a turn being the sea serpent's head and tail.
(Preschool, primary)

4. A fun game to play is "Sea Serpent Search." Ask the children to pretend that they are searching for a huge sea serpent in the ocean. Choose one child to be the sea serpent. Have the rest of the children close their eyes while the sea serpent hides somewhere in the play area. When you call out "Sea Serpent Search!" the children open their eyes and begin to search. When they find the sea serpent, they must run back to a designated spot that represents their ship. If the sea serpent catches someone, that person becomes the new sea serpent.
(Preschool, primary)

5. Older children might enjoy books on sea monsters by Walter Buehr, Ellen Rabinowich, Robert San Souci, Gerald Snyder, and James Sweeney. The children could research modern sea monsters, such as the Loch Ness monster, and compare them to ancient beliefs. Hold a debate between those children who believe there really are creatures like the Loch Ness monster and those who do not. Each group should provide evidence for their stance. For example, the nonbelievers must have a reasonable explanation for all the sightings that have been reported.
(Intermediate)

MYTHS AND LEGENDS

A few reports of ancient explorations have come down to us through the histories by Herodotus and others. Some of the stories have been transformed into myths, such as those of Jason and the Argonauts and Odysseus. We know that parts of Homer's tales are true because in the late 1800s the German archaeologist Heinrich Schliemann discovered the ruins of the city of Troy. If there was a real Troy, perhaps some of Odysseus's travels were real, though obviously exaggerated.

Another legend is about a mythical continent called Atlantis. Plato described this island, which was supposedly out in the Atlantic Ocean, in the fourth century B.C.E. Atlantis reputedly was a highly advanced civilization with a royal city—full of palaces, temples, and public baths—surrounded by rich villages. The belief in Atlantis influenced explorers for centuries to come. Most ancient maps were dotted with such mythical islands, and even Columbus expected to find them. Today, there is still some speculation that Atlantis really existed.

Book List

Abels, Harriette. *The Lost City of Atlantis*. Crestwood House, 1987. (Gr. 3-6)
This title examines the evidence for the existence of the mythical continent of Atlantis.

Bowman, John S. *The Quest for Atlantis*. Doubleday, 1971. (Gr. 5-up)
A scholarly discussion of the possible existence of the mythical land described by Plato.

Connolly, Peter. *The Legend of Odysseus*. Oxford University Press, 1986. (Gr. 4-up)
This title recounts the story of the Trojan War, including Odysseus's adventures returning home.

Fisher, Leonard Everett. *Jason and the Golden Fleece*. Holiday House, 1990. (Gr. 3-6)
Fisher retells this travel myth with beautiful illustrations.

McMullen, David. *Atlantis: The Missing Continent*. Raintree, 1977. (Gr. 3-6)
A recounting of the myth of the ancient continent of Atlantis.

Naden, C. J. *Jason and the Golden Fleece*. Troll, 1980. (Gr. 2-4)
A simplified and illustrated retelling of the myth.

Richardson, I. M. *Odysseus and the Cyclops*. Troll, 1984. (Gr. 3-6)
This title, and others in the series (*Odysseus and the Giants* and *The Voyage of Odysseus*), are retellings of Odysseus' adventures in short, illustrated format.

Storr, Catherine. *Odysseus and the Enchanters*. Raintree, 1985. (Gr. 2-6)
A retelling of Odysseus' adventures in picture-book format.

Related Activities

1. Explain to the children that long ago, storytellers made up strange stories about the travelers of the time. Tell them Odysseus was an ancient traveler who was trying to get back home from a war. Read Catherine Storr's book *Odysseus and the Enchanters*. Let the children make pig masks by gluing features to a paper plate (see fig. 3.4) to pretend they are Odysseus's men being turned into pigs.
(Preschool, primary)

Fig. 3.4.

2. Describe Jason's travels to find the Golden Fleece. Read Leonard Everett Fisher's *Jason and the Golden Fleece*. Explain that the Golden Fleece was the fleece, or wool, of a sheep that was filled with gold dust. Let the children make golden fleeces. Give each child an oval of white construction paper. Show them how to tear up cotton balls and glue the cotton to the ovals to make fleeces. Then sprinkle gold glitter over the cotton.
(Preschool, primary)

3. Describe the legend of Atlantis, using the titles listed above. Then ask the children to imagine that they are archaeologists who find the lost island of Atlantis. Ask them to write a description of their findings that will show what the people of Atlantis and their royal city may have been like. The children could also draw a map or royal city plan of Atlantis.
(Intermediate)

EARLY DISCOVERERS OF THE AMERICAS

Christopher Columbus was not the first European to discover the American continents. Around 1000 C.E., Vikings from northern Europe landed in Newfoundland, among other places, and tried to establish a settlement there. However, they were driven out by the native inhabitants, and the news of their exploits never filtered down to the rest of Europe. Legend has it that even earlier, in the sixth century, Saint Brendan, an Irish abbot, sailed across the Atlantic to the New World. It is also possible that other early peoples, such as the Phoenicians, may have crossed the Atlantic before recorded history began. Some theories even hold that other European sailors in the Middle Ages may have been blown off course and reached the American continents but left no records.

A number of excellent books discuss pre-Columbian exploits and describe how they were possible, arousing a great deal of debate. Most recently, John Dyson has published his book *Columbus: For Gold, God, and Glory*, which contains a fascinating theory that Columbus knew where he was going when he set sail because he had a secret map that he got from a dying seaman who had been blown off course and had ended up in the Caribbean.

Book List

Anno, Mitsumasa. *Anno's U.S.A.* Putnam, 1983. (PreK-5)
In this wordless picture book, Anno introduces the United States in drawings.

Atkinson, Ian. *The Viking Ships*. Lerner, 1980. (Gr. 4-up)
This title discusses the construction and uses of Viking ships.

Barden, Renardo. *The Discovery of America*. Greenhaven Press, 1989. (Gr. 5-up)
This entry in the Great Mysteries series explores the question of who first discovered the North American continent, Columbus or an earlier explorer.

Benchley, Nathaniel. *Snorri and the Strangers*. Harper & Row, 1976. (PreK-3)
This beginning reader tells of Norse explorers trying to establish a settlement in the New World.

Clarke, Helen. *Vikings*. Gloucester Press, 1979. (Gr. 3-up)
This nonfiction title covers Viking history and everyday life.

D'Aulaire, Ingri, and Edgar Parin D'Aulaire. *Leif the Lucky*. Doubleday, 1941. (Gr. 3-6)
This retells, in story form, Leif Eriksson's discovery of America.

Fritz, Jean. *Brendan the Navigator: A History Mystery about the Discovery of America*. Putnam, 1979. (Gr. 3-5)
This is an imaginative recounting of the voyage Saint Brendan may have taken to North America in the sixth century.

Gibb, Christopher. *A Viking Sailor*. Rourke, 1986. (Gr. 3-6)
This heavily illustrated nonfiction title describes the Vikings as sailors and covers how the sea influenced their way of life.

Humble, Richard. *The Age of Leif Eriksson*. Franklin Watts, 1989. (Gr. 4-6)
This story of the Vikings' voyages of discovery includes their colonization of lands discovered by Erik the Red.

Irwin, Constance. *Strange Footprints on the Land: Vikings in America*. Harper & Row, 1980. (Gr. 5-up)
For older readers, this is a fascinating look at the case for early Viking exploration of the North American continent.

Jensen, Malcolm C. *Leif Erikson the Lucky*. Franklin Watts, 1979. (Gr. 4-up)
This biography of Leif Eriksson includes information about his father, Erik the Red, and the Viking explorations.

Krensky, Stephen. *Who Really Discovered America?* Hastings House, 1987. (Gr. 4-6)
The author of this book describes the various people who are believed to have visited the Americas before Columbus.

Lattimore, Deborah. *The Sailor Who Captured the Sea: A Story of the Book of Kells*. HarperCollins, 1991. (Gr. 2-6)
This picture book describes the Viking threat during the creation of the Book of Kells, which was an illuminated manuscript of the four biblical Gospels completed by Irish monks between the middle of the eighth century and the beginning of the ninth.

Lauber, Patricia. *Who Discovered America?* Random House, 1970. (Gr. 4-up)
All the possible predecessors of Columbus are covered in this nonfiction title.

Leon, George deLucenay. *Explorers of the Americas before Columbus*. Franklin Watts, 1989. (Gr. 4-6)
Includes Saint Brendan, the Vikings, and possible ancient visitors to South America.

Maestro, Betsy, and Giulio Maestro. *The Discovery of the Americas*. Lothrop, Lee & Shepard, 1991. (K-5)
This beautiful picture book covers all the early discoverers of America, including the first Stone Age inhabitants, the Phoenicians, Saint Brendan, the Vikings, and Columbus.

Magnuson, Magnus. *Viking Expansion Westward*. Henry Z. Walck, 1973. (Gr. 5-up)
Covers Viking expansion between the ninth and twelfth centuries and examines archaeological discoveries of Viking settlements.

Martell, Hazel. *The Vikings*. Warwick Press, 1986. (Gr. 3-up)
This is a general description of the Viking way of life, including voyages of exploration.

Matthews, Rupert. *Viking Explorers*. Bookwright, 1991. (Gr. 3-6)
A look at early Vikings and their trips of exploration.

Murphy, Barbara Beasley, and Norman Baker. *Thor Heyerdahl and the Reed Boat Ra*. Lippincott, 1974. (Gr. 4-up)
A firsthand account of Heyerdahl's experimental voyage to prove that the early Phoenicians or Egyptians could have reached the American continents.

Neal, Harry Edward. *Before Columbus: Who Discovered America?* Messner, 1981. (Gr. 3-6)
The author examines the claims of the Irish, the Norse, the British, and others as the first discoverers of North America.

Schiller, Barbara. *The Vinlanders' Saga*. Holt, Rinehart & Winston, 1966. (Gr. 3-up)
This adaptation of the Icelandic saga describes the Viking discovery of America.

Simon, Charnan. *Leif Eriksson and the Vikings*. Children's Press, 1991. (Gr. 4-up)
Relates the explorations of Leif Eriksson and the Vikings.

Unstead, R. J. *From Cavemen to Vikings*. Adam and Charles Black, 1982. (Gr. 4-6)
A look at some of the early civilizations that may have visited the American continents.

Related Activities

1. It is hard for very young children to grasp the concepts involved in the exploits of the early explorers. Start by explaining that many different lands exist in the world and that we live in the United States. Show the children Mitsumasa Anno's *Anno's U.S.A.* Then explain that long ago most people did not know that the land we now live in was here. Describe the way early people traveled from place to place by boat and that one day as they were sailing, they came across this land.
(Preschool, primary)

2. *The Discovery of the Americas* by Betsy Maestro and Giulio Maestro is a beautiful picture book that introduces such early travelers as the original Stone Age nomads who crossed a land bridge from Asia, the Phoenicians, Ireland's Saint Brendan, and the Vikings. Let the children act out a voyage of discovery. Use either a large box or a blanket spread on the floor to represent the ship. Have the children sit in the box or on the blanket and pretend they are rowing to the New World. As they sail, they can sing:

Row, Row, Row Your Ship
(Sung to "Row Your Boat")

We row, row, row our ship
On the mighty sea,
Merrily, merrily, merrily, merrily,
To see what we can see.

(Preschool, primary)

3. Introduce older children to the people who discovered the American continents long before Columbus set sail, with the books by Renardo Barden, Stephen Krensky, Patricia Lauber, George deLucenay Leon, and Harry Neal. To help the children understand the sequence in time of these discoverers, have them make an illustrated timeline showing the dates of various explorers, from the ancients through all the possible discoverers of the Americas (see fig. 3.5).
(Primary, intermediate)

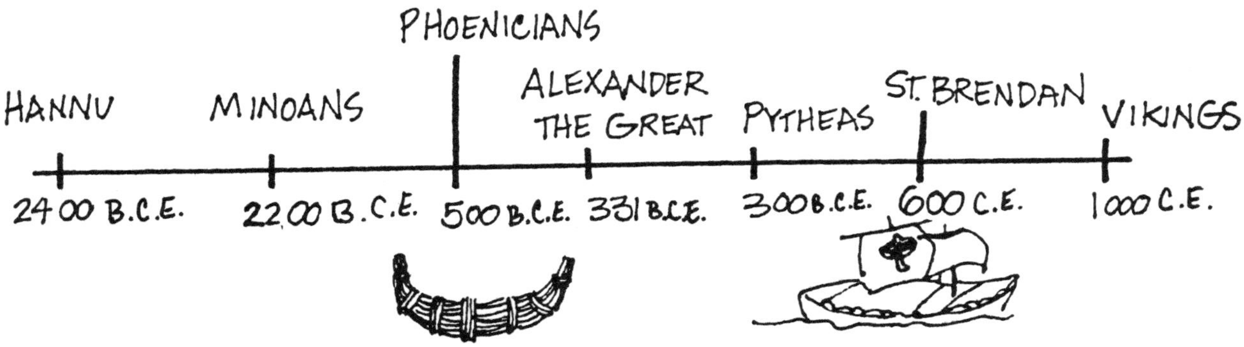

Fig. 3.5.

4. After reading some of the books listed above, hold a discoverer's debate. Let each child pick an early explorer, such as Saint Brendan, Leif Eriksson, a Phoenician, or other possible "firsts." Make sure someone chooses Columbus. Then have each child present the case of the explorer he or she is representing to be awarded the honor of being called the "discoverer of America." After all the debaters have been heard, let the class vote on who was most convincing.
(Intermediate)

5. Talk about the disputed theory that very early explorers such as the Phoenicians could have followed ocean currents to the American continents. Share some of the book *Thor Heyerdahl and the Reed Boat Ra*. Let children experience how amazing Heyerdahl's experiment was by having them try to make a reed boat using straw and string (fig. 3.6). To make a model of a reed boat, collect long dried grass or straw. Each child will need two lengths of wire each about 12 inches long. Around each piece of wire, wrap a bundle of eight-inch straw parallel to the wire. Tie the straw bundles every inch with string. Bend each piece into a boat shape as shown. To connect the two halves, use a piece of wire to weave them together along the boat's keel.
(Intermediate)

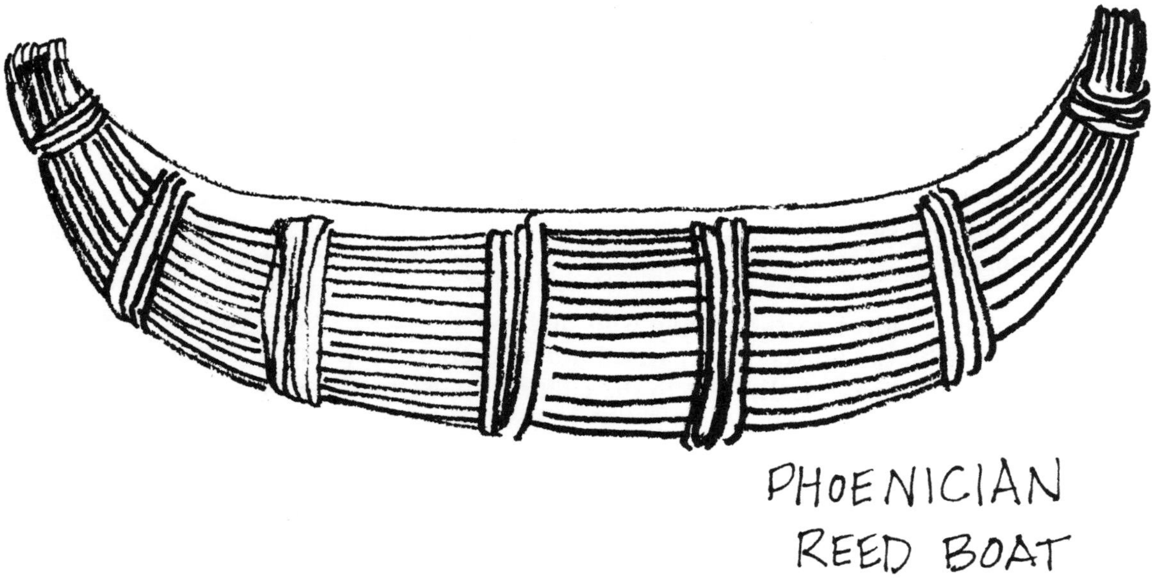

Fig. 3.6.

6. Introduce children to the legend of Saint Brendan by reading aloud Jean Fritz's book *Brendan the Navigator*. You can also use the book *The Sailor Who Captured the Sea* by Deborah Lattimore to introduce both Irish monks and the coming of the Vikings. Saint Brendan's boat would have been a small boat with a wooden frame covered with leather, called a coracle or curragh. Make Saint Brendan's boat using a small box as the wooden frame (see fig. 3.7). Poke holes all around the edges of the box. Cover the box frame with a scrap of leather or burlap and stitch the scrap to the box using the holes in the box. Insert a pencil or wooden dowel for a mast. A lump of clay in the bottom of the box will hold the dowel. To make a realistic sail, cut a sail shape from a piece of cardboard. Trace the shape on a piece of white material folded in half. Cut out the material so that you have two "sails." Glue one of these pieces on each side of the cardboard sail and decorate your "sail" with a cross. Use string to tie the sail to the mast. Finally, make a small figure of Saint Brendan, as shown in figure 3.7. Fold the cutout into a sitting position and insert it in the boat.
(Intermediate)

7. Introduce the Viking explorers by reading Barbara Schiller's *The Vinlanders' Saga*. Because the Vikings are the group for which we have the best evidence of settlement in America, use some of the other titles listed above to introduce children to the Viking way of life.

Fig. 3.7.

Make a Viking longship. Use a piece of posterboard about 12 inches long and 9 inches wide for the hull. Fold the posterboard the long way, and draw an outline of a Viking ship so that the bottom of the ship is on the fold of the posterboard, as shown in figure 3.8. Keeping the posterboard folded, cut out the ship, being careful not to cut through the bottom fold. Decorate the hull, and then glue the ends together where they rise up at the bow and stern. Make shields to decorate the sides of the boat by cutting circles 1½ inches in diameter out of posterboard. Decorate the shields with Viking designs and glue a row of them to each side of the ship. Cut a sail from paper and decorate it with stripes. Use a pencil or dowel for the mast, and poke the mast through the top and bottom of the sail. Tape the mast to the bottom of the boat. Poke a few holes in the sides of the boat between the shields and insert small sticks, such as matchsticks, for oars. Use a tongue depressor glued to the right side in front for a steering oar.
(Intermediate)

8. For younger children, read Nathaniel Benchley's *Snorri and the Strangers*. Then give each child a copy of the Viking ship in figure 3.9 (see page 51) to color, with a slit cut at the dotted line. Give the children precut copies of the Viking in figure 3.9 to insert in their ships.
(Preschool, primary)

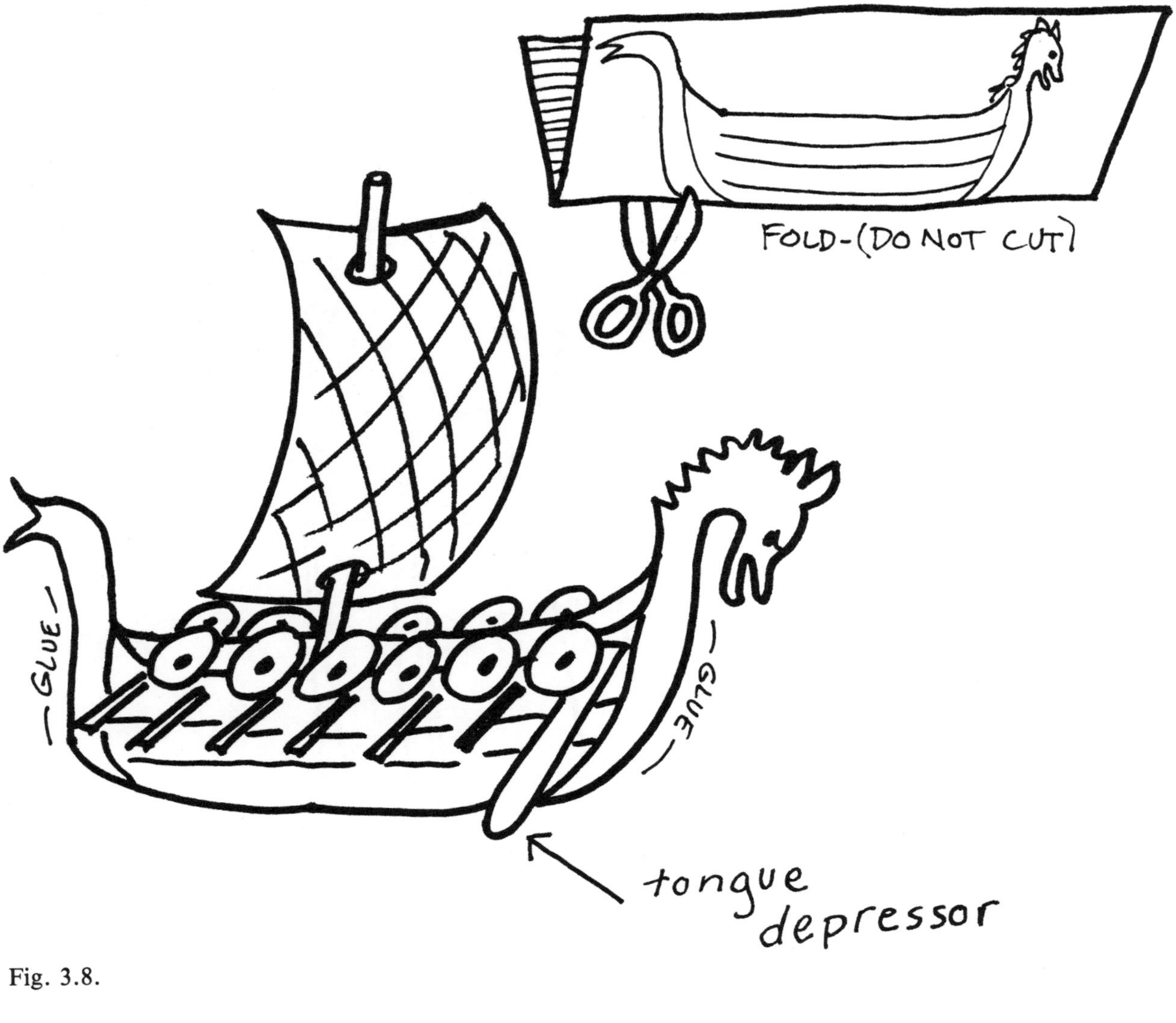

Fig. 3.8.

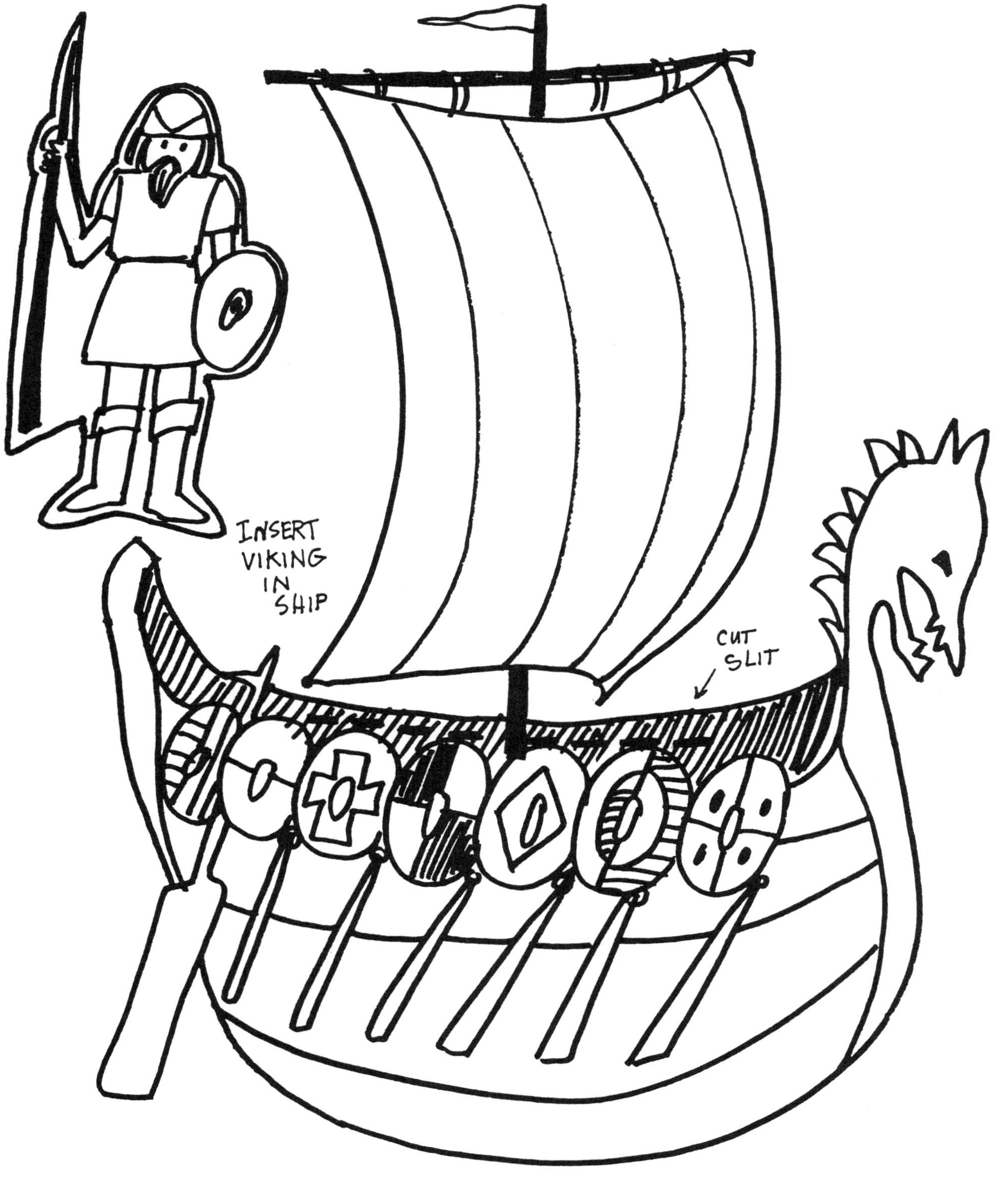

Fig. 3.9.

4

The Medieval World

In this chapter we first cover life in the Middle Ages and how it influenced exploration. Then some of the accounts of travel during this period are looked at. Next, activities are introduced to help children understand the importance of trade from the Indies as a motivation for exploration. Finally, the medieval concept of the world is examined.

LIFE IN THE MIDDLE AGES

During the Middle Ages, the people of Europe had no knowledge of earlier voyages of discovery and held a very limited view of the world. Their lives were strictly governed by the Catholic Church, which did not encourage new ways of thinking. Society was very rigid and little change occurred in the way people did things or in how they envisioned the world. The "known" world at that time consisted mainly of northern Europe and the countries surrounding the Mediterranean Sea. The lands of the Far East were known to exist, but few people had any accurate idea of exactly where they were or what they were like.

Book List

Aliki. *A Medieval Feast*. Crowell, 1983. (Gr. 2-6)

This picture book, which describes a feast in a manor house, can be used to introduce medieval foods and spices.

Bulla, Clyde Robert. *Sword in the Tree*. Crowell, 1988. (Gr. 2-5)

This fiction title introduces England's King Arthur and his knights.

Carrick, Donald. *Harald and the Giant Knight*. Houghton Mifflin, 1982. (Gr. 2-4)

This picture book portrays the injustice of the feudal system when callous knights destroy a family's farm.

Chaucer, Geoffrey. *Canterbury Tales*. Lothrop, Lee & Shepard, 1988. (Gr. 4-8)
An introduction to these classic travelers' tales.

Cosman, Madeleine Pelner. *Medieval Holidays and Festivals*. Charles Scribner's Sons, 1981. (Gr. 5-up)
Describes the customs associated with a number of medieval holidays, including recipes and instructions for costumes and other crafts.

Davies, Penelope. *Growing Up in the Middle Ages*. Wayland Books, 1972. (Gr. 4-6)
Brief paragraphs of text and numerous illustrations describe everyday life during the Middle Ages, including education, home life, work, and entertainment.

dePaola, Tomie. *The Knight and the Dragon*. Putnam, 1980. (PreK-2)
In this picture book, a knight and a dragon prepare for battle.

Edelman, Lynn. *Kings, Queens, Knights, and Jesters: Making Medieval Costumes*. Harper & Row, 1978. (Gr. 4-up)
This title not only includes detailed directions for making medieval costumes but also, in the process, introduces much information about medieval life.

Fradon, Dana. *Sir Dana: A Knight, as Told by His Trusty Armor*. Dutton, 1988. (Gr. 2-6)
In this picture book, a class visits a museum and learns about medieval knights.

Gerrard, Roy. *Sir Cedric*. Farrar, Straus & Giroux, 1984. (PreK-3)
This picture book presents a light-hearted look at a knight of the Middle Ages.

______. *Sir Cedric Rides Again*. Farrar, Straus & Giroux, 1986. (K-4)
This picture book depicts a knight's journey to Jerusalem.

Goodall, John S. *The Story of a Farm*. Macmillan, 1989. (PreK-4)
This wordless picture book shows the changes in an English farm over the centuries.

______. *The Story of an English Village*. Atheneum, 1979. (PreK-4)
This is a wordless look at how an English village changed from medieval times to the present.

Gray, Elizabeth Janet. *Adam of the Road*. Viking, 1942. (Gr. 5-8)
This fiction tale is about a medieval minstrel boy and his adventures.

Lasker, Joe. *Merry Ever After*. Viking, 1976. (Gr. 2-5)
This picture book describes two weddings of the Middle Ages, one of a noble and one of a peasant couple.

______. *A Tournament of Knights*. Crowell, 1986. (Gr. 3-6)
This story tells of a knight going to fight in his first tournament.

Macdonald, Fiona. *The Middle Ages*. Silver Burdett, 1984. (Gr. 4-6)
This is a survey of all aspects of medieval life, including travel and exploration.

Morgan, Gwyneth. *Life in a Medieval Village*. Lerner, 1982. (Gr. 3-up)
This is a nonfiction depiction of village life in the Middle Ages.

Peet, Bill. *Cowardly Clyde*. Houghton Mifflin, 1979. (PreK-2)
Clyde is a knight's horse who is terrified of fighting a dragon.

______. *How Droofus the Dragon Lost His Head*. Houghton Mifflin, 1971. (PreK-2)
This story tells the fate of Droofus the Dragon.

Pierce, Tamora. *Alanna: The First Adventure*. Macmillan, 1983. (Gr. 5-8)
A fiction title concerning knights and the Middle Ages. Also use the sequel, *In the Hand of the Goddess* (1984).

Price, Christine. *Made in the Middle Ages*. Dutton, 1961. (Gr. 4-up)
Covers medieval armor, weapons, clothing, jewelry, furniture, books, and other objects.

Pyle, Howard. *Men of Iron*. Harper and Brothers, 1930. (Gr. 5-8)
A classic about knighthood.

Ross, Stewart. *A Crusading Knight*. Rourke, 1986. (Gr. 3-6)
This heavily illustrated title describes why knights went on the Crusades, their experiences, and the cultural influences they brought back to Europe.

Scarry, Huck. *Looking into the Middle Ages*. Harper & Row, 1985. (Gr. 2-6)
This pop-up book shows medieval castles, cathedrals, and knights.

Skurzynski, Gloria. *Minstrel in the Tower*. Random House, 1988. (Gr. 3-4)
This story concerns the Crusades in the Middle Ages.

Trez, Denise. *The Little Knight's Dragon*. Collins World, 1963. (PreK-1)
This picture book is about knights and dragons.

Williams, Jay. *Life in the Middle Ages*. Random House, 1966. (Gr. 4-up)
This title covers the history and conditions of life in the Middle Ages and includes early travelers such as Marco Polo and other merchant adventurers.

Related Activities

1. To introduce children to the world as it was in medieval times, just before the Age of Exploration, use any of the titles above on the Middle Ages by Fiona Macdonald, Gwyneth Morgan, Huck Scarry, and Jay Williams. You might also share Chaucer's *Canterbury Tales*. Older children can read Elizabeth Gray's *Adam of the Road*. As most of the information about other lands during the Middle Ages came from merchants traveling for trade, let the children make medieval merchant puppets. Give each child two 6-inch paper plates. Cut one plate in half and staple the rim of this half to the other plate, with the convex side of each plate on the outside. This should leave a pocket, as shown in figure 4.1, to insert a hand for manipulating the puppet. On the whole plate, use markers to draw the puppet's face. Use colored construction paper to cut out a floppy-shaped hat like those worn in the Middle Ages (see examples in fig. 4.1). You may want to

trim the hat with feathers or fake fur. Next, use the pattern in figure 4.2 for the puppet's body. Decorate the clothes, cut out the body, and attach the body to the paper-plate head by inserting a paper brad first through the plate in the chin area and then through the black dot on the body pattern.
(Primary, intermediate)

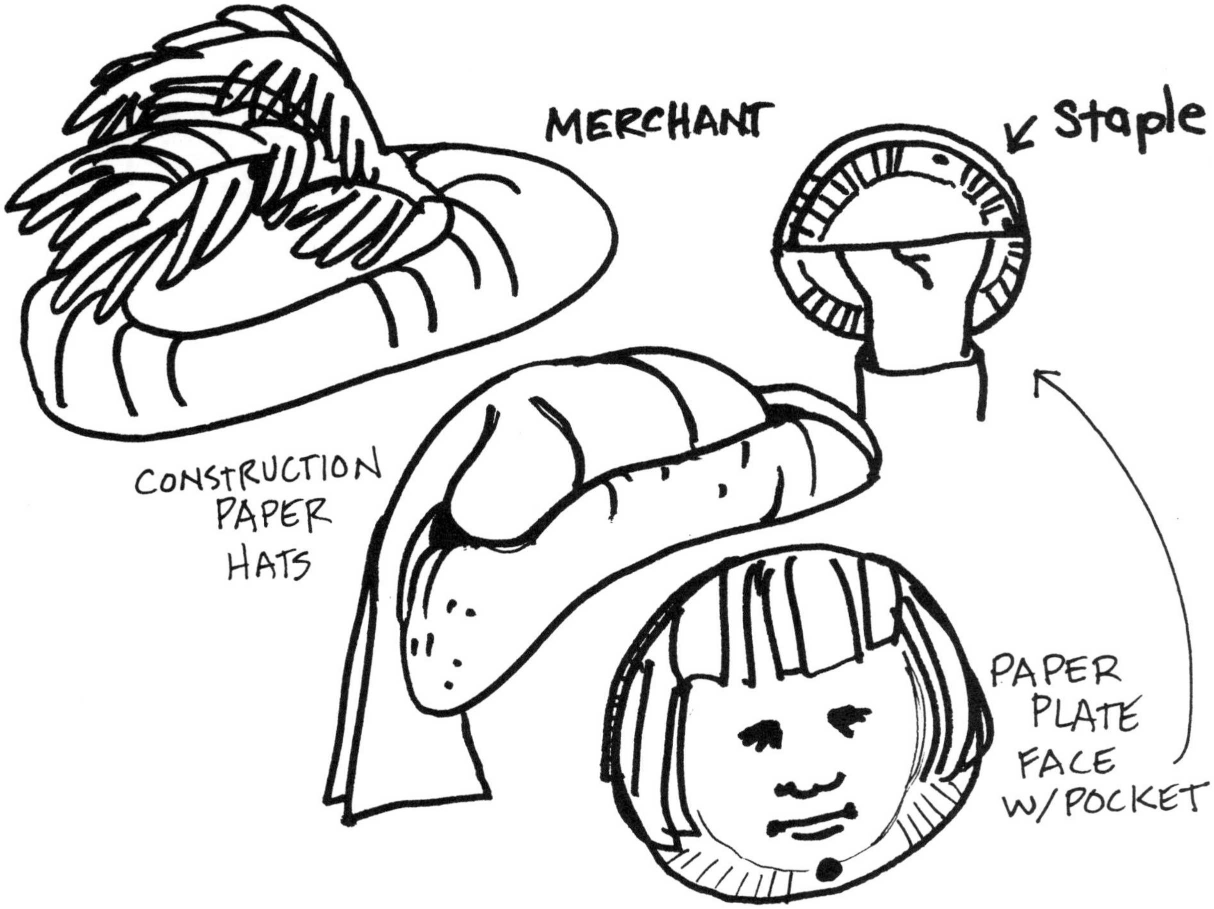

Fig. 4.1.

2. Explain that people did not always live the way we do now. At one time there were no televisions, microwave ovens, or many other things that we have now. Share the books by John S. Goodall, which show the changes that occurred over time in an English farm and village.
(Preschool, primary)

Fig. 4.2.

3. Explain to young children that in the early times known as the Middle Ages, there were people called knights, who rode around the country fighting battles on horseback. Describe a suit of armor by telling children that knights wore these metal suits of armor to protect themselves from harm. Read aloud a couple of the picture books about knights by Tomie dePaola, Roy Gerrard, Bill Peet, and Denise Trez.

Then let the children make their own knights and dragons. Give each child a copy of the knight pattern in figure 4.3, and provide silver crayons so the children can color the armor. Then cut out the pieces and put the knight together with paper brads inserted through the dots on the various parts. Very young children may need help with cutting.

Make dragon stick-puppets in the same way, giving each child a copy of figure 4.4 to color and cut out. Tape each dragon to a popsicle stick. The children can then use these figures to act out an encounter between a knight and a dragon.
(Preschool, primary)

4. Play the game "Knights and Dragons." You will need to make a dragon like the one shown in figure 4.5 (see page 60) from cardboard boxes. Paint the dragon green with tempera paint. For this game, children pretend they are knights and try to "catch" the dragon by tossing rings over the dragon's head. You can make rings by stapling strips of cardboard into a circle.
(Preschool, primary)

5. Knights were also medieval explorers, as they rode off on Crusades against the "infidels" in the East. Introduce knights and the Crusades by reading aloud the books by Donald Carrick, Dana Fradon, Roy Gerrard, Joe Lasker, and Stewart Ross. Older children may want to read *The Sword in the Tree* by Clyde Bulla, *Alanna* by Tamora Pierce, *Men of Iron* by Howard Pyle, *Minstrel in the Tower* by Gloria Skurzynski, or other fiction titles about King Arthur and knights. Then have the children make suits of armor to wear. To make the helmet, use a piece of posterboard about 10" square. Draw on the helmet shape shown in figure 4.6 (see page 60). Draw a visor section with slits to see through and cut out the slits. Either spray the mask with silver spraypaint or cover it with tin foil to make it look like metal. Add a real feather or one cut from construction paper as a plume or crest for the helmet. Poke a hole in either side of the helmet and attach pieces of string to tie the helmet on the head as a mask.

Make a breastplate from another piece of posterboard large enough to cover a child's chest. For primary children you will need a piece of posterboard about 10 inches wide by 12 inches long. For intermediate ages, use a piece about 12 inches by 14 inches. Trim to fit as needed. Cut a neck opening and shape the sides and bottom as shown in figure 4.6. Poke holes in the posterboard on either side at the neck and at the waist. Attach strings long enough to tie around the neck and waist. Cover the breastplate with tin foil. If desired, glue a heraldic design cut from construction paper to the middle of the breastplate.

(Text continues on page 61.)

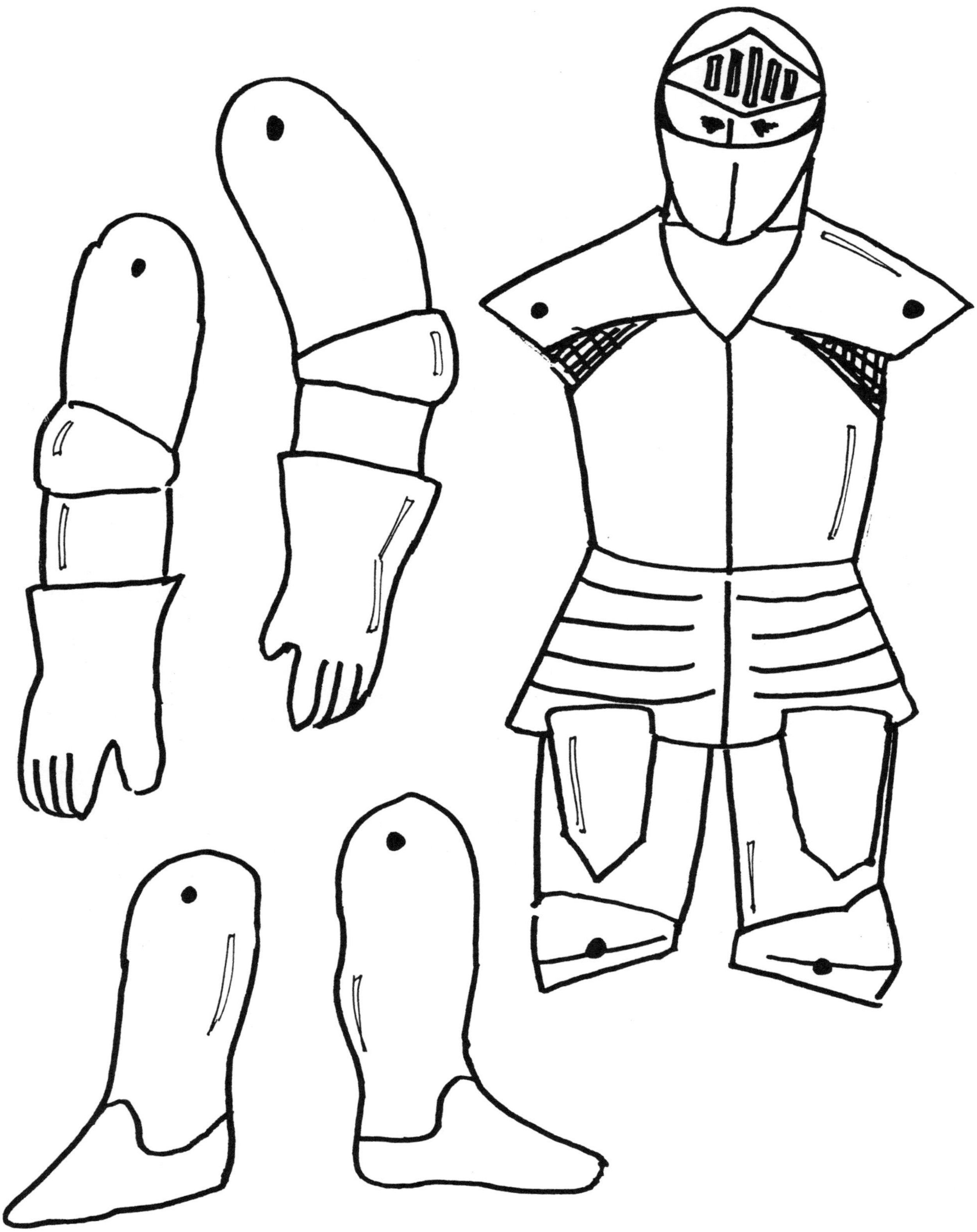

Fig. 4.3.

Fig. 4.4.

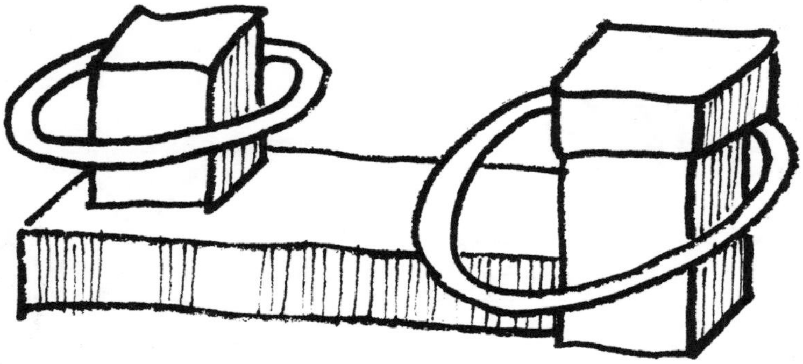

Fig. 4.5. Cardboard dragon.

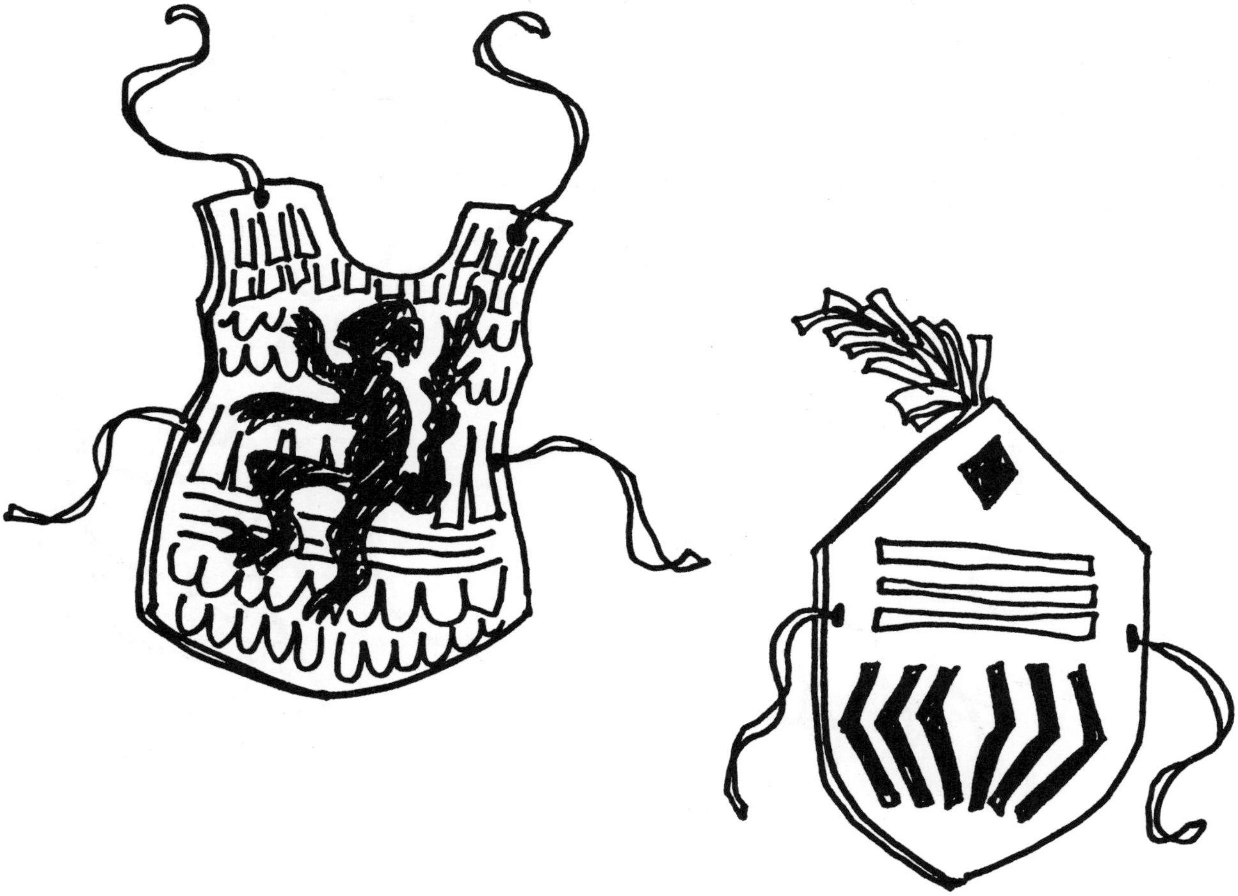

Fig. 4.6.

Also make a shield from posterboard, cut into the shape shown in figure 4.7. Decorate the front with heraldic designs. Staple to the back a loop of cardboard that is large enough to insert an arm into so children can hold up the shield. Finally, cut a sword from cardboard in the shape shown in figure 4.7. Cover the blade with tin foil, and use markers to color the hilt.

Fig. 4.7.

Now, design a knight's horse like the one in figure 4.8. For this project, you need a box large enough for a child to stand in. Remove the top flaps and turn the box upside down. In the sealed bottom of the box, cut a hole large enough for a child's body. Attach shoulder straps on each side of this opening by poking small holes and tying on strings, as shown. From a piece of posterboard, cut out the shape of the horse's head using an enlargement of figure 4.9. Decorate the horse's head using paints or markers. Draw a design on the sides of the box to look like draperies on the sides of knights' horses. At the back of the box, attach a long tassle of yarn as the horse's tail. The child then stands in the box and pulls it up so his or her arms fit through the shoulder straps.

If you want to extend these activities on the medieval period, use Madeleine Pelner Cosman's *Medieval Holidays and Festivals* or Lynn Edelman's book *Kings, Queens, Knights, and Jesters: Making Medieval Costumes*. Edelman's book provides directions for making costumes for all the orders of medieval society, easy enough for intermediate-age children to complete.

Read aloud *A Medieval Feast* by Aliki and *Merry Ever After* by Joe Lasker. Along with Cosman's book, these will present a clear picture of the medieval way of life.
(Primary, intermediate)

Fig. 4.8.

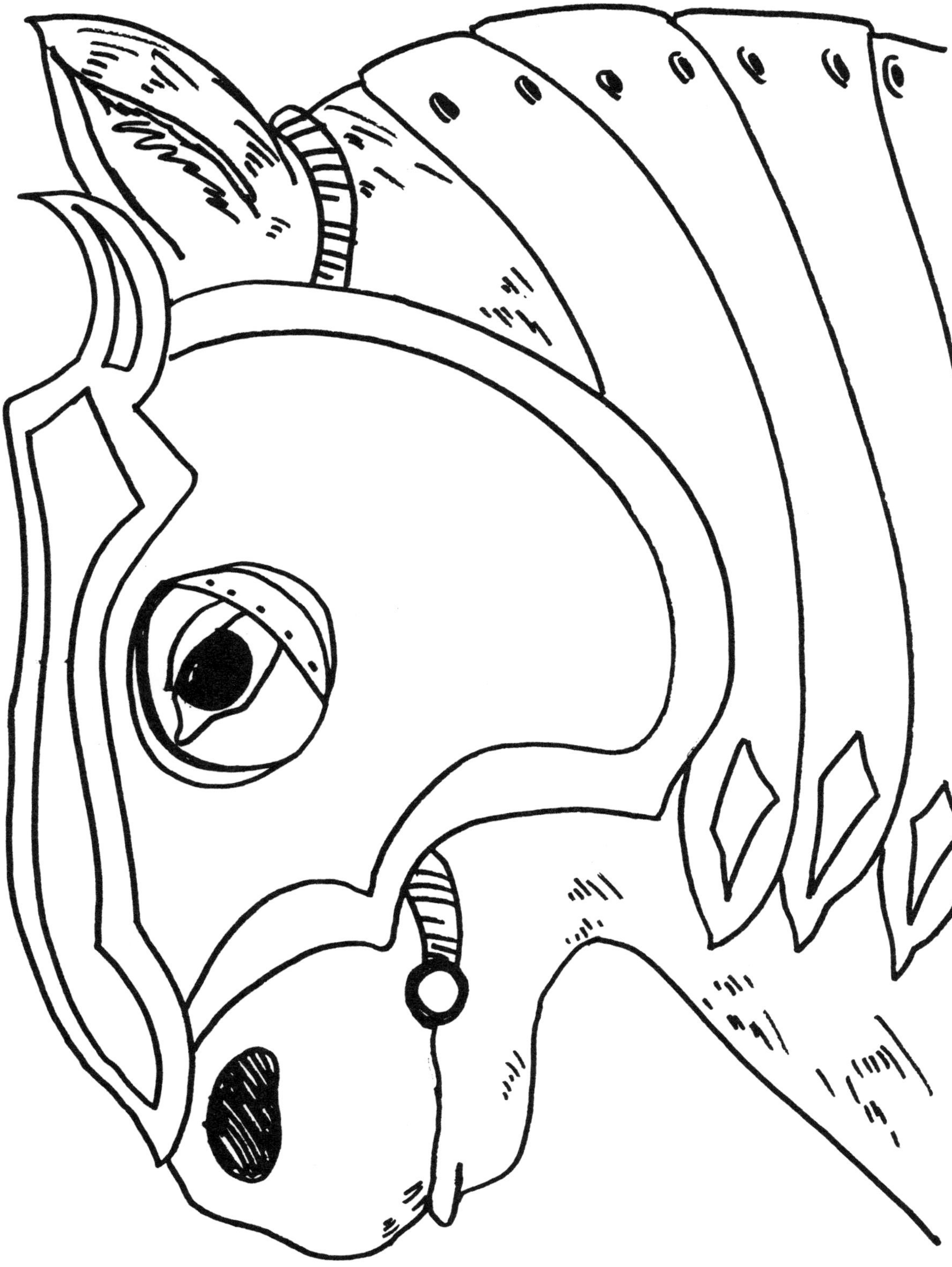

Fig. 4.9.

TRAVEL DURING THE MIDDLE AGES

In 1271, a Venetian, Marco Polo, traveled overland all the way from the eastern shore of the Mediterranean to the capital of the Mongol ruler Kublai Khan, in China. Polo's account of what he saw was so intriguing to Europeans that others, such as Sir John Mandeville, made up their own fabulous stories about life in these faraway lands and presented these stories as truth. Because the Far East was almost completely unknown, such false accounts were believed by many.

Book List

Anno, Mitsumasa. *Anno's Journey*. Collins World, 1977. (K-up)
This wordless book uses drawings to describe a traveler's journey through northern Europe and records (as did Marco Polo) impressions of the land, the people, and the customs encountered.

Balian, Lorna. *The Aminal*. Abingdon, 1972. (PreK-1)
As this story of a creature found by a little boy travels from friend to friend, the tale becomes stranger and stranger.

Barrett, Judi. *Cloudy with a Chance of Meatballs*. Atheneum, 1978. (K-up)
This tall tale of a fantastic land where food drops from the sky is similar to the outlandish stories told by Sir John Mandeville about the fabled East.

Benjamin, Alan. *Ribtickle Town*. Four Winds Press, 1983. (PreK-1)
This picture book describes a trip to a fantastic town.

Ceserani, Gian Paolo. *Marco Polo*. Putnam, 1982. (Gr. 3-6)
In picture-book format, this title follows the journeys of Marco Polo.

Demi. *The Adventures of Marco Polo*. Holt, Rinehart & Winston, 1982. (K-3)
In a swirl of graphic images, Demi introduces the exploits of Marco Polo in picture-book format.

______. *Chingis Khan*. Holt, Rinehart & Winston, 1991. (Gr. 2-5)
In this picture book, Demi tells the story of the fabled Mongol leader who conquered the East in the early thirteenth century. It was his grandson, Kublai Khan, whom Marco Polo traveled to see.

Graves, Charles Parlin. *Marco Polo*. Chelsea Juniors, 1991. (Gr. 3-up)
A biography of Marco Polo for young students.

Greene, Carol. *Marco Polo, Voyager to the Orient*. Children's Press, 1987. (Gr. 3-6)
An excellent biography of the early traveler Marco Polo.

Handford, Martin. *Find Waldo Now*. Little, Brown, 1988. (Gr. 2-up)
This is a picture-book game, with every page depicting a different historical scene, crammed with action, in which the reader must find the tiny figure of Waldo. See also *Where's Waldo?* (Little, Brown, 1987).

Humble, Richard. *The Travels of Marco Polo*. Franklin Watts, 1990. (Gr. 4-6)
This is an introduction to Marco Polo and his journeys.

Johnson, Jane. *Today I Thought I'd Run Away*. Dutton, 1985. (PreK-1)
In this picture book, a young boy packs his special things and travels the world, encountering fantastic creatures.

Lionni, Leo. *Fish Is Fish*. Pantheon, 1970. (PreK-1)
When a frog describes the marvels of life on land, a fish develops a very confused version of reality.

Otsuka, Yuzo. *Suho and the White Horse*. Viking, 1981. (K-4)
This Mongolian folktale introduces the way of life of the Eastern tribesmen among whom Marco Polo traveled.

Polo, Marco. *The Travels of Marco Polo, the Venetian*. Doubleday, 1948. (Gr. 5-up)
The fascinating firsthand account of Polo's travels to the East, as Columbus and other explorers read it.

Roth, Susan L. *Marco Polo: His Notebook*. Doubleday, 1990. (Gr. 3-6)
Roth retells Marco Polo's journeys in a first-person, diary format.

Rugoff, Milton. *Marco Polo's Adventures in China*. American Heritage, 1964. (Gr. 5-up)
Intriguing account of the exploits of Marco Polo and the world of his time.

Seuss, Dr. *I Had Trouble in Getting to Solla Sollew*. Random House, 1965. (PreK-3)
In a series of adventures almost as unusual as Marco Polo's, the hero in this picture book travels to find a land where there are no troubles.

Stefoff, Rebecca. *Marco Polo*. Chelsea House, 1992. (Gr. 5-up)
A biography of Polo for older readers.

Tompert, Ann. *Little Fox Goes to the End of the World*. Crown, 1976. (PreK-1)
Little Fox describes for her mother all the strange places she will discover, and the dangers she will encounter, when she travels to the end of the world.

Related Activities

1. Explain to children that long ago people did not have cars to travel in. They had to walk or ride a horse if they wanted to visit a new place, and it took a long time to get there. They also met many difficulties along the way. Read aloud *Anno's Journey* by Mitsumasa Anno and *Little Fox Goes to the End of the World* by Ann Tompert to introduce the concept of going on a journey.

Now let the children act out a journey. First, give each child a scarf or a bandana to fill with the things they think they will need on their travels. You can let them put in either real objects or pretend ones. Tie up each scarf on the end of a stick. Now the children can travel through an obstacle course you have set up. For example, use tables and chairs as mountains to climb over. Cover a card table with a sheet to make a cave to crawl through. Spread a blanket on the floor as a sea children must cross. As they travel along, they can sing this song:

We're Traveling over the Mountains
(sung to "The Bear Went over the Mountain")

We're traveling over the mountains,
We're traveling over the mountains,
We're traveling over the mountains,
To see what we can see.

(*other verses*)
We're traveling through the caverns...

We're traveling across the ocean...

We're traveling over the desert...

(Preschool, primary)

2. Marco Polo was the most famous explorer before Christopher Columbus. His story was told all over Europe for 200 years after he made his epic journey, and it created a burning curiosity in later explorers to go and see for themselves. Introduce the children to Marco Polo with any of the titles listed above about his adventures.
(Primary)

3. Let the children use the books *Find Waldo Now* and *Where's Waldo?* by Martin Handford. These are popular game books in which the character Waldo travels through different historical periods or through foreign lands, like Marco Polo did. Each page is crowded with detail, and the reader must try to find the figure of Waldo in each scene.

Now play the game "I'm Traveling to the Indies." This is an alphabet game with a travel theme. Seat the children in a circle and ask them to pretend they are merchant travelers like Marco Polo. The first player starts with the letter A and makes up a name, a country, and an item of trade. For example, "A, my name is Antonio, I'm taking a trip to Arabia, and I'm bringing back apricots." The next player must follow the pattern, using the letter B: "B, my name is Bernardo, I'm taking a trip to Bombay, and I'm bringing back baskets." Continue around the circle. If your group is old enough to be somewhat familiar with the geography of the Far East, ask them to try to use place names from there, such as Cathay, Delhi, or Ethiopia. Have a globe or map available to help them.
(Primary, intermediate)

4. Read Samuel Taylor Coleridge's poem "Kubla Khan":

In Xanadu did Kubla Khan
A stately pleasure-dome decree:
Where Alph, the sacred river, ran
Through caverns measureless to man
    Down to a sunless sea.
So twice five miles of fertile ground
With walls and towers were girdled round:
And there were gardens bright with sinuous rills,
Where blossomed many an incense-bearing tree;
And here were forests ancient as the hills,
Enfolding sunny spots of greenery.

Then ask the children to create pictures of what they imagine Kublai Khan's fabulous palace must have looked like. They can either draw their palaces freehand or you can give them an enlargement of the outline in figure 4.10 to fill in. Let children use sequins, greenery, glitter, and other fancy scraps to create a truly fabulous scene.
(Primary, intermediate)

5. Introduce the Mongols with Demi's book *Chingis Khan* and Yuzo Otsuka's *Suho and the White Horse*. Then play the game "Kublai Khan's Treasure." You will need a beanbag, a small purse, or a paper bag that is easy to pick up. One person is chosen to be Kublai Khan's Mongol guard and stand guard over the "treasure" (the beanbag, purse, or paper bag). Everyone else forms a circle around the Mongol guard. The group must try to steal the treasure without being tagged. Those touched by the Mongol guard are out. The Mongol guard must try to defend the treasure with fierce yells, mean looks, and fancy moves. One part of the group may try to lure the Mongol guard away from the treasure so someone else can try to grab the loot. If the Mongol guard stays over the treasure, the group may have to charge, at the sacrifice of some players, in order to get the treasure.
(Primary)

6. Explain that people sometimes heard wild stories about the strange things to be found in other lands. Read aloud *The Aminal* by Lorna Balian or *Fish Is Fish* by Leo Lionni to illustrate how such wild stories might get started, and discuss how the characters in the books got the wrong idea from what they were told. Play a game of "Gossip." Have the children sit in a circle. Whisper a secret message to the first child, such as, "Marco Polo rode a camel all the way to China, where he saw crocodiles and palaces with golden roofs." Ask each child to try to whisper the message to the person sitting next to him or her. The last child to hear the message should repeat it out loud. Compare the final message with your original statement.
(Preschool, primary)

7. Share *Ribtickle Town* by Alan Benjamin, which is about a strange land. You can also use *Today I Thought I'd Run Away* by Jane Johnson. Then let the children design strange creatures they might meet if they went traveling. Children can use crayons, paper scraps, yarn, fake fur, and other items, or they can make combination creatures from parts of people and animals cut out of old magazines. Let children decide whether their creatures are monsters, strange people, odd animals, or whatever else they want the creatures to be.
(Preschool, primary)

8. Explain that after Marco Polo wrote about his exotic travels, several other people, such as Sir John Mandeville, made up fantastic accounts of travels that never really happened. In these stories, the "travelers" claimed to have seen men with one eye in the middle of their heads, headless men with faces in their chests, monopodes (men who had only one large foot), and other fantastic sights.

Read Judi Barrett's picture book *Cloudy with a Chance of Meatballs* and Dr. Seuss's *I Had Trouble in Getting to Solla Sollew*. Then have the children imagine they are travel writers like Sir John Mandeville. Have them describe their own versions of new lands with fantastic customs and strange people. Encourage children to make drawings, as well.
(Primary, intermediate)

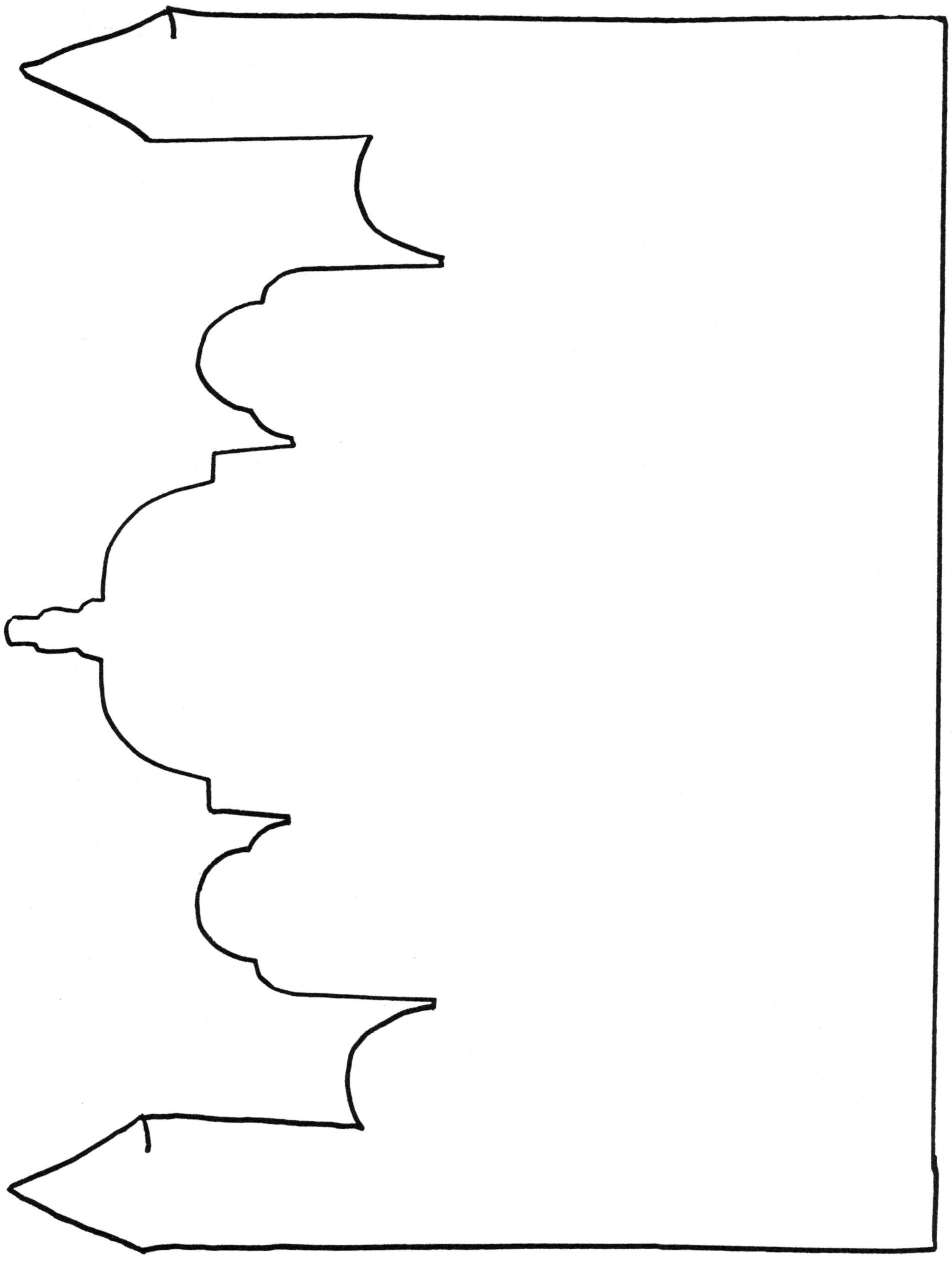

Fig. 4.10.

TRADE FROM THE EAST

The fascination of the Indies, as the lands of the Far East were called, lay in their role as the source of exotic goods brought to Europe by adventurous merchants and traders. The craving of Europeans for items such as spices, silk, jewels, and gold meant enormous profits for anyone who could supply them. The cost of pepper alone increased in value fiftyfold in the journey from east to west. Spices were particularly important because they not only added flavor but also masked the taste of food that had spoiled without refrigeration.

Before the fifteenth century, spices, silk, and other goods were brought to Europe by ships that sailed to the eastern end of the Mediterranean Sea and met traders coming from the other direction, from China, Japan, and India. Italian city-states such as Venice and Genoa were the centers for such trade, and these cities became fabulously wealthy.

Book List

Cole, William. *The Sea, Ships and Sailors: Poems, Songs and Shanties*. Viking, 1967. (Gr. 4-up)
A selection of poems about the sea.

Domanska, Janina. *I Saw a Ship A-Sailing*. Macmillan, 1972. (PreK-1)
This picture book illustrates the familiar nursery rhyme of a ship laden with treasures.

Heyer, Marilee. *The Weaving of a Dream: A Chinese Folktale*. Viking, 1986. (Gr. 1-4)
In this Chinese folktale, a widow's third son retrieves the precious brocade she has woven.

Patz, Nancy. *Gina Farina and the Prince of Mintz*. Harcourt Brace Jovanovich, 1986. (K-3)
In this picture book, Gina Farina, a baker's daughter, leaves home to join a medieval minstrel troupe and bake her spicy pies for them.

Shecter, Ben. *If I Had a Ship*. Doubleday, 1970. (PreK-1)
Like the wealthy traders of the Middle Ages, young Ben imagines that he has a ship and will bring back treasures for his mother.

Siegel, Alice, and Margo McLoone. *The Herb and Spice Book for Kids*. Holt, Rinehart & Winston, 1978. (Gr. 3-6)
Introduces herbs and spices and includes ideas for activities for children.

Zemach, Harve. *Salt*. Follett, 1965. (Gr. 1-3)
A picture book about how Ivan the fool introduces salt to the king and wins the hand of the princess.

Related Activities

1. Read the picture book *Salt* by Harve Zemach and then introduce children to some of the spices that were so highly valued in medieval Europe. Give them copies of figure 4.11, which has pictures of various spice plants. Bring in containers of the spices shown and give the children a small "pinch" of each, one at a time. Have children spread white glue thinned with water on the pictures of the

Spices
CINNAMON
GINGER
PEPPERCORNS
THYME
OREGANO
NUTMEG
MUSTARD SEED
PAPRIKA

Fig. 4.11.

spices you have given them and then sprinkle each spice on the appropriate picture. Let each spice dry before adding the next. Then have children color the background. Discuss the different spices, smell them, and imagine what each one is used for.
(Primary, intermediate)

2. Ask the children to bring in simple foods they made at home to share with the group. Each child should pick a particular spice he or she wants to use. For example, they could make cinnamon cookies, ginger cookies, eggnog with nutmeg, pieces of hot dog spread with mustard, deviled eggs with paprika, small English-muffin pizzas with oregano, or cheese sprinkled with thyme. Let the group taste each item to experience the flavor. Have children compare these spiced foods to bland, unsalted crackers, to help them understand why spices were valued so highly. Then read the picture book *Gina Farina and the Prince of Mintz* by Nancy Patz, in which Gina Farina is famous for her spice pies.
(Intermediate)

3. Read the picture book *The Weaving of a Dream*, about a valuable brocade. Nobles in Europe wanted beautiful silks, satins, velvets, and brocades imported from the East for their clothes. Bring in some articles made of silk and other luxurious fabrics for the children to look at and feel. Then, let the children design their own exotic clothes for paper dolls that they make using the patterns in figure 4.12. Enlarge the patterns and trace the outlines on thin posterboard. Have children color the dolls and the clothes and cut them out. To complete the clothes, the children can glue scraps of rich fabric, sequins, feathers, buttons, and other odds and ends onto the costumes.
(Primary, intermediate)

4. Explain to the children that long ago you could not just go to the store to buy whatever you wanted. Precious goods were brought by ships from faraway lands. Read the picture books *I Saw a Ship A-Sailing* by Janina Domanska and *If I Had a Ship* by Ben Shecter. Then teach this song:

> *I Saw Three Ships*
> (sung to traditional tune)
>
> I saw three ships come sailing by,
> Come sailing by, come sailing by,
> I saw three ships come sailing by,
> With treasure from the Indies.
>
> And what do you think was in them then,
> Was in them then, was in them then,
> And what do you think was in them then,
> What treasure from the Indies?
>
> Gold and silver and pearls were there,
> Pearls were there, pearls were there,
> Jewels and satins and silks were there,
> These treasures from the Indies.

(Preschool, primary)

Fig. 4.12.

5. Children can create treasures imported from the East. "Jewels" can be made by painting small rocks or pebbles with tempera paints. Paint red "rubies," blue "sapphires," green "emeralds," and white "pearls." Jewelry can also be formed from clay and painted when dry. After painting, coat the "jewels" with shellac or clear nail polish to give them a shine. Make lumps of gold by painting some large rocks with gold spraypaint.

Next, let the children make ships to bring home these treasures. Decorate shoeboxes to look like Mediterranean trading vessels, as shown in figure 4.13, and then fill the shoeboxes with the treasures the children have made.
(Preschool, primary)

Fig. 4.13.

6. Read aloud the poem "Cargoes" by John Masefield, from the book *The Sea, Ships and Sailors*, selected by William Cole. This poem describes the exotic treasures brought in by ships of various lands. Play the game "My Ship Is Loaded." Seat the group in a circle, and ask them to imagine that they are sailors going back and forth from the Mediterranean to the Indies, trading a variety of exotic goods. The first player starts by saying, "My ship is loaded with silk" (or any other cargo he or she wishes). The next player repeats what the first one said and adds another item to the list, such as, "My ship is loaded with silk and pearls." Continue around the circle, with each player repeating all the items previously mentioned and adding one of his or her own. If a player fails to repeat all the cargo, he or she is out. Continue playing until you have a winner.
(Primary, intermediate)

THE MEDIEVAL CONCEPT OF THE WORLD

No one thought of trying to find an ocean route to the Far East during the Middle Ages. Such a route was not needed, and the open ocean was believed to be too dangerous to venture on for any distance. Many uneducated people still believed that the world was flat and that by sailing too far on the "Ocean Sea," ships would fall off the edge. Even some of the educated, who knew the world was round, believed that if one sailed over the curve of the Earth, one would never be able to sail back "uphill." Many thought of the ocean as one vast body of water encircling all the known land and believed it was full of sea monsters and other terrors. Few maps existed that portrayed the world beyond the Mediterranean, and there was little curiosity to try to find out more. This, then, was the world before Columbus and the beginning of the Age of Exploration.

Book List

Anno, Mitsumasa. *Anno's Medieval World*. Philomel, 1979. (Gr. 2-5)
In this beautiful picture book, the author describes the superstitions and fears that had to be overcome before the Age of Exploration could begin.

Cohen, Caron Lee. *Whiffle Squeek*. Dodd, Mead, 1987. (PreK-3)
Whiffle Squeek, a seafaring cat, has adventures on the open sea.

Lauber, Patricia. *How We Learned the Earth Is Round*. Crowell, 1990. (Gr. 1-4)
This picture book describes how people in ancient times discovered the shape of the Earth. Covers geography up to the time of Columbus.

Silverstein, Shel. *Where the Sidewalk Ends*. Harper & Row, 1974. (Gr. 3-6)
This collection of humorous poems includes "The Edge of the World," which claims that the Earth is flat, after all.

Related Activities

1. Read aloud the book *How We Learned the Earth Is Round* by Patricia Lauber and the poem "The Edge of the World" by Shel Silverstein. Then explain that in early times, many uneducated people believed that the world was a flat disk and that if ships sailed too near the edge, they would fall off. Let the children create their own versions of this belief. Give them sturdy paper plates to make dioramas of a flat Earth, using paints, markers, and paper scraps. They may color the plates blue to represent the ocean and cut out land shapes to glue onto the plates. Then they can add houses, ships, people, or whatever they want. When they draw their ships and other items, tell the children to add a small rectangle at the bottom of the figure. When they cut out the figure, the tab is cut in half up the middle. Then one half can be folded one way and the other half the other way. When the tabs are glued to the plate, they will provide support so that the figure can stand (see fig. 4.14).
(Primary, intermediate)

Fig. 4.14.

2. Read *Anno's Medieval World* to the children. Then explain that one of the arguments for believing the world was flat was the idea that if it was round, people on the other side would be upside down and therefore would fall off. There was no understanding of gravity at that time. The children can create their own version of a world on which half the people live upside down. First they need to make a globe. This can be done by blowing up a round balloon and covering it with papier-mâché. Make papier-mâché by dipping strips of torn newspaper into a paste made of flour and water. When they are covering the balloon, have children leave a small space so that when the papier-mâché is dry, they can insert a pin to pop the balloon and pull the balloon out. Then children

can paint the globe with tempera paints, showing land and water. When the globe is dry, add stand-up figures on the top and bottom of the globe. The figures on the underside will be upside down. On the sides of the globe, add some ships that are trying to sail "uphill."
(Primary, intermediate)

3. In the Middle Ages, the Atlantic Ocean was sometimes called the "Green Sea of Darkness" because no one knew what was beyond its shores. Children can create pictures of the "Green Sea of Darkness" by using a crayon etching method. Each child needs a piece of paper. First, have them fill the entire paper with heavy blotches of light green crayon. Then children can cover all the light green with a coat of dark green or black crayon. Tell kids to press hard to get a thick covering. Next, kids use a pointed object, such as a large, blunt nail or a paper clip that has been opened, to gently scratch an ocean scene in the dark crayon. The dark color will be scratched off and the lighter green below will show through wherever kids scratch. You could share Caron Lee Cohen's book *Whiffle Squeek* to provide inspiration.
(Primary, intermediate)

5

North America

When we talk about the history of civilization, we all too frequently study the development of European civilization and only include the continents of the Americas after the Age of Exploration brought the New World into the European "fold." This historical chauvinism needs to be corrected. The first section in this chapter introduces the first Stone Age Americans, followed by a section of general books that provide an overview of Native American cultures. In following sections, each group of Native North Americans is examined more carefully.

THE FIRST AMERICANS

The Americas have as long and complex a history as Europe does. We just do not have as much information about it, in part because many of the early American cultures were pre-literate and left no written records, and also because huge amounts of historical records were destroyed by the so-called discoverers when they overwhelmed preexisting American civilizations. The gaps in our knowledge are slowly being filled in by the work of archaeologists.

We know, for instance, that the actual first discoverers of North America were Stone Age peoples who crossed the Bering Strait to this continent as they followed herds of game animals. Over many following centuries, these nomadic peoples drifted down through North and Central America, all the way to the tip of South America. As they spread over both continents, they developed a wide variety of cultures and ways of life.

Book List

Aliki. *Wild and Woolly Mammoths*. Crowell, 1977. (K-3)

This title introduces not only these prehistoric animals but also the Stone Age peoples who hunted them and became the first inhabitants of the Americas.

Baity, Elizabeth Chesley. *Americans before Columbus*. Viking, 1961. (Gr. 5-up)
Describes the peoples of the Americas, from the Ice Age Americans, through the North American Indians and the civilizations of Central and South America, up to the time of Columbus.

Batherman, Muriel. *Before Columbus*. Houghton Mifflin, 1981. (Gr. 2-4)
This title describes the dwellings, tools, clothing, and way of life of the earliest Stone Age inhabitants of the Americas.

Elting, Mary. *If You Lived in the Days of the Wild Mammoth Hunters*. Four Winds Press, 1968. (Gr. 2-5)
The way of life of the Stone Age nomads is described in this nonfiction title.

Gerrard, Roy. *Mik's Mammoth*. Farrar, Straus & Giroux, 1990. (PreK-3)
A Stone Age boy, left behind by his tribe, tames a mammoth.

Martin, Rafe. *Will's Mammoth*. Putnam, 1989. (PreK-2)
A young boy gambols with mammoths in his imagination.

May, Julian. *Before the Indians*. Holiday House, 1969. (Gr. 2-5)
Describes the way of life of the ancestors of the peoples Columbus called Indians.

Merriman, Nick. *Early Humans*. Knopf, 1989. (Gr. 4-up)
Part of the Eyewitness series, this book can be used to introduce older children to the way of life of Stone Age peoples.

Osborne, Chester. *The Memory String*. Macmillan, 1984. (Gr. 5-8)
A fictional account of early human travels from Siberia to Alaska.

Silverstein, Shel. *A Light in the Attic*. Harper & Row, 1974. (Gr. 2-up)
Includes the poem "Prehistoric."

Watson, Lucilla. *An Ice Age Hunter*. Rourke, 1987. (Gr. 3-6)
This title describes the day-to-day life of Ice Age peoples.

Related Activities

1. The original inhabitants of North America were nomads who were following game animals as the animals traveled to this continent. Read aloud the picture books by Aliki, Mary Elting, Roy Gerrard, and Rafe Martin to give the children some idea of these early peoples. Then let children make prehistoric woolly mammoths. Use the pattern in figure 5.1 to make a paper-bag puppet. Glue the mammoth's head to the bottom flap of the bag (the part that folds toward the top of the bag). Then decorate the rest of the bag, using markers or pieces of brown yarn. When the child's hand is inserted, with fingers tucked into the flap, the mammoth's head can be moved up and down. (Preschool, primary)

Fig. 5.1.

2. Read aloud Murial Batherman's book *Before Columbus* and Shel Silverstein's poem "Prehistoric." Share the other titles by Elizabeth Baity, Julian May, Nick Merriman, and Lucilla Watson, which describe the lives of prehistoric peoples and the animals they depended on. Older children might enjoy the novel *The Memory String* by Chester Osborne, about early travelers from Siberia to Alaska. Give the children a copy of the maze in figure 5.2, and, like early nomads, they can follow the woolly mammoths over the land bridge from Asia to North America. (Primary)

NATIVE NORTH AMERICANS: AN OVERVIEW

Though non-Native Americans tend to see the Indians as a homogenous group, this is no more true than it would be to imagine the countries of Europe as being culturally identical. The study of Native American cultures could easily make up an entire book by itself. We simply offer a brief look at the cultures that arose in various geographical areas. These different North American cultures can be very roughly divided into six groups: the Indians of the Northeast Woodlands, the Southeast, the Great Plains, the Southwest, the Pacific Northwest, and Alaska.

Book List

Bernstein, Bonnie, and Leigh Blair. *Native American Crafts Workshop*. Fearon, 1982. (For adults)
Includes a wide variety of Native American crafts, games, and recipes.

Blood, Charles L. *American Indian Games and Crafts*. Franklin Watts, 1981. (Gr. 2-5)
Describes pastimes of the Native Americans.

Connolly, James E. *Why the Possum's Tail Is Bare: And Other North American Indian Nature Tales*. Stemmer, 1985. (Gr. 4-7)
Nature and folklore are combined in thirteen tales.

Curtis, Edward S. *The Girl Who Married a Ghost and Other Tales from the North American Indian*. Four Winds Press, 1978. (Gr. 4-up)
This is an excellent collection of authentic Native American folktales divided by areas of origin and illustrated with the author's outstanding photographs.

D'Amato, Janet, and Alex D'Amato. *Indian Crafts*. Sayre, 1968. (Gr. 3-up)
Includes a wide variety of Native American crafts, including projects to make Indian homes, canoes, clothing, weapons, and more.

de Wit, Dorothy, ed. *The Talking Stone: An Anthology of Native American Tales and Legends*. Greenwillow, 1979. (Gr. 5-up)
An excellent source for locating the folklore of particular tribes, as these are divided by area.

Glubok, Shirley. *The Art of the North American Indian*. Harper & Row, 1964. (Gr. 3-6)
Examples of Native American art from various parts of North America.

Fig. 5.2.

Gorsline, Marie, and Douglas Gorsline. *North American Indians*. Random House, 1978. (Gr. 6-8)
Major tribes are identified and briefly described.

Gustafson, Anita. *Monster Rolling Skull and Other Native American Tales*. Harper & Row, 1980. (Gr. 4-8)
Coyote is narrator and character in these nine stories.

Hofsinde, Robert. *Indian Costumes*. Morrow, 1968. (Gr. 3-6)
Describes the clothing of ten Native American tribes.

Houston, James. *Songs of the Dream People*. Atheneum, 1972. (Gr. 4-up)
Chants and images from the Indians and Eskimos of North America.

Jacobson, Daniel. *Indians of North America*. Franklin Watts, 1983. (Gr. 5-8)
A review of major tribes, customs, and peoples in dictionary format.

Martini, Teri. *Indians*. Children's Press, 1982. (Gr. 1-4)
An introduction to Native Americans for younger children.

Mayo, Gretchen Will. *Earthmaker's Tales: North American Indian Stories about Earth Happenings*. Walker, 1989. (Gr. 4-6)
Legends that center on the Earth.

______. *Star Tales: North American Indian Stories about the Stars*. Walker, 1987. (Gr. 4-7)
Includes fourteen tales about the constellations.

Monroe, Jean Guard, and Ray A. Williamson. *They Dance in the Sky*. Houghton Mifflin, 1987. (Gr. 4-8)
These are Native American star myths.

Oakley, Ruth. *The North American Indians: In the Beginning*. Marshall Cavendish, 1991. (Gr. 4-up)
This title describes Native Americans from the Stone Age on. Several other titles in the North American Indian series also would be useful.

Purdy, Susan, and Cass R. Sandak. *North American Indians*. Franklin Watts, 1982. (Gr. 3-6)
Introduces crafts and other projects.

Schoolcraft, Henry R. *Legends of the American Indians*. Crescent, 1980. (Gr. 5-up)
This book includes authentic Native American legends interspersed with dramatic paintings and photographs.

Tunis, Edwin. *Indians*. Crowell, 1979. (Gr. 5-8)
Revised edition of an excellent overview.

Turner, Geoffrey. *Indians of North America*. Sterling, 1992. (Gr. 5-up)
An overview of the culture and way of life of each Native American tribe by area.

Watson, Jane Werner. *The First Americans: Tribes of North America*. Pantheon, 1980. (Gr. 2-3)
Describes life on this continent before the Europeans came.

Wheeler, M. J. *First Came the Indians*. Macmillan, 1983. (Gr. 2-4)
Poetic introduction to the Indians of North America.

Wolfson, Evelyn. *From Abenaki to Zuni: A Dictionary of Native American Tribes*. Walker, 1988. (Gr. 4-8)
An alphabetical listing of Native American tribes.

______. *Growing Up Indian*. Walker, 1986. (Gr. 5-7)
This title describes what it was like to grow up in the Native American culture before the Europeans arrived.

Wood, Marion. *Spirits, Heroes and Hunters from North American Indian Mythology*. Schocken Books, 1982. (Gr. 4-up)
Beautifully illustrated compilation of Native American myths.

Related Activities

1. Use any of the titles above to introduce Native Americans to the group. *First Came the Indians* by M. J. Wheeler is suitable for reading aloud.

Native American folklore can be introduced using the titles by Connolly, Curtis, de Wit, Gustafson, Mayo, Monroe and Williamson, and Schoolcraft. Shirley Glubok's *The Art of the North American Indian* presents an overview of Native American art. *Songs of the Dream People* by James Houston contains beautiful Native American poetry to share with children.
(Primary)

2. Give each child a copy of a map of North America. They can use the titles above to identify the areas of the various Native North American groups. Each area can be colored in with a different color.
(Primary, intermediate)

3. Use Janet D'Amato and Alex D'Amato's *Indian Crafts* to make the homes of various tribes. This book includes a Seminole grass house, an Iroquois longhouse, a Mandan earth lodge, a tepee, a Pueblo dwelling, and a totem plank lodge.
(Primary, intermediate)

4. Ask each child to pick a tribe to research for a presentation to the rest of the group. Reports should include folklore, shelter, clothing, food, crafts, tribal government, and religious practices. Geoffrey Turner's *Indians of North America* provides an overview of each area.
(Intermediate)

TRIBES OF THE NORTHEASTERN WOODLANDS

In the northeastern woodlands, the predominant tribes included the Chippewa, Iroquois, Ojibwa, and Mohawk. They depended on some agriculture and the gathering of wild foods. They lived in longhouses and wigwams made of birch bark and made birch-bark canoes. Part of their culture included False Face Societies, whose members wore grotesque wooden masks to frighten evil spirits away. Their artwork included wampum belts and other beadwork, masks, quillwork, and stone carvings.

Book List

Bierhorst, John, ed. *The Naked Bear: Folktales of the Iroquois*. Morrow, 1987. (Gr. 4-7)
Sixteen animal stories of the Iroquois tribe.

Bierhorst, John, and Henry Schodcraft, eds. *Ring in the Prairie*. Dial, 1970. (K-3)
This picture book tells a Shawnee legend about a young warrior in love with the daughter of a star.

Bruchac, Joseph. *Iroquois Stories: Heroes and Heroines, Monsters and Magic*. Crossing Press, 1985. (Gr. 5-up)
Retellings of original Iroquois tales.

Doherty, Craig A., and Katherine M. Doherty. *The Iroquois*. Franklin Watts, 1989. (Gr. 4-6)
An introduction to the Iroquois tribe.

Esbensen, Barbara Juster. *The Star Maiden: An Ojibway Tale*. Little, Brown, 1988. (Gr. 3-5)
A star appears in a dream to a young brave, falls to Earth, and becomes a water lily in this picture book.

Fritz, Jean. *The Good Giants and the Bad Pukwudgies*. Putnam, 1982. (K-5)
The giant Maushop and his family form the geography of Cape Cod in their battles with the pukwudgies.

Glubok, Shirley. *The Art of the Woodland Indians*. Macmillan, 1976. (Gr. 3-6)
Describes the art of Northeastern and Great Lakes Indians.

Jones, Hettie. *Longhouse Winter*. Holt, Rinehart & Winston, 1972. (Gr. 3-up)
A collection of Iroquois transformation tales describing how certain natural phenomena came to be.

Sewall, Marcia. *People of the Breaking Day*. Atheneum, 1990. (Gr. 3-6)
This is the story of the Wampanoag people, who lived in Massachusetts before the Pilgrims came.

Siegel, Beatrice. *Indians of the Woodland, before and after the Pilgrims*. Walker, 1972. (Gr. 4-6)
Includes the effects the arrival of the Pilgrims had on these tribes.

Related Activities

1. Read aloud *The Good Giants and the Bad Pukwudgies* by Jean Fritz. Then explain that the people from the area where this story took place lived in wigwams. Help the children make wigwams from paper cups or yogurt containers (see figure 5.3). Turn the cups upside down and paint them with brown tempera paint. When the cups are dry, spread on white glue and stick on pieces of grass and straw.
(Preschool, primary)

Fig. 5.3.

2. Share the folklore of the Woodlands Indians using the books by John Bierhorst, Joseph Bruchac, Barbara Esbensen, and Hettie Jones. *Ring in the Prairie* and *The Star Maiden* are picture books. Ask the children to create their own illustrations for one of these stories using designs of the Woodland tribes, as shown in the books listed above.
(Primary, intermediate)

3. Describe the ways of life of the Woodland tribes, using the titles by the Dohertys, Marcia Sewall, and Beatrice Siegel. As an example of the crafts of these tribes, the children can make a canoe similar to the birch-bark canoes the Indians made. Enlarge the pattern in figure 5.4, and cut the canoes from heavy paper. Then lace up the ends as shown.
(Primary)

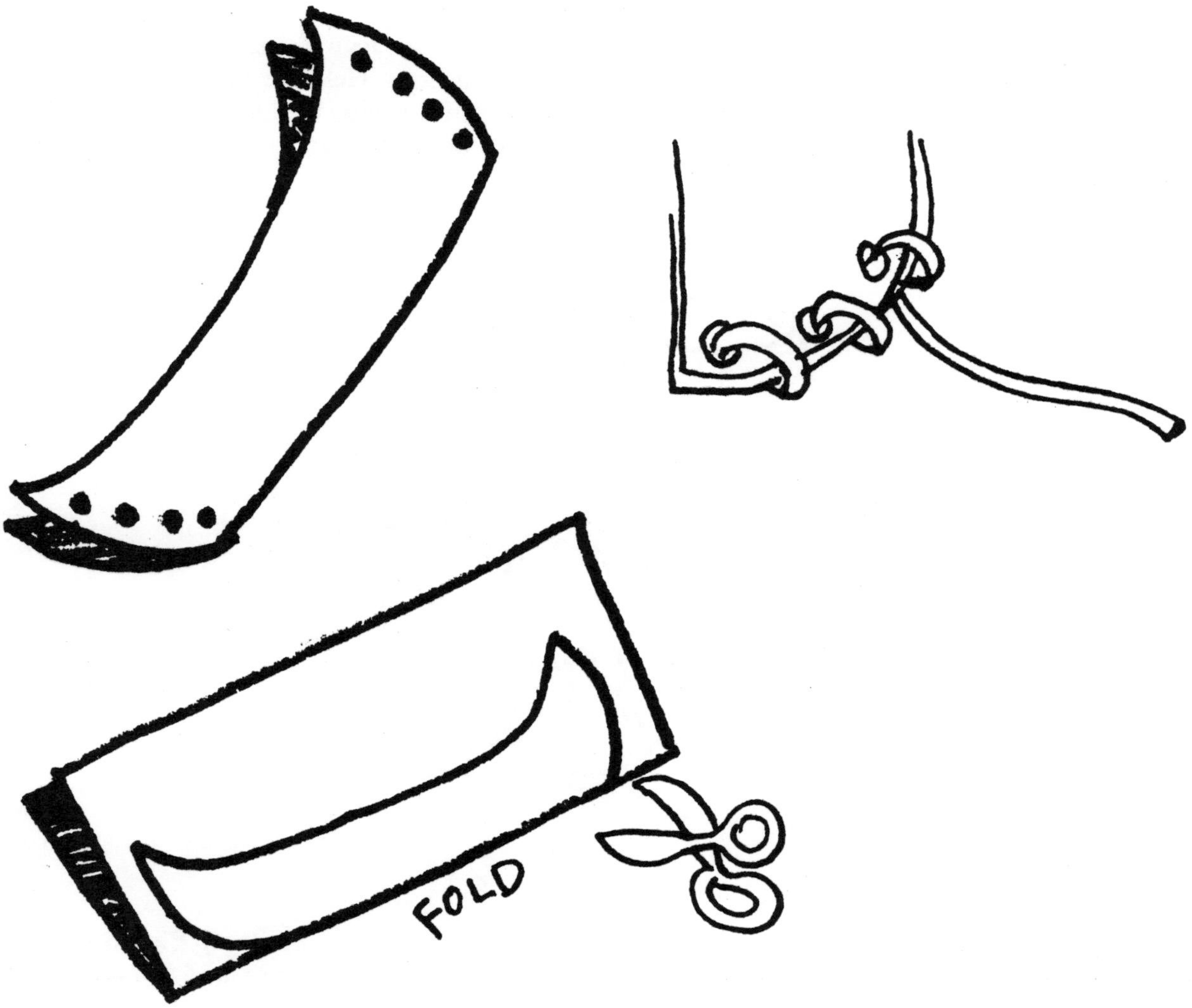

Fig. 5.4.

4. Describe the False Face Societies of the Woodland Indians. Shirley Glubok's book *The Art of the Woodland Indians* has pictures of the masks carved from wood that were worn by these groups. Let the children create their own False Face masks out of papier-mâché. Make papier-mâché by mixing flour and water to create a paste and dipping strips of newspaper into the mixture. The papier-mâché can be molded on a blown-up balloon, and facial details can be added by attaching wadded up pieces of newspaper for noses, eyebrows, etc., and then covering these features with papier-mâché. After the masks are dry, remove them from the balloons and paint the faces. Most False Face masks were painted red. Use black yarn for hair. Drill a hole in each side to attach a string for tying on the mask.
(Intermediate)

TRIBES OF THE SOUTHEAST

In the Southeast, the tribes included the Alabama, Cherokee, Chickasaw, Choctaw, Creek, Natches, and Seminole. The ancestors of these tribes were the Mound Builders, one of the most culturally advanced peoples north of Mesoamerica. These groups lived in large settlements, with a strict class structure, and farmed the land. Their artwork included figures made of clay and stone, copper and mica ornaments, carved stone effigy pipes, masks, and basketry. They decorated their bodies with tattoos.

Book List

Cunningham, Maggi. *The Cherokee Tale-Teller*. Dillon, 1978. (Gr. 3-up)
Folklore of the Cherokee.

Lee, Martin. *The Seminoles*. Franklin Watts, 1989. (Gr. 4-6)
Description of the way of life of the Seminole.

Lepthien, Emilie U. *The Cherokee*. Children's Press, 1985. (Gr. 1-3)
Describes the customs and history of the Cherokee. Also use *The Choctaw* (1988) and *The Seminole* (1985).

Roth, Susan L. *Kanahena*. St. Martin's Press, 1988. (K-3)
A Cherokee tale of how Terrapin outwits the Bad Wolf, retold in a stunning picture book.

______. *The Story of Light*. Morrow, 1990. (PreK-2)
The legend of how Spider brought the sun to the sky, in picture book format.

Steele, William O. *Talking Bones: Secrets of Indian Burial Mounds*. Harper & Row, 1978. (Gr. 3-6)
Describes the early history of the Indians of the Southeast and the mounds they built.

Related Activities

1. Read aloud the picture books by Susan Roth and show the books by Emilie Lepthien. Let the children make a Native American craft from this region by giving each child a lump of clay to use to mold an animal shape. The figures can then be dried in an oven on low heat and painted.
(Preschool, primary, intermediate)

2. Share some of the folklore of the Southeast by using *The Cherokee Tale-Teller* by Maggi Cunningham.
(Primary, intermediate)

3. Some of the titles above show pictures of the body tattoos with which Southeast tribes ornamented themselves. The children can create their own tattoo artwork, either by choosing one member of the group and using washable paints to tattoo him or her or by creating tattoos on paper figures. To make paper figures, the children should lie down on long pieces of butcher paper while a friend traces around their body. Children can cut out the figures and use markers to create the tattoos.
(Primary, intermediate)

4. The ancestors of the native peoples of the Southeast were Mound Builders. Introduce the Mound Builders by sharing William Steele's *Talking Bones*. Then ask the children to make models of these mounds from clay or earth.
(Primary, intermediate)

TRIBES OF THE GREAT PLAINS

The area of the Great Plains covers the center of the North American continent, from the Rocky Mountains to the Mississippi River. The tribes in this area lived mainly by hunting buffalo and included the Arapaho, Blackfoot, Cheyenne, Crow, Iowa, Mandan, Osage, Pawnee, Sioux, Wichita, and others. They lived in tepees that could be put up and taken down easily as they followed the buffalo herds. Their religious practices included sun dance rituals and vision quests. Their art was geometric and nonfigurative. They used beadwork and quillwork in making garments, moccasins, tepees, and other objects. The buffalo provided food, clothing, tools, and houses for these peoples.

Book List

Baker, Olaf. *Where the Buffaloes Begin*. Frederick Warne, 1981. (Gr. 4-6)
A retelling of the legend of the boy who led a stampeding buffalo herd away from his people.

Bierhorst, John, ed. *The Whistling Skeleton: American Indian Tales of the Supernatural*. Macmillan, 1982. (Gr. 4-6)
Nine stories from the Plains Indians.

Dingwall, Laima. *Bison*. Grolier, 1986. (Gr. 2-5)
An introduction to this animal of the Great Plains.

Fichter, George S. *How the Plains Indians Lived*. Morrow, 1962. (Gr. 4-8)
Topics covered include housing, social life, customs, and recreation.

Fradin, Dennis B. *The Cheyenne*. Children's Press, 1988. (Gr. 2-4)
A history of this Native American tribe called "the People." Also use *The Pawnee* (1989).

Glubok, Shirley. *The Art of the Plains Indians*. Macmillan, 1975. (Gr. 3-6)
An overview of the handiwork of the Indians of this area.

Goble, Paul. *Buffalo Woman*. Bradbury, 1984. (Gr. 4-6)
A buffalo turns into a beautiful girl in this legend.

______. *Iktomi and the Boulder: A Plains Indian Story*. Franklin Watts, 1988. (Gr. 3-5)
Iktomi is a trickster in this Sioux tale. You can also use other titles by this author.

Hofsinde, Robert. *Indian Sign Language*. Morrow, 1956. (Gr. 3-6)
Describes the symbols and uses of Plains Indian sign language.

Landau, Elaine. *The Sioux*. Franklin Watts, 1989. (Gr. 4-6)
An overview of the life of this tribe.

Lepthien, Emilie U. *Buffalo*. Children's Press, 1989. (Gr. 2-5)
For young children, this book covers the history and behavior of the buffalo, including its importance for the Native Americans of the Great Plains.

Liptak, Karen. *North American Indian Sign Language*. Franklin Watts, 1990. (Gr. 4-up)
Describes the basic vocabulary of the most common Indian languages.

Luling, Virginia. *Indians of the North American Plains*. Silver Burdett, 1979. (Gr. 5-8)
This title presents a rounded picture of the tribes of the Great Plains.

May, Robin. *A Plains Indian Warrior*. Rourke, 1988. (Gr. 3-6)
Describes the lifestyle of a male Native American from a Plains tribe.

______. *Plains Indians of North America*. Rourke, 1987. (Gr. 4-6)
Covers the lifestyle and customs of the Plains Indians.

Mobley, Jane. *The Star Husband*. Doubleday, 1977. (Gr. 2-6)
A Native American folktale from the Great Plains.

Osinski, Alice. *The Sioux*. Children's Press, 1984. (Gr. 1-4)
Includes history, customs, and social organization of this tribe.

Patent, Dorothy Hinshaw. *Buffalo: The American Bison Today*. Clarion, 1986. (Gr. 3-6)
Describes the present-day life of the buffalo in parks and preserves.

San Souci, Robert D. *The Legend of Scarface: A Blackfeet Indian Tale*. Doubleday, 1978. (Gr. 2-4)
A young brave travels to the Land of the Sun to seek permission to marry the maiden he loves.

Scott, Jack Denton. *The Return of the Buffalo*. Putnam, 1974. (Gr. 4-up)
This book describes the comeback of the buffalo from near extinction, with beautiful photographs by Ozzie Sweet.

Yue, Charlotte. *The Tipi: A Center of Native American Life*. Knopf, 1984. (Gr. 4-7)
Describes the construction of the tepee and its place in the lives of the Plains Indians.

Ziter, Cary B. *The Moon of Falling Leaves: The Great Buffalo Hunt*. Franklin Watts, 1988. (Gr. 3-7)
A fictional description of a buffalo hunt on the Great Plains.

Related Activities

1. The tribes of the Great Plains depended on the buffalo for almost all the necessities of life. Introduce this relationship between the Indians and the buffalo by reading aloud Olaf Baker's *Where the Buffaloes Begin* and Paul Goble's *Buffalo Woman*. Older children can read the fiction title *The Moon of Falling Leaves: The Great Buffalo Hunt* by Cary B. Ziter. Laima Dingwall's *Bison*, Emilie Lepthien's *Buffalo*, Dorothy Hinshaw Patent's *Buffalo*, and Jack Scott's *Return of the Buffalo* describe the buffalo in more detail.
(Primary, intermediate)

2. The titles by John Bierhorst, Jane Mobley, and Robert San Souci can be used to introduce the folklore of Great Plains tribes. Use the other titles above to introduce the way of life of these tribes, and then have the children do an activity related to the buffalo. Janet D'Amato and Alex D'Amato's *Indian Crafts* (in "Native North Americans: An Overview," above) includes directions for making a stuffed buffalo. The children can also create their own stories on buffalo skins. Use either an actual piece of leather or suede or a brown grocery bag. Cut an irregular shape from the bag, soak the piece in water, crumple it up, and wring it out. Spread the shape out flat and let it dry. Then write a story in picture signs, using Robert Hofsinde's *Indian Sign Language* or Karen Liptak's *North American Indian Sign Language* (see figure 5.5).
(Primary, intermediate)

3. For younger children, explain that the Plains Indians hunted the buffalo, and show pictures of buffalo. Then let the children make some buffalo projects. Let them make buffalo masks from paper plates. Each child should cut eyeholes in the plate and then tear brown tissue paper into strips to glue onto the plate as fur (see figure 5.6). Cut the horns and the nose from black construction paper and add some bits of brown yarn to the top of the head. Poke holes on either side of the plate to insert strings, so the mask can be tied on the child's head.
(Preschool, primary)

4. The tribes of the Great Plains played several hoop games. Share one with your group. The Indians made hoops from green sticks, but unless you wish to be completely authentic, you can use a Hula-Hoop™. Lay the hoop on the ground. Use three sticks that are a little shorter than the hoop's diameter. The players should stand about 4 feet away, with their backs to the hoop. They toss the sticks behind them, trying to get the sticks to land inside the hoop. The player who gets the most sticks inside the hoop wins, so keep playing until you have a winner.
(Primary, intermediate)

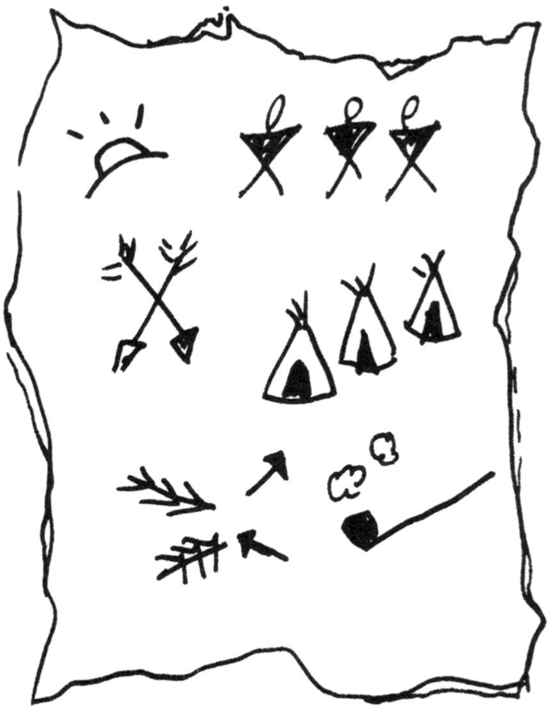

Fig. 5.5.

Fig. 5.6.

TRIBES OF THE SOUTHWEST

The Indians of the Southwest lived in present-day Arizona, New Mexico, and northern Mexico. They included the Apache, Hopi, Comanche, Mojave, Navajo, Pueblo, Shoshoni, Zuni, and others. They built multistory apartment houses focused around subterranean religious rooms called kivas. They were governed by religious organizations that observed ceremonies to celebrate the cycles of the year. They grew corn and ate wild plants and small animals. Their artwork included baskets, featherwork, pottery, weaving, shell and turquoise jewelry, sculptures, masks for kachina dancers, sand paintings, and murals in their kivas.

Book List

Ata, Te. *Baby Rattlesnake*. Children's Book Press, 1989. (PreK-2)
In this Chickasaw tale, Baby Rattlesnake wants his rattle before he is ready for it.

Baylor, Byrd. *Before You Came This Way*. Dutton, 1969. (Gr. 2-4)
Describes prehistoric rock drawings found in the Southwest.

Carter, Alden R. *The Shoshoni*. Franklin Watts, 1989. (Gr. 4-6)
A description of the Shoshoni tribe.

Doherty, Craig A., and Katherine M. Doherty. *The Apaches and Navajos*. Franklin Watts, 1969. (Gr. 4-6)
Describes the ways of life of both these tribes.

Fradin, Dennis B. *The Shoshoni*. Children's Press, 1989. (Gr. 2-3)
This is a history of this Native American tribe of the West.

Hillerman, Tony, ed. *The Boy Who Made a Dragonfly: A Zuni Myth*. Harper & Row, 1972. (Gr. 5-7)
A Zuni boy and his little sister are left behind by their tribe, and survive hunger and deprivation through the intervention of the Cornstalk Being.

McDermott, Gerald. *Arrow to the Sun: A Pueblo Indian Tale*. Viking, 1974. (K-4)
This Caldecott award winner tells of the search of a young Indian boy for his father, the Sun.

McKissack, Patricia. *The Apache*. Children's Press, 1984. (Gr. 1-4)
A description of the history and customs of the Apache.

Osinski, Alice. *The Navajo*. Children's Press, 1987. (Gr. 2-4)
Customs, traditions, history, and religious beliefs are described.

Tamarin, Alfred, and Shirley Glubok. *Ancient Indians of the Southwest*. Doubleday, 1975. (Gr. 5-up)
Describes the early history of the area.

Tomcheck, Ann Heinrichs. *The Hopi*. Children's Press, 1987. (Gr. 2-4)
Describes customs, history, religious beliefs, and present life.

Yue, Charlotte, and David Yue. *The Pueblo*. Houghton Mifflin, 1986. (Gr. 4-up)
Describes the history, daily life, dwellings, and relationship to the land of the Pueblo Indians.

Related Activities

1. Introduce the Native American folklore of the Southwest by reading aloud the Caldecott Medal winner *Arrow to the Sun* by Gerald McDermott, *Baby Rattlesnake* by Te Ata, and *The Boy Who Made a Dragonfly* edited by Tony Hillerman.
(Primary, intermediate)

2. Use any of the titles above to describe the way of life of particular tribes. The Southwest Indians are known for their beautiful coiled pottery. The children can try their hands at this ancient art using modeling clay that dries hard. They begin by making a base for their pot from a slab of clay about ½" thick. Cut a circle from the slab. Next, make coils by rolling the clay between both hands. Each coil should be about ½" thick and about a foot long. Place a coil on the base and pinch the ends firmly to the base. Wind the coil around the base, adding coils one at a time to build up the pot (see figure 5.7). A moist sponge helps the edges stick together. When the pot is finished, smooth the outside with the sponge. If desired, the pot can be painted when dry.
(Primary, intermediate)

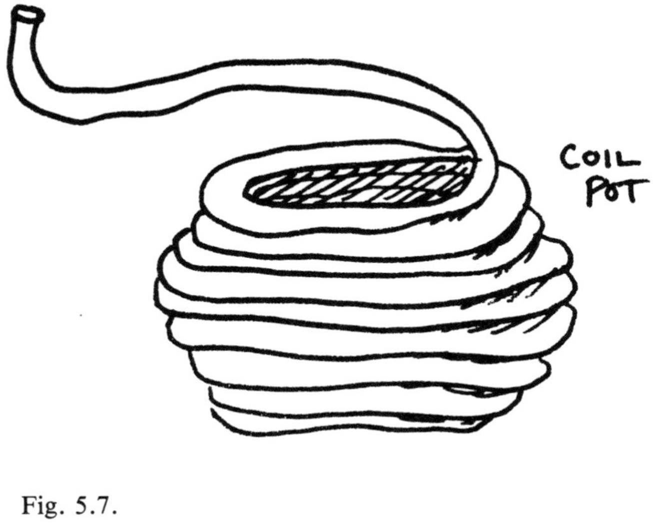

Fig. 5.7.

3. Navajo sand painting was an important part of religious life. Describe this custom to the children, and explain that these paintings frequently were used by medicine men to cure the sick and for other ceremonies. After the paintings were created, the sand was then scattered and the pictures destroyed. Children can make their own more permanent sand paintings by drawing designs on cardboard and then spreading on glue. When sand is shaken onto the design, it will stick to the glue. The easiest way to obtain "colored sand" is to use cornmeal. Put some cornmeal in

several bowls and sprinkle in a few drops of food coloring, mixing with a spoon to color the cornmeal. Let the cornmeal dry. Let children decide where they want the different colors on their designs. Tell them to use only one color at a time and to let the glue dry before they add the next color. The steps are shown in figure 5.8. Several of the books above introduce traditional Southwest Indian designs, such as the thunderbird.
(Primary, intermediate)

Fig. 5.8.

4. Help the children make kachina dolls like that in figure 5.9. Each child needs a paper tube for the doll's body. Show children how to draw a line to separate the head from the body. They should draw on facial features and clothing with Indian patterns. Cut two slits in the head on either side of the paper tube to insert the headdress. Make the headdress from construction paper. You can make feathers from scraps of different colors. Insert the headdress in the slits.
(Preschool, primary)

Fig. 5.9.

TRIBES OF THE PACIFIC NORTHWEST

The cultures of the Pacific Northwest depended on the sea for much of their livelihood. They lived off whales, salmon, and other marine life, as well as game animals, roots, and berries. Wealth was very important in their culture, and they developed the tradition of the *potlatch*, which was a celebration held by wealthy tribal members during which the wealthy gave elaborate and expensive gifts to all their guests. These tribes lived in villages of wooden houses with 100 people or more, and families traced their lineage in the giant totem poles they carved. They celebrated their religious beliefs in dramatic public ceremonies.

Book List

Beyer, Don E. *The Totem Pole Indians of the Northwest*. Franklin Watts, 1989. (Gr. 4-6)
Describes the lifestyle and customs of the Totem Pole Indians.

Glubok, Shirley. *The Art of the Northwest Coast Indians*. Macmillan, 1975. (Gr. 3-6)
A description of the Native American cultural artifacts of this area.

Harris, Christie. *Mouse Woman and the Vanished Princesses*. Atheneum, 1976. (Gr. 3-6)
These are Northwest Coast legends. You can also use *Mouse Woman and the Mischief Maker* (1977), *Mouse Woman and the Muddleheads* (1977), and *Once More upon a Totem* (1977).

Lyons, George. *Pacific Coast Indians of North America*. Messner, 1983. (Gr. 4-7)
Describes these cultures before and after the arrival of European peoples.

Martin, Frances Gardiner. *Raven-Who-Sets-Things-Right: Indian Tales of the Northwest Coast*. Harper & Row, 1975. (Gr. 5-7)
This collection includes nine tales.

Osinski, Alice. *The Nez Perce*. Children's Press, 1988. (Gr. 3-5)
A general description of the way of life of this tribe.

Rand, Gloria. *Salty Sails North*. Henry Holt & Co., 1990. (PreK-2)
On a trip to Alaska, Salty the dog and his master stop at an Indian site in the Pacific Northwest.

Robinson, Gail. *Raven the Trickster*. Atheneum, 1982. (Gr. 4-up)
Trickster tales of the Northwest Native American tribes.

Siberell, Anne. *Whale in the Sky*. Dutton, 1982. (PreK-3)
Describes how Thunderbird punished Whale for chasing Salmon into the river.

Sleator, William. *The Angry Moon*. Little, Brown, 1970. (PreK-4)
Tells how Lupan rescues Lapowinsa when she is captured by the angry Moon.

Related Activities

1. Show the children the book about the Nez Perce Indians by Alice Osinski and other titles to introduce the Indians of the Pacific Northwest. As examples of the folklore of this area, read aloud William Sleator's *The Angry Moon* and some of the tales in the collections by Christie Harris and Frances Martin. You can also share more modern stories, such as *Salty Sails North* by Gloria Rand and *Whale in the Sky* by Anne Siberell.
(Primary, intermediate)

2. Explain to the children that whales and fish were very important to the Indians of the Northwest. Show children how to make stuffed whales like the one in figure 5.10. Cut two whale shapes from black or gray construction paper. Allow the children to add features with crayons. Help children staple all around the edges of their whales, leaving a small opening. Crumple up newspaper and stuff it through the opening until the whale has a three-dimensional shape. Then staple the opening closed.
(Preschool, primary)

Fig. 5.10.

3. Though the totem pole is frequently identified with all Native Americans, it originated with the tribes of the Pacific Northwest. Let the children create their own totem poles. Both Janet D'Amato and Alex D'Amato's *Indian Crafts* (in "Native North Americans: An Overview," above) and Susan Purdy and Cass Sandak's *North American Indians* (same section) include instructions for whittling totem poles from wood. For a simpler project, the children can make totem poles from empty paper-towel rolls, by drawing or painting totem figures on the roll (see figure 5.11). Use either of these books for ideas on designs.
(Primary, intermediate)

Fig. 5.11.

4. Use some of the titles above to introduce the custom of the Potlatch. This was a tradition of proving one's worth by holding a large feast and giving expensive presents to all the guests. Let the children act out a Potlatch, imagining what kinds of gifts they would give each other and what kinds of gifts they would hope to receive.
(Primary, intermediate)

ALASKAN NATIVE AMERICANS

In the Arctic (Alaska), the Inuits and Aleuts survived a hostile environment and developed a flourishing artistic life. Their animal carvings in wood, walrus ivory, bone, antler, and stone adorned utilitarian as well as decorative objects. They were completely dependent on the animals of the region for food and the materials to make everything they needed, and they worshipped and tried to appease the spirits of these animals.

Book List

Cleaver, Elizabeth. *The Enchanted Caribou*. Macmillan, 1985. (Gr. 2-4)
An Indian girl is transformed into a white caribou in this old Inuit tale.

Cobb, Vicki. *This Place Is Cold*. Walker, 1989. (Gr. 2-4)
Cobb describes the land, animals, plants, and climate of Alaska.

Comins, Jeremy. *Eskimo Crafts and Their Cultural Background*. Lothrop, Lee & Shepard, 1975. (Gr. 4-up)
Includes sculpture, stencil prints, appliqué, models, and other crafts.

DeArmond, Dale. *Berry Woman's Children*. Greenwillow, 1985. (Gr. 2-6)
An Eskimo legend of the animals created by Raven and how they came to be.

______. *The Boy Who Found the Light*. Little, Brown, 1990. (Gr. 3-6)
These are three Eskimo folktales about the origins of natural phenomena. Also use *The Seal Oil Lamp* (1982).

Field, Edward. *Eskimo Songs and Stories*. Delacorte, 1973. (Gr. 3-up)
An introduction to the literature of the Eskimos.

Ginsburg, Mirra. *The Proud Maiden, Tungak, and the Sun: How Moon Came to Live in the Sky*. Macmillan, 1974. (Gr. 2-6)
An Eskimo folktale describing the origin of the moon and why the long Arctic night eventually gives way to the day.

Hahn, Elizabeth. *The Inuit*. Rourke, 1990. (Gr. 4-6)
Describes the culture, history, and way of life of these people.

Hewitt, Garnet. *Ytek and the Arctic Orchard*. Vanguard, 1981. (Gr. 3-6)
Another Alaskan folktale.

Houston, James. *Kiviok's Magic Journey*. Atheneum, 1973. (Gr. 3-6)
A tale of the Eskimo folk hero Kiviok and how he takes a wife. Also use *Tikta' Liktak: An Eskimo Legend* (Harcourt Brace Jovanovich, 1965) and *The White Archer* (Harcourt Brace Jovanovich, 1967).

Metayer, Maurice. *Tales from the Igloo*. St. Martin's Press, 1972. (Gr. 3-6)
Folklore of the copper Eskimos, a group of Inuit who live on the harsh Canadian Arctic coast.

Osinski, Alice. *The Eskimo*. Children's Press, 1985. (K-3)
An introduction to the Inuit and Yupik peoples of Alaska.

Purdy, Susan, and Cass R. Sandak. *Eskimos*. Franklin Watts, 1982. (Gr. 3-6)
Contains information about the Eskimo way of life, plus craft projects.

Sloat, Teri. *Eye of the Needle*. Dutton, 1990. (Gr. 3-6)
In this tale, Amik consumes a series of animals.

Smith, J. H. Greg. *Eskimos: The Inuit of the Arctic*. Rourke, 1987. (Gr. 4-6)
Describes the customs and history of the Inuit.

Steltzer, Ulli. *Building an Igloo*. Meadow House, 1981. (K-2)
Describes how an igloo is built.

Yue, Charlotte, and David Yue. *The Igloo*. Houghton Mifflin, 1988. (Gr. 3-6)
Describes the construction and uses of igloos.

Related Activities

1. For young children, explain that the Eskimo Indians live far to the north where it is very cold. Show children pictures of the homes of the Eskimos, using Ulli Steltzer's *Building an Igloo* and Charlotte and David Yue's *The Igloo*. Explain that because the region the Eskimos live in is so cold that trees do not grow, in the past they made their homes from ice and animal skins. Let the children build igloos using squares of white paper you have cut out for them to glue onto a background sheet. They can add people and animals to their scenes if they wish.
(Preschool, primary)

2. Many Alaskan tribes used dogsleds as their major means of transportation. Make sleds by folding a piece of construction paper in half and drawing a sled and dogs along the fold. Each child should make two or three dogs. Then cut out the shapes without cutting through the fold (see figure 5.12). Open the sleds and fold down the runners. Leave the dogs folded so they will stand. The children can color the sleds and dogs. When they are finished, use string to attach the sleds to the dogs.
(Preschool, primary)

Fig. 5.12.

3. Introduce the folklore of Alaska with any of the books by Elizabeth Cleaver, Dale DeArmond, Mirra Ginsburg, Garnet Hewitt, James Houston, Maurice Metayer, or Teri Sloat.
(Primary, intermediate)

4. The Alaskan Indians sculpted figures from stone, wood, or ivory. The children can create similar sculptures from bars of soap. Draw a picture of an animal on the side of a bar of soap (see figure 5.13). Also draw the animal on the ends of the bar, as it would look from front and back. Use a dinner knife to cut out the form. Then, cutting only a little at a time, sculpt the rest of the figure. Use a toothpick to add fine details.
(Intermediate)

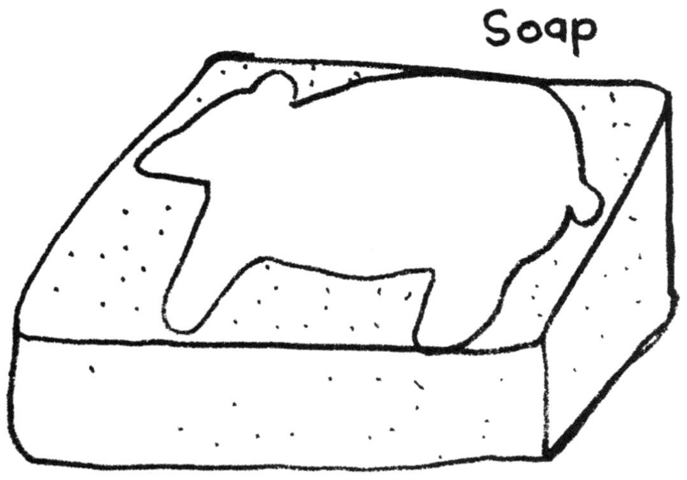

Fig. 5.13.

5. The Eskimos also created special masks to appease the spirits that inhabit all things, as described in Jeremy Comins's *Eskimo Crafts*. Children can make similar masks from paper plates and cardboard. Eskimo masks had a central face with attached carvings of related objects (see figure 5.14). Use the paper plate to make the central face, and then attach pieces of cardboard, with the smaller objects on the ends of them, radiating from the face, as shown.
(Primary, intermediate)

Fig. 5.14.

6

Central and South America

Before Columbus arrived a number of advanced civilizations were flourishing in Central and South America. These civilizations were established by some of the peoples who had gradually been filtering down through the Americas for centuries. In the activities and resources in this chapter, we take a look at the three amazing pre-Columbian civilizations of Central and South America. Because these cultures were so rich, it is hard to give a complete picture of them in a few activities. Encourage children to do further reading on their own, using some of the excellent books listed below.

THE MAYANS

Perhaps the oldest civilization the Spanish encountered was that of the Mayans, who flourished in Central America for fifteen centuries, from about 2500 B.C.E. to 900 C.E. The Mayans built cities that included palaces and pyramids. They developed systems of writing, counting, astronomy, and architecture. They had a structured society, with an elite group at the top who were responsible for religious observances. Mayan civilization began in Guatemala and later moved to the Yucatan Peninsula. By around 900 C.E., the Mayans abandoned their elaborate cities and moved to the forests surrounding them. No one knows why, but it may have been because of disease or crop failure or for a religious reason.

Book List

Beck, Barbara L. *The Ancient Maya*. Franklin Watts, 1983. (Gr. 3-6)
An excellent overview of the history of this civilization.

Bierhorst, John, ed. *The Monkey's Haircut and Other Stories Told by the Maya*. Morrow, 1986. (Gr. 4-6)
Folktales of the Mayans, some of which go back to the *Popol Vuh*, the sacred book of the pre-Columbian Mayan civilization.

Bierhorst, John. *The Mythology of Mexico and Central America*. Morrow, 1990. (Gr. 5-up)
A discussion of the creation myths of the Mayans and Aztecs, with a retelling of some of these tales.

Finger, Charles J. *Tales from Silver Lands*. Doubleday, 1924. (Gr. 3-up)
Folktales with magical themes, from Central and South America.

Gifford, Douglas. *Warriors, Gods and Spirits from Central and South America*. Schocken Books, 1983. (Gr. 5-8)
This title introduces the mythology of the Mayans, Aztecs, and Incas.

Hamilton, Virginia. *In the Beginning: Creation Stories from around the World*. Harcourt Brace Jovanovich, 1988. (Gr. 4-up)
This collection includes the Mayan legend "Four Creations to Make Man," which describes the creation of the Mayans.

Honness, Elizabeth. *The Mystery of the Maya Jade*. Lippincott, 1971. (Gr. 5-7)
This fiction title centers around mysterious thefts at an archaeological site in modern Guatemala.

Karen, Ruth. *Song of the Quail: The Wondrous World of the Maya*. Four Winds Press, 1972. (Gr. 5-up)
A look at this rich culture including religion, sports, and other aspects of everyday life, along with an account of Mayan history from earliest times.

McKissack, Patricia. *The Maya*. Children's Press, 1985. (K-3)
This title briefly describes the history, culture, religion, and way of life of the Mayan civilization.

Meyer, Carolyn, and Charles Gallenkamp. *The Mystery of the Ancient Maya*. Atheneum, 1985. (Gr. 5-up)
This title describes the civilization and unsolved mysteries of the Mayans.

Nougier, Louis-Rene. *The Days of the Mayas, Aztecs and Incas*. Silver Burdett, 1985. (Gr. 4-6)
This title includes information on all three civilizations of Central and South America, with emphasis on their origins.

Odijk, Pamela. *The Mayas*. Silver Burdett, 1989. (Gr. 4-up)
An overview of Mayan history.

Shetterly, Susan Hand. *The Dwarf-Wizard of Uxmal*. Atheneum, 1990. (PreK-3)
This Mayan legend tells how the dwarf-wizard became the ruler of Uxmal.

Stuart, George E., and Gene S. Stuart. *The Mysterious Maya*. National Geographic Society, 1975. (Gr. 5-up)
This history of the Mayans includes many color photographs showing the sites described.

Related Activities

1. To introduce the culture of the Mayans, read any of the nonfiction titles above. *The Mysterious Maya* by George Stuart and Gene Stuart includes beautiful color photographs to share with your group. Several of these books provide pictures of the ruins of ancient Mayan cities that have been found and excavated. It is believed that the pyramids and other buildings were brilliantly colored during the Mayan heyday, instead of the faded gray stone we see today. After you have shared some of these pictures, the children in your group can color an enlargement of the Mayan scene in figure 6.1, making it as authentic as possible.
(Primary, intermediate)

2. The Mayans had legends that described the structure of the world. One myth said that the Earth was flat and square and rested on the back of a giant crocodile floating in a lily pond. Another described the Earth as the floor of a house of giant iguanas. There were thirteen layers of heaven above the Earth and nine underworlds. At the center of the Earth grew a giant ceiba tree, with its roots in the underworld and its branches in heaven. Other creation stories can be found in the folktale collections by John Bierhorst, Douglas Gifford, and Virginia Hamilton. Choose one of these tales to read aloud. Then read the preceding description to your group and ask them to create a mural of the Mayan vision of the world.
(Primary, intermediate)

3. Read *The Dwarf-Wizard of Uxmal*, a picture book by Susan Shetterly with striking color pictures. This story will help your group get an idea of what the Mayan people looked like. The Mayans loved personal adornment. They painted and tattooed their bodies, filed their teeth into points, and used plugs to enlarge their ear lobes. To add to their beauty, mothers bound their babies' heads between boards to flatten the skull and hung beads by strands of hair between their children's eyes to produce crossed eyes, which were considered a mark of beauty.

Have the children make pictures of Mayan noblemen, while you read them the above description of the Mayans. Emphasize that this was the Mayan ideal of beauty.
(Preschool, primary, intermediate)

4. The Mayans developed a hieroglyphic form of picture writing and created books from a paper made of bark. These books, or codices, were folded like an accordion (see figure 6.2 on page 106). Show the children some examples of hieroglyphics from the titles above, and then have children make a codice. To make the book, the children should glue several sheets of paper together at the ends and fold them evenly together like an accordion. Next, they should design their own hieroglyphics to tell a story in their books.
(Primary, intermediate)

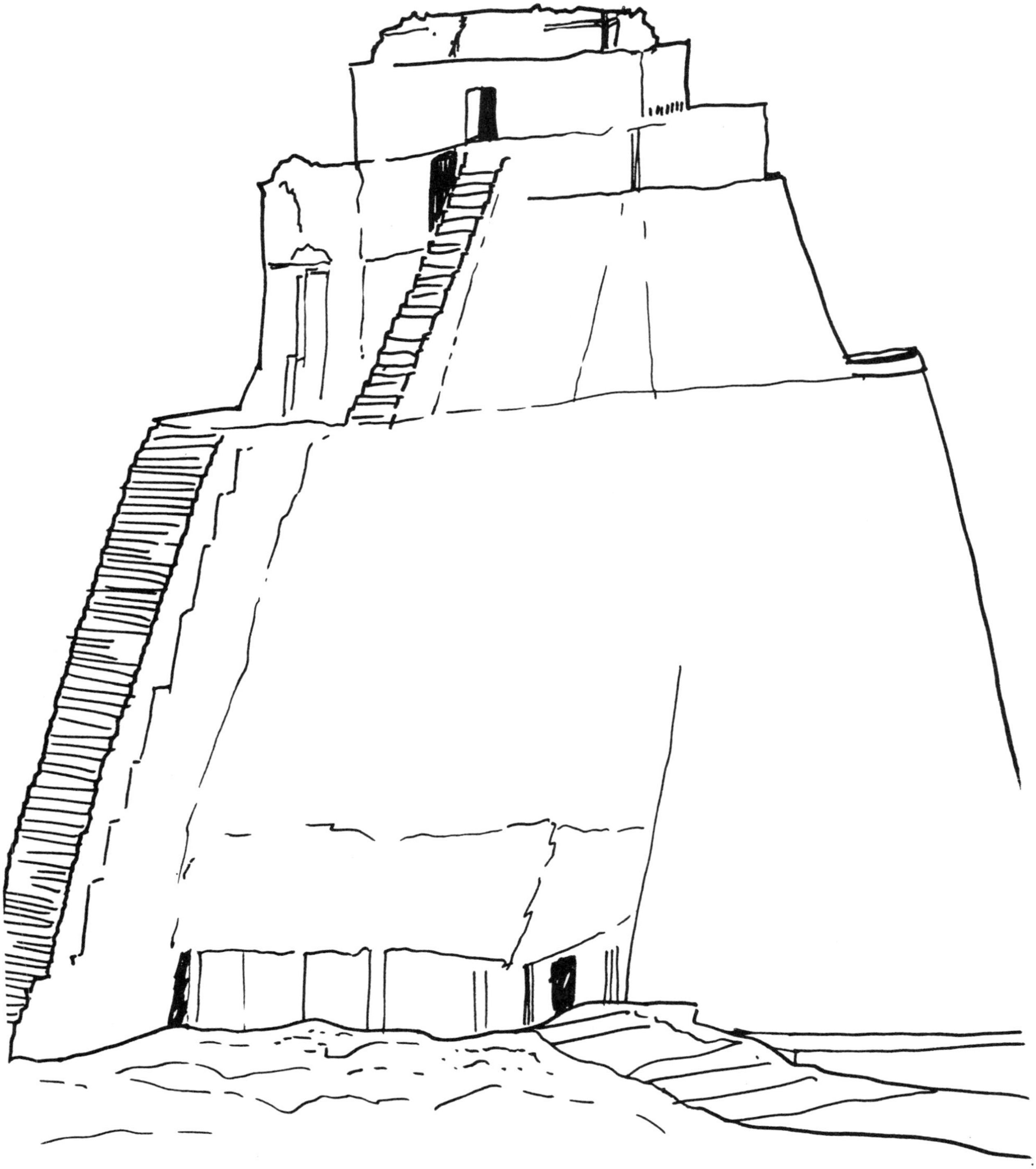

Fig. 6.1.

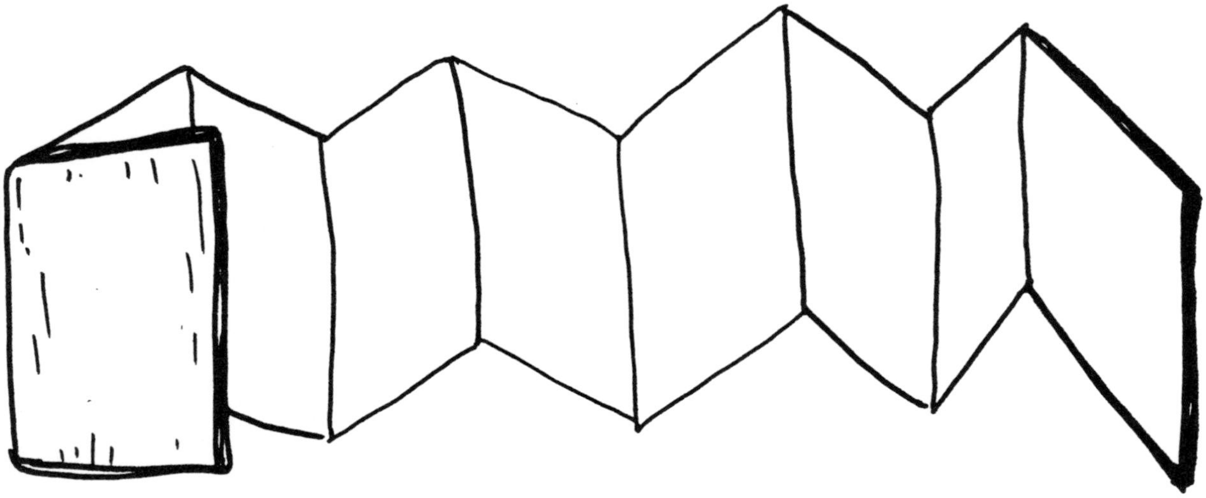

Fig. 6.2.

5. To introduce more of the culture of the Mayans, read other folktales from Charles Finger's *Tales from Silver Lands* and the other collections. Older children might enjoy Elizabeth Honness's *The Mystery of the Maya Jade*, about mysterious events at an archaeological site in Guatemala. Then play a game from Central America called "Drop the Marble." Two children play at a time. Each player starts with five marbles. To begin, each player tosses a marble at a line drawn on the ground. The player whose marble lands closest to the line goes first. The two players face each other. The winner of the toss stands with his or her heels together and toes pointed out. The second player crouches down about 5 feet away. Then the second player tosses a marble toward the spread toes of the first. If a player fails to land a marble between the toes and heels of the other player in three chances, he or she loses one marble. But if a player does shoot a marble between the other player's feet, the standing player drops one of his or her marbles. This player may look down while dropping the marble, but he or she must stand straight and drop the marble from waist height. If this marble hits an opponent's marble, the standing player wins that marble. If the dropped marble misses, the standing player loses both marbles. The players trade off and keep playing until one player has all the marbles. This game can also be played in teams.
(Primary, intermediate)

THE AZTECS

The Aztecs of Mexico started out as a tribe of semi-barbarians who wandered into central Mexico around 1168. Gradually, they absorbed the cultures of the more advanced tribes around them, especially the Olmecs, and became the dominant group. By the end of the 1300s, the Aztecs had built their city of Tenochtitlan in Lake Texcoco and established an empire. The Aztecs were wealthy, and Tenochtitlan was adorned with pyramids and other impressive structures. At the height of their culture under Montezuma II, shortly before the arrival of the conquistadors, the Aztec Empire covered Mexico, Honduras, and Nicaragua and ruled over several million people. However, their control was not secure, as many of their subject tribes were on the verge of rebellion due to the tribute they had to pay and the victims they had to provide for the human sacrifices that were part of the Aztec religion. The stage was set for the arrival of Hernando Cortés.

Book List

Bateman, Penny. *Aztecs and Incas*. Franklin Watts, 1988. (Gr. 3-6)
Describes the history and lifestyles of these two civilizations.

Beck, Barbara L. *The Aztecs*. Franklin Watts, 1983. (Gr. 3-6)
A clear introduction to the history and life of the Aztecs.

Bierhorst, John, ed. *The Hungry Woman: Myths and Legends of the Aztecs*. Morrow, 1984. (Gr. 4-up)
Includes creation myths, the fall of Tula, the founding of Mexico, the period of Montezuma, and the arrival of the conquistadors.

Crosher, Judith. *The Aztecs*. Macdonald Education, 1976. (Gr. 3-6)
A review of the history and culture of the Aztec people.

Fisher, Leonard Everett. *Pyramid of the Sun, Pyramid of the Moon*. Macmillan, 1988. (Gr. 3-6)
This lavishly illustrated title introduces the religious centers of Aztec life.

Hamilton, Virginia. *The Dark Way: Stories from the Spirit World*. Harcourt Brace Jovanovich, 1990. (Gr. 3-up)
This collection of folktales includes an Aztec legend called "The Pretender."

Harris, Nathaniel. *Montezuma and the Aztecs*. Bookwright, 1986. (Gr. 3-6)
This colorful title gives an overview of the Aztec way of life and the conquest of the empire by the Spanish.

Hinojosa, Francisco. *The Old Lady Who Ate People: Frightening Stories*. Little, Brown, 1984. (K-4)
Three of the four stories in this collection are from before the Spanish conquest.

Kurtycz, Marcos, and Ana Garcia Kobeh. *Tigers and Opossums*. Little, Brown, 1984. (K-4)
Mexican animal legends.

Lattimore, Deborah Nourse. *The Flame of Peace*. HarperCollins Children's Books, 1987. (Gr. 3-6)
This folktale describes aspects of Aztec life.

McKissack, Patricia. *Aztec Indians*. Children's Press, 1985. (K-3)
Covers the history, religion, and way of life of the Aztecs for young children.

Odijk, Pamela. *The Aztecs*. Silver Burdett, 1989. (Gr. 4-up)
An overview of the Aztec culture.

Purdy, Susan, and Cass R. Sandak. *Aztecs*. Franklin Watts, 1982. (Gr. 3-6)
Includes crafts and projects on Aztec life.

Rohmer, Harriet. *The Legend of Food Mountain*. Children's Book Press, 1982. (K-4)
Though it is dated from the period after the Spanish conquest, this is an Aztec folktale describing the creation of the human race.

Steel, Anne. *An Aztec Warrior*. Rourke, 1988. (Gr. 3-6)
Describes the typical life of an Aztec warrior.

Related Activities

1. The Aztec civilization included aspects of Mayan culture as well as those of other Central American tribes. The Aztecs' own myths stated that they were sent to found a city by their god Huitzilopochtli, the "Hummingbird Wizard." He told them to settle where they saw an eagle eating a serpent while sitting on a cactus with red, heart-shaped fruit. The sign was revealed to them on an island in Lake Texcoco, and there they built their city. Other myths about the creation of the Aztecs can be found in John Bierhorst's *The Hungry Woman* and Douglas Gifford's *Warriors, Gods and Spirits from Central and South America* (see "The Mayans," above). After reading some of these stories to the group, have children make a mosaic of a serpent, like the one shown on the cover of Barbara Beck's *The Aztecs*. Have them draw the outline of the serpent, as shown in figure 6.3, and then glue on small pieces of torn paper to give it a mosaic appearance.
(Primary, intermediate)

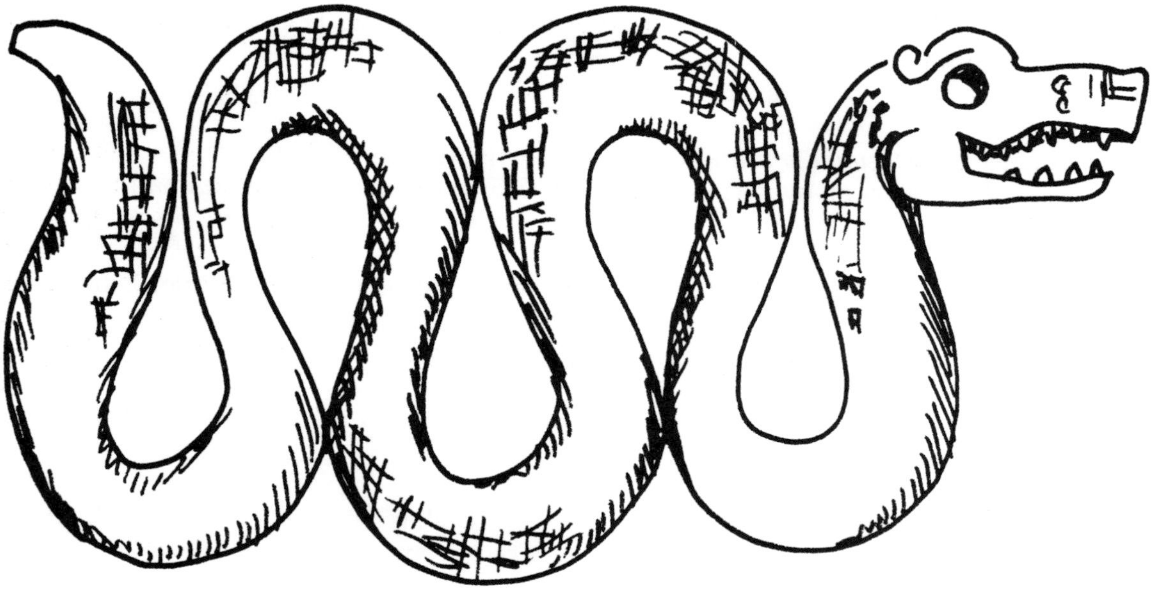

Fig. 6.3.

2. One of the Aztec gods was Quetzalcoatl, the "Feathered Serpent." Play a game that relates to the Aztec interest in both snakes and birds. For the game "Hummingbird and Snake," divide the group into two. The first group forms a chain by holding hands. This group is the snake. The second group are hummingbirds, and they scatter around the play area. The snake tries to capture a hummingbird by encircling it. When a hummingbird is caught, he or she is out. Play until all the hummingbirds are caught, and then reverse roles.
(Primary)

3. The Aztec religion called for human sacrifices on a regular basis. The Aztecs believed that each night when the sun set, it fought a battle against the forces of darkness and only rose again after winning. To keep winning the nightly battle, the sun needed the nourishment of human hearts. These sacrifices took place on sacred pyramids built to honor the Aztec gods. Share Leonard Everett Fisher's *Pyramid of the Sun, Pyramid of the Moon*. Then have the children design their own pyramids. They can make pyramids from folded paper or construct them from clay. Children should add the kinds of decorations shown in Fisher's pictures.
(Primary, intermediate)

4. Corn was very important in the lives of all the Indian tribes of the Americas. Share the story *The Legend of Food Mountain* by Harriet Rohmer, which describes how humans received corn. Then explain that the Aztecs used corn to make tortillas. Bring in some tortillas to share with your group. If you are really ambitious, make your own tortillas with the class, from recipes available in any Latin American cookbook.
(Preschool, primary, intermediate)

5. *An Aztec Warrior* by Anne Steel and several of the other nonfiction titles listed above describe the orders of Aztec society. Read about these different classes, and then have your group make feathered headdresses like those Aztec nobles wore. Real feathers can be obtained from craft and fabric stores, or the children can make feathers from paper, such as tissue paper, for a realistic look. Staple the feathers to a felt headband.
(Primary, intermediate)

6. The Aztecs were very superstitious. They believed everything that happened was controlled by the gods, and they had stories to explain all aspects of life. Read more folktales of the Aztecs in the collections by Virginia Hamilton, Francisco Hinojosa, Marcos Kurtycz, and Deborah Lattimore.

As part of these superstitions, the Aztecs believed that a person's destiny was preordained by the day on which he or she was born. Each day had a different sign or hieroglyphic, such as the crocodile, monkey, or eagle. These day-signs can be found in Barbara Beck's book and in other titles. Ask the children to either choose a day-sign for themselves or see whether they can figure out what their day-sign should be. They can draw a picture of their sign and write out what they think the sign means.
(Primary, intermediate)

THE INCAS

The Inca Empire of South America was based in Peru but stretched to encompass Ecuador in the north and most of Chile in the south. Like the Aztecs, the Incas began as a wandering tribe who gradually became dominant and drove other tribes out of the region. The Inca dynasty began about 1200. During its heyday, the Inca state was an amazingly efficient government. The Incas built incredible cities in the mountains, connected by a network of roads that can still be seen today. They spanned ravines with bridges and carved their hillsides into terraces for planting crops. They had an irrigation system as well. The Inca system was in some ways like a welfare state. It provided security to its people from the cradle to the grave. As the empire grew, many conquered peoples found themselves better off under the Incas than they had been before. Shortly before the arrival of Francisco Pizarro and the conquistadors, the ruling family was torn by strife over who should succeed to the throne, and this lack of unity probably contributed to the Incas' downfall at the hands of the Spanish.

Book List

Alexander, Ellen. *Llama and the Great Flood*. T. Y. Crowell, 1989. (Gr. 3-4)
In this Peruvian folktale, a llama warns of a coming flood.

Arnold, Caroline. *Llama*. Morrow, 1988. (Gr. 2-6)
A description of this animal that was so important in Inca life.

Beck, Barbara. *The Incas*. Franklin Watts, 1983. (Gr. 4-6)
Describes the Inca civilization and its destruction by the Spanish conquistadors.

Clark, Ann Nolan. *Secret of the Andes*. Viking, 1952. (Gr. 4-8)
This Newbery Award winner centers on the life of an Inca boy in the mountains of Peru.

Cobb, Vicki. *This Place Is High*. Walker, 1989. (Gr. 2-5)
This illustrated title describes life in the Andes Mountains and the history of the people living there.

Cohen, Daniel. *Hiram Bingham and the Dream of Gold*. M. Evans & Company, 1984. (Gr. 4-up)
This is a biography of the man who discovered the lost Inca city of Machu Picchu.

Dewey, Ariane. *The Thunder God's Son*. Greenwillow, 1981. (PreK-3)
A Peruvian folktale in picture-book format.

Gemming, Elizabeth. *Lost City in the Clouds: The Discovery of Machu Picchu*. Coward, McCann & Geoghegan, 1980. (Gr. 3-6)
A somewhat fictionalized account of Hiram Bingham's discovery of Machu Picchu.

Karen, Ruth. *Kingdom of the Sun*. Four Winds Press, 1975. (Gr. 5-up)
Discusses daily life, art, and architecture of the Incas.

Lecher, Doris. *Angelita's Magic Yarn*. Farrar, Straus & Giroux, 1992. (PreK-2)
An original folktale set in the South American Andes Mountains.

McIntyre, Loren. *The Incredible Incas and Their Timeless Land*. National Geographic Society, 1975. (Gr. 5-up)
Color photographs illustrate this history of the Incas.

McKissack, Patricia. *The Inca*. Children's Press, 1985. (Gr. 1-3)
Simple text and photos describe the Inca way of life.

Morrison, Marion. *An Inca Farmer*. Rourke, 1988. (Gr. 4-up)
A look at the life of an individual Inca.

Odijk, Pamela. *The Incas*. Silver Burdett, 1989. (Gr. 4-6)
This description of the Inca civilization and way of life includes color photographs.

Roberts, David. *Lost City of the Incas*. Rand McNally, 1977. (Gr. 4-6)
This title describes the finding of the Inca city Machu Picchu, the city's history, and the Spanish conquest.

Related Activities

1. In some ways, the Inca civilization was like a utopia. In fact, there has been speculation that a description of the Inca way of life inspired Thomas More's book *Utopia*. Ask the children to write about what their idea of a utopia would be (after explaining what the term means). After children have completed their own descriptions, use any of the nonfiction titles above to give a picture of the Inca way of life. Ask the group in what ways their ideas are similar to the Inca government and in what ways they are different. Would the children like to live in a civilization like that of the Incas? Why or why not?
(Primary, intermediate)

2. The Incas had no beasts of burden, other than llamas, yet they still managed to build incredible cities high in the Andes Mountains. They used stones for building that were so well put together the buildings could withstand earthquakes, and these buildings can still be seen today. Use some of the titles above to show pictures of Inca architecture, and then have your group create their own model structures by gluing pebbles and rocks into the shapes of walls and buildings. Discuss how difficult it must have been for the Incas to build their cities.
(Primary, intermediate)

3. One of the great cities of the Incas, Machu Picchu, was "lost" until the twentieth century, when archaeologist Hiram Bingham "found" it. Read about the finding of Machu Picchu in the books by Daniel Cohen, Elizabeth Gemming, and David Roberts. Then ask the children what they think this "lost" civilization might have been like after being cut off from the rest of the world for so long.
(Intermediate)

4. Though the Incas had no horses or cattle, they did have llamas, which became an important factor in their lives. Use Caroline Arnold's book *Llama* to find out more about these animals, and read aloud *Llama and the Great Flood* by Ellen Alexander. Older children might enjoy reading *Secret of the Andes* by Ann Nolan Clark. After reading about llamas, let the children make llamas using the outline in figure 6.4. Give children very fine wool to use to glue onto the llamas for coats.
(Preschool, primary, intermediate)

5. All the Central and South American civilizations, including the Incas, had well-developed arts and handicrafts, with strong design elements. The illustrations in the book *The Thunder God's Son* by Ariane Dewey give some idea of these elements. Read this story aloud, and look at some of the pictures of Inca art in other books.

Fig. 6.4.

Then let the children incorporate these graphic elements into tunics they make for themselves (see figure 6.5). To make these, each child needs a rectangle of material such as cotton or felt, about 6 feet by 4 feet (or smaller depending on the size of the children). Children should lay their rectangles out flat and cut a slit in the center as a hole for their heads. Then they should decorate their tunics with Inca designs. They can use fabric paints or crayons or, if you have time, actually embroider the designs on. If you want to make less permanent tunics, give each child a large rectangle of newsprint or butcher paper to draw on.
(Primary, intermediate)

Fig. 6.5.

6. Finally, play a tag game from Peru called "Help!" To decide who is "It," one player stands with his or her hand extended, palm down. The other players place their forefingers on the first player's palm. The player with his or her hand extended suddenly closes his or her fist, and the players whose fingers are caught must try again. The process continues until there is only one player whose finger is caught; he or she is It. Now the game of tag begins. Anyone being chased can call, "Help!" and then another player can take the caller's hand, saving him or her from being tagged. Anyone caught becomes It.
(Primary, intermediate)

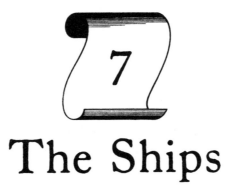

7

The Ships

Humans have used ships as a major means of transportation since earliest times. The first boats were probably logs that fell into the water and that someone thought of riding on. As time passed, humans began to give these primitive boats more shape. They hollowed out tree trunks to make canoes and tied logs together to create rafts. Eventually, they discovered that their boats could be propelled more efficiently with oars and paddles than by hand. Once begun, the evolution of boats and ships has continued throughout human history. We have seen some of the early ships of the Phoenicians, Vikings, and Celts in earlier chapters. In the sections below, we look at the history of ships and shipbuilding, the craft of sailing, and the art of navigation.

THE EVOLUTION OF SHIPS

In the fourteenth century, basically two types of ships were in use. In northern Europe, the Viking longship had evolved into the cog, a sturdy vessel capable of carrying a quantity of cargo but bulky and with one square sail, which made handling difficult in unfavorable winds. In the Mediterranean, the carrack had been developed, also bulky and hard to handle but with a triangular sail that added balance.

Before it was possible to travel out on the open ocean on voyages of exploration, several adaptations needed to be made. A ship was needed that would be sturdy enough to brave the ocean waves, small enough to explore coasts and rivers, large enough to carry supplies and cargo for a long voyage, and relatively easy to handle, so a small crew could be used. The Portuguese were the first to find the solution to these needs, in a ship called a caravel.

Book List

Ames, Lee J. *Draw 50 Boats, Ships, Trucks and Trains*. Doubleday, 1976. (Gr. 3-up)
This book on drawing vehicles includes a variety of ships.

Barton, Byron. *Boats*. Crowell, 1986. (PreK)
Several kinds of boats and ships are depicted.

Berenstain, Michael. *The Ship Book*. David McKay, 1978. (Gr. 2-6)
This picture book presents a historical survey of ships.

Bottomley, Jim. *Paper Projects for Creative Kids of All Ages*. Little, Brown, 1983. (Gr. 3-6)
The craft projects in this book include instructions for making paper-ship models like the ships Columbus sailed.

Chant, Christopher. *Sailing Ships*. Marshall Cavendish, 1989. (Gr. 3-up)
Clear, detailed pictures are the highlight of this history of sailing ships.

Fradin, Dennis. *The Niña, the Pinta, and the Santa Maria*. Franklin Watts, 1991. (Gr. 4-6)
A description of Columbus's ships.

Gay, Michel. *Little Boat*. Macmillan, 1985. (PreK-K)
Shows a little boat experiencing a storm, fishing, and returning home.

Gibbons, Gail. *The Boat Book*. Holiday House, 1983. (PreK-2)
Depicts a variety of kinds of boats.

Goldsmith-Carter, George. *Sailing Ships and Sailing Craft*. Grosset & Dunlap, 1970. (Gr. 4-up)
This guide to all kinds of ships includes historical information.

Humble, Richard. *Ships: Sailors and the Sea*. Franklin Watts, 1991. (Gr. 3-6)
This title provides a history of boats, from Greek galleys to modern vessels.

Kemp, Peter. *The History of Ships*. Orbis, 1978. (Gr. 5-up)
A comprehensive look at the history and development of ships.

Kemp, Peter, ed. *Encyclopedia of Ships and Seafaring*. Crown, 1980. (Gr. 4-up)
An encyclopedia of all kinds of information on ships, including historical development.

Landstrom, Bjorn. *Sailing Ships*. Doubleday, 1969. (Gr. 4-up)
Heavily illustrated guide to the history of sailing ships.

LaPlaca, Michael. *How to Draw Boats, Trains and Planes*. Watermill Press, 1982. (Gr. 2-up)
Instructions on drawing ships are included.

Lasky, Kathryn. *Tall Ships*. Charles Scribner's Sons, 1978. (Gr. 4-6)
This title describes the sailing ships used before the coming of steam power.

Lenski, Lois. *The Little Sailboat*. Henry Z. Walck, 1937. (PreK-K)
The story of a sailor and his boat.

Let's Discover Ships and Boats. Raintree, 1981. (Gr. 3-6)
This reference book covers small boats as well as ships.

Lippman, Peter. *Busy Boats*. Random House, 1977. (PreK-1)
Identifies and discusses the uses of different types of boats.

Robbins, Ken. *Boats*. Scholastic, 1989. (PreK-3)
Describes in text and photos the features of seventeen different kinds of boats and ships.

Rockwell, Anne. *Boats*. Dutton, 1982. (PreK-K)
A picture book showing examples of various kinds of boats and their uses.

Rutland, Jonathan. *Ships*. Warwick Press, 1976. (Gr. 3-up)
Covers the history, design, and building of ships.

Tunis, Edwin. *Oars, Sails and Steam*. Crowell, 1977. (Gr. 3-6)
An illustrated look at early boats and the history of their development.

Wahl, Jan. *The Clumpets Go Sailing*. Parents Magazine Press, 1975. (PreK-K)
The Clumpets build a homemade raft to visit a sick uncle.

Ward, Ralph T. *Ships through History*. Bobbs-Merrill, 1973. (Gr. 3-6)
A history of the development of ships.

Related Activities

1. Explain to the children that boats have improved over time. Tell them that one of the first boats humans used was a raft. Read Jan Wahl's *The Clumpets Go Sailing*, about a family sailing on a homemade raft. Then make rafts from popsicle sticks (see figure 7.1). Use two parallel sticks on one side and layer the other sticks across the two as shown. If you have a tub or plastic swimming pool available, let the children try floating their rafts.
(Preschool, primary)

2. Introduce the historical development of ships by showing Michael Berenstain's *The Ship Book* and other titles listed above. Then make a large group diorama. Cover a table with blue cloth or paper to represent the ocean. Each child can make a boat or ship from a different historical period. You can start with simple logs from prehistoric times, dugout canoes, rafts, reed boats from about 2000 B.C.E., galleys with oars from 1000 to 200 B.C.E., and on forward through history. To make their boats stand up on the "ocean," have the children draw their boats on a piece of paper folded in half, as shown in figure 7.2. The books by Lee Ames and Michael LaPlaca will help the group design their boats.
(Primary, intermediate)

3. Tell the children that boats developed until humans had made the kinds of ships used by the explorers. Let the children make their own explorers' ships using the pattern in figure 7.3. Each child needs a lunch-size paper bag. The flap at the bottom of the bag is decorated as the sail, and the rest of the bag is the hull, as shown in figure 7.4. When the child inserts a hand, the bottom flap can be manipulated up and down to resemble sails filling in the wind.
(Preschool, primary)

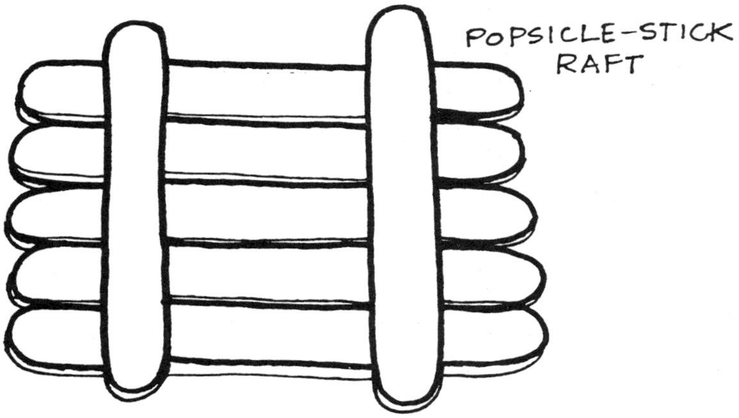

Fig. 7.1.

Fig. 7.2.

Fig. 7.3.

Fig. 7.4.

4. For older children, explain why the caravel was suited to voyages of exploration. Look at Dennis Fradin's book *The Niña, the Pinta, and the Santa Maria*. Then use Jim Bottomley's *Paper Projects for Creative Kids of All Ages* to make individual caravels.
(Intermediate)

5. Take this opportunity to study the wide variety of modern boats. Share with the group Gail Gibbons's and Ken Robbins's picture books. Then assign each child to report on one type of ship or boat. Ask children to make cutout pictures of their ships to hang from the ceiling as a display. Here is a sample list of different types of ships and boats.

Type of Ships and Boats

barge	brig	canoe
catamaran	Chinese junk	clipper ship
cog	coracle	cutter
dhow	ferry	freighter
frigate	galleass	galleon
galley	houseboat	kayak
knorr	lifeboat	liner
longship	outrigger	packet boat
pinnance	raft	rowboat
sailboat	sampan	schooner
sloop	speedboat	steamboat
submarine	tanker	umiak
yacht	yawl	windjammer

(Primary, intermediate)

6. Introduce younger children to the wide variety of boats and ships that exist by sharing the books by Byron Barton, Peter Lippman, and Anne Rockwell. Share the stories *Little Boat* by Michel Gay and *The Little Sailboat* by Lois Lenski. Now make stick puppets. Give the children copies of the different boats shown in figures 7.3 and 7.5 to color and cut out. Tape the boats to popsicle sticks. Have the children act out the motions of the following fingerplay.

What Kind of Boat Am I?

Toot, toot, toot, *(Pull a whistle)*
Chug, chug, chug! *(Make push-and-pull motion)*
What kind of boat am I?
I am a tugboat.

Row, row, row *(Make rowing motion)*
Here we go!
What kind of boat am I?
I am a rowboat.

Putter, putter, putter, *(Steer a boat)*
Hear me mutter.
What kind of boat am I?
I am a motorboat.

Blow a gale, *(Blow)*
Fill my sail!
What kind of boat am I?
I am a caravel!
(Preschool, primary)

Fig. 7.5.

7. Plan a field trip to look at ships. If you live near the ocean or a lake, visit a dock or harbor. Find out whether you can actually board one of the ships. There also may be a nautical museum or a boat dealer in your vicinity to visit.
(Primary, intermediate)

SHIPBUILDING

Unlike modern methods of shipbuilding, which use precise measurements and assembly-line production methods, ancient shipbuilding required highly skilled artisans and was considered an art form. Early ships were not built according to a previously drawn-out plan or blueprint. As a result, each ship was a unique work of art—or a failure. There are records of ships that barely cleared harbor before sinking.

Most wooden ships were built by laying down the keel, or "backbone," first. This was the long piece of wood stretching from stem to stern. Then the posts or ribs were added to give the ship a skeleton of sorts. Finally, a skin of wooden planks was added and covered with pitch or tar to make it watertight. These planks were either attached to the ribs in an overlapping pattern (like shingles on a house) and were said to be "clinker-built," or were placed flush with one another in the carvel style. Ancient ships were open to the elements until the Romans devised decks to provide shelter for people and supplies.

Early in the history of the Mediterranean a nation's power usually depended on the strength and flexibility of its ships. The Phoenicians were aware of this, and only when the Romans began to improve their fleet were they able to become the dominant power in the Mediterranean. As a result, shipbuilders were highly respected craftsmen in their communities.

Overall, the story of shipbuilding is a history of continual refinements of the basic wooden boat. This history reached its climax with the beautiful clipper ships of the eighteenth century.

Book List

Adkins, Jan. *Wooden Ship*. Houghton Mifflin, 1978. (Gr. 4-6)
This title describes the planning and building of a sailing ship, built as a whaler, in the late 1800s. Though this is later than the period being studied, it gives a great deal of information about shipbuilding.

Graham, Thomas. *Mr. Bear's Boat*. Dutton, 1988. (PreK-1)
Mr. Bear builds a boat while his wife sews the sails. They go for a sail and are becalmed at sea.

Grant, Neil. *The Discoverers*. Marshall Cavendish, 1979. (Gr. 4-6)
Includes a clear explanation of early methods of shipbuilding.

Herda, D. J. *Model Boats and Ships*. Franklin Watts, 1982. (Gr. 4-7)
Includes instructions for building several model boats and ships.

Pfanner, Louise. *Louise Builds a Boat*. Orchard, 1989. (PreK-2)
In this picture book, Louise builds a boat exactly to her own specifications.

Rand, Gloria. *Salty Dog*. Henry Holt, 1989. (PreK-2)
Salty's master has a sailboat built and takes Salty for a sail.

Rey, H. A. *Curious George Rides a Bike*. Houghton Mifflin, 1952. (PreK-2)
While delivering papers, Curious George decides to fold them into sailboats.

Silverstein, Shel. *Where the Sidewalk Ends*. Harper & Row, 1974. (Gr. 2-6)
Use the poem "Homemade Boat" from this poetry collection.

Stangl, Jean. *Paper Stories*. Fearon Teaching Aids, 1984. (Adult)
This collection of storytelling ideas includes a paper-folding story.

Steig, William. *Amos and Boris*. Farrar, Straus & Giroux, 1971. (K-3)
This story of adventure at sea begins with Amos building a boat.

Weiss, Harvey. *Ship Models and How to Build Them*. Crowell, 1973. (Gr. 4-8)
Includes step-by-step directions for building models.

Wurmfeld, Hope Herman. *Boatbuilder*. Macmillan, 1988. (Gr. 3-6)
Describes the building of a modern wooden sailboat.

Related Activities

1. For young children, read *Mr. Bear's Boat* by Thomas Graham and *Salty Dog* by Gloria Rand, two stories about building a boat. Then help the children put their own boats together. To make the boats, cut a large triangle from a sheet of paper. Then cut the triangle into four sections, as shown in figure 7.6. Turn the bottom (largest) section upside down to form the hull. The two other sections will be the mainsail and topsail. The tip of the triangle can be used as a flag or anchor. Use a straw or a strip of long, thin paper as the mast. Glue the pieces together and decorate the boat. Glue string to a triangle to make an anchor. As the children make the boats, explain which part is the hull, the mast, and the sail.
(Preschool, primary)

2. Introduce shipbuilding to older children with books such as *Wooden Ship* by Jan Adkins and *Boatbuilder* by Hope Wurmfeld. There is also an excellent explanation of shipbuilding in Neil Grant's *The Discoverers*. Then let children experience modified shipbuilding by building a frame. Cut the shape of a keel, with bow and stern, from heavy cardboard (see figure 7.7). Then add cardboard ribs, as shown. Make the ribs about ¼" wide, and fold the ends up after gluing them to the keel. Curve the ribs up into the shape of the ship and hold them with cardboard supports.
(Primary, intermediate)

3. Read some stories about shipbuilding, such as Louise Pfanner's *Louise Builds a Boat* or William Steig's *Amos and Boris*. Then share Shel Silverstein's poem "Homemade Boat" from *Where the Sidewalk Ends*. Give each child a copy of the blank flag in figure 7.8 on page 124 so he or she can create a personalized ship's flag.
(Primary)

(Text continues on page 125.)

Fig. 7.6.

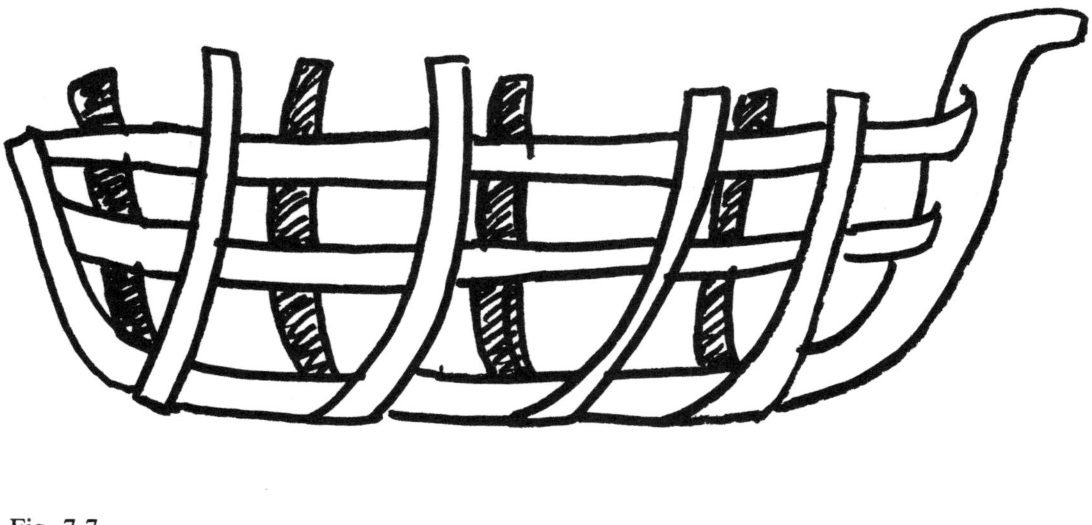

Fig. 7.7.

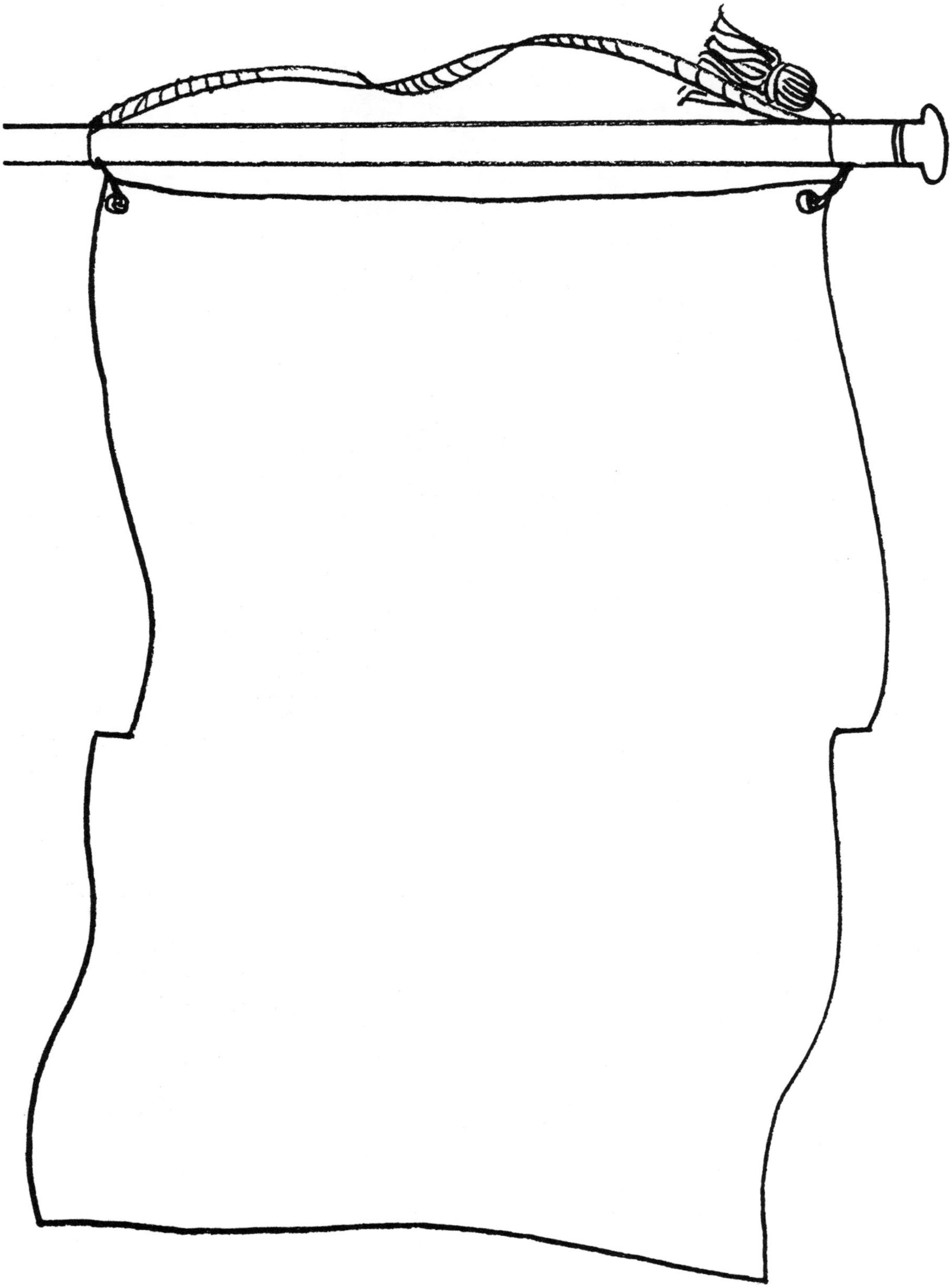

Fig. 7.8.

4. Read aloud *Curious George Rides a Bike* by H. A. Rey. Now tell a paper-folding story. Jean Stangl, in her book *Paper Stories*, has a paper-folding story called "Sailor Boy." Then make paper-fold boats by following the steps described here and shown in figure 7.9. (1) For each boat, you will need an 8½ x 11" piece of paper folded in half from top to bottom. (2 and 3) Fold each of the top corners down to the center. There will be an inch or so left below these folded corners. (4) Fold both the front and back of this long edge up. (5) Push the ends toward the center and flatten the boat in this new shape. (6) Turn the bottom corners up. (7) Push the ends together again and, once more, flatten the boat sideways. (8) Gently pull the top corners open. (9) Shape the sides of the boat. You can float this boat in water.

Share this fingerplay:

Boatbuilder

I am a boatbuilder	*(Tap self on chest)*
Building a boat.	*(Pretend to hammer)*
It is made of paper,	
Watch it float!	*(Make sailing motion)*

(Preschool, primary)

5. If you have space and a willing loaner, bring a small sailboat, canoe, rowboat, or dinghy to your school or library. Perhaps the boat could be on display in your parking lot for a couple of days. Try to find a local sailor who would be willing to make a presentation on sailing, rigging, and other maritime skills to your group. Give the children a copy of the boat in figure 7.10 in this book to diagram, to help them learn the names of the different parts of a ship.
(Primary, intermediate)

6. If the children are interested in models, see whether they would be willing to construct one as a group project or whether anyone has a collection he or she would be willing to share. Instructions for building model ships are included in D. J. Herda's *Model Boats and Ships* and in Harvey Weiss's *Ship Models and How to Build Them*.
(Intermediate)

(Text continues on page 128.)

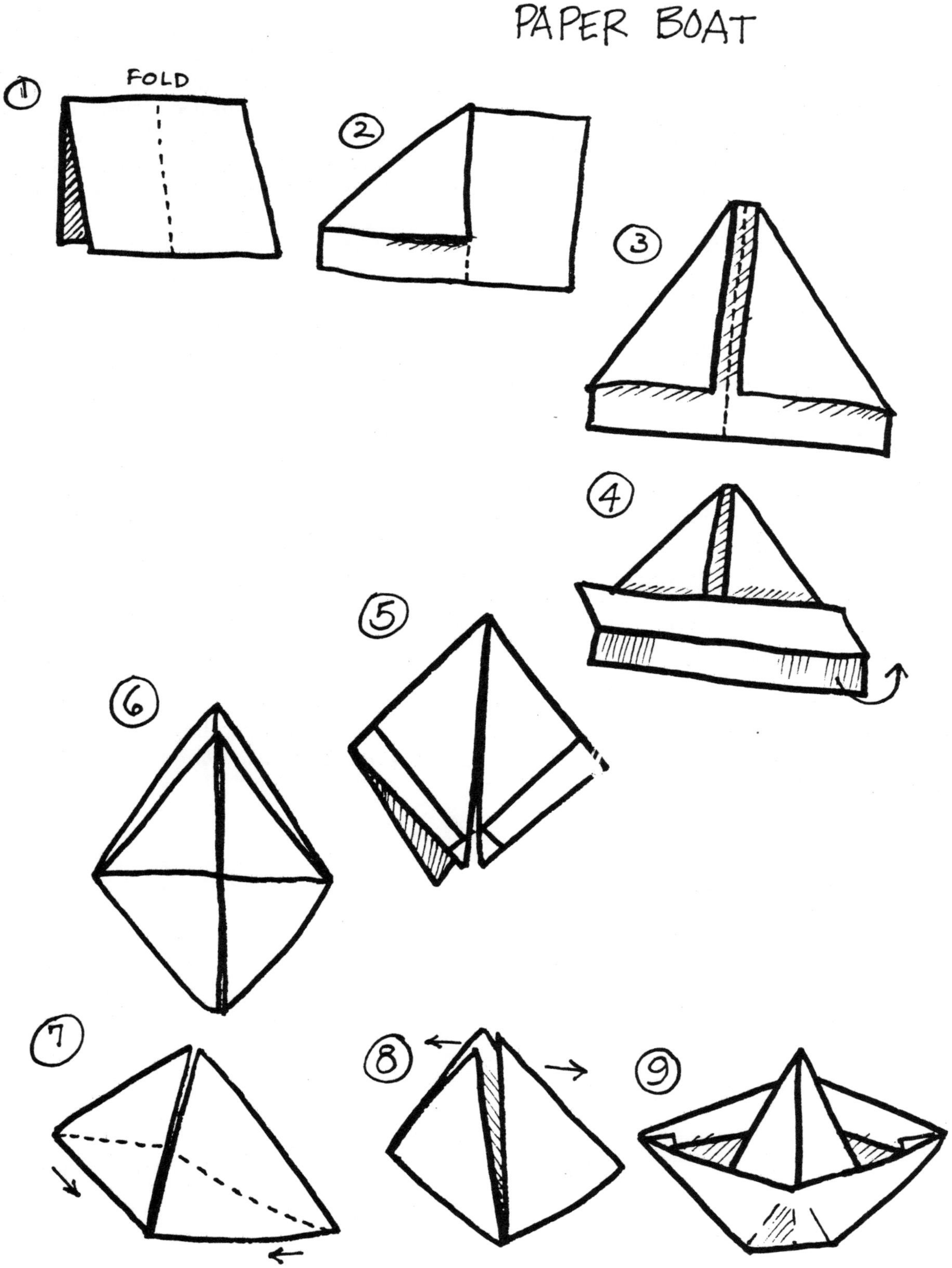
PAPER BOAT
1
FOLD
2
3
4
5
6
7
8
9

Fig. 7.9.

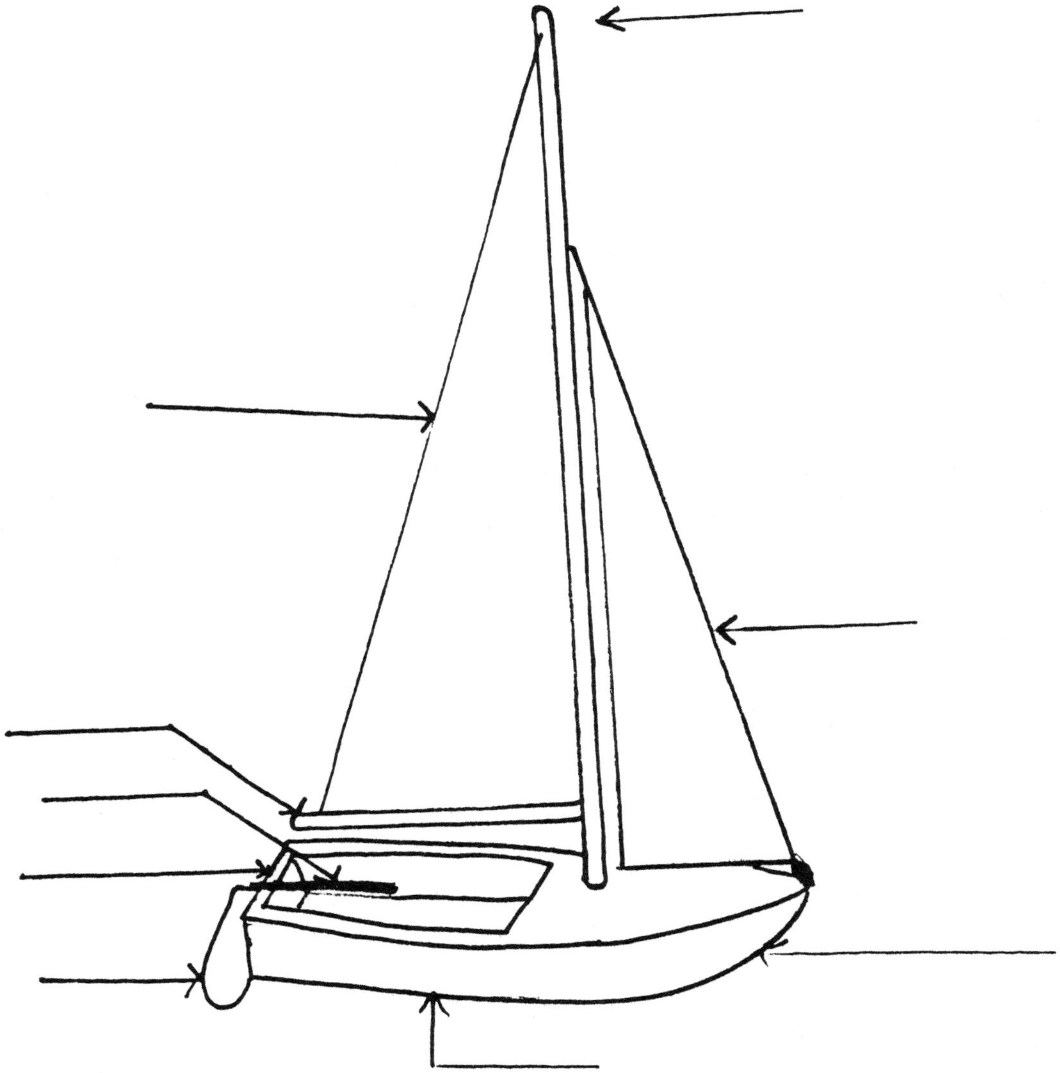

Fig. 7.10.

THE CRAFT OF SAILING

The craft of sailing has developed over the centuries. Very early mariners depended on oars and paddles until they began to understand more about sailing. The earliest sailors discovered, perhaps, that their shirts or cloaks billowed out in the wind, getting the idea to deliberately place a sheet of material to catch the wind.

Gradually it was learned that if the sail was mounted on a mast in such a way that it could be moved depending on which direction the wind was blowing, an element of steering could be introduced. The early ships of the Greeks and Phoenicians had only one sail, but over time sailors learned that more sails could be added to capture even more wind power. The clipper ships of the eighteenth century took this development so far that they used literally dozens of sails of various sizes and heights.

Columbus's caravels probably represent a midpoint in the development of sails. The caravel carried enough sail to power a ship at a steady pace, but not so many sails that a large crew was needed to operate the ship. This was important because food on board was limited.

Eventually, the craft of sailing was overtaken by steam-powered ships, but sailing is still enjoyed by many today as recreation. Other than the first log boat drifting with the current, a sailing boat or ship is the only form of transportation that takes advantage of a natural force, the wind, rather than expending energy to overcome natural forces.

Book List

Adkins, Jan. *The Craft of Sail: A Primer of Sailing*. Walker & Company, 1973. (Gr. 5-up)
This title contains a detailed description of what makes a boat sail, including the scientific principles involved.

Allen, Pamela. *Who Sank the Boat?* Coward-McCann, 1983. (PreK-2)
When too many passengers crowd into a boat, the inevitable happens.

Barrett, Norman. *Sailing*. Franklin Watts, 1988. (Gr. 3-5)
This coverage of sailing techniques includes color photos.

Benjamin, Alan. *A Change of Plans*. Four Winds Press, 1982. (PreK-2)
When too many friends go for a boat ride, they end up swimming.

Blocksma, Mary. *Easy-to-Make Water Toys That Really Work*. Prentice Hall, 1985. (Gr. 2-6)
Instructions for making boats that really float.

Burningham, John. *Mr. Gumpy's Outing*. Holt, Rinehart & Winston, 1971. (PreK-K)
When too many passengers muck about in Mr. Gumpy's boat, over they go.

Cole, William. *The Sea, Ships and Sailors*. Viking, 1967. (Gr. 3-up)
A collection of poems and songs about the sea and ships.

Fisher, Leonard Everett. *Sailboat Lost*. Macmillan, 1991. (K-3)
Two boys sail to an island, where their boat escapes, goes out to sea, and then returns to rescue them.

Glazer, Tom. *Eye Winker, Tom Tinker, Chin Chopper*. Doubleday, 1973. (All ages)
Contains fifty songs with hand movements, including "Sailing at High Tide."

Locker, Thomas. *Sailing with the Wind*. Dial, 1986. (Gr. 1-6)
A young girl sails downriver with her uncle to discover the sea for the first time.

Slocombe, Lorna. *Sailing Basics*. Prentice Hall, 1982. (Gr. 5-8)
A description of the craft of sailing.

Vandervoort, Thomas J. *Sailing Is for Me*. Lerner, 1981. (Gr. 2-5)
A clear explanation of the mechanics of sailing, the parts of a sailboat, and how everything works together.

Weiss, Harvey. *Sailing Small Boats*. Young Scott, 1967. (Gr. 4-6)
A description of sailing techniques.

Related Activities

1. Start by explaining that boats float on water—as long as they stay level and are not too heavy! Harvey Weiss's *Sailing Small Boats* describes what makes a boat float. Read *Who Sank the Boat?* by Pamela Allen and *Mr. Gumpy's Outing* by John Burningham. Let children make boat books. You can either use the patterns in figure 7.11 to illustrate *Mr. Gumpy's Outing* or *Who Sank the Boat?* or create your own sequence. To make the pages of a boat book, cut three or more sheets of 8½" x 11" paper in half. Staple these half-pages together on the left-hand side. Children should add an animal to the boat on each page, until finally the boat tips over on the last page.
(Preschool, primary)

2. Share the following fingerplay with the group:

Sailing

Watch the way, out in the bay,	*(Hand above eyes)*
The boats go sailing by.	*(Make sailing motion)*
With the wind, around the bend,	*(Curve around bend)*
Under the deep blue sky.	*(Sailing motion)*

(Preschool, primary)

Fig. 7.11.

3. Harvey Weiss's book *Sailing Small Boats* gives an explanation of how wind moves a sailboat, and the books by Norman Barrett, Lorna Slocombe, and Thomas Vandervoort also give information on sailing. Read Leonard Everett Fisher's *Sailboat Lost* and Thomas Locker's *Sailing with the Wind* to introduce sailboats. Then let the children make boats that they can actually sail, and float the boats in a tub of water or an inflatable swimming pool to show how this works. There are a number of ways to make simple boats that float. For walnut boats, use empty walnut shells for the hulls (see figure 7.12). Cut sails from paper, and stick a toothpick mast through the "sail." The mast can be glued to the bottom of the boat or you can use a bit of clay to stick it in.

You can also make the body of a boat with a margarine tub. If you want to use the lid, cut a hole in it to put the mast through (see figure 7.13). For other ideas, see Mary Blocksma's *Easy-to-Make Water Toys That Really Work*.

While they sail their ships, have the children sing "Sailing at High Tide" from Tom Glazer's *Eye Winker, Tom Tinker, Chin Chopper*.
(Primary)

Fig. 7.12.

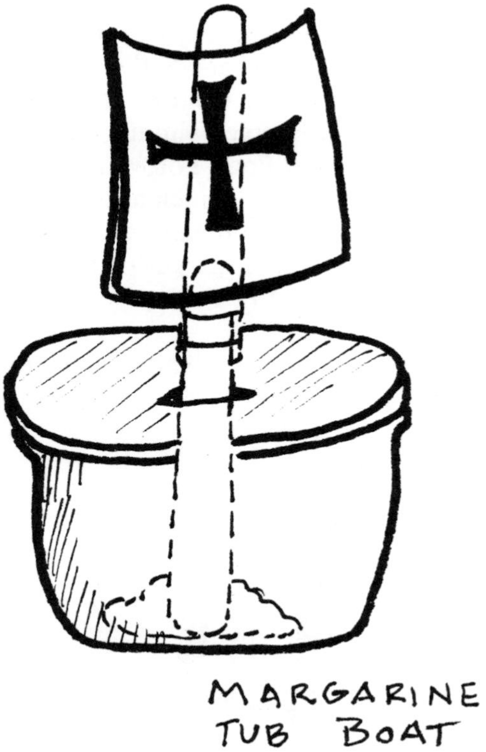

Fig. 7.13.

4. Introduce nautical terms with the poem "Sea Shanty" by Abe Burrows, from William Cole's *The Sea, Ships and Sailors*. Then give the children the crossword puzzle from figure 7.14. (Answers are given in figure 7.15 on page 135.)
(Intermediate)

(Text continues on page 136.)

Sailing Crossword Puzzle

Use these words:

aft	boom	bow
bowsprit	brace	capsize
draft	forward	frame
furl	hold	hull
keel	leeward	mast
moor	poop	port
rigging	rudder	sail
sheet	spar	starboard
stay	stern	tack
windward	yard	

DOWN

1. Below deck; cargo area
2. Main structural piece running the length of the lower hull
3. Rope used to control the foot of the sail
4. Rope used to control the backward and forward swinging movement of a spar
5. An upward-angled "mast" projecting forward from the bow
6. Tip over
7. To secure the boat with cables, anchors, and lines
8. Rope used to brace the mast against backward and forward movement
9. Raised section at the stern
10. Rear or stern of boat
11. Front section of ship
12. Used for steering
13. Back of ship
14. Front of boat or ship

ACROSS

1. Side away from wind
2. Body of ship
3. Depth of the hull between the waterline and the bottom of the keel
4. Vertical supporting pole
5. Ropes and chains for moving sail
6. Spar attached to the foot of a sail
7. Cloth to catch the wind
8. Horizontal or angled length of wood to which head of sail is attached
9. Left side as you are facing front
10. Structural piece rising from the keel to give the hull its shape
11. Make a zigzag course into the wind
12. Alternative name for spar
13. Bunching a sail against its spar and lashing it out of the way
14. Windy side
15. Right side as you are facing front

Fig. 7.14.

(Figure 7.14 continues on page 134.)

Sailing Crossword Puzzle

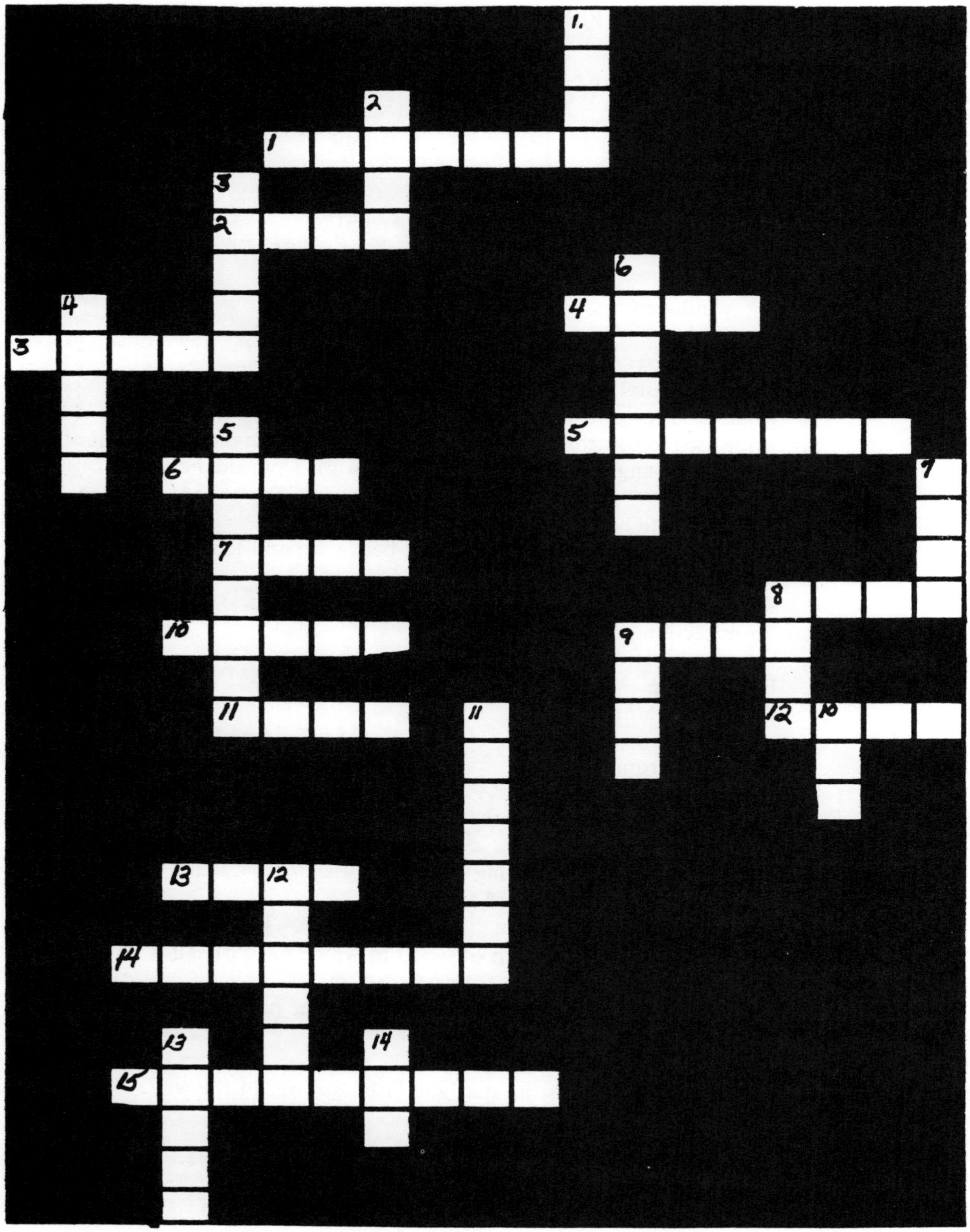

Answers

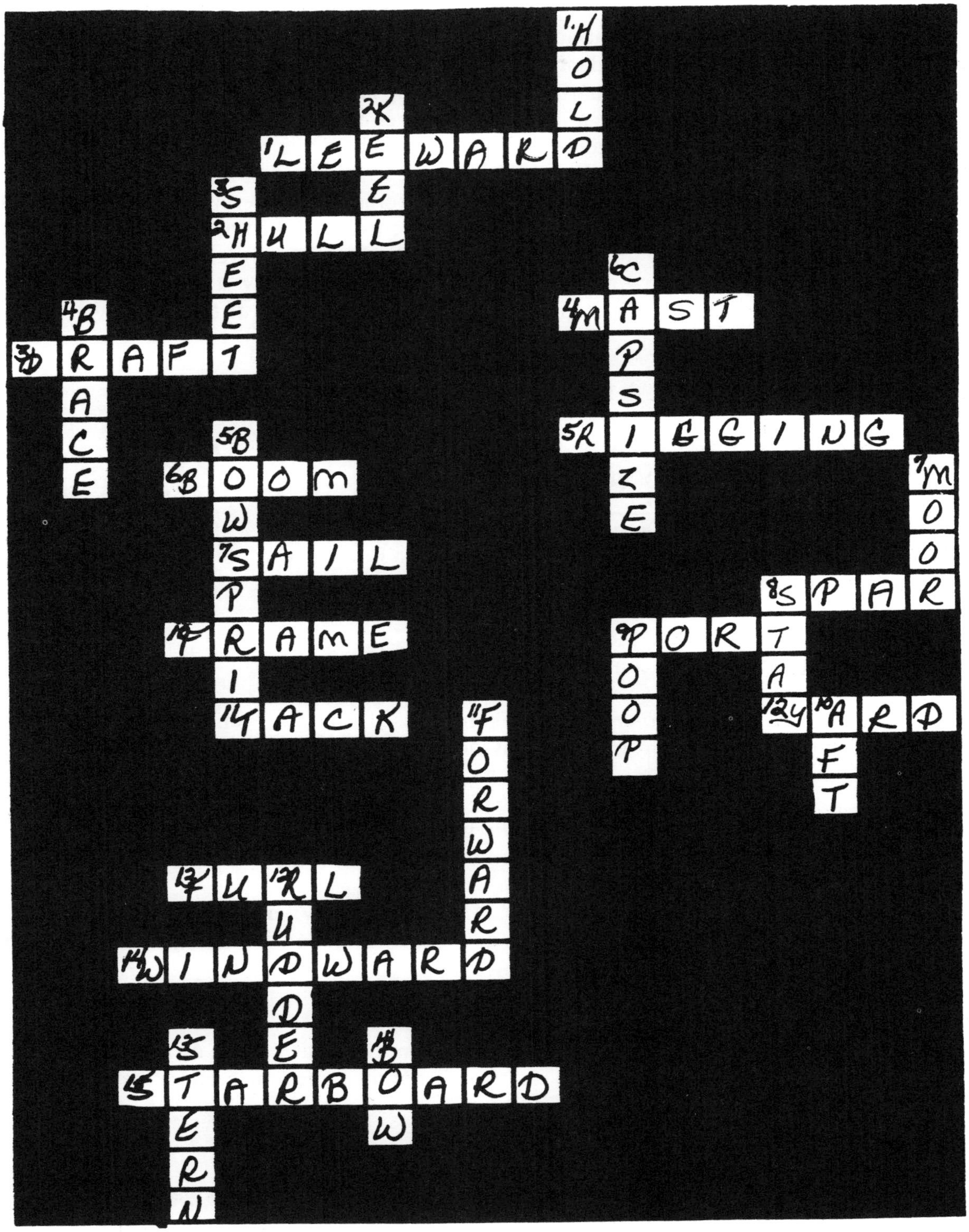

Fig. 7.15.

THE ART OF NAVIGATION

In addition to requiring suitable ships, the task of exploration made it necessary to develop more sophisticated methods of navigation. The earliest mariners used a kind of visual piloting, in which they never lost sight of land and guided their course using coastal landmarks. They sailed by day and anchored their ships at night until the sun came up and they could see the shore again. One of the problems with this kind of navigation was the danger of running aground on shallow shores, so sailors developed the sounding rod and eventually the weighted line, which were used to probe the sea bottom to determine whether the ships had clearance.

Eventually, a method of navigating by "dead reckoning" was developed. This meant that starting from a known point, captains charted their direction with a compass and estimated their latitude using the positions of the sun, moon, and stars. Because there were no chronometers to tell accurate time, sailors guessed at longitude, or the distance east or west they had traveled, by estimating how fast they went in a certain amount of time in a certain direction.

Book List

Brand, Oscar. *Singing Holidays*. Knopf, 1957. (All ages)
This collection includes the song "Sailing on the Sea."

Branley, Franklyn M. *The Big Dipper*. HarperCollins Children's Books, 1990. (PreK-3)
This title describes the constellation that contains the Pole or North Star, used by mariners in navigation.

______. *North, South, East, and West*. Crowell, 1966. (Gr. 1-5)
Clear description of what a compass is and how to find direction.

Heimann, Susan. *Christopher Columbus*. Franklin Watts, 1973. (Gr. 4-up)
This well-illustrated biography of Columbus includes quite a bit of information on navigational skills.

Hellman, Hal. *Navigation: Land, Sea & Sky*. Prentice Hall, 1966. (Gr. 3-6)
Though some of this title is dated, it presents a clear description of nautical navigation.

Hirsch, S. Carl. *On Course! Navigating in Sea, Air, and Space*. Viking, 1967. (Gr. 4-7)
As with the title above, the chapters on air and space navigation are dated, but the beginning, on sea navigation, is useful.

Kandoian, Ellen. *Is Anybody Up?* Putnam, 1989. (PreK-3)
Although Molly in the United States is far away from the Inuit woman of Baffin Bay and the lonely sailor off the coast of Chile, they all eat breakfast at the same time because they are all in the same time zone, or longitude.

______. *Under the Sun*. Dodd, Mead, 1987. (PreK-3)
Molly's mother answers Molly's questions about where the sun goes each night by taking her on a visual journey around the world, all at the same latitude.

Pollard, Michael. *Finding the Way*. Schoolhouse Press, 1986. (Gr. 3-6)
This title describes various methods of navigation.

Ryan, Peter. *Explorers and Mapmakers*. Dutton, 1989. (Gr. 3-6)
Includes a chapter on navigational instruments.

Taylor, Mark. *The Case of the Purloined Compass*. Atheneum, 1985. (PreK-3)
This is part of the Henry the Explorer series, in which Henry's dog, Angus, finds Henry's lost compass.

Related Activities

1. Talk about the need to have directions to where you are going, especially when traveling someplace you have never been. Play the game "Directions." Have the children take turns being the "navigator" and act out giving directions to various places. You may need to prompt them by questions such as, "Do I pass any big buildings on the way?" "Are there any bridges I have to cross?" "When I get to the corner, do I turn right or left?"
(Preschool, primary)

2. The most important instrument sailors had to help them find their way across the unknown ocean was the compass. They did not have any of the sophisticated navigational equipment available today, such as radios, sonar, radar, barometers, and telescopes. Let the children make a working compass, like the one shown in figure 7.16, to see how Columbus used it. Use a darning needle as the marker. Rub a magnet over the needle, in one direction, about fifty times to magnetize the needle. Push the needle through a cork and float the cork and needle in a bowl of water. No matter which way the bowl is turned, the needle will point north.
(Primary, intermediate)

Fig. 7.16.

3. Read Mark Taylor's *The Case of the Purloined Compass* and explain that a compass is used to find direction. To make a nonworking compass model like the one in figure 7.17, cut the bottom off of a salt or similar container, or use a lid with a wide lip. This piece is the compass case. Place the case on a piece of paper and trace around it. Cut out the circle in the piece of paper and draw the points of the compass onto the circle. Attach a compass arrow to the middle of the circle with a small paper brad. Put glue around the edges of the circle on the back, and glue the circle into the compass case. Make sure the glue is only around the edges so the needle can move. Remember to tell the children that this is not a working compass.
(Preschool, primary)

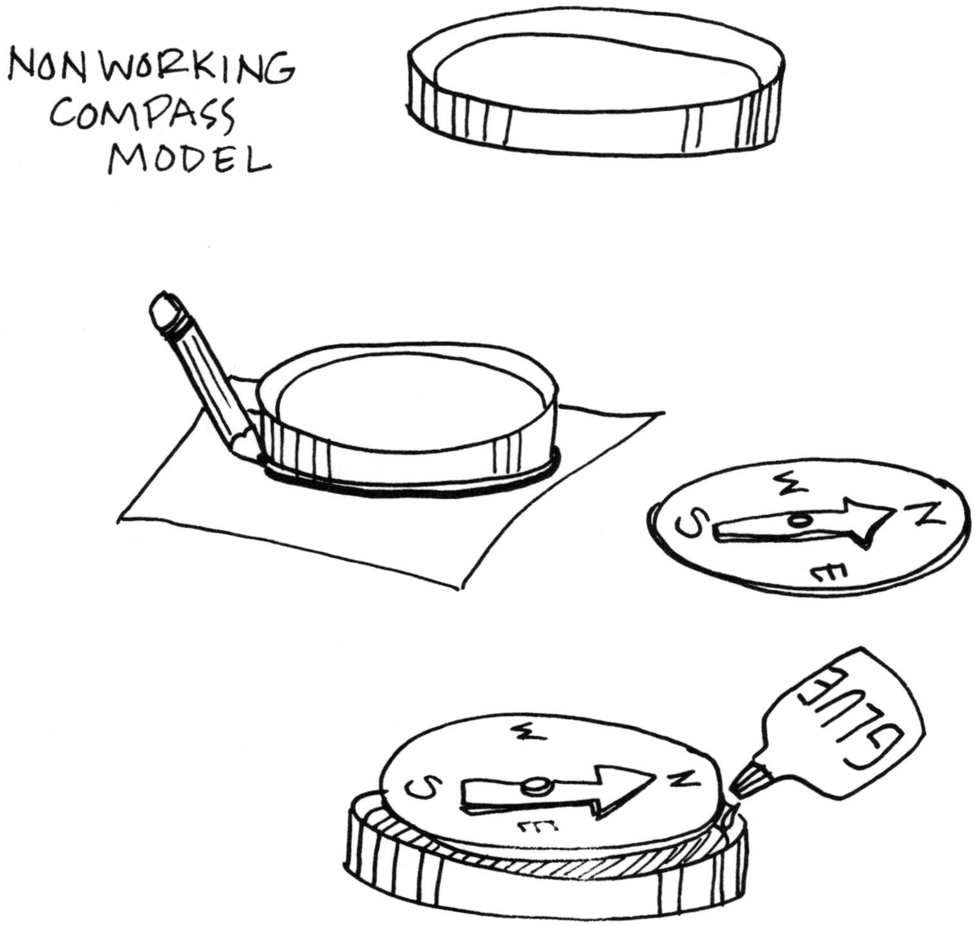

Fig. 7.17.

4. Teach the children the song "Sailing on the Sea" from Oscar Brand's *Singing Holidays*, which describes the difficulties Columbus faced in navigating to the New World. Point out that the song is wrong in saying that Columbus did not have a compass—but that is about all he did have!
(Primary)

5. Play a game called "Compass." The group should stand facing one player, who acts as the pilot reading the compass. The pilot indicates which way the group should turn by calling out a direction, such as "North!" Quickly, all the players should turn to the corner of the room that has been designated as north. At first the pilot may help the group by turning with them, but later he or she may try to confuse them by turning in a direction different from the one he or she calls. Anyone who turns the wrong way is out. After awhile, halfway points on the compass can be added, such as northeast and southwest.
(Primary)

6. Use a globe or map marked with parallels and meridians to explain what latitude and longitude are. Then ask the children to plot the latitude and longitude of where they live. Read the picture books by Ellen Kandoian to clarify the ideas of longitude and latitude.
(Primary, intermediate)

7. Because there were no accurate ship clocks during the time of Columbus, it was very difficult for sailors to plot their longitude. They estimated how far east or west they had traveled by estimating their speed. To judge the speed at which they were sailing, early mariners used a log, or a "corredera." This was basically a piece of wood tied to a line, and the line had knots tied in it at regular intervals. The piece of wood was thrown overboard, and the number of knots that passed through the hand of the sailor holding the line, within a certain amount of time, told the speed of the ship. This is why even today a ship's speed is measured in "knots." Let the children make a corredera with a piece of wood and a length of string.
(Primary, intermediate)

8. To use a corredera (see activity 7), sailors had to have a way of keeping time. Because there were as yet no accurate chronometers available, they used an ampolleta, which was basically an hourglass filled with sand that ran through to the other side every half hour. The ship's boys had to watch the ampolleta and turn it over every time it emptied. Children can make a paper ampolleta using the pattern in figure 7.18. Coat one-half of the ampolleta with white glue thinned with water. Then sprinkle sand over the paper. When the glue is dry, shake the excess sand off. Then share these songs that were sung by the ship's boys as they called the watch.

> Good is that which passeth,
> Better that which cometh,
> Seven is passed and eight floweth,
> More shall flow if God willeth,
> Count and pass makes voyage fast.
>
> Blessed be the hour
> In which God was born,
> Saint Mary who bore Him,
> Saint John who baptized Him,
> The watch is called,
> The glass floweth;
> We shall make a good voyage
> If God willeth.

Fig. 7.18.

One glass is gone
And now the second floweth
More shall run down
If my God willeth.

(Primary)

9. Navigation instruments early mariners used included the quadrant and the astrolabe, which were used to find the ship's latitude with the help of the North Star. Use some of the titles above by Franklyn Branley, Hal Hellman, S. Carl Hirsch, Michael Pollard, and Peter Ryan to show pictures of these early instruments. Then have the children make simplified quadrants and astrolabes, like those shown in figures 7.19 and 7.20.

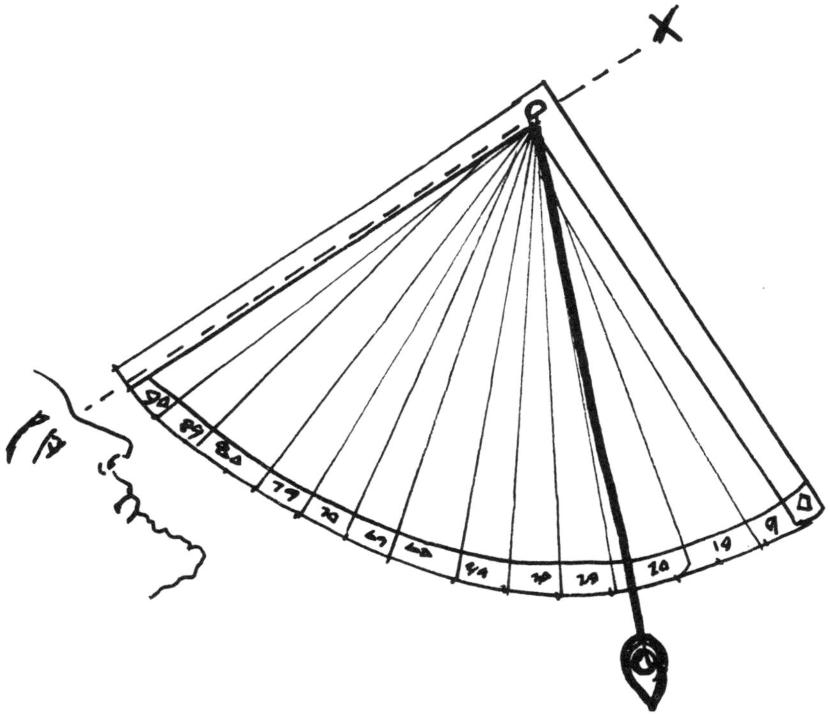

Fig. 7.19. Quadrant.

The quadrant, shaped in a quarter-circle, was marked with degrees from 0 to 90. The altitude of the object in view (such as the North Star) was determined by sighting along one side. A thread with a small weight (such as a metal washer or bolt) hanging from it indicated the angle of elevation. Make a quadrant from cardboard.

To make an astrolabe, use a paper plate or a cardboard circle. Mark the circle with 360 degrees. Attach a drinking straw at the midpoint of the circle (see figure 7.20) to sight along. Use a paper brad to attach the straw so the straw can be moved. Tape a ring to the top by which to hold the astrolabe. Latitude would be found by sighting along the straw at the North Star and noting the degree reading.

Read Franklyn Branley's *The Big Dipper* to help show the importance of the North Star in early navigation.
(Intermediate)

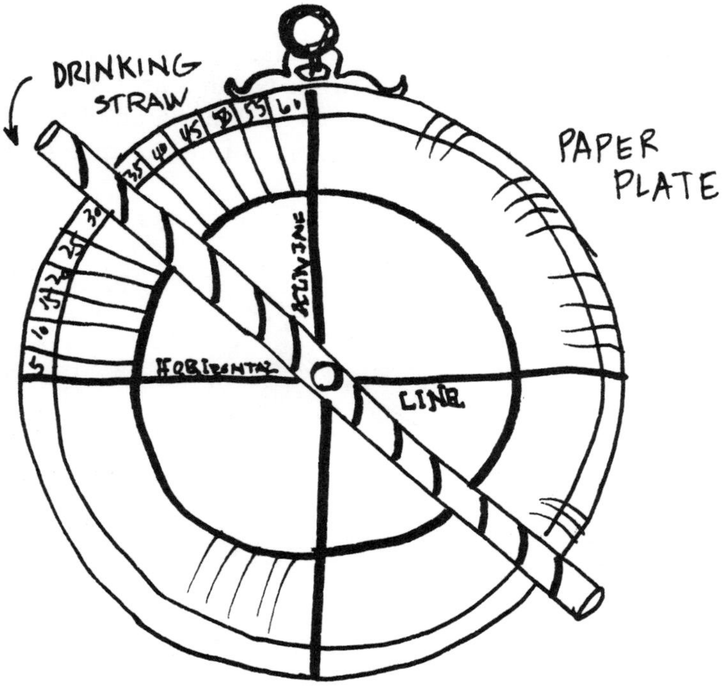

Fig. 7.20. Astrolabe.

THE PORTUGUESE SEAFARERS

In the 1400s, Portugal was the hub of the seafaring world, due partly to its location, perched precariously on the edge of the Atlantic, and to the fact that it was dependent on the sea for survival. Portugal's preeminence was also due to the efforts of Prince Henry the Navigator and to a shift in the focus of trade away from the Mediterranean. In 1454, when the Moslems captured the city of Constantinople, the overland routes to the Far East were closed. This is what sparked the desire for overseas exploration—the need for a new route to the lands of treasure.

Prince Henry, third son of the king of Portugal, established what has been called a "school of navigation." He gathered the finest cartographers, astronomers, navigators, sailors, shipbuilders, explorers, and anyone else who might have information for him. He began sending ships down the coast of Africa, looking for a sea passage to the east. The exploration of the African coast proceeded in stages and took many years to complete. Each voyage went a little bit farther than had the one before. However, Prince Henry died in 1460, without seeing his dream of a passage to India realized.

Finally, in 1488, Bartholomew Dias rounded the Cape of Good Hope. He had been caught in a storm at sea and blown far to the south. When the storm was over, Dias turned east, but he found nothing but water. He finally turned north and found the tip of the continent. He was not able to complete the trip to India, however, because his sailors mutinied and insisted on returning home.

It was not until almost ten years later, in 1497, that Vasco da Gama set sail for India once more. His fleet included the flagship *São Gabriel*, plus the *São Rafael*, the *Berrio*, and the *São Maria*, with a total crew of about 150 sailors. The voyage was long and hazardous. The crew suffered from scurvy, caused by lack of fresh fruit and vegetables. They were also involved in several battles, as all the countries on the eastern coast of Africa were controlled by hostile Arabs. After many dangers, they finally reached India on May 20, 1498, but still their troubles were not over. They had to overcome both hostility to this incursion on the local trade monopoly and da Gama's own limited ideas of dealing with "foreigners." Though da Gama was responsible for creating Portugal's India trading monopoly, he probably also was responsible for the later downfall of that monopoly, in that he established a tradition of relating to the Indians only by force. However, this trip was the beginning of Portugal's trading empire and established the country, along with Spain, as one of the leaders of the Age of Exploration.

Book List

Buehr, Walter. *The Portuguese Explorers*. Putnam, 1966. (Gr. 3-6)

This title describes the exploits of Prince Henry and the Portuguese sailors who explored the western coast of Africa.

Carlson, Nancy. *Loudmouth George and the New Neighbors*. Carolrhoda, 1983. (PreK-2)

When new neighbors move in, George has already made up his mind about them before he even meets them.

Chubb, Thomas Caldecot. *Prince Henry the Navigator and the Highways of the Sea*. Viking, 1970. (Gr. 5-up)

This biography describes Prince Henry of Portugal's influence on the history of sea exploration.

Fisher, Leonard Everett. *Prince Henry the Navigator*. Macmillan, 1990. (Gr. 3-6)
In picture-book format, Fisher introduces the life of Prince Henry and the prince's impact on the history of navigation.

Jacobs, W. J. *Prince Henry the Navigator*. Franklin Watts, 1973. (Gr. 4-up)
This biography of Prince Henry includes a number of illustrations.

Knight, David. *Vasco da Gama*. Troll, 1979. (Gr. 3-6)
A somewhat uninspired biography of this explorer but one of the few available.

Rutland, J. P. *The Amazing Fact Book of Ships and Boats*. Creative Education, 1979. (Gr. 3-6)
Includes a description of a Portuguese muletta.

Sharmat, Marjorie Weinman. *Gila Monsters Meet You at the Airport*. Macmillan, 1980. (PreK-3)
When a boy is forced to move to the West Coast of the United States, he worries about all the stereotypes he has ever heard.

Sterling, Thomas. *Exploration of Africa*. American Heritage, 1963. (Gr. 4-up)
The first chapters of this title describe the exploits of the Portuguese explorers in the time of Prince Henry.

Syme, Ronald. *Vasco da Gama: Sailor toward the Sunrise*. Morrow, 1959. (Gr. 3-6)
Unfortunately, very few biographies of Vasco da Gama are available, and this one is not particularly objective.

Related Activities

1. The concept of Portuguese exploration is a difficult one to convey to very young children, but you can explain that the Portuguese were people who lived by the sea and that they painted eyes on their boats so that they could "see" where to go. Give the children copies of the Portuguese *muletta* in figure 7.21 and tell them to draw on eyes.
(Preschool, primary)

2. To describe Prince Henry's accomplishments, use any of the titles above on his life. *Prince Henry the Navigator* by Leonard Everett Fisher is in picture-book format and suited for use with a group.
(Primary, intermediate)

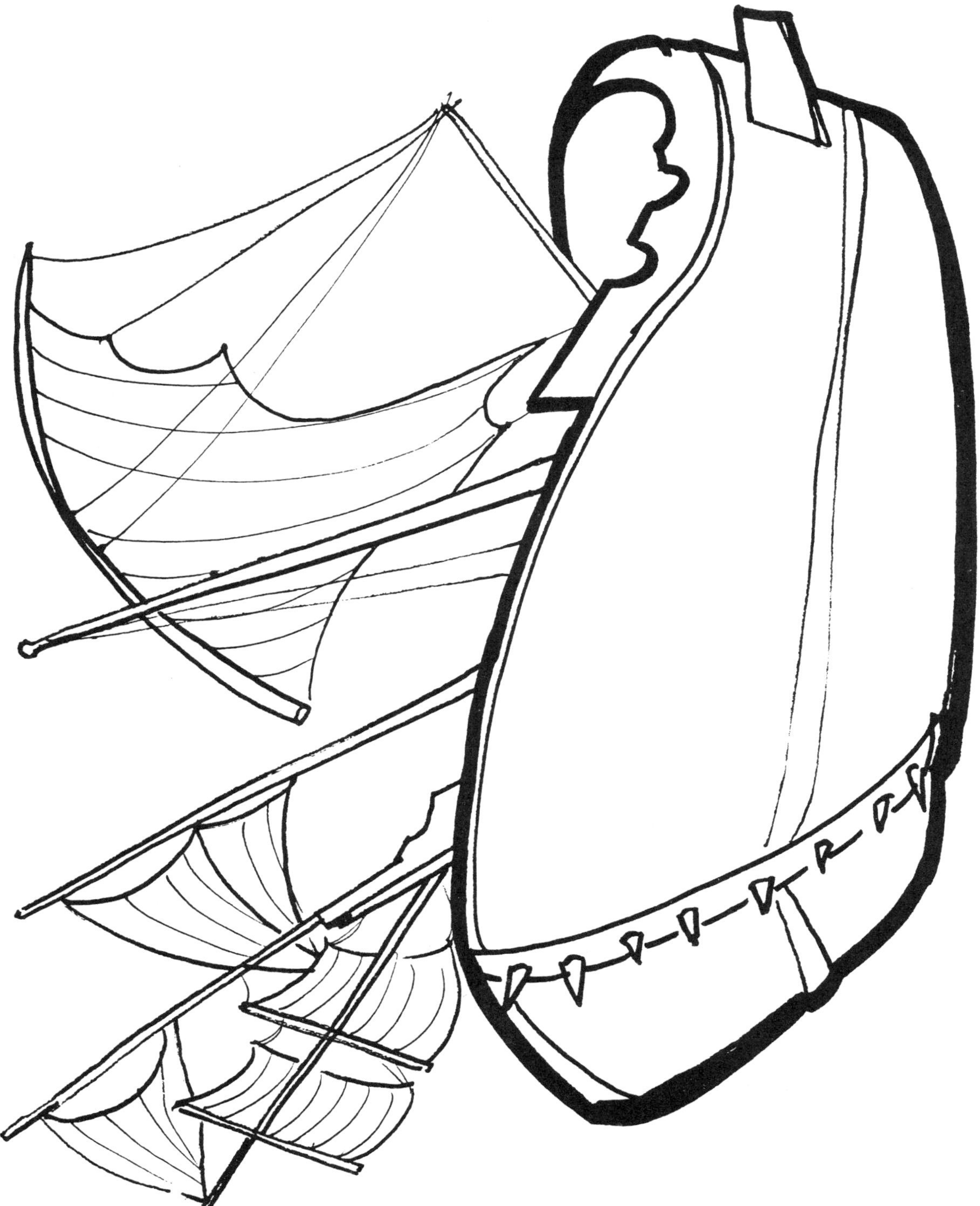

Fig. 7.21.

3. Describe the exploits of the Portuguese using the books by Walter Buehr and Thomas Sterling. Then give the children copies of the map of Africa in figure 7.22 to use for charting the different voyages of the various explorers. Use a different color marker for each voyage.
(Primary, intermediate)

4. Timbuktu was one of the places in Africa the Portuguese wanted to know more about. Play the game "Off to Timbuktu." Ask the children to stand in a circle and hold hands, moving clockwise, as they recite this verse:

> We are off to Timbuktu.
> Would you like to go there, too?
> All the way and back again,
> You must follow the leader then.

One player walks outside the moving circle, going in the opposite direction. At the end of the verse, this player asks the player closest to him or her, "Would you like to go to Timbuktu?" The player responds, "Yes, I would." The first player asks, "Would you like to take a friend?" The second player responds, "Yes," and turns to the next player in the circle, asking, "Would you like to go to Timbuktu?" This third player responds, "Yes, I would." These two players join hands with the first player. The game is continued with the last player in line asking the closest person in the circle whether he or she would like to go to Timbuktu. Repeat until all the players are in line and the circle has reversed itself.
(Primary)

5. Probably the most famous explorer to sail for Portugal was Vasco da Gama. Use the biographies above to introduce his personality. Then explain that da Gama began a tradition of trying to "ride roughshod" over all foreigners. Use Nancy Carlson's *Loudmouth George and the New Neighbors* and Marjorie Sharmat's book *Gila Monsters Meet You at the Airport* to introduce the concept of stereotypes. Ask the children to make a list of stereotypes, such as "all women can cook" and "all men can fix cars." Then explain how such stereotyping hampered the Portuguese in their dealings with the Indians.
(Primary, intermediate)

6. Describe da Gama's encounters with the Arab and Indian rulers he met. These powerful leaders of wealthy trading cities were used to being given extravagant gifts when someone wanted to win their favor. However, because of his stereotyped ideas about foreigners, da Gama had brought with him only cheap cloth and trinkets. When da Gama offered these tacky gifts, the local officials were insulted and did not take him seriously. Ask the children to imagine that they are going to a previously unknown country and want to bring gifts to win the friendship of the local population. What kinds of things might they take, and what do they think their choices say about their preconceived ideas about the people they will meet?
(Intermediate)

7. Let the children make sample trinkets to take on the voyage for trading, as da Gama did. To make simple beads, cut triangles from paper, about 12" long and about 1½" wide at the base (see figure 7.23). You can use colored construction paper or pages torn from magazines. Thread a darning needle with a piece of string. Wrap the triangles around pencils, starting at the wide end. When the triangle is completely wrapped, use a dot of glue to secure the end. Then take the pencils out of the "beads," and thread them onto the string. If desired, alternate beads with buttons or macaroni.
(Primary, intermediate)

Fig. 7.22.

Fig. 7.23.

8

Christopher Columbus before the Voyage

Christopher Columbus has been called a man of mystery. Little is known of his early life, and even generally accepted information, such as his birth in Genoa, Italy, are still debated. Some of the mystery comes from the lack of information or because information was lost. Recordkeeping in the fifteenth century was not as standardized as it is today, and some information about Columbus's early years may never have been written down. In addition, 500 years of political upheavals, natural disasters, and misplacing of documents account for the lack of records.

Many scholars also debate whether Columbus himself may have deliberately obscured his past. Information we have, written by him and about him, mentions almost nothing of his personal life. Theories by historians attempting to account for this reticence are far ranging. Perhaps he was ashamed of his humble origins. One theory holds that he was a Jew and hid his background to escape persecution. Another theory holds that his family had been allied to political parties that had lost favor, so he hid his past. Whatever the explanation, the mystery of what made the man Columbus who he was is an intriguing one to explore.

In this chapter, we look first at Columbus's youth. The second section covers his stay in Portugal and how this influenced the creation of his grand plan. Finally, Columbus's long petition to the Spanish court is covered.

COLUMBUS'S YOUTH

Though many details of Christopher Columbus's childhood are unknown, it is generally believed that he was born in Genoa, Italy, and was the son of a weaver. He learned the weaving trade as a boy, but he had higher ambitions and a love of the sea. Genoa was one of the great merchant cities of Italy at the time, and its cosmopolitan way of life must have influenced him. It is guessed that when he was about thirteen years old, Columbus began making short trading voyages for his father. He eventually left home for good to become a sailor on the Mediterranean.

Book List

Adler, David A. *A Picture Book of Christopher Columbus*. Holiday House, 1991. (Gr. 2-4)
This simple biography details Columbus's life from birth to death.

Anno, Mitsumasa. *Anno's Italy*. Collins World, 1978. (PreK-4)
A wordless introduction to Italy.

Caselli, Giovanni. *A Florentine Merchant*. Peter Bedrick, 1986. (Gr. 3-6)
A somewhat fictionalized account of the everyday life of an Italian merchant and his household in the late fifteenth century.

Cole, William. *The Sea, Ships and Sailors*. Viking, 1967. (Gr. 3-up)
A collection of poems and songs about the sea and ships.

D'Aulaire, Ingri, and Edgar Parin D'Aulaire. *Columbus*. Doubleday, 1955. (Gr. 1-4)
This brief biography begins with a vivid description of Columbus as a boy and is illustrated in picture-book format.

dePaola, Tomie. *Charlie Needs a Cloak*. Prentice Hall, 1973. (K-3)
Charlie shears his sheep; cards, spins, and dyes the wool; and weaves a new cloak.

Fritz, Jean. *Where Do You Think You're Going, Christopher Columbus?* Putnam, 1980. (Gr. 3-6)
This biography for older children also begins with a description of Columbus's early life.

Gilbreath, Alice. *Fun with Weaving*. Morrow, 1976. (Gr. 3-6)
This book provides a variety of weaving projects using various methods for children to try.

Heller, Nicholas. *The Adventure at Sea*. Greenwillow, 1988. (PreK-3)
Two brothers and their sister use a cardboard box to create an adventure at sea.

Kelly, Karin. *Weaving*. Lerner, 1973. (Gr. 3-up)
A book to teach the craft of weaving.

Kraus, Robert. *The Gondolier of Venice*. Dutton, 1976. (K-2)
Gregory the gondolier comes up with a plan to keep Venice from sinking.

Lasky, Kathryn. *The Weaver's Gift*. Frederick Warne, 1980. (Gr. 3-6)
Describes the process of weaving a blanket, from shearing the sheep, through carding, spinning, and dying the wool, to weaving the final product.

Lindgren, Barbro. *Wild Baby Goes to Sea*. Greenwillow, 1982. (PreK-1)
While his mother cleans, baby Ben sets sail in a wooden box and has many adventures.

Lionni, Leo. *Matthew's Dream*. Knopf, 1991. (PreK-1)
Matthew turns a dream into a reality when he decides to become a painter.

Marshall, James. *George and Martha Round and Round*. Houghton Mifflin, 1988. (PreK-2)
In the story "The Trip," George and Martha use their imaginations to go on a sea trip.

Powell, Anton. *Renaissance Italy*. Warwick Press, 1979. (Gr. 4-up)
A look at the events in Italy during the Renaissance that were to have an effect on Columbus and later explorers.

Rubenstone, Jessie. *Weaving for Beginners*. Lippincott, 1975. (Gr. 3-up)
A book on weaving that covers various methods, handmade looms, and a variety of projects for children to complete.

Schauffler, Robert Haven, ed. *Days We Celebrate*. Dodd, Mead, 1940. (Gr. 3-up)
Poems and plays to use for holidays, including Columbus Day.

Ventura, Piero. *Venice: Birth of a City*. Putnam, 1987. (Gr. 3-6)
This nonfiction title describes the history of Venice with full-color illustrations.

Related Activities

1. To familiarize children with Columbus as a boy, read aloud David Adler's biography *A Picture Book of Christopher Columbus*, or read the first few pages of the biographies by Ingri D'Aulaire and Edgar D'Aulaire and Jean Fritz. Then read aloud the poem "The Young Columbus" by Nancy Byrd Turner, from *Days We Celebrate*, edited by Robert Haven Schauffler. You could also use "Sea Fever" by John Masefield, from *The Sea, Ships and Sailors*, selected by William Cole.
(Primary, intermediate)

2. Explain to the children that Columbus was born and grew up in Italy, a country that is very different from ours, where they speak a different language. To give young children some idea of what Italy is like, share the books *The Gondolier of Venice* by Robert Kraus and *Anno's Italy* by Mitsumasa Anno. For older children, introduce life in Italy in the fifteenth century with the books *A Florentine Merchant* by Giovanni Caselli, *Renaissance Italy* by Anton Powell, and *Venice: Birth of a City* by Piero Ventura.
(Preschool, primary, intermediate)

3. Tell the group that when Columbus lived, children were expected to grow up to do the same kind of work their parents did. Because Columbus's father was a weaver, Columbus learned to weave. Let the children play a charade game about what their own parents do. They can take turns acting out occupations (giving a shot for a doctor, squirting a hose for a firefighter, making driving motions for a bus driver, etc.). Ask children whether they want to do the same kind of work their parents do when they grow up.
(Preschool, primary)

4. To familiarize children with the work of a weaver, read *Charlie Needs a Cloak* by Tomie dePaola and *The Weaver's Gift* by Kathryn Lasky. Though Lasky's book is about a present-day weaver, interestingly, she and her husband have twice sailed their own boat across the Atlantic.

If you are interested in introducing the children to the craft of weaving, find a local weaver to come and give a demonstration. Titles to teach children to weave are *Fun with Weaving* by Alice Gilbreath, *Weaving* by Karin Kelly, and *Weaving for Beginners* by Jessie Rubenstone.

For a simpler activity, have the children weave with paper. Start with two different colors of paper, each the same size. Cut one sheet into strips about 1½" wide. Fold the other sheet in half and, starting at the fold, cut slits across the paper, but stop about 1½" before you reach the end, as shown in figure 8.1. Open the paper. Now weave the cut strips in and out of the slits, starting the first strip going into the first slit from the top and the second strip coming out of the first slit from the bottom.
(Preschool, primary, intermediate)

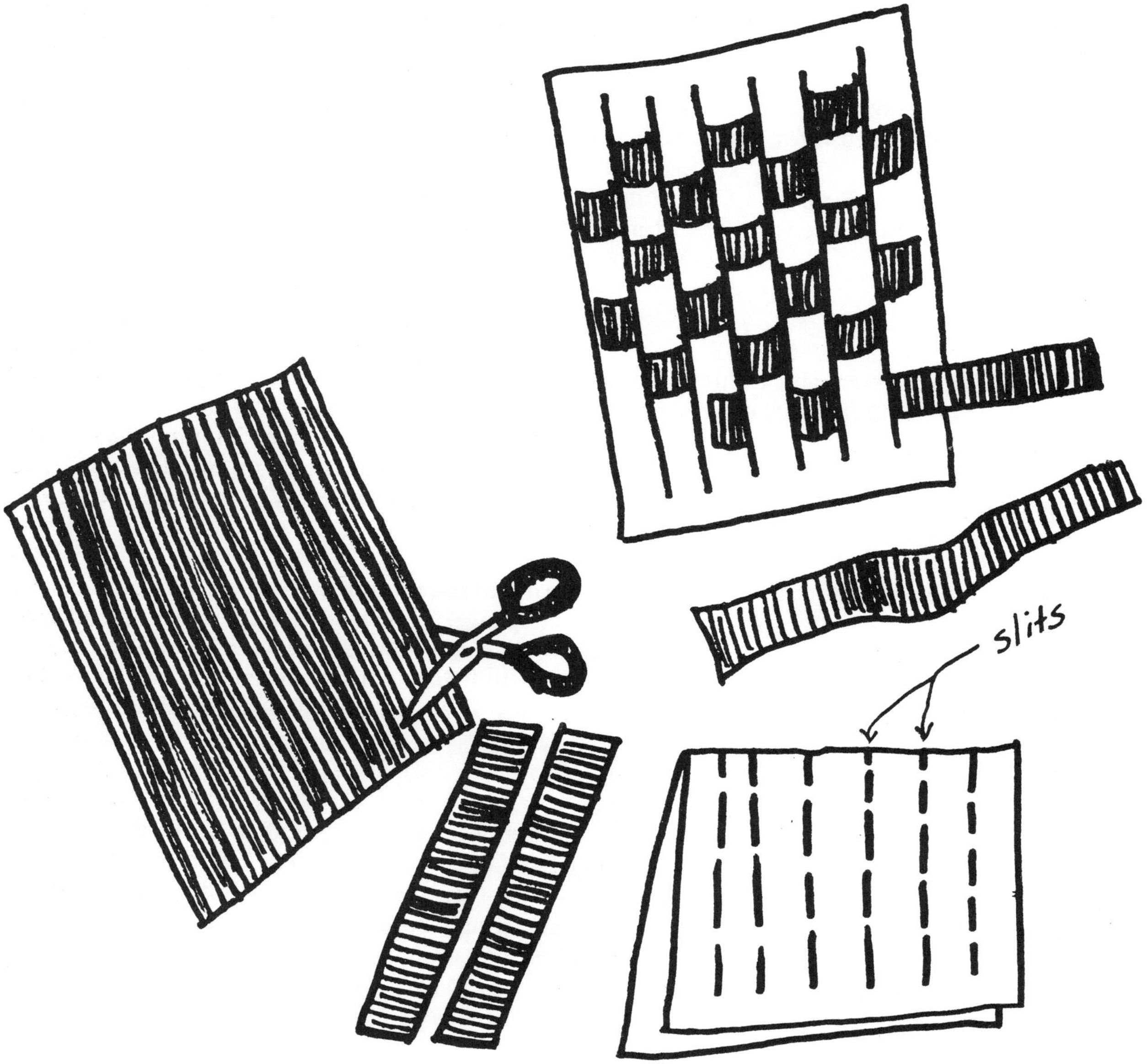

Fig. 8.1.

5. Have a "weaver's relay." Divide the group into two equal teams. Each team forms a circle, holding hands. At the signal, a designated player begins to weave in and out around the circle. He or she goes into the circle under one pair of arms and out through the next. When the entire round is completed, the player takes his or her place in the circle, and the next player to the right begins weaving. Continue play until every player has gone weaving. The team to finish first wins. (Primary)

6. Columbus did not want to be a weaver. He dreamed of being a sailor. Explain that a daydream is imagining something you wish might happen; it is like pretending. Read the books *The Adventure at Sea* by Nicholas Heller and *Wild Baby Goes to Sea* by Barbro Lindgren or the story "The Trip" from *George and Martha Round and Round* by James Marshall. If you have a large box, let the children take turns sitting in the box and imagining where they would like to go in their own daydreams. Share *Matthew's Dream* by Leo Lionni to show how a dream can be turned into reality. (Preschool, primary)

COLUMBUS IN PORTUGAL

Sometime around 1476, Columbus was a member of a fleet of trading vessels sailing off the Portuguese coast, headed for northern Europe. They were attacked by an enemy fleet, and Columbus's ship went down. Columbus, though wounded, made his way to the Portuguese coast and, when he recovered, went on to Lisbon.

Columbus settled in Portugal and went to work with his brother, Bartholomew, as a mapmaker. Eventually, he married and lived on one of the Madeira Islands. At this point in his life he probably began to conceive his dream of sailing west around the world to find the fabled wealth of the Far East.

New ideas were beginning to emerge during the late 1400s, and Columbus was influenced by these ideas. Johannes Gutenberg of Germany had discovered the process of printing using movable type (at least as far as the European world was concerned) about 1450. Many books had become newly available, such as works by Ptolemy and other classical scholars and the account of Marco Polo's travels. Before this, books had been copied out and illustrated by hand, a process that resulted in beautiful works of art but could take years to produce a single volume. In addition, such hand-printed books were much too expensive for most people to own. With the advent of printing and the publication of books that more people could afford, a new spirit of learning arose. Columbus learned to read and write in several languages, and he began to study geography, cartography, and navigation.

Book List

Anderson, Joan. *Christopher Columbus: From Vision to Voyage*. Dial, 1991. (Gr. 3-6)
A recounting of Columbus's life, from boyhood up to the time of his great voyage.

Arnold, Caroline. *Maps and Globes*. Franklin Watts, 1984. (Gr. 3-6)
This nonfiction title explains the uses of maps and globes.

Bell, Neill. *The Book of Where or How to Be Naturally Geographic*. Little, Brown, 1982. (Gr. 3-6)
This title introduces maps, globes, and other geographical concepts.

Carey, Helen H. *How to Use Maps and Globes*. Franklin Watts, 1983. (Gr. 4-up)
An introduction to maps and how they are used.

Cartwright, Sally. *What's in a Map?* Coward, McCann & Geoghegan, 1976. (K-2)
This title explains what a map is for very young children.

Caselli, Giovanni. *A German Printer*. Peter Bedrick, 1986. (Gr. 3-6)
In this fictionalized history, a young German boy learns the printing trade, and his friend, Albrecht Durer, plans to become a painter.

Donnelly, Judy. *All around the World*. Grosset & Dunlap, 1991. (Gr. 2-6)
A discussion of maps and globes.

Freschet, Berniece. *Bernard Sees the World*. Charles Scribner's Sons, 1976. (K-3)
After reading travel books, Bernard goes to sea to see the world and ends up seeing all of it on the first trip to the moon.

Fritz, Jean. *The Man Who Loved Books*. Putnam, 1981. (Gr. 2-4)
This is the story of Saint Columba of Ireland, who hand-copied many books in the sixth century.

Hartman, Gail. *As the Crow Flies: A First Book of Maps*. Bradbury, 1991. (PreK-1)
Very simple, clear illustrations of what a map is, in picture-book form.

Helldorfer, M. C. *The Mapmaker's Daughter*. Bradbury, 1991. (Gr. 2-4)
The daughter of a mapmaker undertakes a journey through an enchanted land to rescue the king's son.

Knowlton, Jack. *Maps and Globes*. Harper & Row, 1985. (Gr. 2-5)
A description of the uses of maps and globes.

Kramer, Ann, and Simon Adams. *Exploration and Empire*. Warwick Press, 1990. (Gr. 4-up)
This nonfiction title includes a section on the invention of printing.

Lehner, Ernst, and Johanna Lehner. *How They Saw the New World*. Tudor Publishing, 1966. (Gr. 4-up)
A collection of old maps and engravings of the world before and during the Age of Exploration.

McFall, Christie. *Maps Mean Adventure*. Dodd, Mead, 1972. (Gr. 3-up)
Somewhat dated when it comes to modern information, but a good overview of maps.

Mango, Karin N. *Mapmaking*. Messner, 1984. (Gr. 3-6)
This includes a clear description of how maps are used today, as well as chapters on the history of mapmaking.

Menton, Theodore. *The Illuminated Alphabet*. Dover Publications, 1971. (All ages)
This book of patterns for letters from an illuminated alphabet can be used for craft projects or simply to show what this art form looked like.

Miquel, Pierre. *The Age of Discovery*. Silver Burdett, 1980. (Gr. 4-up)
This title also includes a section on Gutenberg and his printing press, with illustrations.

Moore, Patrick, and Henry Brinton. *Exploring Maps*. Hawthorn Books, 1967. (Gr. 4-6)
Although somewhat dated, this title introduces the use of maps and includes a number of projects children can do.

Schere, Monroe. *The Story of Maps*. Prentice Hall, 1969. (Gr. 3-6)
Although an older title, this book details the history of mapmaking.

Weiss, Harvey. *Maps: Getting from Here to There*. Houghton Mifflin, 1991. (Gr. 3-6)
Includes information on finding direction, distance, what map symbols mean, and latitude and longitude.

Where in the World Is Geo? Barrons, 1991. (PreK-2)
This large-format board book introduces a little bear learning to find his way around.

Wiesner, David. *Free Fall*. Lothrop, Lee & Shepard, 1988. (Gr. 1-6)
After reading an adventure story, a young boy falls asleep and dreams of exciting journeys.

Related Activities

1. When he arrived in Portugal, Columbus went to work with his brother in a mapmaker's shop. Read M. C. Helldorfer's *The Mapmaker's Daughter*. Introduce children to maps and the study of geography with any of the books on maps and globes listed in the previous section. Then let the children try their hands at making a map. Let them choose an area they want to map, such as the route from their homes to a local park, candy store, or school. They can use "paces" (the number of steps it takes to get to a certain location) as a unit of measurement. They should include landmarks such as city blocks, unusual buildings, large trees, and other outstanding items along the route. This activity can be expanded by having the children exchange maps and try to follow the directions to the destinations.
(Primary, intermediate)

2. For young children, read the books *What's in a Map?* by Sally Cartwright, *As the Crow Flies* by Gail Hartman, and *Where in the World Is Geo?* Give each child a copy of the map in fig. 8.2 so they can draw in pictures of places they would like to go. If the children are very young, you may need to help them draw squares to represent the places they are thinking of. If they have small toy cars, they can now use their cars on the maps.
(Preschool, primary)

Fig. 8.2.

3. While he was in Portugal, Columbus taught himself to read, write, and speak several languages so he would be able to learn more about theories of navigation, cartography, and geography. As a young boy he spoke Genoese, which was a spoken, not written, dialect of Italian. It is also probable that as an adult he learned to read and write Portuguese, Spanish, and Latin. Let the children hear tapes of these different languages, and perhaps learn an identical phrase from each, to appreciate what Columbus accomplished.
(Primary, intermediate)

4. Introduce children to the importance of Gutenberg's invention of printing by reading them the chapters on printing in Ann Kramer and Simon Adams's book *Exploration and Empire* and in Pierre Miquel's book *The Age of Discovery* and by sharing Giovanni Caselli's *A German Printer*. Compare the method of mechanical printing to hand copying a manuscript by reading Jean Fritz's *The Man Who Loved Books*.

Then let the children try their hands at book illumination and hand copying. Show *The Illuminated Alphabet*. Give each child a copy of the capital C from an illuminated manuscript, shown in figure 8.3, to color. If possible, include gold crayons or paints for children to use. Have them handwrite a page from a book of their choice to understand how time-consuming this process was.

Next, let them make a vegetable print. Cut a potato in half. Using a pencil, have the children trace their initials in the flat section of potato, but in reverse, as if they were seeing the letters in a mirror. Then cut away the parts of the potato around the letters so the letters are raised above the rest of the potato. Press the letters on an ink pad and then on a piece of paper to print them. Explain that this is how metal letters worked.
(Primary, intermediate)

5. Explain what an important influence books were on Columbus. He created his dream by reading a number of newly available books. Illustrate this by reading two picture books about dreams of exploration that are influenced by reading, Berniece Freschet's *Bernard Sees the World* and David Wiesner's *Free Fall*.
(Primary, intermediate)

6. While living in Portugal, Columbus visited a number of islands in the Atlantic, from which he could look out across the "Ocean Sea," and this also influenced his plan. Let the children play the game "Musical Islands." Cut islands from pieces of construction paper. You will want one less island than the number of players. Turn on some music and let the children dance. Then suddenly stop the music. Everyone must try to find an island to stand on. Whoever is not on an island is out. Remove one island and repeat the game until you have a winner.
(Primary)

7. To help children understand Columbus's obsession with his dream and how he formed his "Great Enterprise," read aloud *Christopher Columbus: From Vision to Voyage* by Joan Anderson.
(Intermediate)

Fig. 8.3.

COLUMBUS AT THE SPANISH COURT

In 1484, Columbus approached King John II of Portugal to request backing to attempt his plan to sail west to the Indies. When King John II refused, Columbus moved to Spain and began the long wait while he tried to persuade King Ferdinand and Queen Isabella to sponsor his voyage. The commission they appointed to study the plan originally turned it down because they believed Columbus was vastly underestimating the size of the world—and they were right! Columbus, however, was persistent, and, finally, in 1492, after their defeat of the Moors in Granada, Ferdinand and Isabella had the time and money to consider Columbus's plan. They agreed to sponsor the voyage.

In the end, two things convinced the king and queen. One was their desire to spread Christianity. They were fanatical Catholics and had only recently begun the Inquisition and forced all Jews into exile from Spain. The other reason was their desire for the gold and riches they would win if Columbus proved himself right. Columbus's dream was about to become a reality.

Book List

Burch, Joanne. *Isabella of Castile: Queen on Horseback*. Franklin Watts, 1991. (Gr. 4-6)
A biography of Queen Isabella of Spain.

Finkelstein, Norman H. *The Other 1492: Jewish Settlement in the New World*. Charles Scribner's Sons, 1989. (Gr. 5-up)
Describes Ferdinand and Isabella's expulsion of the Spanish Jews in the same year as Columbus's voyage.

Foreman, Michael. *Land of Dreams*. Holt, Rinehart & Winston, 1982. (Gr. 1-4)
In the Land of Dreams, uncompleted dreams are revived and sent out into the world again.

Foster, Genevieve. *The World of Columbus and Sons*. Charles Scribner's Sons, 1965. (Gr. 4-up)
While placing Columbus in his historical context, Foster also clearly portrays the personalities and motives of Ferdinand and Isabella.

Hewitt, Kathryn. *King Midas and the Golden Touch*. Harcourt Brace Jovanovich, 1987. (K-4)
The traditional story of a king so greedy that he forfeits the thing he loves most for gold.

Hutchins, Pat. *King Henry's Palace*. Greenwillow, 1983. (PreK-2)
This picture book shows life at King Henry's royal palace.

Related Activities

1. After being refused by King John II of Portugal, Columbus went to Spain to ask for the support of King Ferdinand and Queen Isabella. As he approached the Spanish court, he must have been feeling a combination of emotions—disappointment over King John's refusal to help; hope that in Spain he would receive the aid he needed; embarrassment that he, the son of a weaver, was approaching royalty with this request; arrogance because he was convinced his plan was right; and even a little hostility because he had to beg for help. Ask the children to imagine that they are Columbus about to approach the king and queen with his proposal. Let them use the activity sheet in figure 8.4 to write down how they think they would feel in this situation. You can share the picture book *Land of Dreams* by Michael Foreman to illustrate a dying dream being revived. (Intermediate)

Fig. 8.4.

2. Tell younger children that before Columbus could go on the wonderful trip he had planned, he had to ask the king and queen for permission. Explain that the king and queen were the rulers who ran the country. Read *King Henry's Palace* by Pat Hutchins, to give the children an idea of how royalty live. Give children copies of the castle pattern in figure 8.5 to color. After they have colored the pictures, help children cut out the doors and windows so they open. Be sure to cut only on the dotted lines. Next, show the children how to put glue around the edges of the castle and glue it to a piece of paper the same size or larger. Now they can draw pictures in the open doors and windows. When the doors are shut, the pictures will be hidden.
(Preschool, primary)

3. Introduce children to the personalities of Ferdinand and Isabella using background from books such as Joanne Burch's *Isabella of Castile* and Genevieve Foster's *The World of Columbus and Sons*. The impression most historians give is that Ferdinand was not really interested in Columbus or his plan but was more concerned about war and power. Isabella was more intellectual and sincere, and it was she who was inclined to listen to Columbus. Have the children try to imagine what Ferdinand and Isabella were like using the activity sheets in figures 8.6 and 8.7 on pages 163 and 164. If you prefer, you could give the children a choice of which sheet to use: King Ferdinand or Queen Isabella. For whichever they choose, they should try to describe what these historical figures might have been like as people, remembering that history is enacted by human beings with distinct personalities, fears, hopes, and dreams. Ask children to include what they imagine the king and queen liked to do, what they were looking forward to, what they were worried about, and what their attitudes were toward Columbus.
(Intermediate)

4. Columbus had to wait in Spain for six or seven years before Ferdinand and Isabella made up their minds to help him. Though he must have felt frustrated and impatient, he refused to give up his plan and continued to make his requests. Let the children act out how Columbus, the king, and the queen must have been feeling with the following games.

Columbus was determined to "bowl the castle over" and make them agree to his grand enterprise, so play "Bowl the Castle Over." The children will need to make castles from empty 1-quart milk cartons. Give them 12" x 16" pieces of construction paper on which to draw castle outlines. Have them cut out the outlines and glue them around the milk cartons.

To play the game, set up the cartons like bowling pins. Let the children take turns pretending they are Columbus and trying to bowl over the castle, using a rubber ball.

Now let the children play "The Royal Headache" (which is probably what Ferdinand and Isabella thought Columbus was by this time). Choose one player to be the king or the queen and sit in a chair in the middle of the play area, with his or her eyes closed. The rest of the children line up on one side. One at a time, the players must try to get from one side of the room to the other so quietly that the king or queen cannot hear them. If the king or queen does hear someone crossing the room, it makes the headache worse and the king or queen moans. If the king or queen moans, the player trying to cross the room has been too loud and is out. Keep playing until everyone has had a turn.
(Primary)

(Text continues on page 165.)

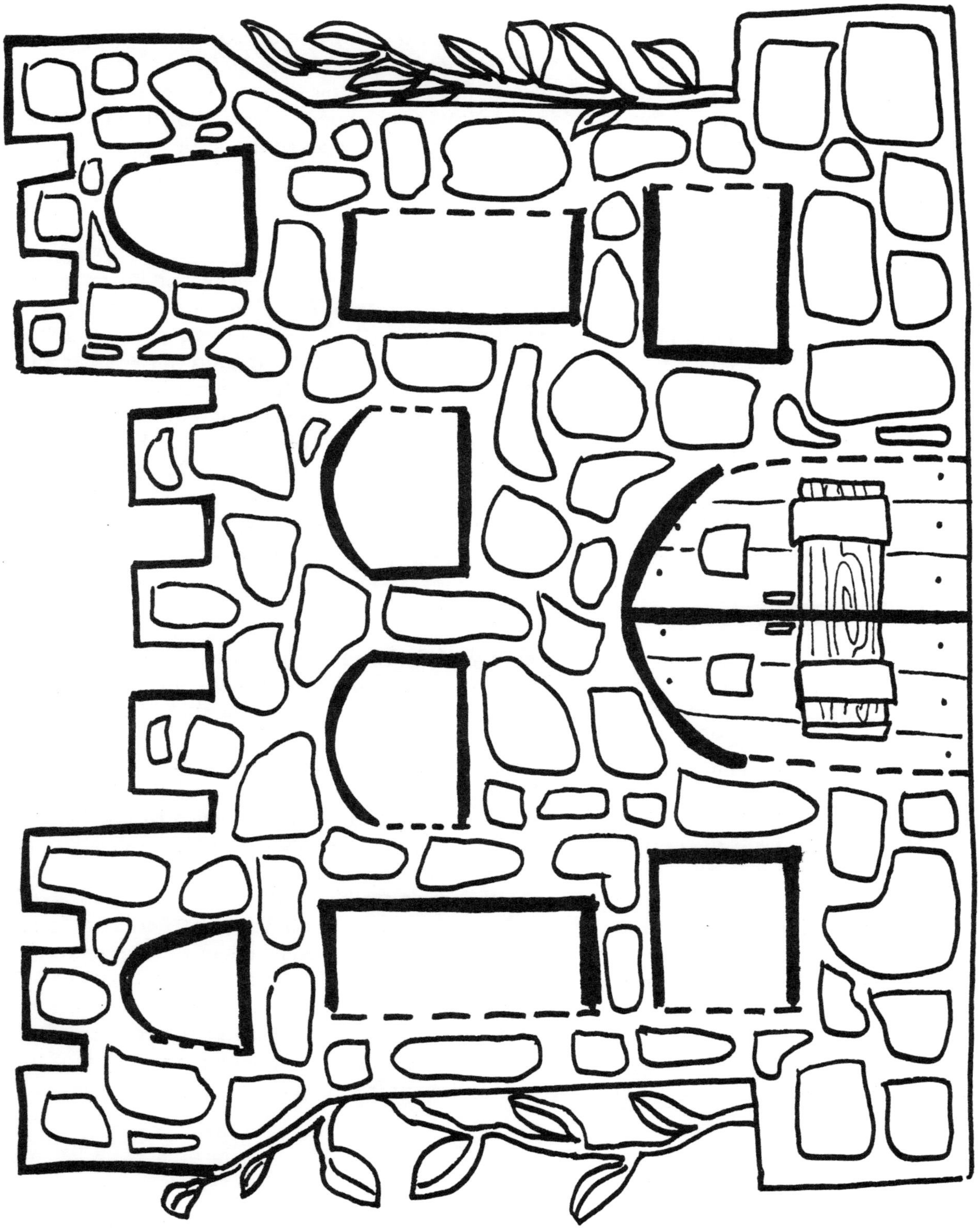

Fig. 8.5.

King Ferdinand

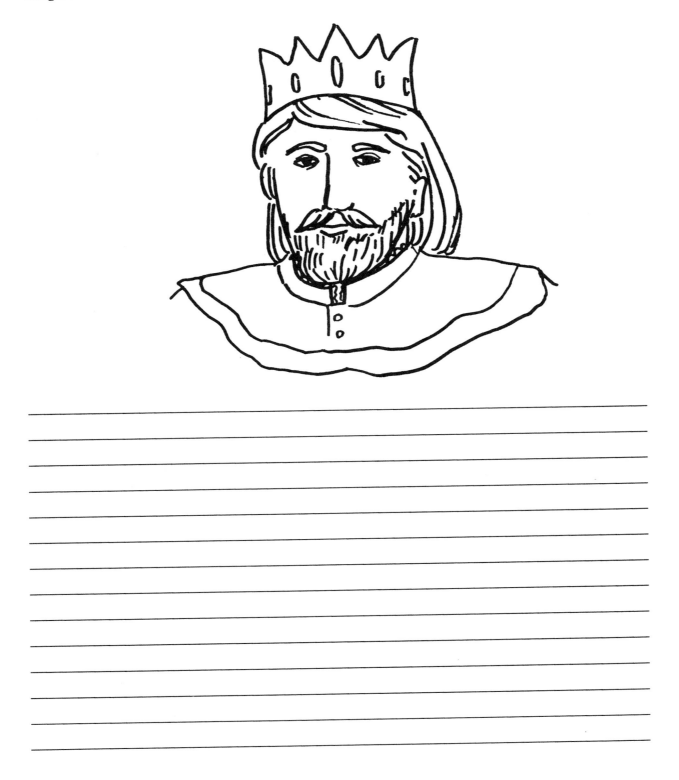

Fig. 8.6.

Queen Isabella

Fig. 8.7.

5. Queen Isabella and King Ferdinand debated for several years about whether or not they would finance Columbus's voyage. They even established a commission to study his plan. Ask the children to imagine themselves as the king or queen trying to make this decision. How would they decide? What factors would influence the decision? What would be the drawbacks and advantages of approving the plan? Whom would they consult? What might be some of the primary arguments against the plan?

Let the children act out this debate. Choose players to be Columbus, Isabella, Ferdinand, and the councillors to the throne. Have the children dress up as these characters, as shown in figure 8.8. To make a costume for Columbus, use a long-sleeved shirt, tights, and boots. Make a knee-length tunic to wear over this costume with two towels. Pin the towels at the child's shoulders so that one towel covers the front and the other one covers the back. Tie a sash around the waist. To make a hat, start with a cardboard headband, sized to fit. For the top of the hat, place the headband over a piece of cloth. Pinch the center of the cloth and bring it up through the headband, so that the cloth flops over the edge. Staple the cloth to the headband. Add a feather to the hat.

The king, queen, and councillors can all wear capes. Make ankle-length capes from rich-looking material. Drape the capes over the childrens' shoulders and pin them closed at the neck with jewelry pins. The king and queen should also wear crowns. Let the children make crowns from posterboard. They will each need a piece about 8 inches high and wide enough to go around their heads and be stapled in back. Cut the posterboard into the crown shape shown in figure 8.9. The children can decorate the crowns with sequins, glitter, foil, fake jewelry, and other odds and ends.

At the end of the debate, let the children sing this song.

What Shall We Do with Chris Columbus?
(sung to "What Shall We Do with the Drunken Sailor?")

What shall we do with Chris Columbus?
What shall we do with Chris Columbus?
What shall we do with Chris Columbus?
Early in the morning?

Dreams fill the head of Chris Columbus,
Dreams fill the head of Chris Columbus,
Dreams fill the head of Chris Columbus,
Nighttime, noon, and morning.

(Continue the pattern with these verses)
Give him three ships and send him sailing...
Send him off to find the Indies...
He'll find a New World before he's finished...

(Intermediate)

(Text continues on page 168.)

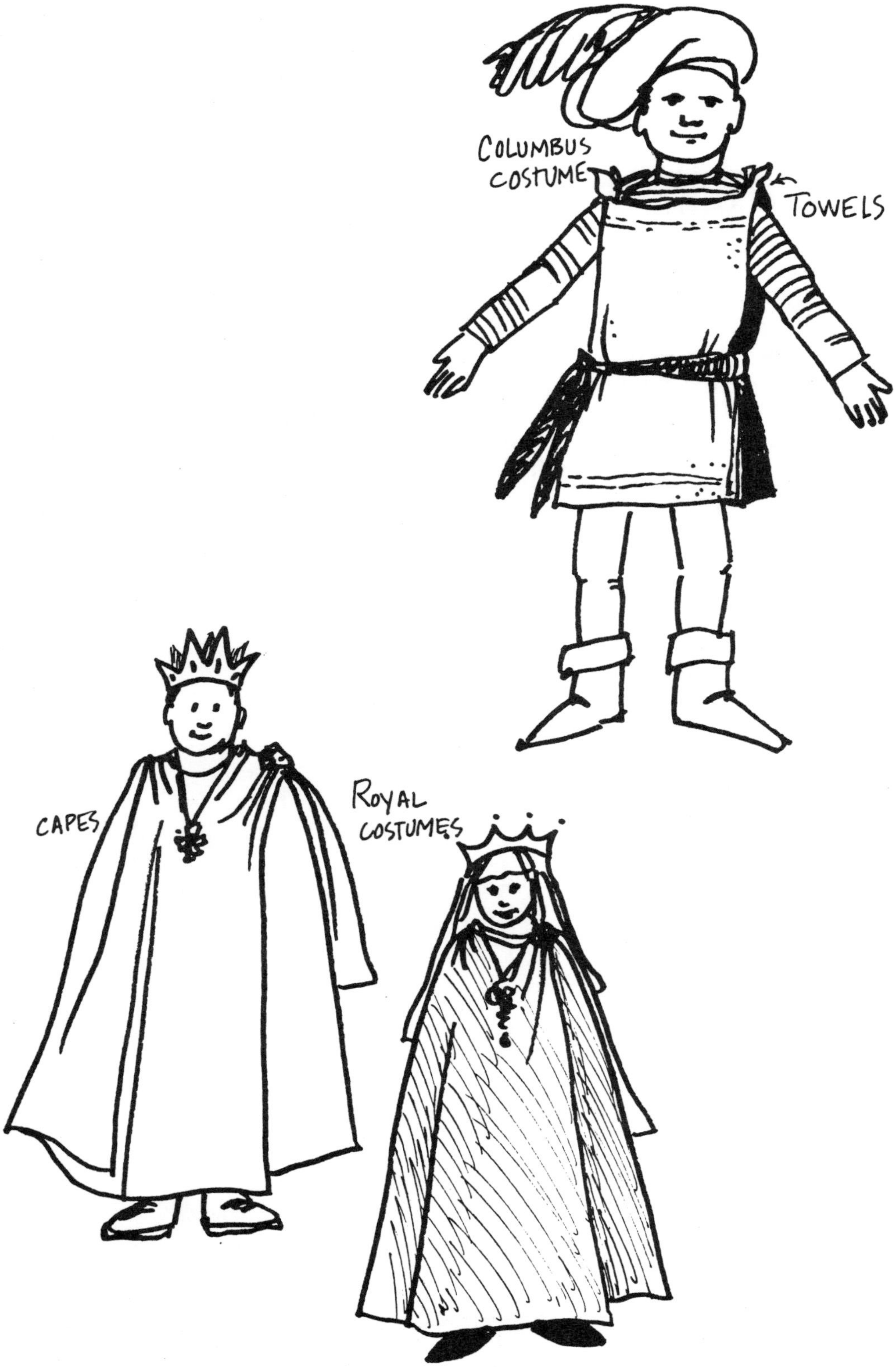
COLUMBUS
COSTUME
TOWELS
CAPES
ROYAL
COSTUMES

Fig. 8.8.

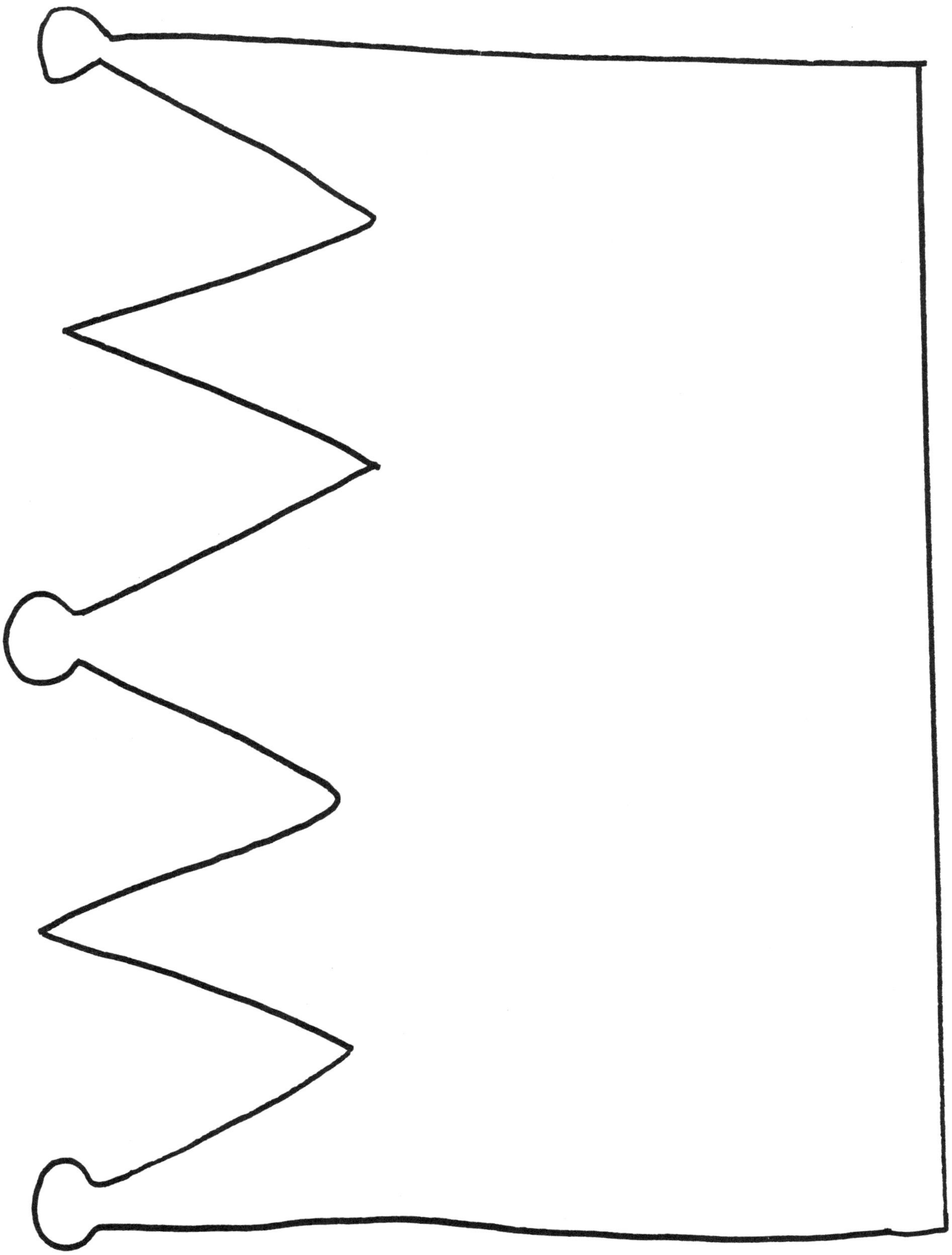

Fig. 8.9.

6. One of Queen Isabella's primary motives in supporting Columbus was her desire to spread Christianity among the peoples he might encounter. She felt that Catholic Christianity was the only acceptable religion and that everyone else's beliefs should give way to it. The Mongols, on the other hand, had extended religious tolerance to the peoples whose lands they conquored. Mangu Khan, brother of Kublai Khan, expressed the Mongols' beliefs by saying, "We believe there is only one God. But just as God has given the hand a variety of fingers, so has He given mankind a variety of ways" of worshipping Him (Evan S. Connell, *A Long Desire*, Long Point Press, 1988, p. 84).

Encourage the children to compare Queen Isabella's religious beliefs to those of Mangu Khan. Does one seem more reasonable than the other or more devoted? Compare how each promotes cooperation. To help show the results of Isabella's beliefs, use Norman Finkelstein's *The Other 1492: Jewish Settlement in the New World*.
(Intermediate)

7. To emphasize the importance of religion for Ferdinand and Isabella (and for Columbus himself) as a motivation for Columbus's voyage, the children can make the kind of elaborate, ornate crosses created in medieval times. Have the children cut the shape of a cross from cardboard. It can be covered with tin foil or gold wrap and then heavily decorated with sequins, buttons, fake jewels, etc.
(Primary, intermediate)

8. To emphasize the desire for gold as a motivation for Columbus's voyage, read aloud Kathryn Hewitt's version of *King Midas and the Golden Touch*, about another greedy king. Then play the game "The Golden Touch," played like "Button, Button, Who Has the Button?" Choose one child to be the king or queen, and seat the others in a circle around him or her. The king or queen then gives the command to open hands and close eyes, and the children place their hands, palms up, on their laps. When everyone's eyes are closed the king or queen quietly walks around the circle and deposits a gold coin in someone's hand. Then the king or queen commands all hands to be closed and eyes to be opened. The king or queen says to a player, "Gold, gold, I must have the gold!" That player has two guesses about who has the gold. If he or she misses, the king or queen calls on someone else. The player who guesses correctly becomes the new king or queen.
(Primary)

9. It has been estimated that the equivalent in modern-day money of what Ferdinand and Isabella provided for Columbus's voyage is $151,780. Ask the children the question, "What if you received a gift of $100,000 cash, like Columbus did? What would you do with the money?" They can either take turns telling the group about their answers or write about what they would do.
(Primary, intermediate)

10. Recount the story of when Queen Isabella finally decided to support Columbus, she said that, if necessary, she would pawn her jewels to finance the voyage (it was not necessary). Now play the relay game "The Queen's Necklace." Divide the group into two teams. Each team should select a player to be the queen. Give each queen the same number of buttons or beads as there are players on her team. The queens stand about 10 feet from the other players, who line up facing them. Each player in line is given a couple of pieces of macaroni. Give the first player in each line a darning needle threaded with string. On the signal "go," the players start threading their macaroni pieces onto the string. Each player runs to the queen and adds one of the beads she is holding to the string. Then the player runs back to the line and gives the needle and thread to the next player, who repeats the actions. The first team to complete their necklace, tie it off, and hang it around the queen's neck wins.
(Primary)

11. Finally, the king and queen decided to give Columbus permission to go on his voyage. Recite this altered nursery rhyme together:

Where Have You Been?

Little boy, little girl, where have you been?
I've been with Columbus to visit the queen.
Little boy, little girl, what gave she you?
Three ships to sail on the ocean blue!

(Primary)

9

Columbus's First Voyage

In the following sections, we look first at the preparations Columbus made for the voyage. Next we look at the voyage itself and at how Columbus and his men must have been feeling. A variety of resources and activities are then presented to introduce ocean life. Finally, the sighting of land is covered.

PREPARATIONS FOR THE VOYAGE

Once Columbus had persuaded the Spanish monarchs to finance his voyage, he still had much to do to prepare for the trip. He needed ships, provisions, instruments, and a crew. Ferdinand and Isabella provided Columbus with his three ships by extracting the ships from the town of Palos as a penalty for some previous infraction. The ships were the *Niña* (the smallest), the *Pinta* (the fastest), and the *Santa Maria* (the flagship).

Columbus packed his ships with all the provisions he thought he would need for his long voyage. He took sea biscuits, meat, cheese, raisins, salt, beans, honey, rice, almonds, sardines, anchovies, water, and wine. Firewood, cannons, muskets, and crossbows were packed. He took small trinkets, such as bells, beads, and mirrors, to trade with the people he expected to meet. He took letters of introduction from Ferdinand and Isabella to the rulers of the countries he expected to find. He even took cats to kill the rats that flocked on ships in those days. All these provisions were packed into his very small ships, and he also needed room for himself and his crew.

At first Columbus had difficulty recruiting a crew for what was considered a crazy plan. But when the highly respected Martin Alonzo Pinzon signed on, others followed. When the whole crew was signed, there were forty men on the *Santa Maria*, twenty-six on the *Pinta*, and twenty-four on the *Niña*. Columbus's fleet departed early on the morning of August 3, 1492. Upon leaving Spain, Columbus sailed first to the Canary Islands off the coast of northern Africa, to replenish his provisions before setting out across the unknown ocean.

Book List

Haas, Irene. *The Maggie B.* Atheneum, 1975. (PreK-1)
On a make-believe sailing trip, Margaret and her brother have everything they could need on board.

Jonas, Ann. *Now We Can Go*. Greenwillow, 1986. (PreK)
A small child gathers special belongings before a trip.

Lasker, Joe. *Tales of a Seadog Family*. Viking, 1974. (PreK-3)
The history of ocean exploration is covered by showing the adventures of a sea-going dog family that includes Eric the Rover, Christopher Collie, Sir Francis Seadog, and Commodore Byrd-Dog.

Levinson, Nancy S. *Christopher Columbus: Voyager to the Unknown*. Lodestar, 1990. (Gr. 4-up)
This biography includes a list of the names of the crew members on Columbus's ships.

Ventura, Piero. *Christopher Columbus*. Random House, 1978. (Gr. 2-6)
This description of Columbus's voyage includes a cut-away view of the interior of one of his ships.

Williams, Vera B. *Three Days on a River in a Red Canoe*. Greenwillow, 1981. (PreK-2)
This story of a canoe trip includes the packing of the provisions.

Related Activities

1. To introduce young children to the preparations needed for going on a voyage, read aloud the picture books *The Maggie B.* by Irene Haas, *Now We Can Go* by Ann Jonas, and *Three Days on a River in a Red Canoe* by Vera Williams. Ask the children to tell you what they would want to take on a trip. Remind them to name things they would need as well as things they would want. Children also can make collages representing the packing they would do.
(Preschool, primary)

2. Columbus's ships were very small by modern standards. Illustrate this for the children in your group by giving them a copy of the *Santa Maria* in figure 9.1. Tell them to draw forty sailors on board, approximately the size of the one shown. The ship and the sailor are drawn roughly to scale, so this project gives the children a clear idea of how crowded conditions were.
(Primary, intermediate)

3. For older readers, read the list given in the introduction of all the things Columbus packed on board for his trip. Ask the children to make lists of what kinds of provisions they would pack for a long voyage. Have them each make two lists, one of provisions they feel they would have needed for a voyage in 1492 and another list of items they would take today. They should include items necessary for survival and also articles of personal significance. Compare the lists, and discuss why they are different.
(Primary, intermediate)

4. After they make their lists of necessary provisions, let the children design the interiors of their own ships, as shown in figure 9.2. To help them prepare for this project, share the book *Christopher Columbus* by Piero Ventura. Have each child draw a ship's hull on a piece of construction paper.

(Text continues on page 174.)

Fig. 9.1.

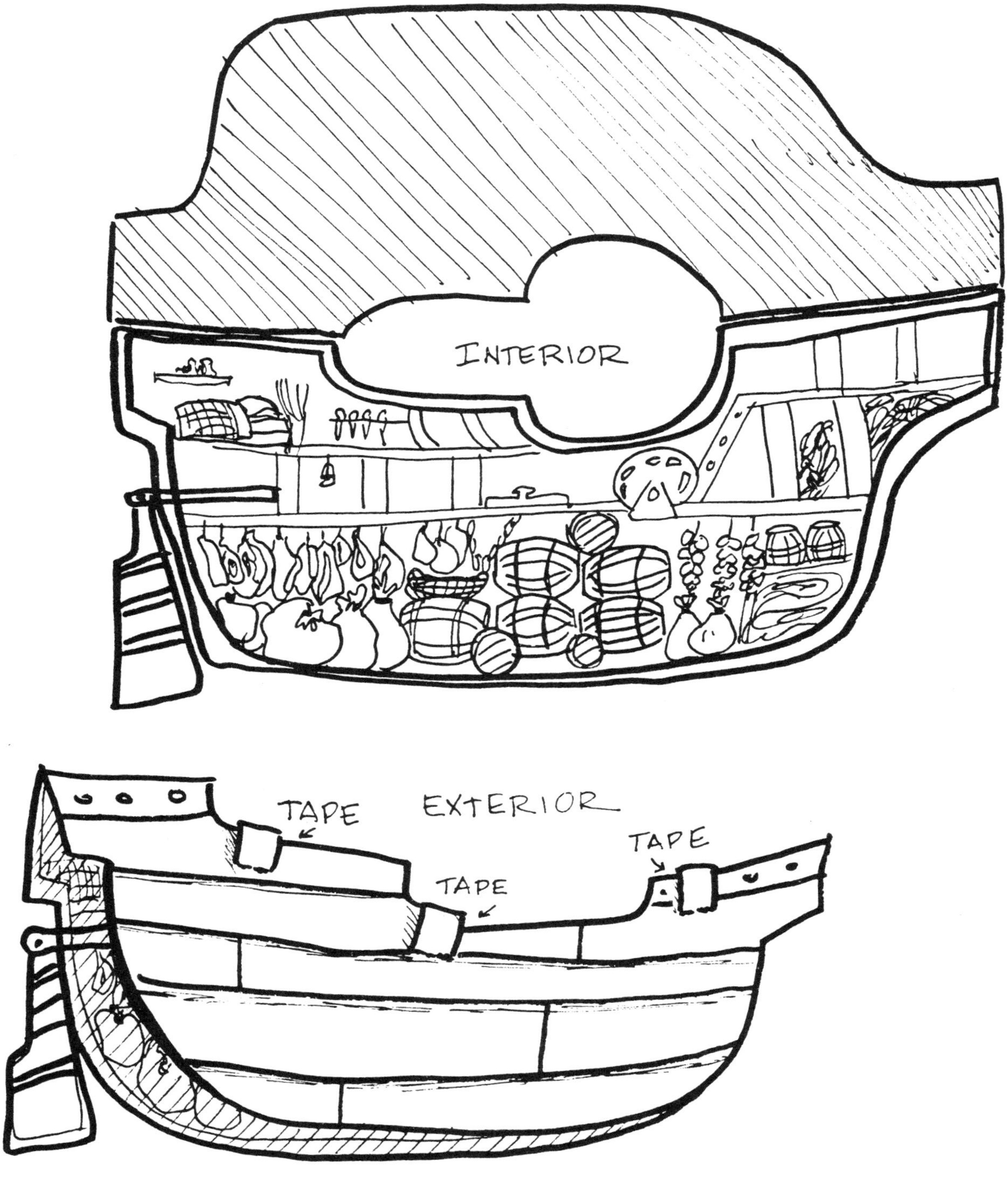

Fig. 9.2.

Cut out the hull, and place it on another piece of paper. Trace around it, and then set the cutout hull aside. Using the hull outline, the children design the interior as a cut-away view, as if the ships had been sliced in half from bow to stern. Sections should be marked off for ballast, cargo, food, the crew, and other items. After designing the interiors, children draw in the upper decks and sails. Next, they should decorate the hulls they previously cut out. These hulls can be taped over the interior views so that they can be lifted up to see inside (see figure 9.2).
(Primary, intermediate)

5. In addition to supplies, Columbus needed a crew to man the ships, but most sailors of Palos considered the idea of a voyage west to the Indies crazy. Ask the children to imagine that they are responsible for finding a crew. They should create an advertisement that Columbus could have used to recruit his sailors. Tell children to include all the advantages of signing on for the voyage that they can think of and to put the ad together as if it were going to appear on a billboard in Palos.
(Primary, intermediate)

6. Many of Columbus's difficulties in convincing local seamen to sail with him were overcome when the Pinzon family got behind the voyage. The Pinzons were a local seafaring family who were highly regarded in the Palos community. Introduce this family who were to have so much influence on the voyage, and then read Joe Lasker's *Tales of a Seadog Family*, about another seafaring family.
(Primary)

7. Have each child in your group pick a sailor from the following list and assume that identity.

- Captain: Each ship needs a captain, who has authority over all the sailors. The captain on the *Santa Maria* was Columbus; on the *Pinta*, Martin Alonso Pinzon; and on the *Niña*, Vicente Yanez Pinzon.
- Ship's master: Each ship needs a master as second-in-command, who sees to the maintenance of the ship. On the *Santa Maria*, the master was the ship's owner, Juan de la Cosa. On the *Pinta*, the master was Francisco Pinzon, and on the *Niña*, it was Jean Nino.
- Pilot: The pilot of the ship is the navigator, who must understand astronomy and chart the ship's course. The pilots were, for the *Santa Maria*, Paralonso Nino; for the *Pinta*, Rafael Sarmiento; and for the *Niña*, Sancho Ruiz.
- Crew: Other crew members should include the boatswain, who looks after the cargo; the steward, in charge of the food; a ship's boy or gromet; carpenters; caulkers; painters; coopers; cooks; and regular sailors. The names of those who signed on for the trip have been recorded, and a list can be found in Nancy Levinson's *Christopher Columbus: Voyager to the Unknown*.

In addition, on the *Santa Maria*, Columbus took an interpreter named Luis de Torres who spoke Arabic (Columbus believed the people he would meet in the Indies would understand Arabic because they traded with the Arabs). He also took an officer in charge of punishment, Diego de Harana; a secretary and notary, Rodrigo de Escobedo; an inspector for the crown, Rodrigo Sanchez; and the king's majordomo, Pedro Gutierrez, who may have come along as a spy. Each child can assume one of these identities.

Let each child create a personality for the sailor he or she has chosen to become. In their new identities, children should write a description of why they chose to go on the voyage, what skills they bring to the expedition, what job they do, what they hope to find, what they think of Columbus, and their private hopes and fears. Give each child a copy of figure 9.3 for this activity.

I Sail with Columbus

Imagine you are one of Columbus's sailors. Describe who you are, what you do, and how you feel about the voyage.

My name is ______________________________

My age is ______________________________

I would describe myself as (personality traits) ______________________________

____

____

My job on-board ship is ______________________________

____

My special skills include ______________________________

____

My background before the voyage was ______________________________

____

____

I signed on for this voyage because ______________________________

____

____

I hope to find ______________________________

____

I think Columbus is ______________________________

____

My biggest fear is ______________________________

____

When we return, I'll ______________________________

____

Fig. 9.3.

With their personalities in place, the children can dress up as sailors (see figure 9.4). Spanish sailors in the fifteenth century frequently wore red woolen caps or scarves around their heads. The children can wear blue jeans rolled up to the knees and shirts with the sleeves rolled to the elbows. Tell them to leave their shirttails out, and tie pieces of rope around their waists.
(Primary, intermediate)

Fig. 9.4.

THE VOYAGE

Columbus's voyage loses some of its drama when viewed from a modern perspective. In the twentieth century, we know about the whole world, and it is hard for us to imagine what an amazing feat this trip was. The closest thing in modern memory is the moon landing of 1969, but even this fails to fully convey Columbus's adventure. The astronauts on the flight to the moon were in constant communication with their home base. They knew where they were going and they knew how to get home.

Columbus's voyage was closer to a modern science fiction story about a spaceship randomly taking off for parts unknown, like the television series "Star Trek." The men who sailed to the New World in 1492 had no real knowledge of what they would encounter. The voyage must have been an experience of complete isolation, such as few people today have had. Modern humans are almost never out of contact with others. But as Columbus and his men floated on the surface of the vast Atlantic, they must have been awed by the knowledge that they were all alone, attempting a voyage that, to their knowledge, no one before them had ever tried.

Book List

Ardizzone, Edward. *Ship's Cook Ginger*. Macmillan, 1977. (PreK-2)
A Little Tim story about the rigors of life on-board ship.

Brand, Oscar. *Singing Holidays*. Knopf, 1957. (Gr. 3-up)
This collection of songs includes "Christopher Columbo."

Columbus, Christopher. *The Log of Christopher Columbus*. International Marine, 1987. (Gr. 6-up)
A new translation by Robert Fuson of Columbus's log from the first voyage.

______. *The Log of Christopher Columbus's First Voyage to America in the Year 1492 as Copied out in Brief by Bartholomew Las Casas*. Linnet Books, 1989. (Gr. 3-6)
These excerpts from Columbus's log, with illustrations by J. O'H. Cosgrave II, reveal much about life on-board ship.

Conrad, Pam. *Pedro's Journal: A Voyage with Christopher Columbus, August 3, 1492—February 14, 1493*. Boyds Mills Press/Caroline House, 1991. (Gr. 3-6)
The fictional story of a young boy sailing with Columbus, in journal form.

Crews, Donald. *Harbor*. Greenwillow, 1982. (PreK)
The variety of boats that come and go in a busy harbor are shown.

Dor-Ner, Zvi. *Columbus and the Age of Discovery*. Morrow, 1991. (Adult)
Full of information and wonderful illustrations, this is the companion volume to the public television series.

Dupasquier, Philippe. *Dear Daddy...* Bradbury, 1985. (PreK-2)
The top portion of each double-page spread shows Sophie's father on a long sea voyage, and the bottom portion shows her activities at home as she is describing them to her father in a letter.

______. *Jack at Sea*. Prentice Hall, 1987. (PreK-3)
When Jack follows his friend on-board ship, he learns how hard life at sea can be.

Dyson, John. *Westward with Columbus*. Scholastic, 1991. (Gr. 3-7)
Historical fiction that retells the voyage through the eyes of a ten-year-old cabin boy.

Foreman, Michael. *The Boy Who Sailed with Columbus*. Arcade, 1992. (Gr. 3-6)
A fictional account of Columbus's voyage in picture-book format for young children.

Lewis, Thomas. *Hill of Fire*. Harper & Row, 1971. (Gr. 1-3)
This picture book retells the eruption of Mt. Paricutin in Mexico.

Maestro, Betsy. *Big City Port*. Four Winds Press, 1983. (PreK-K)
Lifting cargo onto ships and boats pulling in and out of the docks is clearly illustrated in this book about a busy harbor.

Martin, Susan. *I Sailed with Columbus: The Adventures of a Ship's Boy*. Overlook Press, 1991. (Gr. 5-up)
Columbus's voyage is told from the point of view of the ship's boy, Diego, in this fiction title.

Marx, Robert F. *Following Columbus: The Voyage of the Niña II*. World, 1964. (Gr. 4-up)
A description of a 1962 voyage replicating Columbus's voyage from Spain to San Salvador.

Marzollo, Jean. *In 1492*. Scholastic, 1991. (PreK-2)
A rhyming picture book about Columbus's voyage.

Schlein, Miriam. *I Sailed with Columbus*. HarperCollins, 1991. (Gr. 3-6)
Columbus's voyage told from the viewpoint of a twelve-year-old ship's boy.

Sendak, Maurice. *Outside Over There*. Harper & Row, 1981. (K-3)
When Papa goes away to sea, Anna must watch over her baby sister and protect the baby from the goblins.

Simon, Seymour. *Volcanoes*. Morrow, 1988. (Gr. 1-up)
Simon describes what makes a volcano erupt and shows examples.

Sis, Peter. *Follow the Dream: The Story of Christopher Columbus*. Knopf, 1991. (K-4)
A beautiful picture-book version of Columbus's dream and his voyage.

Smith, Barry. *The First Voyage of Christopher Columbus*. Viking, 1992. (Gr. 1-4)
Told from the point of view of one of Columbus's sailors, this picture book tells the story of the first voyage to the New World and includes a fold-out map.

Soule, Gardner. *Christopher Columbus on the Green Sea of Darkness*. Franklin Watts, 1988. (Gr. 4-up)
Excellent biography of Columbus for middle grades.

Williams, Vera B. *Stringbean's Trip to the Shining Sea*. Greenwillow, 1988. (Gr. 2-up)
Stringbean describes his trip to the West Coast of the United States in a series of postcards.

Related Activities

1. Read Peter Sis's *Follow the Dream*, and make paper-plate puppets of Columbus waving good-bye. Use the pattern of Columbus in figure 9.5. Let the children color their own copies of the pattern and glue them to 6" paper plates. They should also color Columbus's hands and glue them to the edges of the plate to make it look like he is waving good-bye. You can turn these into puppets either by taping a popsicle stick to the plate or by stapling a half paper plate to the back to form a pocket for the hand (see figure 9.5).
(Preschool, primary)

2. Your group can reenact Columbus's voyage, either on an impromptu basis or by actually writing and performing a script. You can incorporate the personalities children developed in activity 7 in the previous section and use the activities, games, and songs included here. Make a setting for your reenactment by turning a large table, such as a picnic table, into a ship (see figure 9.6). Use a broom or a wooden pole as the mast and a piece of an old sheet as the sail. Share Robert Marx's *Following Columbus*, about a voyage undertaken in 1962 to replicate Columbus's trip, or Jean Marzollo's *In 1492*.
(Primary, intermediate)

3. Set the mood for setting sail with the following song.

Down by the Ocean
(sung to tune of "Down by the Station")

Down by the ocean early in the morning
See Christopher Columbus set sail in his ships,
The *Niña*, the *Pinta*, the *Santa Maria*,
Three ships to take him on a discovery trip.

(Preschool, primary)

4. Ask your group to imagine what it must have been like for Columbus and the sailors at port on August 3, 1492, as they anticipated what they were about to undertake. Describe the sights, sounds, and smells the sailors must have experienced: dawn breaking, a fresh wind beginning to fill the sails, the creaking of the ship, the sound of the waves, and the smells of the sea. For very young children, share the books *Harbor* by Donald Crews and *Big City Port* by Betsy Maestro, to help them envision a port and a ship's departure.

Ask the children to remember a time when they were just about to start something new and felt a similar thrill of anticipation. The experience might be preparing for a trip, starting at a new school, taking up a challenging activity, or speaking or performing in public for the first time. Ask the children to write about their feelings at the time, using as much description as possible.
(Preschool, primary, intermediate)

5. While the fleet was in the Canary Islands, a volcano on Tenerife erupted, frightening the crew, who believed the eruption was a bad omen. Ask the children to imagine how strange a volcanic eruption would be to people who had never heard of such a thing. Share some books about volcanoes. You can read aloud Thomas Lewis's *Hill of Fire* and show the pictures from Seymour Simon's *Volcanoes*.

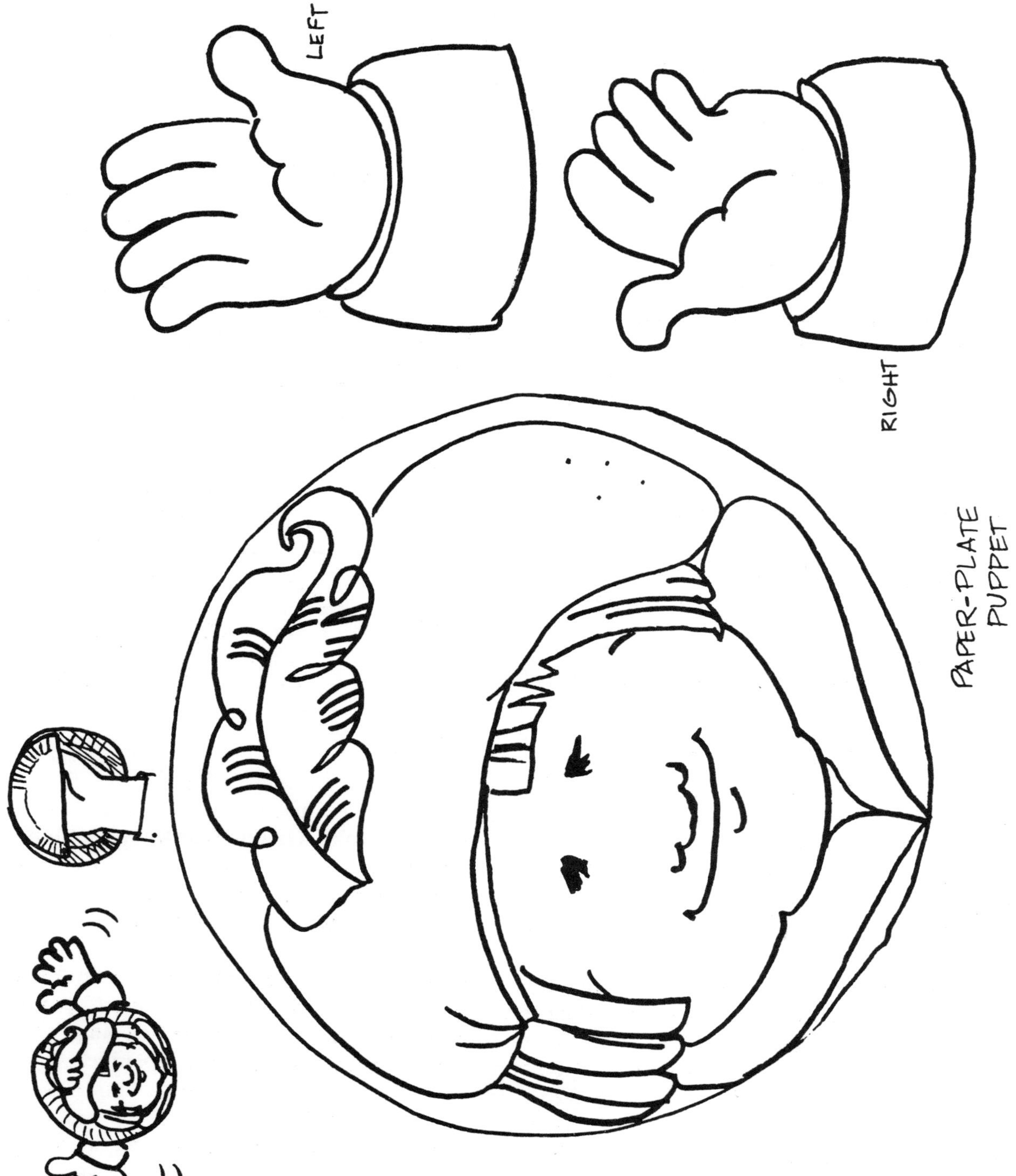

Fig. 9.5.

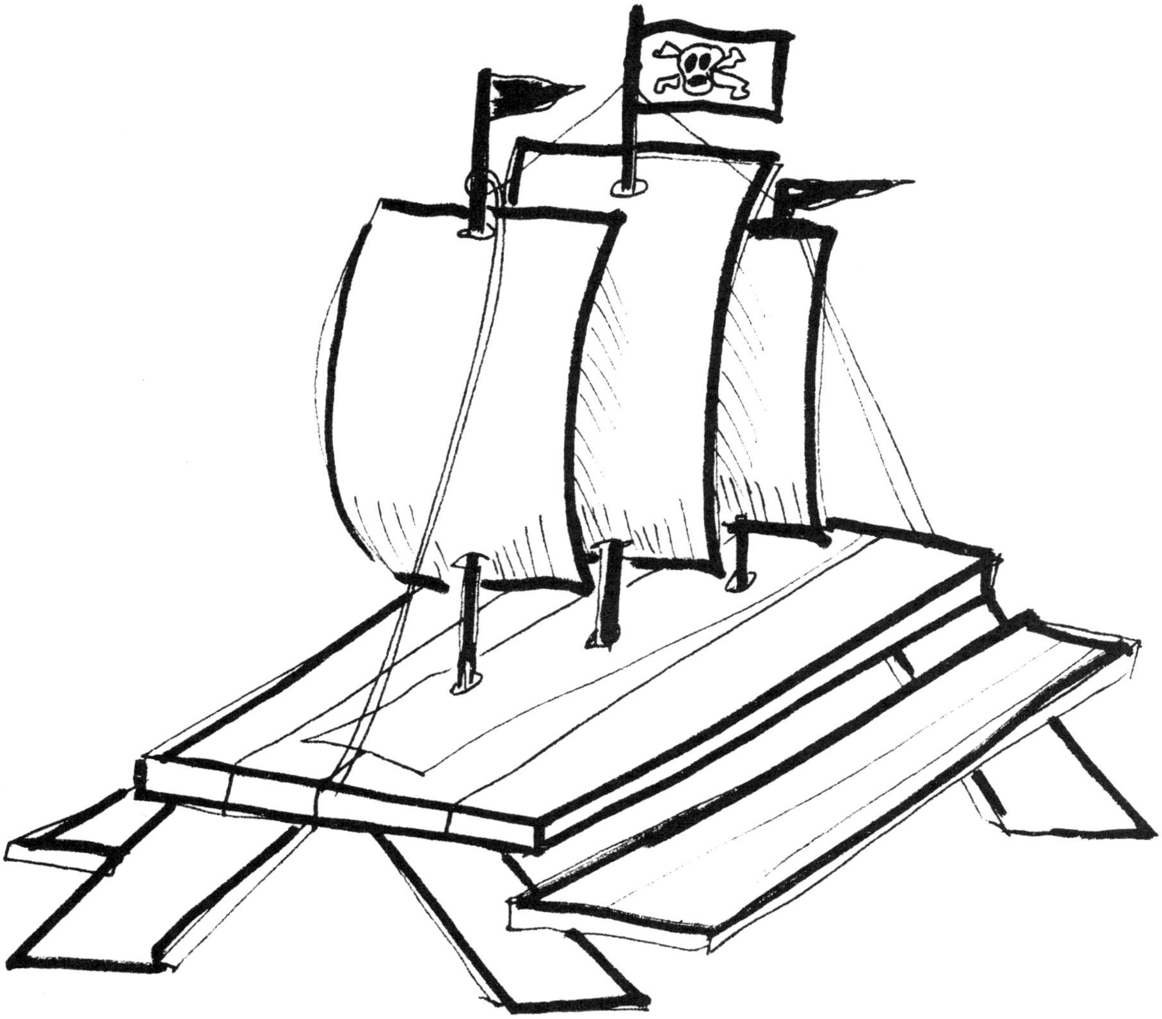

Fig. 9.6.

Make a class volcano. Start with a box at least a foot square with sides that are not very high. Place an empty tin can in the middle of the box and surround the can with damp sand. Form a "mountain" around the can, but do not cover the opening. Put ¼ cup of baking soda in the can. In a separate container, make a mixture of 1 cup of water, ¾ cup of vinegar, and ½ cup of dishwashing liquid. If you add 10 drops each of red and yellow food coloring, your lava will be orange. Now, have the children take turns pouring some of this mixture into the can of baking soda to make the lava flow.
(Primary, intermediate)

6. Once they left the Canary Islands, Columbus's fleet was committed to the "great enterprise." In the biography entitled *Christopher Columbus on the Green Sea of Darkness*, Gardner Soule opens the book with a very evocative chapter. He describes what it must have been like for Columbus and his men, out at night on the sea, with only the lanterns hanging from the masts of the three ships visible and with the knowledge that, as far as they knew, no one had attempted before what they were trying to accomplish.

Ask the children to imagine themselves on such a voyage, standing on the deck at night with only these three lights in view. What would be their feelings, hopes, fears, and expectations? To help them imagine what the sailors must have been feeling, let children write about how they would feel if they were about to set off into space to discover a new planet, which is probably the closest modern-day equivalent to what Columbus and his men faced.
(Primary, intermediate)

7. Because travel was so slow and difficult in the fifteenth century, sailors faced long separations from friends and family. For example, when Columbus left Genoa to become a sailor, he may not have seen his parents more than one other time for the rest of his life. He did not see his brother Bartholomew for many years until they met in Lisbon. When Columbus was older and decided to approach the king and queen of Spain for assistance, he left his five-year-old son, Diego, in the monastery of Rabida and may not have seen him again for almost seven years. The picture books *Dear Daddy* by Philippe Dupasquier and *Outside Over There* by Maurice Sendak will help small children understand separations due to sea travel.

For older children, explain that if we reach the point of sending astronauts on long-distance space exploration, they will face the same long-term separations from family and friends. Such separation might even be forever. As a group, imagine you are astronauts. What might be the motivations that would enable you to face this separation, what would be your feelings, and how would you reconcile yourself to the possibility of never seeing your family again?
(Primary, intermediate)

8. When Columbus first left home to go to sea, he may have been no more than thirteen years old. Later, during his famous voyage, there were ship's boys with him who also were very young. Several fiction titles have been written about Columbus's voyage told from the point of view of a ship's boy, including Pam Conrad's *Pedro's Journal*, John Dyson's *Westward with Columbus*, Susan Martin's *I Sailed with Columbus*, and Miriam Schlein's *I Sailed with Columbus*. Share these with your group.

Ask the children to think about what it must have been like to be so young, away from family, assigned a full-time job on-board ship, and completely responsible for yourself. The children can write biographies of themselves as ship's boys (or girls) on one of Columbus's voyages.
(Primary, intermediate)

9. Life on-board ship was very hard for sailors in the fifteenth and sixteenth centuries. Only the ship's captains had quarters assigned to them. The rest of the crew slept on the open deck or tried to find a spot in the dark, cramped hold. There were no sanitation facilities, other than the sea. Cooking was difficult because of the danger of fire. They cooked over a metal firebox in a bed of sand, but this could not be used when the sea was very rough. Fresh water was kept in wooden barrels and quickly became foul. Weevils and worms got into the food. Read a description of life on board from Zvi Dor-Ner's *Columbus and the Age of Discovery*. Dor-Ner excerpts an account from a Spanish noble named Eugenio de Salazar, who sailed across the Atlantic on a Spanish ship in 1573. For younger children, share *Ship's Cook Ginger* by Edward Ardizzone and *Jack at Sea* by Philippe Dupasquier to help them picture the hardships faced.
(Primary, intermediate)

10. Share a ship's meal with your group. Bring in a small cooker to heat up soup or hot dogs. As you cook, ask the children to imagine how difficult preparing this meal would be on a rolling ship's deck.

You can also make authentic ship's biscuits to share. Mix ½ pound of flour with ½ teaspoon of salt. Add water, a drop at a time, and mix until you have a stiff dough. Roll out the dough on a board sprinkled with flour, to a thickness of about ⅓ of an inch. Cut the dough into squares or use the rim of a glass to cut it into circles. Use a fork to prick the top of the biscuits. Now bake them in a 375-degree oven until they turn lightly brown.

Share these along with some of the other foods Columbus took with him, such as raisins, cheese, almonds, and sardines, with plain water to drink. Ask the children whether they feel they would get tired of this fare after a couple of weeks.
(Primary, intermediate)

11. One of the reasons we know so much about Columbus's voyage was because he kept a log in which he wrote down his course and what happened each day. Read some of Columbus's log aloud to the group, and then have the kids write their own logs for a make-believe voyage. An example of keeping a record of a trip can be seen in Vera Williams's *Stringbean's Trip to the Shining Sea*. If kids need ideas to get started, give them copies of the form in figure 9.7.
(Primary, intermediate)

12. Make quill pens such as those Columbus must have used for writing in his log. Each child needs a large feather (available in craft stores). Use scissors to snip the tip off the feather, cutting it on a diagonal (see fig. 9.8). Hollow out the tip with a toothpick. The children can dip the pens in ink and use them for writing a log. Ask the children to describe how difficult they find writing with this kind of pen.
(Primary, intermediate)

13. Along with keeping their own logs of the voyage, the children can chart Columbus's course across the Atlantic. Give each child a copy of the map of the Atlantic shown in figure 9.9 on page 185, to chart the course individually, or make a map on a bulletin board and mark the course as you read through Columbus's log. Read one entry a day, and use a piece of yarn pinned to the board to chart each day's course. Pin paper copies of the ships to the board and move them each day.
(Primary, intermediate)

14. As part of a reenactment of Columbus's voyage, the children can sing the seafaring songs below. You can also use "Christopher Columbo" from Oscar Brand's *Singing Holidays*.

99 Miles
(sung to the tune of "99 Bottles of Beer")

Oh, we're 99 miles from Spain,
We're 99 miles from Spain,
We'll sail awhile and rest awhile,
We're 99 miles from Spain.

Oh, we're 100 miles from Spain...

(Text continues on page 186.)

THE LOG OF ______________________________

The date is ______________.

We are sailing to ______________.

We have been at sea for ______________ days.

Our speed has been ______________.

I estimate we are about ______________ miles from home.

Today we saw ______________________________

______________________________.

The weather has been ______________________________

______________________________.

The ship is ______________________________

______________________________.

The food is ______________________________

______________________________.

The sailors are feeling ______________________________

____

______________________________.

They want to ______________________________

____

______________________________.

I am afraid ______________________________

____

______________________________.

We expect to sight land by ______________.

Fig. 9.7.

QUILL
PEN
INK

Fig. 9.8.

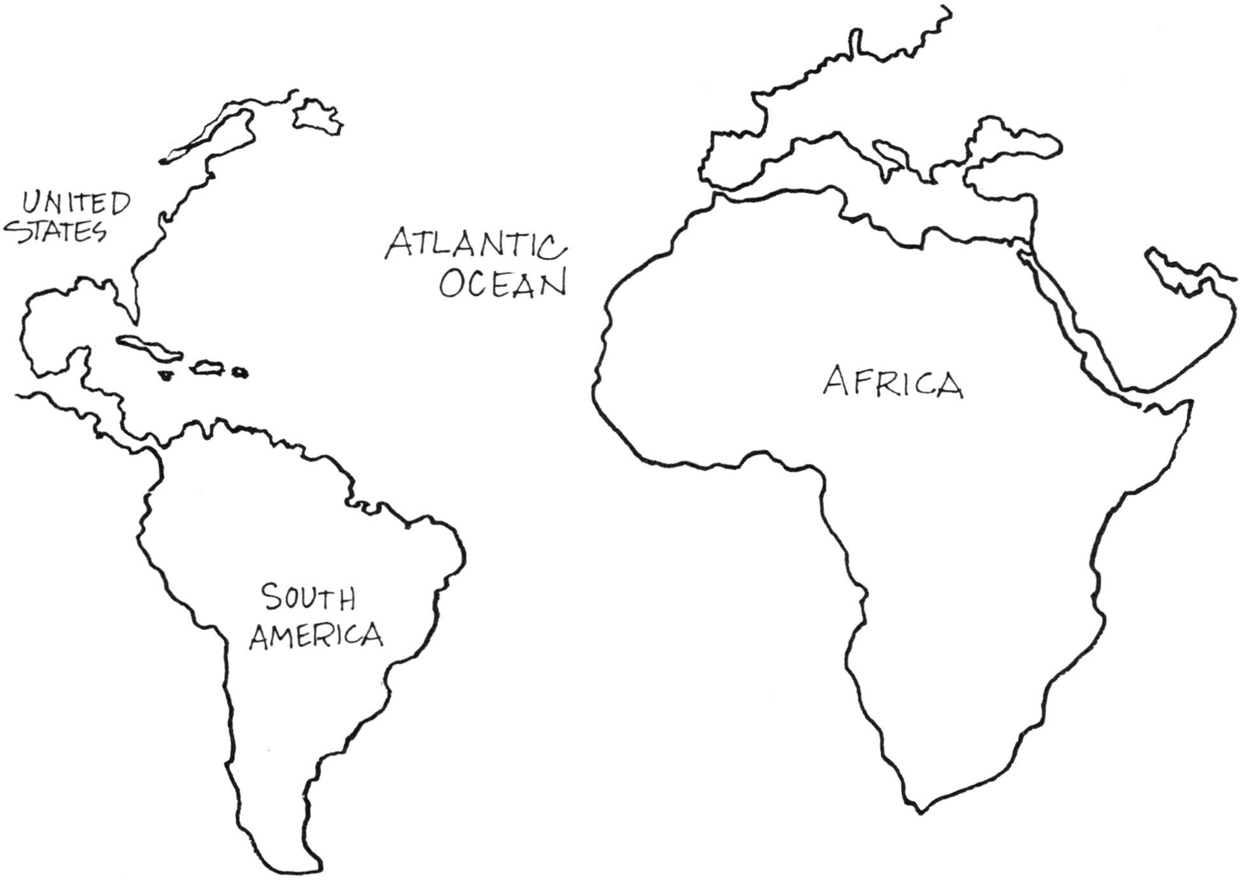
UNITED
STATES
ATLANTIC
OCEAN
AFRICA
SOUTH
AMERICA

Fig. 9.9.

Sail Your Ship
(sung to tune of "Row, Row, Row Your Boat")

Sail, sail, sail your ships
Across the ocean blue,
The *Niña*, the *Pinta*, the *Santa Maria*,
Sail to a world that's new.

(Preschool, primary)

15. Preschoolers will enjoy a special Columbus Day rhyme.

Rub-a-Dub-Dub

Rub-a-dub-dee
Three ships on the sea,
And who do you think they be?

The *Niña*, the *Pinta*,
The *Santa Maria*,
Off on adventure all three!

(Preschool)

SEA CREATURES COLUMBUS ENCOUNTERED

Columbus described in his log the variety of marine life he observed during the voyage. He was very interested in the flora and fauna he encountered and regretted that he was not more learned in biological subjects. Many people, including some of his crew, probably expected the ships to come across the sea monsters described in old tales. Instead, they found octopi, jellyfish, whales, sharks, flying fish, and even crabs in mid-ocean. Many of these creatures are as exotic as the creatures of legend, but are more fascinating to children because they are real.

Book List

Ames, Lee J. *Draw 50 Sharks, Whales, and Other Sea Creatures*. Doubleday, 1989. (Gr. 3-up)
Instructions on how to draw a variety of sea animals.

Brandenberg, Franz. *Otto Is Different*. Greenwillow, 1985. (PreK-2)
Otto the octopus realizes he has different talents.

Carrick, Carol. *Octopus*. Clarion, 1978. (K-3)
This picture book describes the life cycle of a female octopus.

Clements, Andrew. *Big Al*. Picture Book Studio, 1988. (PreK-2)
Big Al is a huge, ugly fish who frightens all the other fish away until one day when he saves them all.

Coldrey, Jennifer, and David Shale. *The World of Jellyfish*. Gareth Stevens, 1987. (Gr. 2-6)
This title covers the physical habits and environment of the jellyfish.

Cole, Joanna. *Hungry, Hungry Sharks*. Random House, 1986. (K-4)
Information about sharks is presented in a colorful, early-reader format.

Day, Edward. *John Tabor's Ride*. Knopf, 1989. (K-2)
John Tabor is taken for a ride—on a whale!

Demi. *Find Demi's Sea Creatures*. Grosset & Dunlap, 1991. (PreK-2)
Large, beautiful illustrations introduce a number of sea animals.

Frame, Paul. *Drawing Sharks, Whales, Dolphins and Seals*. Franklin Watts, 1983. (Gr. 2-up)
More instructions for drawing sea creatures.

Heller, Ruth. *How to Hide an Octopus and Other Sea Creatures*. Grosset & Dunlap, 1985. (PreK-3)
Includes a variety of fish that use camouflage.

James, Simon. *My Friend the Whale*. Bantam, 1991. (PreK-3)
A picture-book look at whales.

Kalan, Robert. *Blue Sea*. Greenwillow, 1979. (PreK)
A graphically striking look at the order of things in the sea.

Kraus, Robert. *Herman the Helper*. Prentice Hall, 1974. (PreK)
Herman is an octopus who uses his arms to help his family and friends.

Lauber, Patricia. *An Octopus Is Amazing*. Crowell, 1990. (K-3)
An introduction to this unusual animal.

Lionni, Leo. *Swimmy*. Pantheon, 1963. (PreK-K)
Swimmy is a little fish who learns how to stay safe and have fun, too.

Marshak, Susan. *I Am the Ocean*. Arcade, 1991. (PreK)
A look at the variety of life under the sea.

Pallotta, Jerry. *Ocean Alphabet Book*. Charlesbridge, 1986. (PreK-1)
An alphabet's worth of sea creatures.

Ryder, Joanne. *Winter Whale*. Morrow, 1991. (K-3)
This nature writer turns her sights to whales.

Selsam, Millicent E., and Joyce Hunt. *A First Look at Sharks*. Walker, 1979. (Gr. 1-3)
A nonfiction introduction to sharks.

Seymour, Peter. *What's in the Deep Blue Sea?* Henry Holt, 1990. (PreK-3)
A pop-up book introducing sea creatures.

Sheldon, Dyan. *The Whale's Song*. Dial, 1991. (K-3)
A little girl learns about the whale's song from her grandmother.

Soloff-Levy, Barbara. *How to Draw Sea Creatures*. Watermill, 1987. (Gr. 2-6)
More instructions on drawing creatures of the sea.

Tashjian, Virginia. *Juba This and Juba That*. Little, Brown, 1969. (K-4)
Includes the chants "Who Did?" and "If You Ever."

______. *With a Deep Sea Smile*. Little, Brown, 1974. (K-4)
This collection of rhymes includes "The Fish with a Deep Sea Smile."

Weller, Frances Ward. *I Wonder If I'll See a Whale*. Philomel, 1991. (K-3)
Out at sea, a young girl experiences the excitement of seeing whales.

Related Activities

1. As part of a group dramatization of Columbus's voyage, create an ocean scene in your room. Partition off a corner with fishnet. The children can make some of the sea creatures below to hang from the ceiling, along with green and yellow streamers to represent seaweed. For inspiration, read some of these books about sea creatures: *Find Demi's Sea Creatures* by Demi, *I Am the Ocean* by Susan Marshak, *Ocean Alphabet Book* by Jerry Pallotta, and *What's in the Deep Blue Sea?* by Peter Seymour.
(Preschool, primary)

2. Read some picture books about fish. Use Robert Kalan's *Blue Sea* and Leo Lionni's *Swimmy*. Share the poem "The Fish with a Deep Sea Smile" by Margaret Wise Brown, from *With a Deep Sea Smile* compiled by Virginia Tashjian. To make fish to hang up, the children can draw around their hands, as shown in figure 9.10, or use the drawing books listed above. They can decorate their fish in various ways. For example, they could cover the fish with scales made from tin foil, colored paper, or sequins. Columbus and his sailors also encountered flying fish that actually flew on board their ships. Figure 9.11 shows how to make flying fish.
(Preschool, primary)

3. In the Sargasso Sea, which is a huge floating bed of seaweed in the middle of the Atlantic, Columbus and his men were amazed to find crabs living on the seaweed. Make crabs from small paper plates and attach pincers and legs (see fig. 9.12 on page 191). For Sargassum fish, the children can make fish with shaggy lumps and fins, as shown in figure 9.13 on page 191. Read Andrew Clements's *Big Al* for inspiration.
(Preschool, primary)

4. You can make beautiful jellyfish by covering paper plates with colored cellophane (see fig. 9.14 on page 192). Tape streaming tentacles of cellophane to the plates. Show the children examples of these strange sea creatures from Jennifer Coldrey and David Shale's *The World of Jellyfish*.
(Preschool, primary)

(Text continues on page 192.)

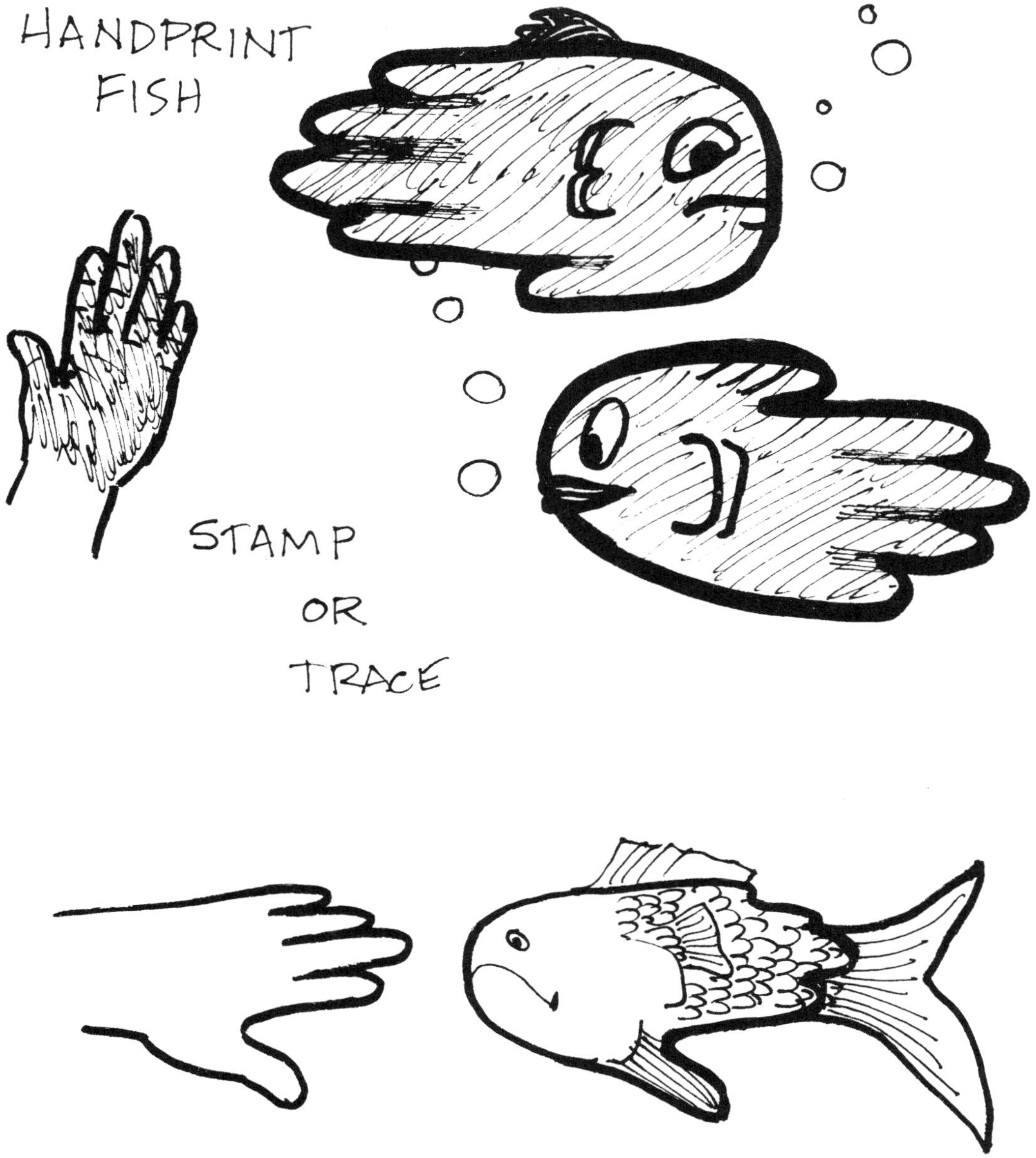
HANDPRINT FISH
STAMP OR TRACE

Fig. 9.10.

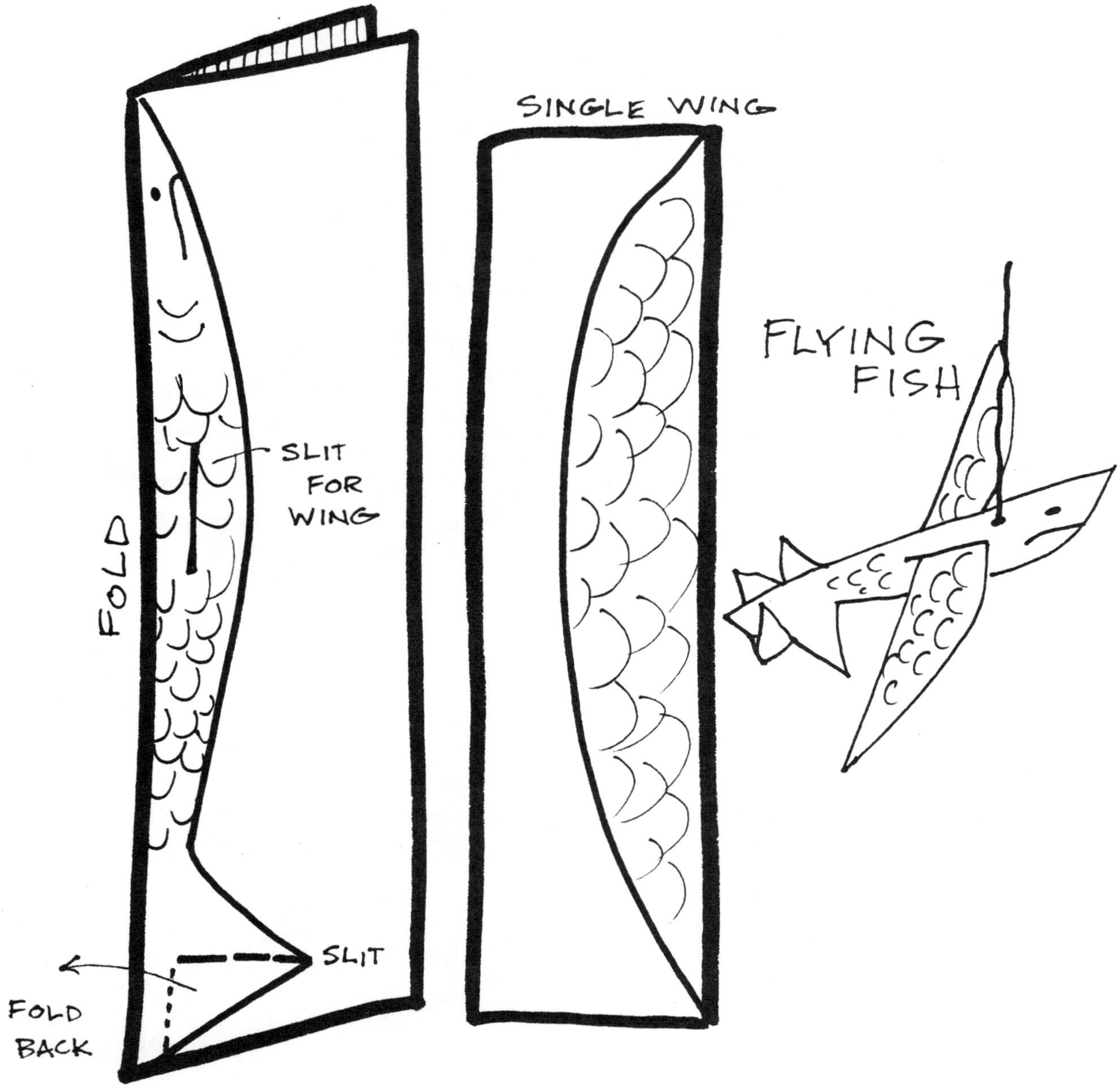

SINGLE WING
FLYING FISH
SLIT FOR WING
FOLD
SLIT
FOLD BACK

Fig. 9.11.

Fig. 9.12.

Fig. 9.13.

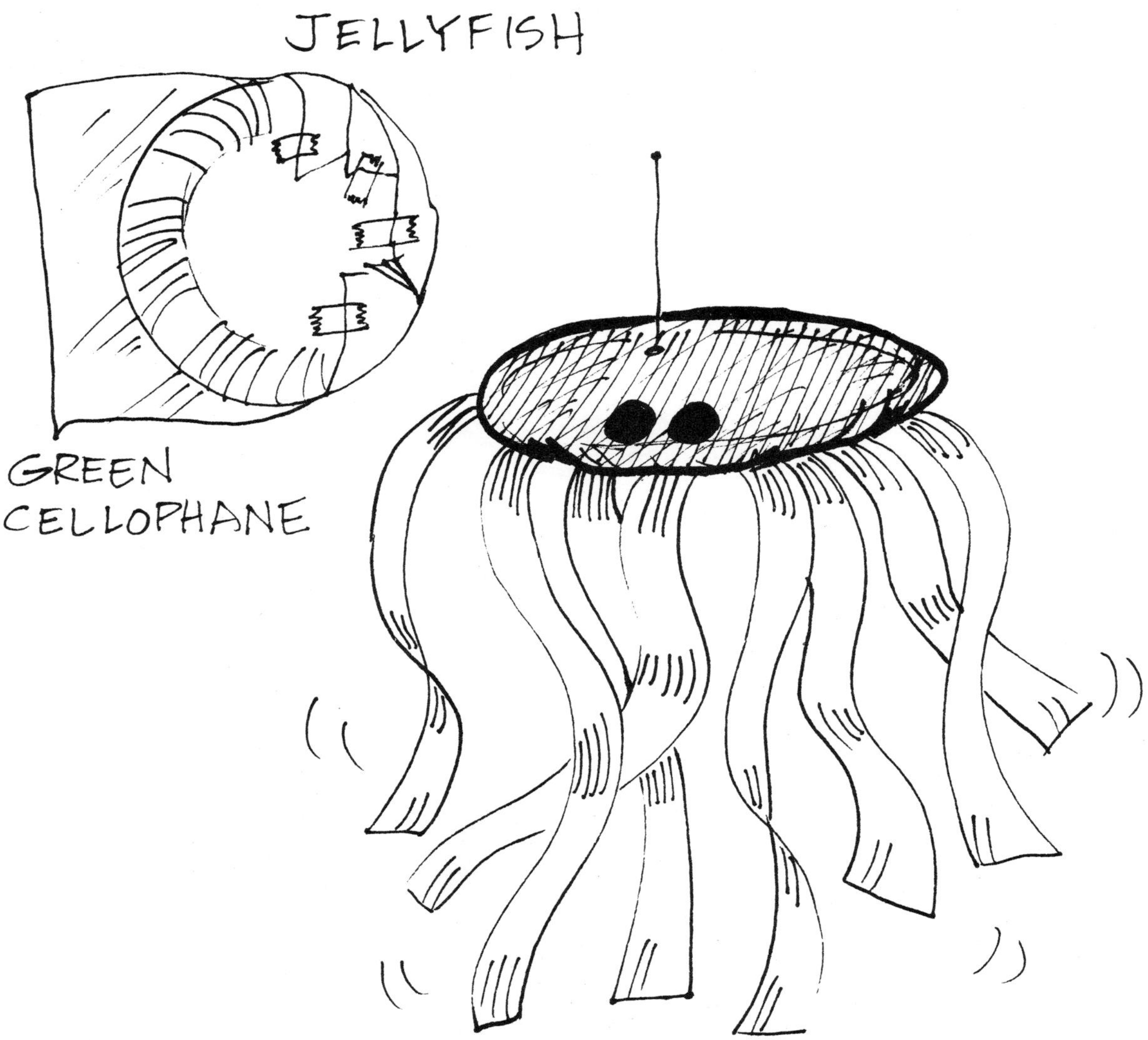

Fig. 9.14.

5. Enjoy a "Sea Creature Relay." Before starting, make a list of various sea creatures whose movements can be imitated by the players, such as crabs, lobsters, sharks, and jellyfish. Divide the children into two teams behind a starting line. The leader calls out the name of a sea creature, such as "crab." The first child in each line moves sideways like a crab toward the finish line. The winner scores a point for his or her team. The leader calls out another sea creature, such as "jellyfish," and the next child on each team races to the finish, wobbling and slithering like a jellyfish. Play until everyone has had a turn. The team with the most points wins.
(Preschool, primary)

6. The octopus is a fascinating animal to many children. Introduce this creature with the books *Otto Is Different* by Franz Brandenberg, *Octopus* by Carol Carrick, *How to Hide an Octopus and Other Sea Creatures* by Ruth Heller, *Herman the Helper* by Robert Kraus, and *An Octopus Is*

Amazing by Patricia Lauber. Show the children how to make an octopus from a paper plate. Cut legs from a second plate and attach them with paper brads to the body so the legs are movable. An octopus can also be made from an upside-down margarine tub. Tape streamers or folded paper strips to the inside for legs (see fig. 9.15).
(Preschool, primary)

Fig. 9.15.

7. Introduce whales by using the group chants "If You Ever" and "Who Did?" in Virginia Tashjian's *Juba This and Juba That*. Read aloud any of these picture books: *John Tabor's Ride* by Edward Day, *My Friend the Whale* by Simon James, *Winter Whale* by Joanne Ryder, *The Whale's Song* by Dyan Sheldon, and *I Wonder If I'll See a Whale* by Frances Weller. Have the children make whales from stuffed lunch bags, as shown in figure 9.16. Stuff a bag with wadded newspaper and tie off the end. This end is the whale's tail. Color the whale black or gray, and cut a water spout from blue paper to glue on top of the whale.
(Preschool, primary)

8. Show a couple of books about sharks, such as Joanna Cole's *Hungry, Hungry Sharks* and Millicent Selsam's *A First Look at Sharks*. Make shark puppets from envelopes as shown in figure 9.17. Each child needs one standard-size business envelope. Seal the envelope shut. Cut a triangle out of one end, as shown, and cut a strip off the other end. Use the triangle as the shark's fin; tape the "fin" to the top of the envelope and then decorate.

Fig. 9.16.

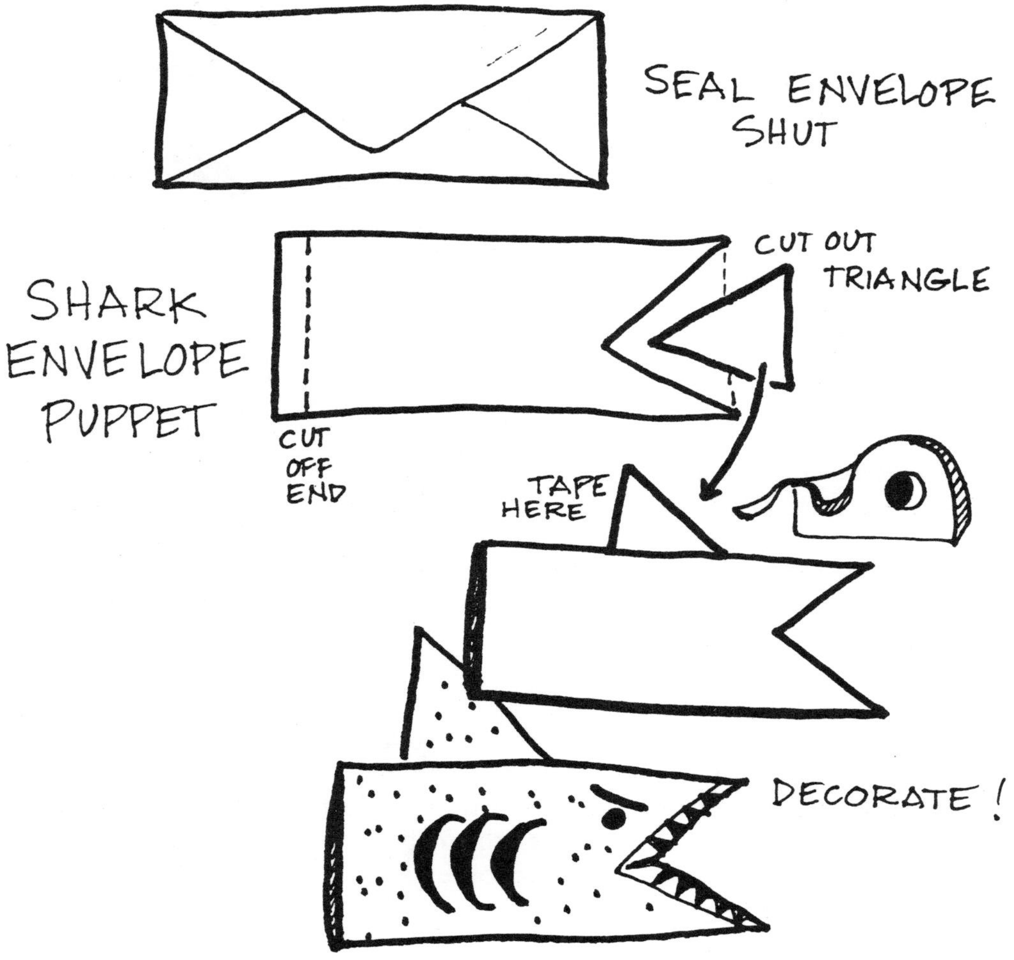

Fig. 9.17.

Play the game "Sharks." Begin by marking off a large area to represent the boat. Divide the group into sailors and sharks. The sailors stand inside the boat. The sailors try to pull the sharks into the boat, and the sharks try to pull the sailors out of the boat. If you are pulled into the circle, you become a sailor. If you are pulled out of the circle, you get eaten!
(Preschool, primary)

LAND HO!

Life on such a voyage of discovery was often very hard on the crew and, even at best, boring. On this particular voyage, the crew was also unsettled by the fact that they were sailing blindly into the unknown. After a few weeks, the sailors became restless and anxious, and false sightings of land became frequent. At one point, Columbus barely had control of his fleet. Finally, about 2:00 in the morning of October 12, 1492, a sailor on board the *Pinta*, Rodrigo de Triana, gave the call, "Land ho!" Indeed, the white beach of an island could be seen in the moonlight.

The king and queen of Spain, before the fleet set out, had offered a reward to the first sailor to sight land, but the money did not go to Triana. As it turned out, Columbus himself received the reward. He claimed to have seen a light out in the darkness at about 10:00 the night before. For years, historians have debated about this light. Some say it might have been a bonfire on San Salvador, but others state that the ships were still too far away to have possibly spotted a fire on shore. Some believe it was an illusion created by Columbus's strong desire to find land, and some believe he simply made it up because he could not stand not getting the credit for actually sighting the land he had come so far to find.

When dawn came, Columbus and his captains were rowed to shore, and Columbus officially claimed the land for Spain in a formal ceremony. He planted the flags of the Spanish monarchs and led the group in prayer. The secretary of the fleet notarized his actions.

Book List

Brown, Marc. *The True Francine*. Little, Brown, 1981. (Gr. 1-3)
Francine faces a dilemma when her best friend claims the work Francine did.

Freeman, Don. *Come Again, Pelican*. Viking, 1961. (PreK-1)
A boy makes friends with a pelican during his vacation.

Fritz, Jean. *The Great Adventure of Christopher Columbus*. Putnam, 1992. (Gr. 2-up)
Jean Fritz describes Columbus's great enterprise in this pop-up book illustrated by Tomie dePaola.

Geisert, Arthur. *The Ark*. Houghton Mifflin, 1988. (PreK-2)
A retelling of the story of Noah and the ark.

Hart, Jane. *Singing Bee! A Collection of Favorite Children's Songs*. Lothrop, Lee & Shepard, 1982. (All ages)
This collection includes the song "Three White Gulls."

Pomerantz, Charlotte. *Flap Your Wings and Try*. Greenwillow, 1989. (PreK)
A young seagull learns to fly.

Ross, Tony. *The Boy Who Cried Wolf*. Dial, 1985. (PreK-3)
A humorous retelling of the old tale of the boy who falsely cried for help once too often.

Schaffler, Robert Haven. *The Days We Celebrate*. Dodd, Mead, 1940. (Gr. 3-up)
This collection includes the poem "Landfall" by Dorothy Brown Thompson.

Taylor, Mark. *Henry the Explorer*. Little, Brown, 1966. (PreK-1)
After reading a book about exploring, Henry puts together an explorer's kit and sets out with his dog, Angus, to discover the world, taking flags to claim all the lands he finds.

Wharton, Anthony. *Discovering Sea Birds*. Franklin Watts, 1987. (Gr. 4-6)
Text and clear photos describe a variety of sea birds.

Wildsmith, Brian. *Pelican*. Pantheon, 1982. (PreK-2)
When a pelican hatches from the large egg Paul finds, he must teach the bird how to fish.

Related Activities

1. As Columbus's voyage grew longer, the sailors grew more uneasy. Finally, around October 9, they threatened mutiny. They said that if Columbus would not turn around, they would throw him overboard. After much debate, he convinced the crew to give him three more days, saying that if they had not found land by then, he would agree to turn back for Spain. Ask the children to devise a speech like the one Columbus must have made to convince his crew to sail on. What must he have said or threatened to convince them?
(Intermediate)

2. Columbus saw many birds while he was at sea and often believed they were signs of approaching land. One of the birds he saw was a pelican. Pelicans are very interesting birds, so share a couple of picture books about them: *Come Again, Pelican* by Don Freeman and *Pelican* by Brian Wildsmith. Have the children make their own pelicans. Using the pattern in figure 9.18, have kids color and cut out the pieces. The upper beak should be attached to the lower with a paper brad inserted at the dots. The wing is inserted in a slit cut along the dotted line on the pelican's body. Cut out some fish to stick in the pelican's mouth. If you glue the pelican to a background sheet of paper, put just a bit of glue around the edge of the large, lower beak, so you can insert fish into the beak. Do not glue the upper beak, so it can move freely.
(Preschool, primary)

3. Research some of the other birds Columbus saw, such as petrels, albatrosses, herons, terns, frigate birds, and boobies, using Anthony Wharton's *Discovering Sea Birds*. Each child can draw a different bird and cut it out. Ask the children to color their birds on each side, and attach the birds together to create a group mobile.
(Primary)

Fig. 9.18.

4. The sailors were finally convinced they were really nearing land because they saw branches with green leaves floating by the ships, and a number of birds flew over as if going to land. Columbus's description of the birds and branches as harbingers of land is similar to the story of Noah's ark. Read aloud a version of Noah's ark, and then make seagulls using the pattern in figure 9.19.

Share the book *Flap Your Wings and Try* by Charlotte Pomerantz, about a seagull. Then sing a song about seagulls, "Three White Gulls" by Marguerite Wilkinson, found in *Singing Bee! A Collection of Favorite Children's Songs* compiled by Jane Hart.
(Preschool, primary)

5. After being at sea for many days, the sailors became very anxious for the voyage to end. The king and queen of Spain had offered a large reward to the first man to sight land. As a result, there were some false alarms. On several occasions land was hailed, but it turned out to be only a low-lying cloud. Finally, Columbus declared that the man who raised the next false cry of land would forfeit the reward even if he later actually sighted land. Read the book *The Boy Who Cried Wolf* by Tony Ross, as an example of the consequences of giving a false warning too many times.
(Preschool, primary)

6. The sailors kept a lookout for land from the top of the mast. You can reenact this search for land by placing a basket on a table that you have turned into a ship and letting a "sailor" sit in the basket to keep a lookout.

Land was actually sighted at 2:00 a.m., October 12, 1492, by Rodrigo de Triana. Read the poem "Landfall" by Dorothy Brown Thompson, from *The Days We Celebrate* by Robert Haven Schaffler.
(Primary, intermediate)

7. Describe Columbus's claim to be the first to sight land, because of the light he said he had seen the night before. Tell the group about the various explanations historians have put forward, such as Columbus sighting a fire on the shore, imagining the light because he was so anxious to find land, and making the story up because he wanted the credit of being the one to sight the "Indies." In his book *Columbus on the Green Sea of Darkness*, Gardner Soule suggests that Columbus may have seen palolo worms. These segmented worms, which can be up to 16" long, live in coastal areas, in rocks and coral below the tideline, but once a year in October they migrate out to sea to reproduce. The rear segments that become the new worms glow with a fluorescent light. Have the class debate these various explanations of the light Columbus saw and vote on which one they feel is true.

Cut palolo worms from fluorescent paper, and tape them to the walls of your room. Then turn out the lights in the room to help you imagine whether this could be what Columbus saw.
(Primary, intermediate)

8. How must Rodrigo de Triana have felt when Columbus claimed the reward for sighting land? Have a group discussion about whether the children think it was fair of Columbus to take the money after not speaking up at the time he supposedly saw the light. Do children think this action increased or decreased the sailors' respect for Columbus? Ask whether someone else has ever claimed credit for something the children did. If so, how did they handle it? To help young children understand this issue, read *The True Francine* by Marc Brown.
(Primary, intermediate)

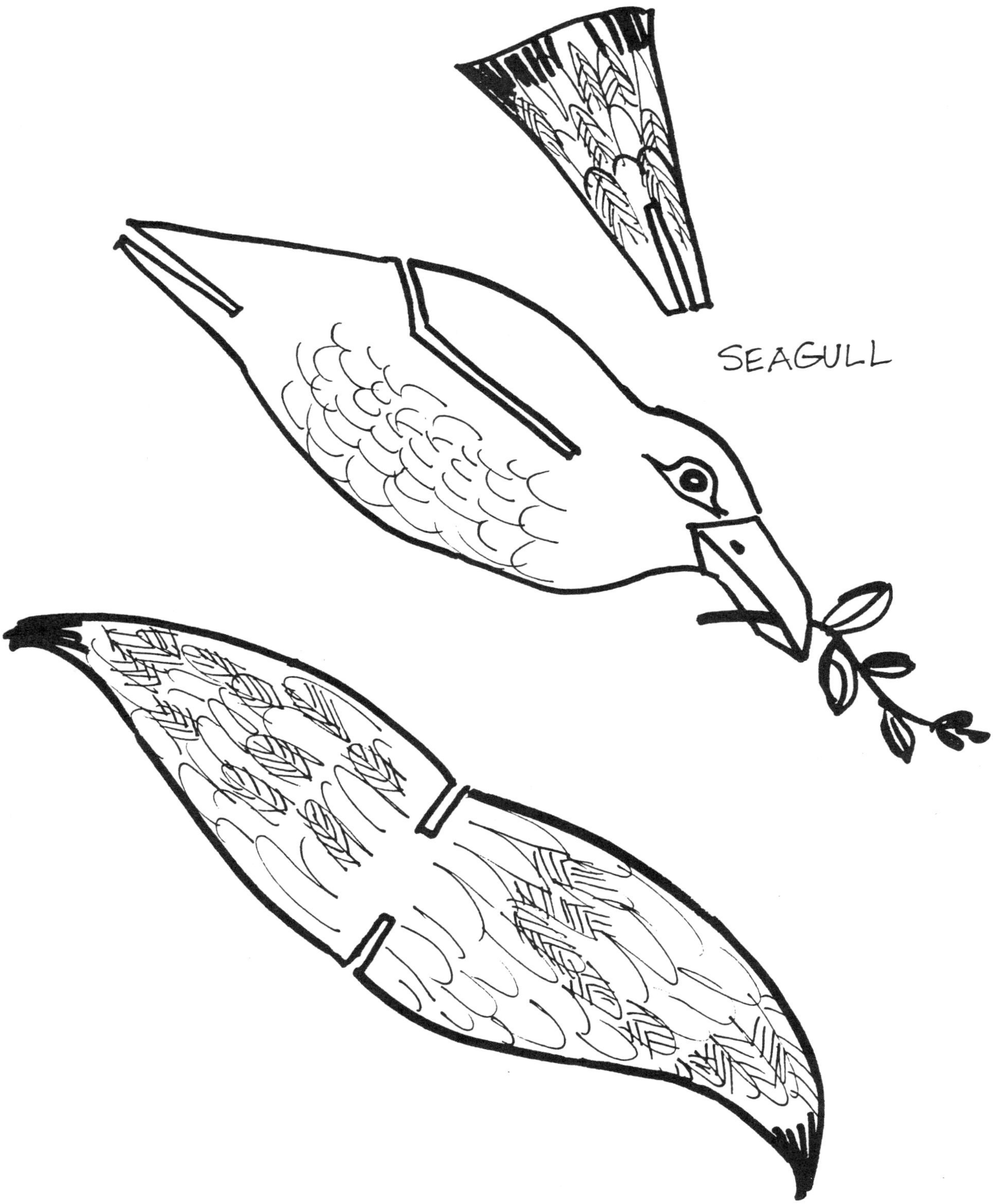

Fig. 9.19.

9. With preschoolers, share this fingerplay. Start with your fist closed, and lift one finger for each verse.

Five Sailors

Christopher Columbus needed sailors and ships
To sail across the ocean on his discovery trip.

The first brave sailor waved Spain good-bye,
Then looked ahead at the endless sea and sky.

The second brave sailor looked into the deep
Where the whales and fish and the sea serpents sleep.

The third brave sailor cried, "We're surely lost!"
For all he could see were the waves on which they tossed.

The fourth brave sailor looked out on the sea,
Saw leaves and branches floating by:
"Somewhere the land must be!"

The fifth brave sailor was the first to know
The long voyage was over. He cried, "Land, ho!"

Columbus had found new lands to explore,
As his three ships rested on the New World's shore.

(Preschool)

10. When he landed on San Salvador, Columbus immediately claimed the land for Spain. Later, other explorers also claimed the lands they found for their home countries. Have a discussion about why these discoverers felt that they could take over land where people were already living.
(Primary, intermediate)

11. Even in modern times, explorers have performed "landing" ceremonies when they arrive at new destinations. Edmund Hillary planted a flag on Mt. Everest, and the U.S. astronauts who first landed on the moon left a flag and a plaque. In some ways, this desire to "make a mark" is similar to that of people who write graffiti on bridges over a highway or carve their initials in a tree. Talk about what makes people want to leave a mark like this. Jean Fritz's pop-up book *The Great Adventure of Christopher Columbus* shows Columbus's landing ceremony. Share the picture book *Henry the Explorer* by Mark Taylor. Then let each child design a banner and form a proclamation that they would use if they were making a new discovery. Ask them to decide whether they would copy the proclamations of earlier explorers and claim the land as their own, or instead create a new kind of discovery ceremony.
(Primary, intermediate)

THE WEST INDIES

When Columbus landed, he was expecting to encounter a wealthy and sophisticated Chinese culture. Instead, he found an island paradise and a people he described as peaceful and innocent. He was greeted by Arawak Indians, who must have been amazed at the arrival of these strange creatures from over the sea in their "floating houses." Some of the Indians Columbus first saw were wearing gold ornaments. The sight of these ornaments seems to have sparked what was to become a continuous search for gold for the rest of Columbus's life.

One of the first things Columbus did on landing at San Salvador was capture several Indians, both to use them as guides and to take them back to Spain to show to Ferdinand and Isabella, as "specimens" of what he had found. He explored several islands and described the local flora and fauna. We know much about what he found because of the detailed account he gives in his log.

On each island Columbus visited he asked the natives about gold; each time he was told he would find gold farther on. At one point, Martin Alonso Pinzon deserted the fleet with the *Pinta* and sailed off on his own to find gold. With only two ships now, Columbus continued his search. At last he thought he had reached the source of the gold when he came to the island of Hispaniola, today's Dominican Republic and Haiti. The Indians seemed wealthier than any he had met up to then, and he spent time exploring the island.

Book List

Charlip, Remy, and Mary Beth Ancona. *Handtalk*. Macmillan, 1974. (K-5)
Introduces sign language with colorful photographs.

Cole, William. *The Sea, Ships and Sailors*. Viking, 1967. (Gr. 3-up)
This collection includes the old English song "The Mermaid."

Darling, Kathy. *Manatee on Location*. Lothrop, Lee & Shepard, 1991. (Gr. 3-up)
An up-close look at this unusual animal.

Davis, Gibbs. *Fishman and Charlie*. Houghton Mifflin, 1983. (Gr. 6-up)
In this story, a boy makes friends with a manatee.

dePaola, Tomie. *The Popcorn Book*. Holiday House, 1978. (K-3)
Presents a variety of facts about popcorn and includes two recipes.

Goodall, John. *Paddy under Water*. Atheneum, 1984. (PreK-3)
In this wordless picture book, Paddy Pig goes deep-sea diving and encounters tropical fish, an octopus, a sea monster, mermaids, and finally a sunken ship, where he finds treasure.

Haley, Gail E. *Sea Tale*. Dutton, 1990. (K-4)
A young sailor's love for a mermaid is preserved in the ring she fashions for him from a strand of her hair, but he finds himself in a dire dilemma when he remembers he has promised a lock of his sweetheart's hair to a mysterious old woman.

Jacobs, Francine. *The Tainos: The People Who Welcomed Columbus*. Putnam, 1992. (Gr. 4-up)
This is a description of the history and culture of the people Columbus first encountered on reaching the New World and covers the disastrous results of this meeting for the Tainos.

Kellogg, Steven. *The Island of the Skog*. Dial, 1973. (PreK-3)
To escape the persecution of cats, a band of mice sail away to find a new land. They find an island, but it is already inhabited.

Lauber, Patricia. *Snakes Are Hunters*. Crowell, 1988. (PreK-3)
Describes the habits of snakes.

Lawson, Robert. *I Discover Columbus*. Little, Brown, 1941. (Gr. 3-6)
In this fictional story, a parrot named Aurelio claims to have been a major factor in Columbus's voyage to the New World.

Lessac, Frane. *My Little Island*. Lippincott, 1984. (K-3)
A young boy goes with his best friend to visit the Caribbean island where he was born.

MacDonald, Golden. *The Little Island*. Doubleday, 1946. (PreK-1)
Describes a peaceful little island and what goes on there.

McCarthy, Patricia. *Ocean Parade*. Dial, 1990. (PreK-K)
Some of the beautiful patterns of the sea are introduced in this counting book.

McDermott, Gerald. *Papagayo the Mischief Maker*. Windmill Books, 1980. (PreK-2)
Papagayo the parrot causes trouble in the jungle.

McGovern, Ann. *Nicholas Bentley Stoningpot III*. Holiday House, 1982. (PreK-4)
A little rich boy is shipwrecked alone on a deserted island. He sets up a new life for himself there and is very happy.

Noble, Trinka Hakes. *Hansy's Mermaid*. Dial, 1983. (K-4)
A storm brings a mermaid to a Dutch family, who put her to work for them. But the young son, Hansy, longs to help her return to her home in the sea.

Obrist, Jurg. *The Miser Who Wanted the Sun*. Atheneum, 1984. (PreK-3)
A rich man loves gold so much that he wants to own the sun.

Overbeck, Cynthia. *The Fish Book*. Lerner, 1978. (Gr. 3-up)
An introduction to tropical fish.

Rohmer, Harriet. *The Invisible Hunters*. Children's Book Press, 1987. (Gr. 1-5)
This folktale from Nicaragua describes the diastrous results suffered by indigenous people on coming into contact with the "outside" world. Text in English and Spanish.

Rohmer, Harriet, and Jesus Guerrero Rea. *Atariba and Niguayona*. Children's Book Press, 1988. (K-5)
A folktale of the Taino people of Puerto Rico.

Sherlock, Philip. *The Iguana's Tail*. Crowell, 1969. (Gr. 4-up)
Folktales of the West Indies.

Singer, Marilyn. *Exotic Birds*. Doubleday, 1990. (Gr. 3-6)
Introduces some of the unusual birds Columbus must have encountered.

Tompert, Ann. *Charlotte and Charles*. Crown, 1979. (K-3)
Charlotte and Charles are two giants who long for visitors to their island. But after taking Charlotte and Charles's help, the newcomers turn against them.

West, Colin. *Have You Seen the Crocodile?* Lippincott, 1986. (PreK)
All the animals are looking for the crocodile.

Wiseman, Ann. *Making Things, Book II*. Little, Brown, 1975. (Gr. 3-6)
This craft book includes instructions for making a hammock.

Yolen, Jane. *Encounter*. Harcourt Brace Jovanovich, 1992. (Gr. 2-up)
In this picture book, a young Taino boy describes his fears and their justification on encountering Columbus.

Yorinks, Arthur. *Company's Coming*. Crown, 1988. (K-2)
A middle-aged couple invite a group of aliens for supper.

Related Activities

1. Introduce the life of the Caribbean with the books *The Iguana's Tail* by Philip Sherlock, which contains West Indian folktales; *Atariba and Niguayona* by Harriet Rohmer and Jesus Guerrero Rea, a tale of the Taino Indians; and *My Little Island* by Frane Lessac, about a modern-day visit to a Caribbean island. Share *The Little Island* by Golden MacDonald to give the children some idea of the "unspoiled" scene Columbus must have found.
(Preschool, primary, intermediate)

2. For a reenactment of this part of Columbus's voyage, decorate the library or classroom as a Caribbean island. Start by stringing brown twine back and forth across the ceiling so it looks like vines. Then let the children color and cut out the foliage shown in figures 9.20 and 9.21 and hang it from the vines. If you are holding an explorers' reading program, the children could fill out a piece of foliage for each book they read. If you have support posts in your room, turn them into palm trees. Wrap them with fringed paper bags to represent bark, and add cardboard palm leaves at the top.

Columbus even claimed he saw a tree that grew different species of leaves from the same trunk. He got this impression because the foliage grew so densely that it became intertwined. Make a tree of many species for your classroom. Tape a cardboard tree trunk to the wall, and let each child make a leaf from a different species of plant to add to the tree.
(Preschool, primary, intermediate)

3. Share the book *Nicholas Bentley Stoningpot III* by Ann McGovern, about finding a deserted island. Then the children can draw and write about what they would do if they found an island paradise of their own. Ask them to name their island, set up a government for it, and decide who would be allowed to live with them.
(Primary, intermediate)

(Text continues on page 206.)

Fig. 9.20.

Fig. 9.21.

4. Ask the children to imagine that, like the Arawaks, they witness the arrival of an alien civilization to their land. They can imagine that these unknown travelers come from another planet, from under the sea, or from the center of the earth. Ask them to decide what these aliens look like and what their customs are. For example, do they have any strange landing ceremony, like Columbus performed? Use the book *Company's Coming* by Arthur Yorinks to get imaginations going. (Primary, intermediate)

5. To illustrate how the sight of the ornaments worn by the natives aroused Columbus's lust for gold, the children can make gold nose rings by cutting rings from posterboard and coloring them yellow or gold. Then they should cut a slit in the ring to insert in their noses. Now read the book *The Miser Who Wanted the Sun* by Jurg Obrist about a wealthy man's greed for gold.

Tell the children to imagine that the aliens they described in activity 4 were very greedy for their rings and other jewelry. How would it make them feel? How would the greediness of the newcomers affect the way the children think of the newcomers? Would they feel willing to help the strangers find more gold?
(Primary, intermediate)

6. When Columbus arrived on San Salvador, he discovered that his interpreter was useless. The natives did not speak Arabic or any language Columbus and his men knew. Therefore, they had to communicate through sign language. If the children in your group are not familiar with sign language, show them a book of signs, such as Remy Charlip and Mary B. Miller's *Handtalk*. Explain that sign language is used both by people who cannot hear and by groups who speak different languages, such as Native American tribes.

However, Columbus and his men did not even have an organized system of signs known to both the Europeans and the Arawaks. They had to come up with gestures that would convey their meaning, and it must have been difficult. To experience what this must have felt like, break the children into groups of four. Each group should come up with a "script"—a message they want to convey to the rest of the children. They should write the message out and give it to you and then decide how they are going to convey this message, using only hand gestures, without words. Let each group present their "script" to the entire class. The class should try to interpret the message. You could give a small prize to each group who successfully gets their message across.
(Primary, intermediate)

7. Most of the Indians who greeted Columbus were friendly and welcomed the strangers. At first, Columbus returned their friendship, but on leaving he took several people with him, to act as guides and as "specimens" to show to Ferdinand and Isabella. Introduce the Tainos people with the book *The Tainos* by Francine Jacobs. Use the book *Charlotte and Charles* by Ann Tompert to describe the trusting way the Indians greeted Columbus and the book *The Island of the Skog* by Steven Kellogg to show how Columbus returned their trust. Jane Yolen brings this meeting of cultures to life in her book *Encounter*, and Harriet Rohmer's *The Invisible Hunters* shows what a disastrous effect such a meeting can have on indigenous cultures. Have a discussion about encountering a different culture for the first time. Is it possible to build a relationship on trust? Is it naive?
(Primary, intermediate)

8. As Columbus traveled around the islands, he was frequently greeted by natives rowing out to his ships in their dugout canoes. The group can make individual canoes by scooping out blocks of plastic foam or clay.

Play the game "Canoes on the Ocean." Divide your group into teams. Each team needs a broomstick or a pole about 2 yards long. As many teams as you like may take part in the contest. Two teams at a time race against each other. The teams pretend they are rowing canoes on the ocean, avoiding rocks, reefs, and sharks, without letting the waves turn them over. Start and finish lines are marked on the ground about 15 yards apart. Obstacles such as chairs or cartons are placed in the path to represent natural hazards and to make a "wavy" course. The teams stand holding the sticks between their legs and with their backs to the finish, except for the navigator for each team, who faces forward. On the starting signal, the crews run backwards trying to follow the directions of the navigators and make their way around the obstacles to the finish line as quickly as possible. If you have more than two teams, the winners of each race can have a playoff.
(Primary)

9. At various times, Columbus and his men landed and examined the villages and homes of the Indians they met. As a group project, make a table-top diorama of an Arawak village. Make canoes by scooping out blocks of plastic foam or clay, and place the canoes in the ocean. Then make a shore with a village beside it. Make houses like the ones Columbus described seeing on the Caribbean islands he visited. As shown in figure 9.22, start with a round oatmeal or salt box, a tin can, or a tube made from posterboard. Make a cone from construction paper using the pattern and place it over the top of the tube, and glue it in place. Spread glue on the cone in small sections at a time, and stick on straw or dried grass, layering it from the lower edge up until the roof is covered with grass.

The Arawaks actually made their homes of royal palms, with the trunks used to build walls and the fronds used for roofs. Make palm trees to add to the diorama. The leaves are made by folding a green piece of paper over once and cutting it like the teeth of a comb, as shown in figure 9.23. Do not cut through the fold. Then the leaves are taped inside the trunk, which is made the same way, by folding a brown piece of paper over once and cutting notches in the sides.
(Primary, intermediate)

10. One of the things Columbus found in the Arawak homes was hammocks. This find turned out to be a great boon to future sailors, as hammocks became standard equipment on board ships from this time on. This meant the crew no longer had to sleep on the deck. Bring in a hammock for the group to see. If you can get one with a frame, or if you have support posts in your library or classroom, hang the hammock so the children can experience swinging in it. If you are really ambitious, you could make a hammock as a group project, using the instructions in *Making Things, Book II* by Ann Wiseman.
(Preschool, primary, intermediate)

11. Some of the plants the crew discovered were sweet potatoes, pineapple palms, maize (corn), pumpkins, manioc, tobacco, beans, and cotton. Let the children grow their own sweet potato and pineapple plants.

To grow a sweet potato plant, stick toothpicks into a sweet potato in a circle around the middle. Then place the potato in a glass of water. The toothpicks should hold the potato up by resting on the rim of the glass. Put the glass and potato on a window sill, and in about a week the potato will start to sprout leaves.

To grow a pineapple, cut off the top of the fruit, with the leaves on it, and set the top in a shallow dish of water until roots start to form. Then plant the fruit in a pot, and water it regularly.
(Preschool, primary, intermediate)

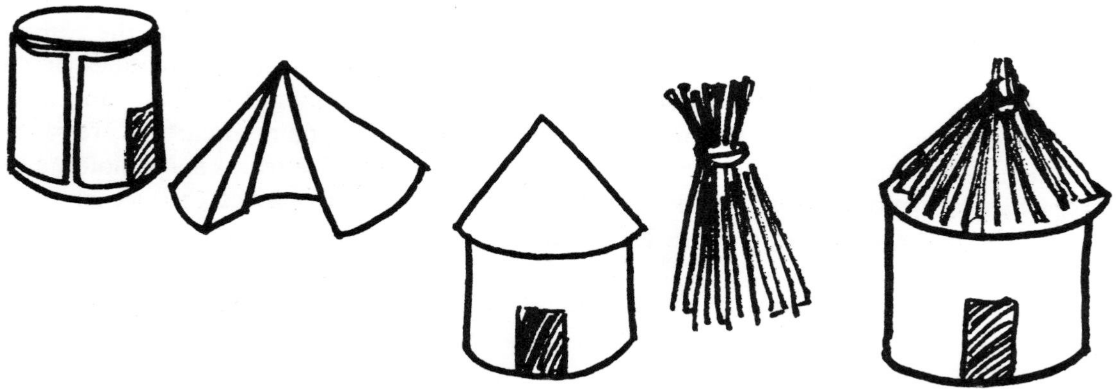

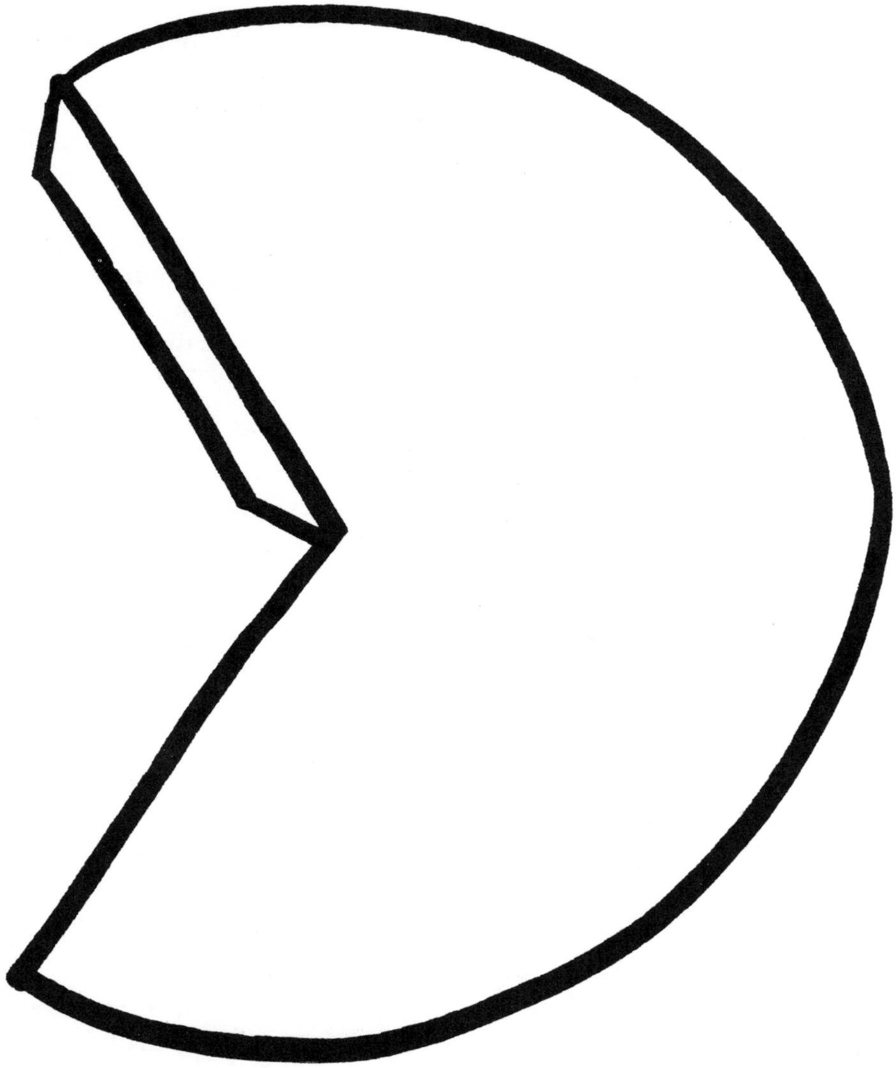

Fig. 9.22.

Fig. 9.23.

12. Another new discovery for Columbus and his men was maize, or corn. This plant, previously unknown to the European world, was to become very important. Some of the Indians popped the corn they grew and wore it as a corsage. Share Tomie dePaola's *The Popcorn Book*. Then let the children pop a batch of popcorn and string it to make necklaces. Of course, the group will want to snack on it, too!
(Preschool, primary)

13. Columbus reported that the Indians ate fish, birds, crabs, spiders, white worms, iguanas, coon oysters, lobsters, and hutia (rats). Though many of these items seem strange to us, the Arawaks had a very healthy diet. Ask the group to describe the strangest things they have ever eaten. If possible, get some samples of exotic foods, such as chocolate-covered ants, and bring them in to share with the group. Make lobsters from egg cartons, as shown in figure 9.24. For each lobster, cut a strip of four or five cups for the lobster's body. Paint it red. Cut claws from red construction paper and tape them on underneath the body. Make antennae from red pipe cleaners.
(Preschool, primary, intermediate)

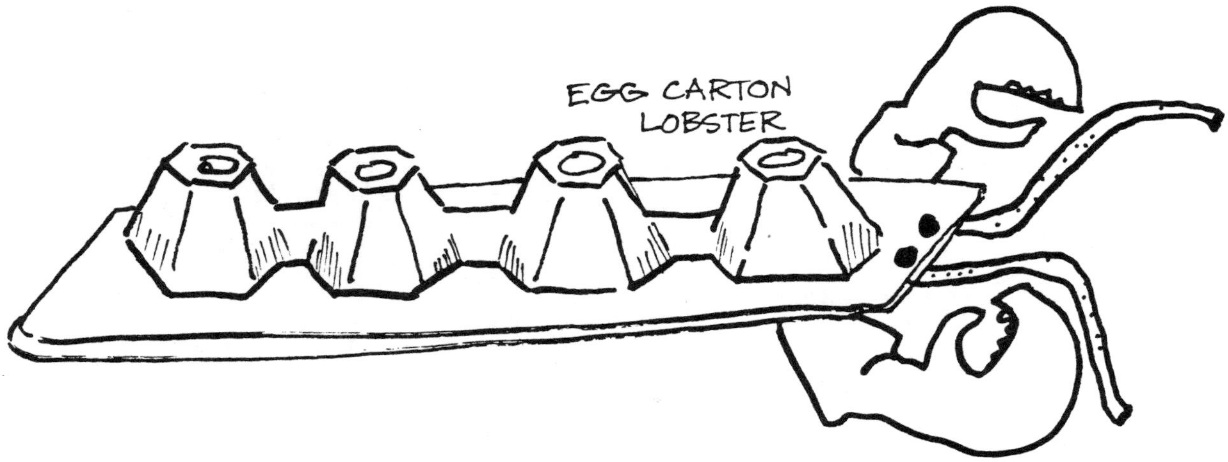

Fig. 9.24.

14. Columbus wrote about how much he admired the marine life of the coral reefs around the islands he visited. Share some books on tropical fish with the group to give them an idea of how colorful these fish are, such as Patricia McCarthy's *Ocean Parade* and Cynthia Overbeck's *The Fish Book*. If possible, bring in fish from an aquarium or pet store. Use the patterns in figure 9.25 and let the children make their own colorful fish to hang around the library or classroom.
(Preschool, primary, intermediate)

15. Much of the animal life he found on the islands he visited was strange to Columbus. He described large "serpents" that were actually iguanas, and other snakes and reptiles. Share a couple of picture books, such as *Have You Seen the Crocodile?* by Colin West and *Snakes Are Hunters* by Patricia Lauber. Let the children make some of these creatures. Cut iguanas from a folded piece of

Fig. 9.25.

paper, as shown in figure 9.26, and decorate them. Use the snake pattern in figure 9.27 for the children to color, cut out, and hang.

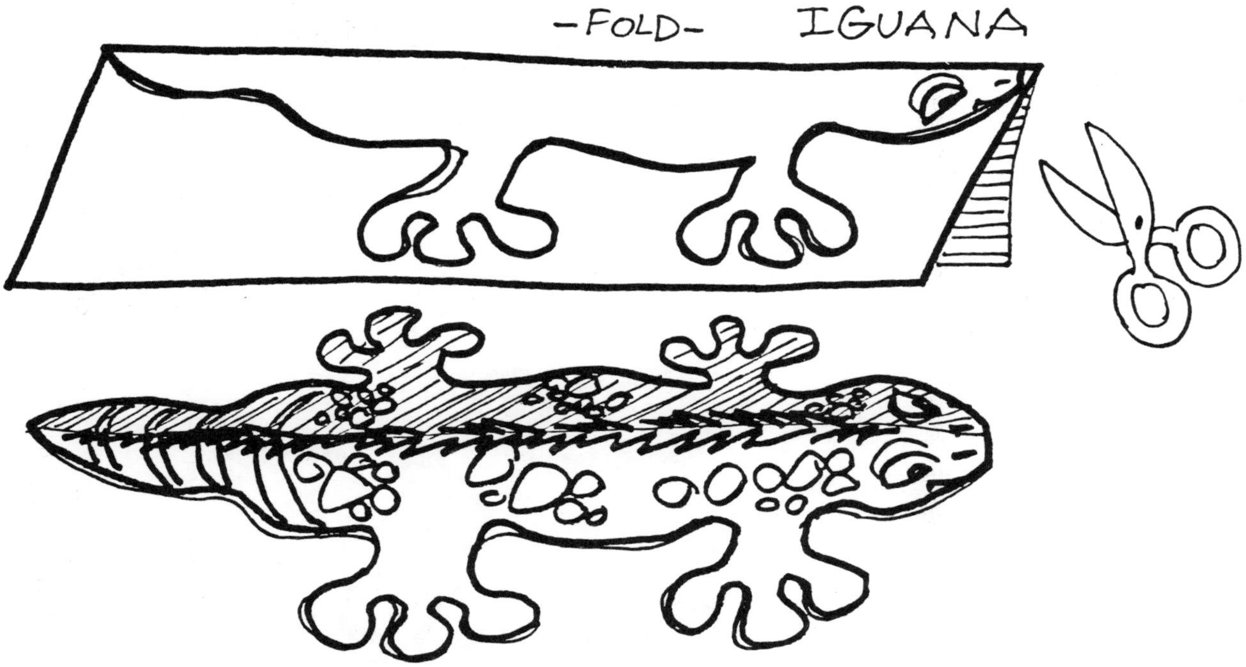

Fig. 9.26.

Make alligators from cardboard. You can make small versions from posterboard or large, "life-size" ones from heavier cardboard. Cut out the body in the shape shown in figure 9.28, cutting two slits on the bottom of the body. Make the legs separately, with slits that can be inserted into the slits on the body. After assembly, the alligator can be decorated with torn scraps of green paper or painted with poster paint.
(Preschool, primary)

16. Everywhere Columbus went, the islanders brought him colorful parrots as gifts. Share some books about parrots with the group, such as *Exotic Birds* by Marilyn Singer and *Papagayo the Mischief Maker* by Gerald McDermott. The book *I Discover Columbus* by Robert Lawson is about a parrot who aids Columbus on his voyage.

(Text continues on page 215.)

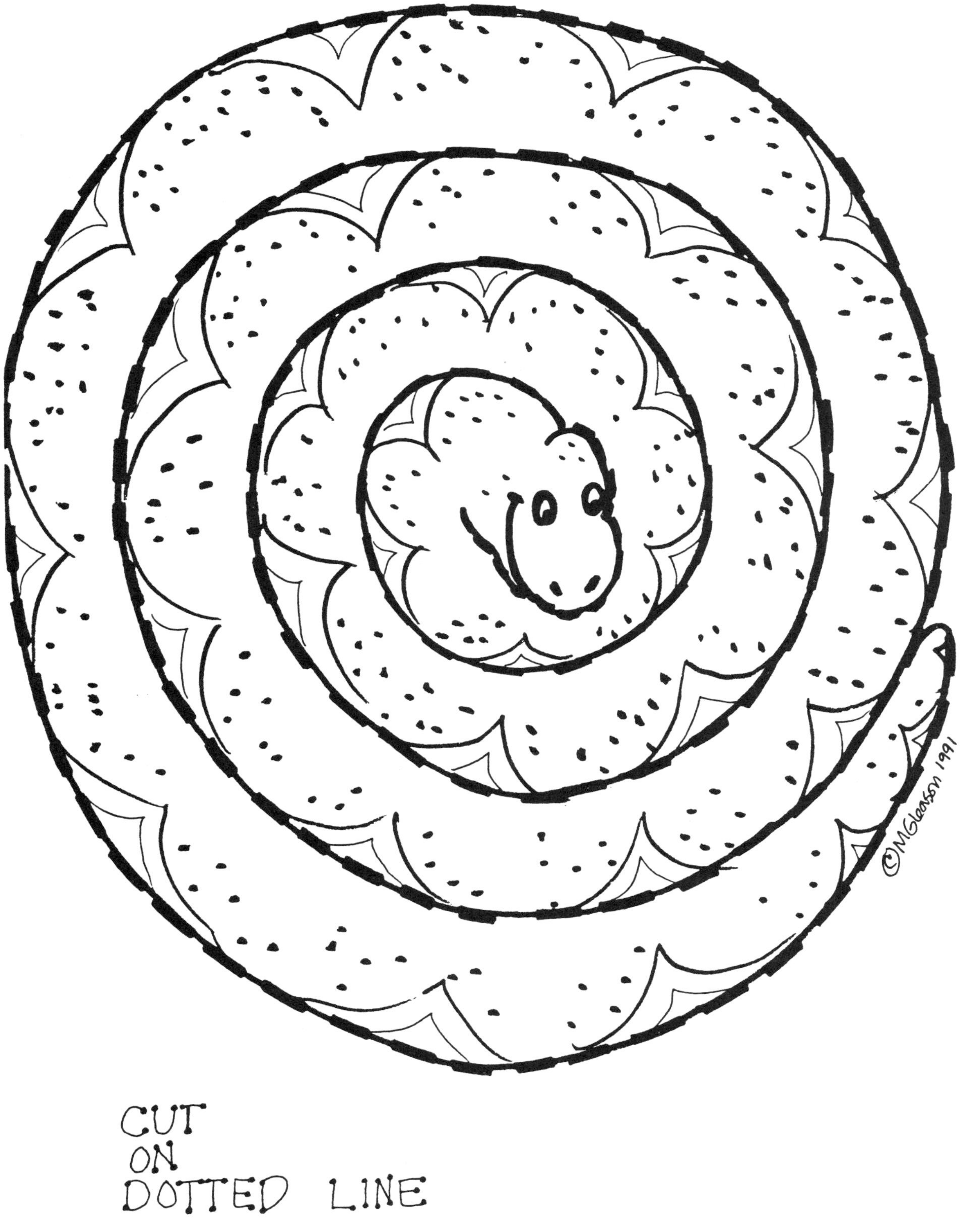

Fig. 9.27.

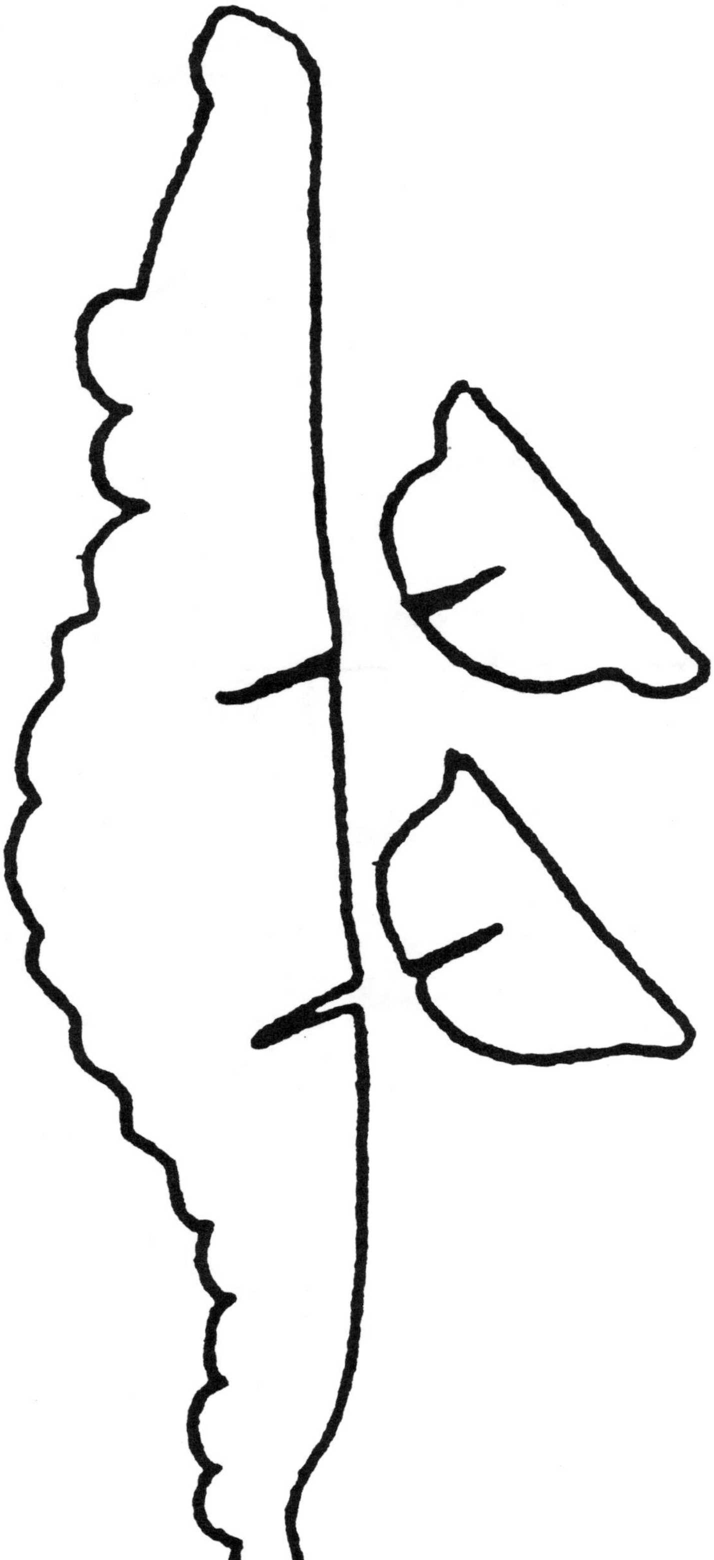

Fig. 9.28.

The group can make parrots from homemade clay that has been rolled out and cut into the shape shown in figure 9.29. Before drying the clay, use a drinking straw to poke holes for the eye, wings, and tail, as shown. Decorate the parrot shapes with paints. Thread a string, yarn, or ribbon through the eye for hanging. Wing and tail feathers can be made from thin strips of fabric or ribbons.
(Primary, intermediate)

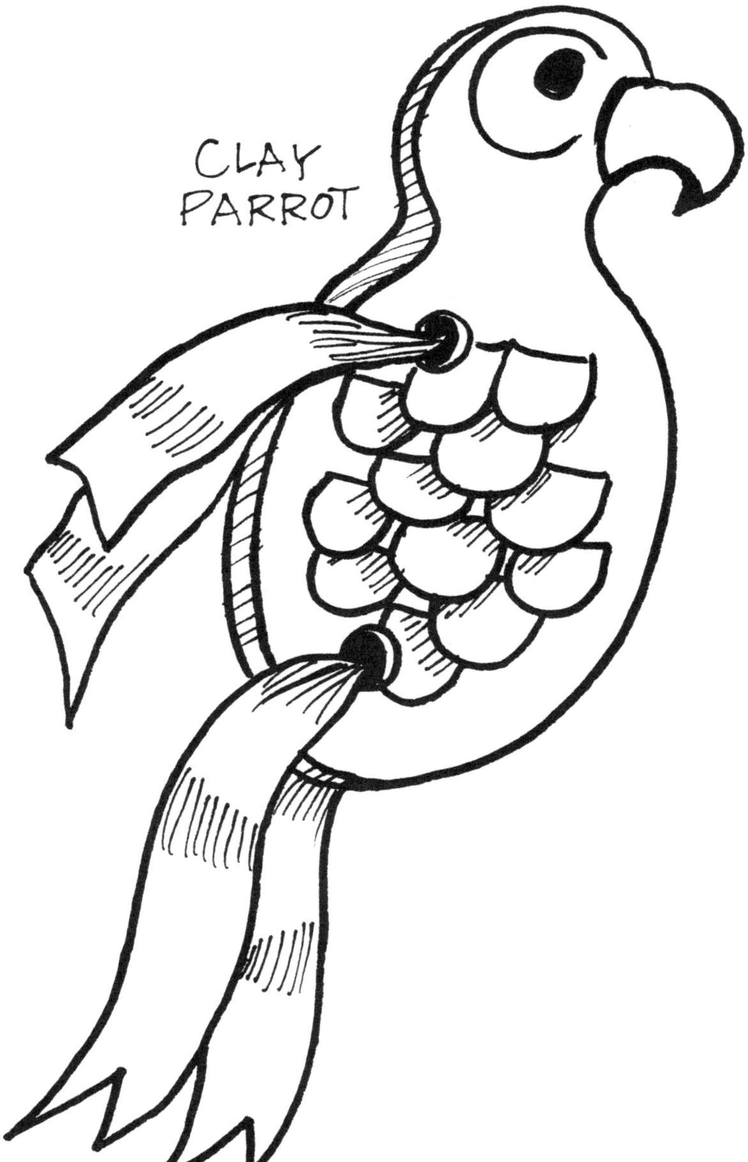

Fig. 9.29.

17. Columbus believed he saw mermaids in the Caribbean, but they were actually sea cows, or manatees. Show the children a picture of a manatee from a book such as Kathy Darling's *Manatee on Location*, and ask whether they think it looks like a mermaid. Older children might enjoy the novel *Fishman and Charlie* by Gibbs Davis, about a pet manatee.

Read about mermaids and make mermaids from bathroom-tissue rolls. You can share the books *Paddy under Water* by John Goodall, *Sea Tale* by Gail Haley, and *Hansy's Mermaid* by Trinka Hakes Noble. William Cole's collection *The Sea, Ships and Sailors* includes the song "The Mermaid." To make a mermaid, draw a line about one-third of the way down the bathroom-tissue roll. Above this line, wrap the roll with pink construction paper. Below the line, wrap green construction paper (see fig. 9.30). The upper part is the mermaid's body. Wrap a thin strip of construction paper (any color) around the body to resemble a bathing-suit top. Cut two paper arms from pink construction paper and attach them to either side of the body. Make the head from a small, plastic foam ball or a ping-pong ball, glued to the top of the tube. Use yarn to create hair, and draw on facial features with markers. Finish the bottom two-thirds by covering it with small pieces of tin foil as scales. You can cut a tail fin from cardboard or construction paper and add it to the side of the tube. (Preschool, primary, intermediate)

Fig. 9.30.

18. When Columbus reached the island of Hispaniola, he met one of the wealthiest tribes he had encountered. He exchanged gifts with the king, or cacique, giving him a red cloak and gloves, along with other items. In return, the king, Guacanagari, gave Columbus a mask of hammered gold. The children can make similar masks from aluminum foil, like the one shown in figure 9.31. One method is to cut a mask from posterboard and cover it with foil. To etch in a design, use a pencil on the posterboard inside of the mask.
(Primary, intermediate)

Fig. 9.31.

THE SHIPWRECK

On the night of December 24, 1492, the *Santa Maria* was sailing along the coast of Hispaniola. Columbus was sleeping, having left the ship in charge of the master, Juan de la Cosa. When de la Cosa became tired, he turned the ship over to one of the ship's boys. While everyone was asleep, the ship ran aground. Despite Columbus's efforts to save it, the *Santa Maria* was wrecked on the coral reef. Though all the men were saved, Columbus found himself stranded with only one ship and too many men to carry on her.

Though at first this seemed like a disaster, Columbus convinced himself that it was really a sign from God that he should start a colony on Hispaniola. He used the timber from the wrecked ship to build a fort and left thirty-nine men on the island to continue the search for gold while he sailed back to Spain. As he was preparing to depart, the *Pinta* sailed back into view. Pinzon claimed to have become accidentally separated from the fleet but said he had found gold. The two ships departed together.

The return trip to Spain was much more difficult than the outward voyage. By this time, a feeling of jealousy and distrust had arisen between Columbus and Pinzon. Each wanted to be the first to return and claim credit for their discoveries. When their ships were separated in a severe storm, Columbus worried that Pinzon would arrive first and steal his glory. One storm drove Columbus ashore on an island of the Azores, and because this was Portuguese territory, several of his men were promptly arrested. Columbus talked his way free and set off again, but another storm forced him to land in Portugal before reaching home. While there, he had an audience with King John, who must have been frustrated at Columbus's success after he had refused to sponsor the voyage.

The *Pinta* was not lost but arrived on the north coast of Spain before Columbus returned. Pinzon sent a message to Ferdinand and Isabella, but they refused to see him without Columbus, so he continued to Palos. The *Niña* and the *Pinta* arrived back in Palos on the same day. Martin Alonso Pinzon was said to be so disappointed in not receiving credit for his discoveries that he left his ship, went directly to his home, and died almost immediately. Columbus went on to a glorious reception in Spain.

Book List

Ardizzone, Edward. *Little Tim and the Brave Sea Captain*. Henry Z. Walck, 1952. (PreK-2)
Tim runs away to sea and encounters many adventures, including a shipwreck.

Fine, John Christopher. *Sunken Ships and Treasure*. Macmillan, 1986. (Gr. 5-up)
A description of how sunken ships are excavated.

Gennings, Sara. *The Atocha Treasure*. Rourke, 1988. (Gr. 4-up)
A look at a real-life treasure hunt.

Gibbons, Gail. *Sunken Treasure*. Crowell, 1988. (Gr. 2-5)
In picture-book format, Gibbons examines the finding of the Spanish galleon *Atocha*.

Hayes, Geoffrey. *The Secret of Foghorn Island*. Random House, 1988. (PreK-3)
In this story, Otto and his uncle investigate shipwrecks.

Johnson, Sylvia. *Coral Reefs*. Lerner, 1984. (Gr. 3-up)
Stunning color photographs and clear text help children understand what a coral reef is like.

O'Byrne-Pelham, Fran, and Bernadette Balcer. *The Search for the Atocha Treasure*. Dillon, 1989. (Gr. 4-7)
Another look at the discovery of this sunken ship.

Tayntor, Elizabeth, Paul Erickson, and Les Kaufman. *Dive to the Coral Reefs*. Crown, 1986. (Gr. 3-up)
Beautiful color photographs accompany this description of the formation and life of a coral reef.

Related Activities

1. On Christmas Eve, while everyone except a cabin boy slept, the *Santa Maria* ran aground on a coral reef. Despite Columbus's effort to save it, the ship was wrecked. Show the children what a coral reef looks like with the books *Coral Reefs* and *Dive to the Coral Reefs*. Then read a couple of books about shipwrecks, such as Geoffrey Hayes's *The Secret of Foghorn Island* and Edward Ardizzone's *Little Tim and the Brave Sea Captain*.
(Preschool, primary)

2. All his life, Columbus saw events as acts of God to show him the way he should go, as he saw the wreck of the *Santa Maria*. He believed that he was named Christopher for its meaning in Latin, "Christ-bearer," indicating he was destined to bring the word of Christ to the unconverted Indians.

Have a discussion about fate. Do the children in your group believe people are predestined to act in certain ways? Or do they feel that Columbus was simply unable to acknowledge the mistake of his shipwreck and was trying to make a bad situation look like something he had planned?

Explain the expressions "Every cloud has a silver lining" and "If life gives you lemons, make lemonade." Tell the children that Columbus followed this philosophy. Is this a realistic way to look at life? Always? Sometimes? Are there circumstances when this might not be a useful outlook?

Play a game in which you give an example of a catastrophe, such as having a tree fall on your house, having your car roll into the ocean, or missing an important appointment. Let the children take turns trying to come up with reasons that these events may have outcomes that could be interpreted as useful or beneficial.
(Preschool, primary)

3. The remains of the *Santa Maria* have been searched for off the coast of San Salvador but have never been found. According to accounts that have come down to us, the Indians of the island helped Columbus and his men remove all the supplies from the ship. The only remains of the *Santa Maria* to have been found is her anchor. Let the children make anchors. Cut an anchor shape from a piece of black posterboard and attach it to a piece of twine.
(Preschool, primary)

4. Ask children to pretend they are underwater archaeologists who find the *Santa Maria*, discovering many items left on the wreck. They can write about what they imagine they might find. To get them started, share some of the books listed above about searches for sunken ships.
(Primary, intermediate)

5. Columbus left thirty-nine of his men at Fort Navidad on Hispaniola when he returned to Spain. The men were all very anxious to stay because they believed they would soon find the source of the islanders' gold. Before he left, Columbus appointed leaders for the group and gave them a list of rules:

- The men should pray and thank God.
- They should obey the captains.
- They should show respect for the Indians.
- They should do the Indians no harm.
- They should stay together.
- They should suffer their solitude (in other words, try not to become downhearted because of their isolation).
- They should discover the gold mines, barter with the Indians for more gold, and settle a new village.
- Finally, he promised to ask the Spanish sovereigns to favor them.

Ask the children to imagine that they are Columbus, leaving for Spain after setting up Fort Navidad. Do they think his rules were useful? What other rules might he have made? Ask them to create their own rules for the colonists using copies of figure 9.32.
(Intermediate)

Fort Navidad – Rules for Government

I, Christopher Columbus, leave you, my men from the shipwrecked *Santa Maria*, with the following rules to govern you during my absence to Spain.

1. ______________________________

2. ______________________________

3. ______________________________

4. ______________________________

5. ______________________________

6. ______________________________

7. ______________________________

8. ______________________________

Fig. 9.32.

6. Ask the children whether they would have been willing to be left behind in a strange land. What inducement would they need to make them want to stay, as Columbus's men had the inducement of finding gold? Ask them to imagine themselves in a similar situation while traveling with a shuttle fleet to a new planet. If they were chosen to be left behind, how would they feel? (Intermediate)

THE WELCOME HOME

When Columbus arrived back in Spain, it was to great acclaim. Ferdinand and Isabella summoned him to court to report on his adventures, and as he traveled through the countryside, his progress was like a parade. He had with him several Indians and caskets of gold, along with gaudy parrots and strange plants.

When Columbus arrived at the court, he was heaped with the highest honors. Ferdinand and Isabella gave him a seat next to them and confirmed all the rewards they had promised him. This period was to mark the high point of Columbus's life. He made three more voyages to the New World, but, although his discovery attracted fame, he faded further and further into disfavor and obscurity.

Book List

Burningham, John. *John Patrick Norman McHennessy—The Boy Who Was Always Late*. Crown, 1987. (K-3)
John Patrick Norman McHennessy's teacher never believes his excuses for being late.

Crews, Donald. *Parade*. Greenwillow, 1983. (PreK-1)
A colorful look at the excitement of a parade.

Schauffler, Robert Haven. *Days We Celebrate*. Dodd, Mead, 1940. (Gr. 4-up)
This collection includes the poems "Boob Ballads" and "Q.E.D."

Zemach, Harve. *The Judge*. Farrar, Straus & Giroux, 1969. (K-3)
The judge never believes any of the witnesses who describe a catastrophe approaching—until it is too late.

Related Activities

1. According to one legend, when Columbus returned from his first voyage, someone stated that anybody could have done what he did. He replied by asking everyone present to try to stand an egg on its end. No one could do it. Then Columbus took the egg, tapped it on the table to flatten part of the shell, stood the egg on end, and said, "It's easy once you know how."

Tell the children this story and then ask them to pretend to be Columbus and write a how-to for explorers. They should imagine someplace they are planning to send an exploration party and describe each step the explorers should take to reach their destination, in order, with illustrations. (Primary, intermediate)

2. Columbus was called to court, and as he traveled through Spain he was greeted in each town as a hero. Share the picture book *Parade* by Donald Crews to help the children imagine what it must have been like. Jean Fritz's *The Great Adventure of Christopher Columbus* (listed in the section "Land Ho!") also presents a graphic picture of this triumphal procession. When Columbus arrived at court, Ferdinand and Isabella gave him a seat next to them and asked him all about his voyage. They confirmed all the rewards they had promised him. This was probably the proudest and happiest day of Christopher Columbus's life. Ask the children to imagine their own day of triumph and to describe it. They could describe something that has already happened or what they imagine it would be like to have their most cherished dream come true.
(Preschool, primary, intermediate)

3. After his first voyage, Columbus began to sign his name on all written documents in the way shown in figure 9.33. Although no one knows exactly what all of these symbols meant, the last line

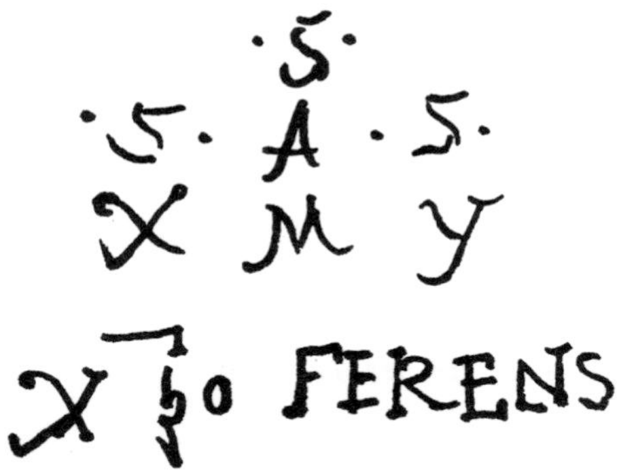

Fig. 9.33.

probably indicates the name *Christopher*, because it shows the Greek letters *XNO*, meaning "Christ," and *ferens*, which is the Latin word for "bearing." The first four letters may stand for the Latin words *servus sum altissima salvatoris*, which means "Servant am I of the most high Savior." The *X* in the third line may stand for Christ again.

After showing children this mysterious signature, ask them to design their own secret signatures. The symbols must refer to things about themselves that they think are significant. They could use a variant of their name or the version of their name from another language. They can include a secret code if they want.
(Primary, intermediate)

4. As a result of his discovery, Columbus was made a nobleman and given the title "Don Christobal Colon, Admiral of the Ocean Sea." He received a coat of arms, which included the castle of Castile, the lion of Leon, a group of islands to represent his discovery, and anchors to symbolize his admiralty. A picture of the coat of arms is included in many of the books about Columbus. Show one of these pictures to the children, and then give them copies of the blank coat of arms in figure 9.34 to design one of their own. Tell them the symbols should actually be related to something about themselves.
(Primary, intermediate)

Fig. 9.34.

5. Share two poems from Robert Haven Schauffler's *Days We Celebrate*: "Boob Ballads" by Berton Braley and "Q.E.D." by Dorothy Brown Thompson. Also use the picture books *John Patrick Norman McHennessy—The Boy Who Was Always Late* by John Burningham and *The Judge* by Harve Zemach. All of these express what Columbus must have felt—"I told you so!" (Primary, intermediate)

10

Columbus's Later Voyages

The activities and resources in this chapter are designed to help children understand this late period of Columbus's life. First, the second voyage and establishment of a colony are covered. The story of his continued search for the Indies is looked at next, including his experience of being marooned on the island of Jamaica for a year. The final section looks at his death and tries to evaluate who he was.

THE SECOND VOYAGE OF COLONIZATION

On Columbus's second voyage, he was still full of high hopes, sure that he would find the Indies around the next bend. It was this voyage that Columbus saw as his great colonizing effort. He sailed with 17 ships and over 1,200 men. He also took sheep, pigs, cows, chickens, horses, and seeds for growing crops. One plant he took with him was to have a far-reaching impact on the future of both the New World and the Old. The cultivation of sugarcane ushered in one of the darkest periods in the history of the Americas—that of slavery.

This importation of new foods and animals into the American continents was to change the New World forever. Many of the most enduring stereotypes of the Americas—cowboys, horses, cattle ranches, citrus fruits—were born in this meeting of worlds, having traveled across the Atlantic with Columbus. In addition, the products of the New World inevitably changed the Old, also creating new customs that people today see as ancient characteristics about certain countries but that were actually born in 1493. Before this date, corn, potatoes, tomatoes, and many other foods were totally unknown in Europe.

On arriving back at Hispaniola, Columbus expected to find a thriving colony at Fort Navidad. Instead, he discovered that all the men he had left there were dead. This was the beginning of a series of disasters for Columbus. He established a new colony called Isabella and continued his search for the actual landmass of the Indies, which he was sure lay somewhere in the area.

Book List

Aliki. *Corn Is Maize: The Gift of the Indians*. Crowell, 1976. (Gr. 2-4)
An introduction to the origins and uses of corn.

Barbour, Karen. *Little Nino's Pizzeria*. Harcourt Brace Jovanovich, 1987. (PreK-3)
A picture book about an Italian-American family's pizza parlor.

Dutton, Cheryl. *Not in Here, Dad*. Barron's, 1989. (K-3)
A family will not let Dad smoke in the house.

Fischetto, Laura. *All Pigs on Deck*. Delacorte, 1991. (K-3)
A picture-book description of Columbus's second voyage to the New World.

Freedman, Russell. *Farm Babies*. Holiday House, 1988. (Gr. 2-4)
An introduction to farm animals.

Ipcar, Dahlov. *Horses of Long Ago*. Doubleday, 1965. (Gr. 3-6)
This title presents the history of the horse and how the horse has affected history since earliest times.

Jurmain, Suzanne. *Once upon a Horse: A History of Horses and How They Shaped Our History*. Lothrop, Lee & Shepard, 1989. (Gr. 4-up)
A history of the horse.

Khalsa, Dayal Kaur. *How Pizza Came to Queens*. Crown, 1989. (K-3)
Pizza returns to the New World with an Italian visitor.

Maestro, Betsy. *Ferryboat*. Crowell, 1986. (PreK-2)
A ferry boat is introduced when a family goes for a ride on one.

Mitgutsch, Ali. *From Cacao Bean to Chocolate*. Carolrhoda, 1981. (Gr. 1-3)
A look at how the cacao bean becomes chocolate.

Peet, Bill. *Chester the Worldly Pig*. Houghton Mifflin, 1978. (K-3)
Chester is saved from becoming dinner when someone notices that his spots resemble a world map.

Politi, Leo. *Three Stalks of Corn*. Scribner's, 1976. (K-3)
A young Hispanic girl learns about corn from her grandmother.

Seixas, Judith S. *Tobacco: What It Is, What It Does*. Greenwillow, 1981. (Gr. 1-4)
Describes the history of tobacco and the consequences of smoking.

Tobias, Tobi. *The Quitting Deal*. Viking, 1975. (K-3)
A young girl makes a bargain with her mother to quit smoking.

Ventura, Piero. *Man and the Horse*. Putnam, 1980. (Gr. 4-up)
Covers the uses of horses throughout history including their introduction into the New World.

Williams, Garth. *Baby Farm Animals*. Western, 1983. (Gr. 1-3)
Describes various farm animals.

Young, Ruth. *Daisy's Taxi*. Orchard, 1991. (PreK-2)
Daisy runs a ferry boat that takes a large variety of goods back and forth for people living on an island.

Related Activities

1. Ask the children to imagine that they are Columbus trying to recruit colonizers for the West Indies. Ask them to devise a publicity campaign that could have been used. How could Columbus get the word out that he was looking for people to sail back to Hispaniola with him? What group should he target? What kinds of people would make good colonists? What skills should they have? How should Columbus describe Hispaniola? What would be the advantages of going? What would be the disadvantages, and how could they be made to sound minimal?
(Primary, intermediate)

2. Ask the children to imagine that they have signed up to go to Hispaniola as colonists. Let them write about their decision. Why did they decide to go? What and whom are they leaving behind? What do they expect to find? What do they think they will need to take with them? Do they anticipate returning to Spain in the future? Do they realize that they will be cut off from the Old World for long periods and will depend on ships from Spain for the kinds of goods they have been accustomed to? You might want to share the books *Ferryboat* by Betsy Maestro and *Daisy's Taxi* by Ruth Young, to help children understand what living on an island is like.
(Primary, intermediate)

3. Columbus took with him on the second voyage a variety of livestock and seeds, to enable his settlement to sustain itself. Pigs, horses, cows, sheep, goats, and chickens were some of the animals he took. Introduce this second voyage with the book *All Pigs on Deck* by Laura Fischetto. For very small children, talk about farm animals, and explain that their presence in the Americas is the result of Columbus's voyage. Use books such as Russell Freedman's *Farm Babies* and Garth Williams's *Baby Farm Animals*.

The children can make a diorama of what it must have been like on board. Use a tabletop as your ship, and have the children make clothespin animals, as shown in figure 10.1. Cut animal shapes from construction paper without including the legs. Draw on details and color. Clip on two clothespins where the animals' legs should be and stand the animals on the table.

Ask your group to decide how they would manage the animals on board. How would they keep the horses and cows from being tossed about and getting hurt? How would they feed the animals?
(Preschool, primary, intermediate)

4. Just for fun, read Bill Peet's book *Chester the Worldly Pig*, about a pig who goes off to seek his fortune and finds out it is on his back all the time. Then give the children outlines of pigs and tell them to draw maps on the pigs' backs. Ask the group to do some research to find out what became of some of the pigs that escaped and ran wild. (Hint: What is a razorback?)
(Primary, intermediate)

Fig. 10.1.

5. Horses were another import from Europe that permanently and radically changed the face of the New World. As we will see below, the conquistadors used horses to devastating effect in conquering the New World. But horses have had a profound effect on the whole history of humans. Use the books *Horses of Long Ago* by Dahlov Ipcar, *Once upon a Horse* by Suzanne Jurmain, and *Man and the Horse* by Piero Ventura to introduce the effects the horse has had on history. Younger children might enjoy making hobbyhorses. To make hobbyhorses, stuff grocery bags with newspaper for the heads and draw on features. Insert a long wrapping-paper tube into the bag and tie it on. The children can ride their horses by attaching a string as a bridle around the bags.
(Primary, intermediate)

6. We often have fixed ideas of what certain countries are like and assume that they have always been that way. For example, ask the children in your group to tell you what foods come to mind when they think of Italy. Chances are they will say pizza and spaghetti and meatballs with tomato sauce. Point out that before Columbus, tomatoes had not been introduced to Europe, so these foods were unknown at that time. Share some books about pizza, such as *Little Nino's Pizzeria* by Karen Barbour and *How Pizza Came to Queens* by Dayal Kaur Khalsa. Share a pizza to commemorate this transfer of culture.
(Preschool, primary, intermediate)

7. Corn is another product that made the transfer from the New World to the Old. Before Columbus, such foods as polenta and other corn-based dishes were not part of the diet of Europeans. Use the books *Corn Is Maize* by Aliki and *Three Stalks of Corn* by Leo Politi to introduce corn. Then let the children make ears of corn using the pattern in figure 10.2. Tear small pieces of red, brown, yellow, and orange paper to glue on as kernals.
(Preschool, primary)

Fig. 10.2.

8. One plant that caused a kind of revolution when it was introduced into Europe from the West Indies was tobacco. In his log, Columbus describes seeing the Indians he met smoking rolled leaves of this plant. He brought these leaves back to Europe, where tobacco smoking became immensely popular. Start a discussion about tobacco and smoking using the books *Not in Here, Dad* by Cheryl Dutton, *The Quitting Deal* by Tobi Tobias, and *Tobacco: What It Is, What It Does* by Judith Seixas.

Ask your group to imagine what life would be like if tobacco had never been discovered. You could research the topic to find out how much money is spent yearly on tobacco, on cancer research, on medical services to smokers, and on advertising. Have your group try to find out why smoking has never been prohibited by law. What effect has the growing of tobacco had on U.S. agriculture? (Intermediate)

9. Several products that were introduced to Europe from the Americas include beans, peanuts, papaya, cacao beans, pineapple, pepper, strawberries, and avocados. Plants introduced to the Americas from Europe include oranges, lemons, limes, mangos, bamboo, bananas, coconuts, and sugarcane. Assign various plants to members of your group to research. Ask them to find out about the plants' origins, locations, climate needed, commercial uses, and food uses. Then explain that this whole transfer of goods is called the "Columbian exchange." Your group can plan and share a meal that includes only foods found in Europe before Columbus's voyage and one with only pre-Columbian foods of the Americas.

One book to share is *From Cacao Bean to Chocolate* by Ali Mitgutsch. Make paper chains of fruits and vegetables to hang around your room. First, fold a long strip of paper accordion-wise. Draw a simple outline of a food on one end of the long strip, making sure the top and bottom of the item meet the folds (see fig. 10.3). Cut out the shapes, but do not cut through the folds. Open for a long chain, and let the children decorate the chains.
(Primary, intermediate)

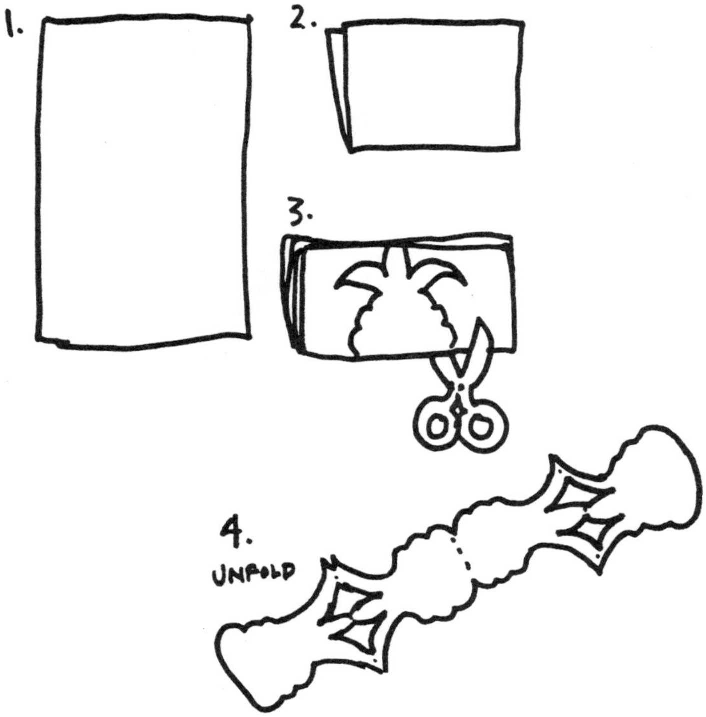

Fig. 10.3.

COLUMBUS'S CONTINUING QUEST FOR THE INDIES

It is hard for us to comprehend in retrospect Columbus's inability to perceive the truth of his discovery. To the end of his life he was convinced that he had found the Indies—he just could not locate them exactly. Because of this misconception, he was more concerned with continuing his explorations than he was with the more mundane but necessary business of governing the colony. When he found Cuba, he was convinced it was part of the Chinese mainland and even made his men take an oath to that effect.

During his third voyage, he actually landed on the coast of South America, but rather than admit that he had found a new continent, at one point he decided he had found the Garden of Eden. It would be another man, sailing with one of the rebels from Hispaniola in 1499, who would correctly identify what Columbus had discovered and pass his name on to it—Amerigo Vespucci.

Book List

Alper, Ann Fitzpatrick. *Forgotten Voyager: The Story of Amerigo Vespucci*. Carolrhoda, 1991. (Gr. 4-7)
A biography of the man who gave his name to the New World.

Baker, Nina Brown. *Amerigo Vespucci*. Knopf, 1959. (Gr. 3-6)
Another look at this other discoverer of the Americas.

Davis, Maggie S. *The Best Way to Ripton*. Holiday House, 1982. (PreK-2)
An old man seeking directions is told all the ways *not* to get to Ripton.

Heine, Helme. *The Pearl*. Atheneum, 1985. (K-3)
The finder of an oyster imagines that it might contain a pearl.

Syme, Ronald. *Amerigo Vespucci: Scientist and Sailor*. Morrow, 1969. (Gr. 4-6)
Syme presents Vespucci, who in many accounts is a man of somewhat questionable character, as the epitome of honor and truth.

Related Activities

1. Though Columbus is often praised for his imagination and vision in coming up with the idea to sail west to reach the East, he was very limited in his concept of geography. He had convinced himself that the world was arranged in a certain way, and he could not admit that the reality might be different. Share the picture book *The Best Way to Ripton* by Maggie Davis, in which a man is given instructions on the best way not to get to Ripton, and explain that Columbus seemed to have discovered the best way not to reach the Indies.

On his third voyage to the Caribbean, Columbus actually reached the shores of South America but could not reconcile it with his view of the world. Therefore, he decided he must have found the Garden of Eden. Have the children write a travelogue for the Garden of Eden as if it were a real place one could sail to.
(Primary, intermediate)

2. During his explorations along the coast of Central and South America, as he searched for a way to the Indies, Columbus discovered Indians who fished for pearl oysters in the Gulf of Paria. By this time, he had become so focused both on gold and the Indies that he virtually ignored this source of wealth. Read Helme Heine's book *The Pearl*, about greed and the destruction it can conceivably bring about. Then use the pattern in figure 10.4 to make pearl oysters. Give each child a fake pearl, found at craft shops, to glue inside his or her oyster.
(Primary, intermediate)

3. North and South America were not named for Columbus, even though he is considered the man who found them in that he was the first European to establish lasting contact with the New World. The honor of having the New World named for him went to Amerigo Vespucci, another Genoese explorer. In 1499, Vespucci sailed across the Atlantic with Alonso de Ojeda, one of Columbus's former colonists, and reached the shore of South America. He later wrote a letter describing the new lands he had reached and stating that he believed they were not just an extension of the Far East, but another world altogether. In 1510, the German cartographer Martin Waldseemüller printed a map with the name *America* on it, because of what Vespucci had written. For many years, it was believed that Vespucci was a fraud and that he had never actually visited the New World, and thus stole Columbus's glory. However, his history has been reexamined and many people do believe he actually did what he said.

Have your group read some of the biographies listed above about Vespucci, and hold a debate about whether or not they think Vespucci was telling the truth.
(Primary, intermediate)

4. Hold a debate to decide what the Americas should really have been named. Should they have been named Columbia, after Columbus, or should they have been named for some earlier or later explorer? Or should they have received a name that acknowledged the original inhabitants of the continents? Have your group vote on a name, and then make a large class map labeled with this new name.
(Primary, intermediate)

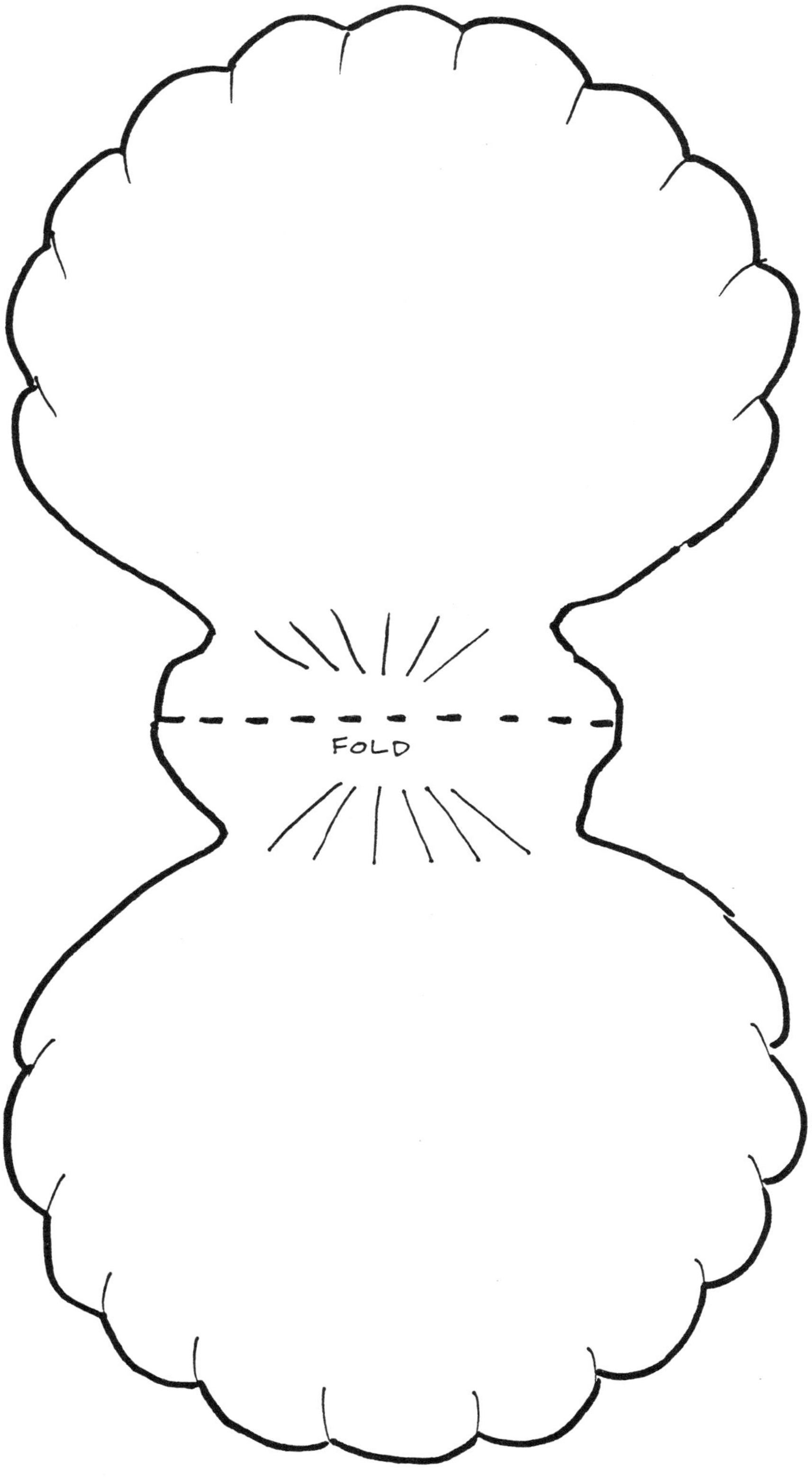

Fig. 10.4.

REBELLION, SLAVERY, AND GREED

While Columbus continued his explorations, the colony of Isabella was floundering. The colonists were unruly, did not want to work, and had expected instant wealth. Instead, they found themselves far from home and known comforts, in an "uncivilized" land. They acted accordingly. They plundered, abused, and enslaved the Indians, rebelled against Columbus's government, and complained of conditions to Spain.

In addition, another devastating exchange was going on—that of diseases. Many colonists fell ill of fevers and malaria. The Indians suffered even more. Because they had never encountered European diseases and therefore had no immunities, whole tribes were wiped out by epidemics of smallpox, measles, and flu.

Columbus tried to set up a new colony in a more healthful location, called Santo Domingo. But the whole "great enterprise" Columbus had envisioned had become a mad rush for plunder. Greed was the primary motivation of most of the colonists, many of whom were the younger sons of noble Spanish families. They had no future in Spain, as they did not inherit anything from their families, and so they came to the New World looking for glory and gain. But not work—they considered themselves above that.

Eventually the situation deteriorated so much that Ferdinand and Isabella sent a replacement governor to Santo Domingo to investigate. He arrived on the island to find a scene of chaos. A number of Spaniards had rebelled and were hanged for treason. The new governor promptly sent Columbus home in chains. Though Columbus was pardoned when he arrived in Spain and explained the situation to Ferdinand and Isabella, they did not return the governorship of Hispaniola to him. In fact, on his fourth voyage, he was forbidden by them to land on Hispaniola until he was on the way home.

Book List

Anderson, Joan. *A Williamsburg Household*. Ticknor & Fields, 1988.
This photo essay contrasts the lives of slaves and their owners.

Avi. *Something Upstairs: A Tale of Ghosts*. Franklin Watts, 1988. (Gr. 5-7)
When Kenny moves to a new house, he discovers the ghosts of slaves in his attic.

Carle, Eric. *Rooster's Off to See the World*. Picture Book Studio, 1972. (PreK-1)
A number of animals follow Rooster off to see the world, until they realize he has made no plans for taking care of them.

Christopher, John. *Empty World*. Dutton, 1978. (Gr. 5-8)
A boy is left alone in a world decimated by disease.

dePaola, Tomie. *Bill and Pete*. Putnam, 1978. (PreK-3)
When William Everett, a crocodile, is captured to become a suitcase, his friend and toothbrush rescues him.

Evitts, William. *Captive Bodies, Free Spirits*. Messner, 1985. (Gr. 5-up)
This is a history of slavery in the U.S. South.

Grimm, Jacob, and Wilhelm K. Grimm. *The Fisherman and His Wife*. Picture Book Studio, 1988. (PreK-4)

The fairy tale about a greedy woman and her brow-beaten husband who encounter a magic fish.

Hamilton, Virginia. *The House of Dies Drear*. Macmillan, 1968. (Gr. 5-8)

Thomas and his father investigate their rented house, which was a station on the Underground Railroad.

Lester, Julius. *To Be a Slave*. Dial, 1968. (Gr. 6-up)

An account of being a slave.

Liestman, Vicki. *Columbus Day*. Carolrhoda, 1991. (Gr. 2-4)

A thoughtful look at the events behind the legend.

Meltzer, Milton. *All Times, All Peoples*. Harper & Row, 1980. (Gr. 4-up)

A review of slavery throughout human history.

Rey, H. A. *Curious George*. Houghton Mifflin, 1941. (PreK-2)

George is a little monkey who is captured from Africa and brought back to the United States by the Man in the Yellow Hat.

Shulevitz, Uri. *The Treasure*. Farrar, Straus & Giroux, 1979. (K-4)

A man travels seeking treasure, only to find it at home.

Smith, Roger. *Empty Island*. Crocodile, 1991. (PreK-2)

A family on an undiscovered island manages to drive all the inhabitants away.

Smucker, Barbara. *Runaway to Freedom*. HarperCollins Children's Books, 1979. (Gr. 3-5)

Two slave girls run away to Canada and freedom.

Winter, Jeannette. *Follow the Drinking Gourd*. Knopf, 1988. (K-3)

Runaway slaves follow the Big Dipper to freedom.

Yates, Elizabeth. *Amos Fortune: Free Man*. Dutton, 1967. (Gr. 6-8)

The Newbery award winner about a slave who buys his freedom.

Yorinks, Arthur. *Hey, Al*. Farrar, Straus & Giroux, 1986. (K-4)

Al and his dog flee their humdrum existence and fly to an exotic island, only to discover it is not all they thought.

Related Activities

1. One of the areas in which Columbus failed was as a successful founder of a colony. His first colony disappeared with no survivors. Later attempts under his direction were plagued by discontent, disease, thievery, and conflict with the native population. Ask your group to imagine that they have discovered a new land and wish to start a new colony. What elements do they feel would be necessary to operate a successful new society from "scratch"?
(Primary, intermediate)

2. Columbus imported sugarcane to the West Indies, envisioning it as a crop that would stabilize the colonies and provide them with a commercial base (besides gold). The growing and making of sugar did have these effects, but it also had much more devastating ones. Sugarcane may be the foremost reason that slavery became such an entrenched part of commerce and agriculture in the New World. Have older children read some books about slavery, such as *A Williamburg Household* by Joan Anderson, *Something Upstairs* by Avi, *Captive Bodies, Free Spirits* by William Evitts, *The House of Dies Drear* by Virginia Hamilton, *To Be a Slave* by Julius Lester, *All Times, All Peoples* by Milton Meltzer, *Runaway to Freedom* by Barbara Smucker, and *Amos Fortune: Free Man* by Elizabeth Yates. Also have them read biographies of freedom fighters such as Frederick Douglass, Harriet Tubman, and Sojourner Truth. Ask the children to imagine themselves in the position of an African captured and sold into slavery. How would they feel? What do they imagine their future life would be like? What justifications did the Europeans use to condone this act?
(Primary, intermediate)

3. Younger children can be helped to understand the issue of enslaving people against their will by reading *The Drinking Gourd* by Jeannette Winter. Start a discussion by reading *Curious George* by H. A. Rey and *Bill and Pete* by Tomie dePaola. Though Curious George is a beloved character who is happy in his new home, his original capture is ethically questionable. Ask the children to talk about how they would feel if they were Curious George. Would they be happy to be taken from their home? Would it depend on how they were treated? Even if they were treated well, do they believe someone else should have the right to take them to a new land? Tomie dePaola's *Bill and Pete* has a similar theme, when a trader captures Bill the crocodile to make him into a suitcase.
(Preschool, primary)

4. Not all the Spanish approved of the way the Indians were being treated. Bishop Bartholomew de Las Casas worked to improve conditions for the Indians and wrote a book about their treatment that had great impact throughout Europe.

Tell the children to imagine that they are the king of Spain and suddenly become aware of what is going on in the New World after reading Bishop de Las Casas's book. What would they do as king to correct conditions? How would they reconcile the needs of both the Spanish and the Indians? How would they handle Columbus?
(Primary, intermediate)

5. The colonists rebelled against Columbus's leadership. In fact, they became lawless and simply did as they pleased. Their society had very little structure. This was in part because Columbus was not a good leader and did not really know how to govern. Read *Rooster's Off to See the World* by Eric Carle, in which Rooster convinces the other animals to travel off with him to see the world. But when they discover Rooster has no long-term plans for their welfare, they go back home. Ask the children to imagine living in a society that had no rules or laws. How would they decide what to do? How would they ensure fair treatment for everyone? How would they protect themselves?
(Primary, intermediate)

6. Because conditions in the West Indies were so bad, many of Columbus's colonists returned to Spain, full of complaints about his leadership. Read Uri Shulevitz's *The Treasure*, about a man who goes out to seek his fortune but decides it is really back home after all—the same experience the colonists had.
(Primary, intermediate)

7. Some of Columbus's problems were due to so many of his colonists falling ill. The Spaniards were unused to the climate of Hispaniola and developed malaria and other fevers. Mosquitoes spread disease rapidly. Many colonists returned home, complaining of conditions in Hispaniola. Things got so bad that Columbus's sons, who were pages at the Spanish court, were called the sons of the Admiral of Mosquitos. Read aloud *Hey, Al* by Arthur Yorinks, about another man who found out his island paradise was not all he hoped it would be. Then make clothespin mosquitoes, as shown in figure 10.5. They can be decorated with scraps of paper, pipe cleaners, and other odds and ends.
(Primary, intermediate)

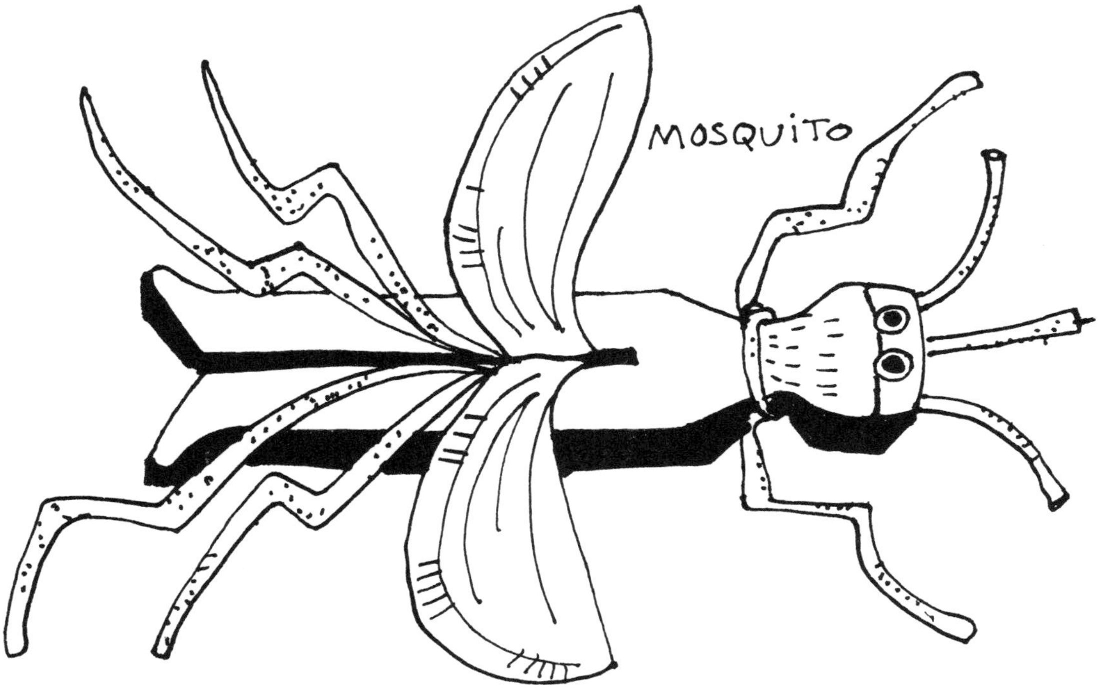

Fig. 10.5.

8. It is hard for us to realize in this day of medical miracles just how much the Indian population was devastated by European diseases. Within fifty years of the arrival of the Spanish, the indigenous population of the islands Columbus reached was almost extinct. Have your group research some of the diseases that were so deadly for the Indians, such as smallpox, measles, and influenza (flu). With young children, share the picture book *Empty Island* by Roger Smith. Though the people in this story do not empty the island because of disease, they do get rid of the inhabitants. Older children can read John Christopher's *Empty World*, about a boy who is left alone when the world's population is decimated by disease.
(Primary, intermediate)

9. The Spanish exploration efforts were almost totally motivated by greed. Their desire for instant wealth was so great that it blinded them to all other considerations. Develop a scenario so your group can try to understand the power that greed had in the events that took place. Ask children to imagine that they suddenly find an island with incredible riches in gold and silver. Because of their advanced technological skills, they can control the local population and do whatever they want. They suddenly have the ability to fulfill their wildest and most extravagant dreams. How would they balance this greed and the sudden ability to fulfill it with the needs and rights of the native people? Compare this greed with the madness that seized the panhandlers during the California gold rush. Share *The Fisherman and His Wife* by the Brothers Grimm, another story of greed.
(Primary, intermediate)

10. Sing the following song with the group to help them realize that despite his fame, Columbus had some tragic flaws in the way he treated other people. You could also share the book *Columbus Day* by Vicki Liestman, which touches on some of these issues.

Columbus Sailed over the Ocean
(sung to tune of "My Bonnie Lies over the Ocean")

Columbus sailed over the ocean
With three tiny ships for his crew
He forced his men on for a long time,
Sailing on the ocean blue.

Chorus:
Sail on, sail on,
Oh, sail on, Columbus, for me, for me!
Sail on, sail on,
Oh, sail on, Columbus, for me!

Columbus was quite a good sailor,
An explorer with many a dream,
But sometimes the great and the famous
Are not always all that they seem.

Chorus

Columbus was not a good leader,
When he started a town on the shore,
His men were too greedy for riches,
And all that they thought of was, "More!"

Chorus

Columbus mistreated the people
He met on the islands he found.
He took them as slaves to the Spanish
To show his discoveries around.

Chorus

He wanted to spread his religion
But didn't care much for their own.
He never was able to realize
The islands he found were their home.

Chorus

Oh, Columbus thought he'd reached the Indies.
He said it was new land for Spain.
But how can a land that is lived in
Be free for someone else's claim?

Chorus

If we go on trips of discovery
Leaving our own world behind,
We always should try to remember
To respect all the life that we find.

(Primary, intermediate)

11. Finally, the complaints they received got so bad that Ferdinand and Isabella sent a new governor to Hispaniola to investigate what was happening. On his arrival, he found that several Spaniards had been hanged for treason. He was so outraged that he immediately had Columbus clapped in chains and sent back to Spain. Columbus never recovered from this humiliation. Even after he explained the circumstances to Ferdinand and Isabella and they pardoned him, he kept his chains as a bitter reminder of his mistreatment. Make paper chains by taping strips of black construction paper into interconnecting circles. The children can attach these chains around their wrists and ankles with paper clips to get an idea of how Columbus must have felt.
(Primary, intermediate)

MAROONED!

Columbus called his fourth and final voyage the "High Voyage," but it was to mark the low point of his life. He was sent out with a fleet less seaworthy than the first one had been, to continue his fruitless search for gold and the Indies. When he arrived in the West Indies, a hurricane was brewing, and he asked permission to land. The new governor, Ovando, refused permission, denying that a storm was coming. Columbus's fleet huddled together as best they could and weathered the storm, but the governor's fleet that had been preparing to depart for Spain was destroyed.

After this unpropitious beginning, things proceeded to get worse. Columbus's fleet explored the coasts of Honduras, Nicaragua, Costa Rica, and Panama, searching for a passage to the Asian mainland. They encountered fierce storms and hostile natives, but no passage. Eventually, the fleet, riddled with holes from shipworms, tried to reach Hispaniola but did not make it. They were forced to land on the island of Jamaica, just barely making it to shore. They were now marooned miles from the nearest outpost of their countrymen, with no hope of rescue.

They ran their ships on shore and lived in them, getting food from the local Indians. Eventually, in desperation, they came up with an almost hopeless plan. Columbus's lieutenant, Diego Mendez, set out to sea with a group of natives in dugout canoes. He was driven back by other natives, but he agreed to make a second try. Miraculously, he made it to Santo Domingo. But Ovando was in no rush to rescue Columbus. It took him three months to send a ship to find them.

While Columbus and his men were stranded, the natives became tired of them and refused to keep feeding them. To save the group, Columbus played a hoax on the Indians. By consulting an almanac he had on board, Columbus knew an eclipse of the moon was due. He told the Indians that his god was angry with them because of their refusal to help him and so was taking away the moon. The Indians were frightened, and Columbus told them he would return the moon for their continued help. The ploy was successful. After being stranded on Jamaica for a year, Columbus and his crew were finally rescued.

Book List

Anderson, Lonzo. *The Day the Hurricane Happened*. Scribner's, 1974. (K-3)
A family on the island of St. Thomas experiences a hurricane.

Branley, Franklyn M. *Eclipse: Darkness in Daytime*. Crowell, 1988. (Gr. 2-4)
Though what Columbus foretold was an eclipse of the moon rather than the sun, this title will help children understand this phenomenon.

Defoe, Daniel. *Robinson Crusoe*. Putnam, 1963. (Gr. 5-8)
The classic story of a castaway on a desert island.

Lane, Carolyn. *Ghost Island*. Houghton Mifflin, 1985. (Gr. 4-up)
When a group of campers are marooned, one of them suspects the island of being haunted.

Litowinsky, Olga. *The High Voyage: The Final Crossing of Christopher Columbus*. Delacorte, 1991. (Gr. 5-8)
A recounting of Columbus's final voyage, on which he took his younger son, Fernando.

Ross, Katherine. *Bear Island*. Random House, 1987. (PreK-2)
When Bear and his friend are sailing, they are shipwrecked on a deserted island and decide to stay.

Steig, William. *Abel's Island*. Farrar, Straus & Giroux, 1985. (Gr. 4-6)
Abel the mouse is marooned during a storm and must learn to fend for himself.

Taylor, Mark. *Henry the Castaway*. Atheneum, 1972. (PreK-2)
When Henry finds an empty canoe, he goes for a ride, but then he becomes marooned on an island.

Wyss, Johann D. *Swiss Family Robinson*. Putnam, 1949. (Gr. 5-8)
Classic story of a shipwrecked family.

Related Activities

1. Columbus had high hopes for his final voyage and called it the "High Voyage." He even took one of his sons with him. Read Olga Litowinsky's *The High Voyage* to get an idea of what it was like.
(Intermediate)

2. Columbus's trouble started when his fleet was refused shelter by the governor at Santo Domingo with a hurricane brewing. Read Lonzo Anderson's *The Day the Hurricane Happened*, and ask the group whether any of them have ever experienced a hurricane or a really bad storm.
(Preschool, primary)

3. After exploring the coast of Central America, Columbus's ships became so worm-eaten that he had to beach them on Jamaica, where he and his crew were marooned. Share some books about being marooned on an island, such as *Abel's Island* by William Steig, *Bear Island* by Katherine Ross, and *Henry the Castaway* by Mark Taylor. Older children would enjoy reading *Robinson Crusoe* by Daniel Defoe, *Ghost Island* by Carolyn Lane, and *Swiss Family Robinson* by Johann Wyss. Several of these are available in film or video formats and would make an enjoyable presentation.
(Preschool, primary, intermediate)

4. Ask the children to imagine that like Columbus, they have been marooned on a desert island. Their most crucial needs of food and water have been met. What other things do they feel would be indispensable for their survival? If they could suddenly be granted a wish for five things from home to have with them on the island, what would these five things be?
(Primary, intermediate)

5. Columbus tricked the Indians on Jamaica into continuing to help him by telling them that the eclipse of the moon was actually an act by his angry god. Read Franklyn Branley's book about eclipses, and have the children make a diagram of how a lunar eclipse works.
(Primary, intermediate)

COLUMBUS'S DEATH

After his final voyage, Columbus returned to Spain a disappointed, ill, and embittered man. Though he had made his fortune in the West Indies, he had not received the many rewards he had been promised. He petitioned the monarchs to grant him an audience, but his ally, Isabella, was dying. After her death, Ferdinand had no more use for Columbus. Columbus was to spend the rest of his life (only two years) following the court, trying to get his just desserts, as he saw them, and feeling sorry for himself. There is some evidence that he even suffered from delusions—imagining that he was leading a force against Jerusalem. When he died, Columbus had faded from the public view. His "great enterprise" had become a success, but not for him.

Who was Columbus? Many biographers have described him as a man of mystery, a man who revealed almost nothing of his past. In keeping with this persona, historians are not even sure where he is buried. His obscurity was to last for 200 years, before a new nation would revive him as its hero.

Book List

dePaola, Tomie. *The Clown of God*. Harcourt Brace Jovanovich, 1978. (K-3)
The story of an old juggler who presents a final show for the Christ child.

Giardini, Cesare. *The Life and Times of Columbus*. Curtis, 1967. (Gr. 5-up)
This biography for older children includes many portraits of Columbus.

Livingston, Myra Cohn. *Celebrations*. Holiday House, 1985. (Gr. 2-6)
A collection of poems about holidays by this prestigious poet.

Van Allsburg, Chris. *The Wreck of the Zephyr*. Houghton Mifflin, 1983. (Gr. 1-6)
A young boy who considers himself the best sailor in the world sails his boat to a land where boats fly through the air.

Related Activities

1. Some people see Columbus as a hero who braved the unknown and found the New World as a result. Some see him as an ambitious man determined to increase his own importance and wealth. To some he was a genius, and to some, a madman. The true man was probably a combination of all these traits. Like the boy in the book *The Wreck of the Zephyr* by Chris Van Allsburg, Columbus wanted to be the first and the best. Share this story with your group, and discuss what they believe Columbus was like.
(Primary, intermediate)

2. Have the children create portraits of Columbus as they see him. No portrait was ever painted of him during his lifetime, so no one really knows what he looked like. Records have hinted that he had red hair as a young man, which later turned white. His eyes were probably blue or gray. Most likely he was clean-shaven. Show the children some of the many portraits that have been painted of Columbus since his death (a good source is Cesare Giardini's *The Life and Times of Columbus*), and explain that all of them are really just the results of how the artists imagined Columbus might have looked. The children can create their own portraits of Columbus using any of a number of methods, such as sketching, painting, collage, or cutting from paper. The portraits can be full-length or show just the head.
(Primary, intermediate)

3. As a group project, create a picture tapestry about Columbus. Assign each child a different event in Columbus's life, such as his birth, his work as a weaver, when he became a sailor, etc., and ask the student to draw a picture depicting that event. When all the pictures are completed, assemble them in order on your wall or bulletin board.
(Primary, intermediate)

4. Columbus died almost alone, his accomplishments unrecognized. Several of the biographies of him offer poignant descriptions of his death that you could read aloud to your class. In addition, read Tomie dePaola's *The Clown of God* to convey the pathos some see in Columbus's death.
(Preschool, primary, intermediate)

5. Whoever he was, Columbus remained a man of mystery even in death. Historians are not even sure where he was buried. Have the children do some research about where Columbus's body may lie, and then have a debate about which one they think is the actual place.
(Primary, intermediate)

6. Share Myra Cohn Livingston's poem "Columbus Day." It provides a fitting ending to the study of Columbus's life because it neither praises nor condemns him but recognizes his dream.
(Primary, intermediate)

11

Later Explorers

THE CONQUISTADORS

Though Columbus passed from the stage on which the "collision of worlds" was being enacted, the drama did not end. The Spanish continued to explore the New World. Some of the major figures in this enterprise are listed below.

- In 1513, Vasco Núñez de Balboa became the first European to see the Pacific Ocean.
- In 1514, Juan Ponce de León discovered Florida while searching for the legendary fountain of youth.
- In 1521, Hernando Cortés led a small force of men and sixteen horses into Mexico and in less than two years conquered the Aztec Empire.
- Francisco Pizarro led an even smaller force of men into South America and conquered the Incas in 1532.
- Álvar Núñez Cabeza de Vaca was a Spanish explorer who wandered the region of the U.S. Southwest from 1528 to 1536.
- Hernando de Soto was the Spanish explorer credited with the discovery of the Mississippi River and with exploring the southeastern United States.
- Francisco Vásquez de Coronado was the brutal conquistador who explored the U.S. Southwest while searching for the legendary Seven Golden Cities of Cibola.

How could such small forces conquer such large and sophisticated civilizations and have such a tremendous effect on two continents? There does not seem to be one answer, but rather a combination of factors that came together to spell the downfall of the indigenous Americans.

In the case of the Aztecs, the Spaniards gained an initial advantage because the Aztec King Montezuma believed the Spaniards were gods. It had been foretold that the Aztec god Quetzalcoatl would return to Mexico in the year 1519, and the god was believed to be a white man with a beard. This prophecy seems to have greatly weakened Montezuma's will to resist the Spanish, because he saw his fate as preordained.

In addition, the Spanish had a small number of horses that they used in battle against the Aztecs. Having never seen horses before, the Aztecs were terrified of the animals. They believed man and horse to be one animal and fled in fear.

The Aztecs also had a tradition in battle of trying to capture rather than kill their enemies. This was because they wanted to take prisoners to use as religious sacrifices. Even against Cortés they were not able to break this tradition, and so even though they greatly outnumbered the Spanish, they did not "go for the kill."

In addition, the Spanish were aided by a number of other groups who had been conquered by the Aztecs and hated them. They gladly joined Cortés to overthrow their oppressors. One of those who turned against the Aztecs was Cortés's guide and interpreter, Marina.

Finally, the Spanish had a secret weapon they did not even know about—disease. Lacking immunities to European diseases such as smallpox, influenza, and measles, the Aztecs were decimated by the epidemics that swept through their society. The fact that they died and the Spanish did not may have convinced the Aztecs that the gods were on the side of the Europeans.

In the case of the Incas, many of the same factors were at work and, in addition, the Inca monarchy was divided by a feud over succession to the throne.

As a result of all these factors, the Spanish were able to conquer and plunder both of these civilizations. They destroyed the Indians' cities, stole their treasures, and enslaved or killed their people. In Central America, most of the native Indian population was exterminated or mixed with the Spanish to create the mestizo race, a combination of Indian and Spanish. So complete was the devastation wrought by the conquistadors that even to this day, much of Central and South America remain in a Third-World state.

Many modern feelings of racism also stem from this period. To justify their treatment of both the Indians they enslaved and the Africans they captured and imported, the conquerors convinced themselves that both were inferior races. Because of the exploitation they have suffered, these races often are unable to advance economically, which in turn contributes to their being seen as less productive than, and therefore inferior to, the dominant white race. A vicious cycle of oppression is thus perpetuated.

These are complex issues to present to children, but they are as crucial today as they were in the sixteenth century. Our ability to overcome prejudice and extend full rights, privileges, and dignity to all ethnic populations is crucial to our continued growth as a nation, and crucial also to our relationships with our neighbors in Central and South America.

Book List

Aesop. *The Goose That Laid the Golden Egg*. Andre Deutsch, 1986. (PreK-3)
The fable about a couple whose greed destroys the source of their fortune.

Allen, Pamela. *The Hidden Treasure*. Putnam, 1989. (PreK-1)
Two brothers are split when they find hidden treasure.

Ash, Maureen. *Vasco Núñez de Balboa*. Children's Press, 1990. (Gr. 3-up)
Biography of the Spanish conquistador who discovered the Pacific Ocean.

Babbitt, Natalie. *Tuck Everlasting*. Farrar, Straus & Giroux, 1975. (Gr. 3-6)
The Tucks own the spring of eternal life.

Bellairs, John. *The Treasure of Alpheus Winterborn*. Bantam, 1985. (Gr. 5-7)
To avoid his family problems, Alpheus searches for treasure.

Berger, Josef. *Discoverers of the New World*. American Heritage, 1960. (Gr. 5-up)
Berger covers most of the major figures in the exploration of the Americas.

Carson, Robert. *Hernando de Soto: Expedition to the Mississippi*. Children's Press, 1991. (Gr. 4-up)
An overview of the exploits of one of the Spanish conquistadors.

Cooper, Susan. *The Silver Cow*. Macmillan, 1983. (K-4)
A farmer's greed causes the loss of his silver cows, which were the source of his wealth.

Hunter, Nigel. *Expedition of Cortés*. Bookwright, 1990. (Gr. 4-6)
An overview of Cortés's conquest of the Aztecs.

Jensen, Malcolm. *Francisco Coronado*. Franklin Watts, 1974. (Gr. 4-up)
Standard biography of this conquistador.

McGraw, Eloise. *The Money Room*. Macmillan, 1981. (Gr. 5-7)
Two kids search for their grandfather's hidden treasure.

Moeri, Louise. *Journey to the Treasure*. Scholastic, 1986. (Gr. 4-6)
In this novel, the main character follows as ailing Grandfather searches a cave for treasure.

Nevins, Ann. *Super Stitches: A Book of Superstitions*. Holiday House, 1983. (Gr. 4-6)
An explanation of a variety of superstitions.

Perl, Lila. *Don't Sing before Breakfast, Don't Sleep in the Moonlight: Everyday Superstitions and How They Began*. Ticknor & Fields, 1988. (Gr. 5-8)
This book gives the sources of many common superstitions.

Schwartz, Alvin. *Gold and Silver, Silver and Gold: Tales of Hidden Treasure*. Farrar, Straus & Giroux, 1988. (Gr. 4-8)
A collection of stories about hidden treasure.

Stadler, John. *Gorman and the Treasure Chest*. Bradbury, 1984. (PreK-2)
When Gorman finds a treasure chest, he also finds many other creatures anxious to help him open it.

Stein, R. Conrad. *Hernando Cortés*. Children's Press, 1991. (Gr. 4-6)
An excellent biography of the complex man who conquered the Aztecs.

Van Allsburg, Chris. *The Wretched Stone*. Houghton Mifflin, 1991. (Gr. 3-up)
Though there are many meanings to this allegorical tale, one is that greed can turn people into beasts.

Vidal, Beatriz. *The Legend of El Dorado*. Knopf, 1991. (Gr. 2-6)
A retelling of the legend of the treasure of El Dorado in South America.

Whitman, Sylvia. *Hernando de Soto and the Explorers of the American South*. Chelsea House, 1991. (Gr. 5-up)
This look at the conquistadors is for older readers.

Related Activities

1. After Columbus charted the way, the rush was on for the Spanish and Portuguese, both racing to the New World to find riches. Play the game "Race to the Islands" to emphasize this. Each player needs a copy of a map of the Caribbean area. Divide the group into two or more teams. Call out locations in this area, such as the names of Caribbean Islands and parts of Florida, Mexico, and Central and South America. The first player to find the place on the map scores a point for his or her team.
(Primary, intermediate)

2. Ask the children to create their own islands to discover from paper cups. They can draw island scenery and tape it inside the cup as a backdrop. Then they can create island animals, or people, and cut them out. They should attach these "characters" to the ends of plastic drinking straws inserted through the bottom of the cup as shown in figure 11.1. These characters can now be used as pop-up puppets.
(Preschool, primary)

Fig. 11.1.

3. Because of the discoveries of Cortés and others, Spanish explorers arriving in the New World expected to find streets paved with silver and houses roofed with gold. Many legends sprang up about fabulously wealthy hidden cities that inspired much of the Spanish exploration of the New World such as *The Legend of El Dorado* by Beatriz Vidal. The children can make their own houses of gold. Use small milk cartons and cover them with gold wrapping paper (see fig. 11.2). If you want, you could combine their houses in a tabletop diorama of Eldorado or one of the Seven Golden Cities of Cibola.

Fig. 11.2.

Older children might enjoy reading some books about treasure hunts, such as *The Treasure of Alpheus Winterborn* by John Bellairs, *The Money Room* by Eloise McGraw, *Journey to the Treasure* by Louise Moeri, and *Gold and Silver, Silver and Gold* by Alvin Schwartz.
(Primary, intermediate)

4. In 1514 the aging Juan Ponce de León began his fruitless search for the fountain of youth and instead discovered Florida. Ask your group to imagine that they have found the fountain of youth, and discuss whether or not they would drink from it. If they would, how do they think it would change their lives? What would be the drawbacks and benefits of having everlasting life? Older readers would enjoy Natalie Babbitt's book *Tuck Everlasting*, about a family who have a spring of water on their property that gives everlasting life. Ask whether anyone has seen the Disney film *The Flight of the Navigator*, in which a boy suddenly finds himself still a child in a world that has grown older.
(Primary, intermediate)

5. One reason Cortés was able to conquer the Aztecs against overwhelming odds is that their leader, Montezuma, seemed to have seen their downfall as preordained. He was initially influenced by a prophecy that the Aztec god Quetzalcoatl would return in 1519, as a white man with a beard. In addition, Montezuma was disturbed by several omens that had been observed at the time, including a comet, a speck on the face of the sun, and the sound of ghostly crying in the streets at night. Montezuma was obviously someone who believed in fate and signs and who felt they could not be fought against.

Have a discussion of superstitions, using the books by Ann Nevins and Lila Perl. Ask your group whether they believe any superstitions. Do they feel these beliefs affect their actions? Can someone be too superstitious?
(Primary, intermediate)

6. One factor in Cortés's success was his foresight in bringing sixteen horses with him when he invaded Mexico. The Aztecs were terrified of these creatures, believing man and horse to be a single animal. Have your group draw pictures of what such a creature would look like. You might have your class do some research about similar mythical creatures such as centaurs.
(Primary, intermediate)

7. The Spaniards' greed was so great they even fought against each other. For example, Balboa was falsely accused and executed with the help of Francisco Pizarro, who wanted a free hand to invade the Inca Empire. While Cortés was fighting Montezuma, he was also fighting a rear war against other Spaniards. There was a mentality of "every man for himself." In many cases, the Indians suffered from the same kinds of divisions. The Aztecs were overthrown with the help of other tribes who allied themselves with the Spanish. In fact, Cortés's interpreter and guide, Marina, was from one of these tribes.

Ask the children to imagine that they are members of one of the Mexican states under the Aztecs who decide to join the Spanish against Montezuma. Ask them to list their reasons and why they think life would be better with the Spanish as overlords instead of the Aztecs. Do they feel they are being disloyal or are fighting for their rightful independence? Does the end justify the means?
(Intermediate)

8. Assign each child in your group a conquistador to research. Here is a partial list to get you started:

Juan Ponce de León	Alonso de Ojeda
Pedro Álvars Cabral	Vasco Núñez de Balboa
Francisco Pizarro	Hernando Cortés
Álvar Núñez Cabeza de Vaca	Hernando de Soto
Francisco Vásquez de Coronado	Pedro de Alvarado

After assigning a conquistador, ask the children to describe what he did, what his motivations may have been, and where and when he was active. The books listed above should be helpful.
(Intermediate)

9. Children could make paper figures of the conquistadors using the outline in figure 11.3, and then look through some of the books to get an idea of how the conquistadors looked. After drawing on features and coloring them, children can turn their figures into marionettes. Each child needs a small square of cardboard, folded in half. Staple a long string between the halves. The ends that hang down on either side of the cardboard can be taped to the back of the conquistador. Lay out a large map on a table and have each child "walk" his or her conquistador over the map on the route he took.
(Primary, intermediate)

Fig. 11.3.

10. Ask members of your group to volunteer to take on the roles of various conquistadors, such as Cortés and Pizarro. You should also get students to act out Bartolomé de Las Casas, the Spanish bishop who agitated for Indian rights; Montezuma II, ruler of the Aztecs; Atahualpa, the Inca ruler; Marina, Cortés's interpreter; and others in the drama of the conquistadors. Ask the children to have a debate with each other. Start them off by asking Las Casas to launch an attack against the conquistadors. Conquistadors should answer with whatever justifications they can think of, including the fact that the Indians also fought each other. Then have Montezuma, Marina, and other Indian characters justify their actions as well. Have the children try to reach a resolution to the debate. Do they think the problems were the fault of one person or group, or do they think they were due to a combination of factors?
(Intermediate)

11. To justify their actions, each side (the Spanish and the Indians) viewed the other as alien and less than human. And in some ways they were right. The Aztec religion with its constant demand for human sacrifice was abhorrent to the Spanish. At the same time, the Aztecs and Incas saw the Spanish, with their lust for gold, as little better than beasts. Read Chris Van Allsburg's *The Wretched Stone*, and ask in what ways the group thinks it relates to the issue of greed. Does the blind worship of any idea or object inevitably dehumanize us?
(Intermediate)

12. When Pizarro conquered the Incas, he imprisoned their ruler, Atahualpa, and demanded that a ransom be paid for him. The Incas were to fill a room with gold to buy Atahualpa's release. The Incas kept their part of the bargain, but Pizarro executed Atahualpa anyway. Read the picture books *The Silver Cow* by Susan Cooper and *The Goose That Laid the Golden Egg* by Aesop, and discuss why all these characters kill the very source of their fortunes.
(Primary, intermediate)

13. Ask the children to take a look at what the countries invaded by the Spanish are like today. In what ways can Spanish and Portuguese influences still be seen throughout the U.S. Southwest, the West Indies, Mexico, and Central and South America? Children should consider issues such as language, religion, dress, food, architecture, and other aspects of culture and government.
(Intermediate)

PIRATES!

Piracy has always been a part of seafaring. The early Greeks and Phoenicians battled pirates as they sailed the Mediterranean. During the Middle Ages, the threat of being robbed at sea became so great that many Italian merchant vessels were escorted by battleships from port to port. At the time when Columbus sailed, ships from other countries were always considered fair game for raiding. This was why the Spanish and Portuguese tried so hard to stay out of each other's way as they sailed the Atlantic.

During the late 1500s the rivalry between Spain and England became fierce. When the two countries were not actually at war with each other, English sea captains waged a kind of guerrilla warfare against Spanish ships whenever they found time. Men such as Sir Francis Drake and Sir John Hawkins sailed with the unofficial blessing of Queen Elizabeth, who encouraged their "privateering."

When the conquests of the conquistadors resulted in enormous wealth for Spain, piracy really reached its height. Most people, when they think of pirates, envision the typical swashbucklers of the seventeenth and eighteenth centuries who terrorized the Caribbean and preyed on Spanish galleons carrying New World treasures back to Spain.

These are the pirates of the Spanish Main (the northern coast of South America, under Spanish rule), men such as Blackbeard and Captain Kidd, who inspired romantic legends as they ruled the seas. Of course, the reality was not really so romantic. Many men became pirates not to win glory, but to escape desperate poverty. And when "pickings" were slim, they faced the same hardships all seafarers faced: starvation, scurvy, rat-ridden ships, weevil-eaten food, shipworms, and boredom. In addition, there was the added threat that if caught, they would be hanged.

But to balance these drawbacks, there was the freedom of the pirate's life. Though many stories describe strong pirate captains who dominated their crews, in actuality there was a good deal of democracy on a pirate ship, with the men voting on most decisions. An unpopular or unsuccessful captain was quickly gotten rid of. And piracy does not seem to have discriminated on the basis of sex. Anne Bonney and Mary Reade were two of the better-known pirates of the Spanish Main.

The reality of these brigands was often no romantic tale for their victims, either. Books and movies sometimes depict the pirates' prey as deserving their fate, but if we look at piracy in a modern-day context, it was the equivalent of today's sky-jacking.

Despite the grim realities of the age of piracy, it offers an opportunity to have some fun as we study the history of discovery on the high seas. Below are some projects to help children learn more about the period of piracy and also several activities just for fun. So, "Yo, ho, ho, on a dead man's chest," set sail!

Book List

Allen, Pamela. *I Wish I Had a Pirate Suit*. Viking, 1990. (PreK-1)
A little boy longs for a pirate suit like his big brother's.

Baum, Louis. *JuJu and the Pirate*. Peter Bedrick, 1983. (PreK-2)
When JuJu the parrot learns that she is descended from a pirate's parrot, she sets off to find a pirate of her own.

Brewton, John E., comp. *Gaily We Parade*. Macmillan, 1940. (Gr. 3-6)
This poetry compilation includes the pirate poem "The Pirate Don Durk of Dowdee."

Burningham, John. *Come Away from the Water, Shirley*. Crowell, 1977. (PreK-1)
When Shirley visits the beach with her parents, her imagination leads her into adventures with pirates.

Collington, Peter. *The Angel and the Soldier Boy*. Knopf, 1987. (PreK-1)
In this wordless book, a toy angel and soldier battle pirates.

Dewey, Ariane. *Lafitte the Pirate*. Greenwillow, 1985. (Gr. 2-4)
This title includes several tales of this legendary pirate.

Dyke, John. *Pigwig and the Pirates*. Methuen, 1977. (PreK-2)
When his nephew is kidnapped by pirates, Pigwig sets out to save him and wins a treasure in the bargain.

Faulkner, Matt. *The Amazing Voyage of Jackie Grace*. Scholastic, 1987. (PreK-2)
Jackie sails off in his tub for a fantastic voyage, complete with pirates, storms, and shipwreck.

Fleischman, Sid. *The Ghost in the Noonday Sun*. Greenwillow, 1965. (Gr. 5-7)
All the elements of a pirate story are here, including the wicked captain, a kidnapped boy, and buried treasure.

Hutchins, Pat. *One-Eyed Jake*. Greenwillow, 1979. (PreK-2)
A greedy pirate plunders one ship too many.

Johnson, Charles. *Pieces of Eight*. Discovery, 1989. (Gr. 5-7)
Blackbeard's ghost appears in this story of pirates.

McCall, Edith. *Pirates and Privateers*. Children's Press, 1980. (Gr. 3-up)
A nonfiction look at these robbers of the sea.

McNaughton, Colin. *Anton B. Stanton and the Pirates*. Doubleday, 1979. (K-3)
Anton B. Stanton is no bigger than a tea cup, but he takes on the fierce rat pirates when they kidnap the princess of the water rats.

______. *Jolly Roger and the Pirates of Abdul the Skinhead*. Simon & Schuster, 1988. (Gr. 1-4)
A boy named Roger is shanghaied by a band of pirates and, through his adventures with them, reunites his family.

Mahy, Margaret. *The Man Whose Mother Was a Pirate*. Viking, 1986. (PreK-3)
Straitlaced Sam sails the seas with his pirate mom.

Marrin, Albert. *Sea Rovers: Pirates, Privateers, and Buccaneers*. Atheneum, 1984. (Gr. 3-up)
A nonfiction account of these buccaneers.

Moerbeek, Kees. *When the Wild Pirates Go Sailing*. Price Stern Sloan, 1988. (PreK-2)
This pop-up picture book offers surprise creatures.

Paul, Korky, and Peter Cart. *Captain Teachum's Buried Treasure*. Oxford University Press, 1989. (PreK-3)
Captain Teachum is a really fierce pirate—or is he?

Peppe, Rodney. *The Kettleship Pirates*. Lothrop, Lee & Shepard, 1983. (PreK-1)
Pip Mouse sets sail on a pirate ship and finds buried treasure.

Ross, Tony. *The Treasure of Cozy Cove*. Farrar, Straus & Giroux, 1990. (PreK-1)
Sailing for adventure, two travelers meet pirates and discover that the true treasure is finding a home.

Shub, Elizabeth. *Cutlass in the Snow*. Greenwillow, 1986. (Gr. 2-5)
The characters in this story stay up all night talking about pirates on Fire Island and the next day find a cutlass in the snow.

Stevenson, Robert Louis. *Treasure Island*. Macmillan, 1981. (Gr. 5-up)
This is the classic pirate story of buried treasure, desert islands, and kidnapping.

Woychuk, Denis. *Pirates!* Lothrop, Lee & Shepard, 1992. (PreK-1)
When Mimi the hippo is kidnapped by pirates, Gustav the mouse must rescue her.

Related Activities

1. To decorate your library or classroom while you are reading about pirates, create a pirate scene like the one in figure 11.4 from a large piece of cardboard about 4 feet square. Draw a couple of pirates digging up buried treasure, but instead of drawing on the pirates' faces, cut out holes in the cardboard where the faces would be. Paint the scene. Now let the children stand behind the scene and put their faces in the openings, so that they appear as the pirates in the scene. Take pictures with an instant camera.
(Preschool, primary, intermediate)

Fig. 11.4.

2. Learn about some famous pirates. Use the books by Edith McCall and Albert Marrin, along with other sources from your collection, to research some pirates from history such as Blackbeard, Sir Henry Morgan, Captain Kidd, Black Bart, Calico Jack, Charles Vane, Stede Bonnett, Edward England, Anne Bonney, Mary Reade, Jean Lafitte, and Henry Every. Read aloud Ariane Dewey's *Lafitte the Pirate*. Older children would enjoy reading Charles Johnson's novel *Pieces of Eight* or Elizabeth Shub's *Cutlass in the Snow*.
(Primary, intermediate)

3. Read some stories about being attacked by pirates, such as Peter Collington's *The Angel and the Soldier Boy*, John Dyke's *Pigwig and the Pirates*, Matt Faulkner's *The Amazing Voyage of Jackie Grace*, and Colin McNaughton's *Anton B. Stanton and the Pirates*.

With this inspiration, concoct "wanted" posters for these brigands. Most wanted posters have pictures of the criminals on them, and, if you want, you could use the pictures taken of the children in the pirate scene from activity 1. Each child should make a poster that includes the pirate's name, his or her crimes, the name of the ship, where the crime took place, any identifying information, and the amount of the reward for capturing the pirate.
(Primary, intermediate)

4. Although we know that pirates were actually criminals, playing "pirate" is great fun. Let your group become a pirate band and act out some adventures. Read the picture books *I Wish I Had a Pirate Suit* by Pamela Allen and *JuJu and the Pirate* by Louis Baum. Share the poem "The Pirate Don Durk of Dowdee" by Mildred Plew Meigs, from the collection *Gaily We Parade* compiled by John Brewton.

Now let the kids dress up as pirates as shown in figure 11.5. For a pirate costume, wear black trousers shredded at the knees, a red sash tied around the waist, boots, an eyepatch of cloth or paper, and a head scarf. For an earring, use a large metal curtain ring. Tie a loop of thread to the curtain ring and hang it over the ear. Make a sword like the knight's sword in the chapter on the medieval world. Make pirate hats from black posterboard. For each child, you need two pieces of posterboard. Fold each piece of posterboard in half and draw the shape shown in figure 11.6. Cut the shapes out without cutting through the fold. Staple the two pieces together at the ends to fit. The children can draw skulls and crossbones on paper to cut out and glue onto their hats.
(Preschool, primary, intermediate)

5. Pirates almost never used their real names, both as protection against getting caught and to save their loved ones the shame of having a pirate in the family. Have your group come up with new names for themselves. Read Colin McNaughton's *Jolly Roger and the Pirates of Abdul the Skinhead* for ideas on pirate names.
(Primary)

6. For a pirate ship, make a boat from a large box. Use an empty refrigerator box, and cut an opening in one side. Make a sail like the one used for the picnic-table ship (page 181). The children can use this boat for acting out pirate raids or as a spot for quiet reading. Share the books *The Man Whose Mother Was a Pirate* by Margaret Mahy, *When the Wild Pirates Go Sailing* by Kees Moerbeek, *The Kettleship Pirates* by Rodney Peppe, and *Pirates!* by Denis Woychuk.
(Preschool, primary)

Fig. 11.5.

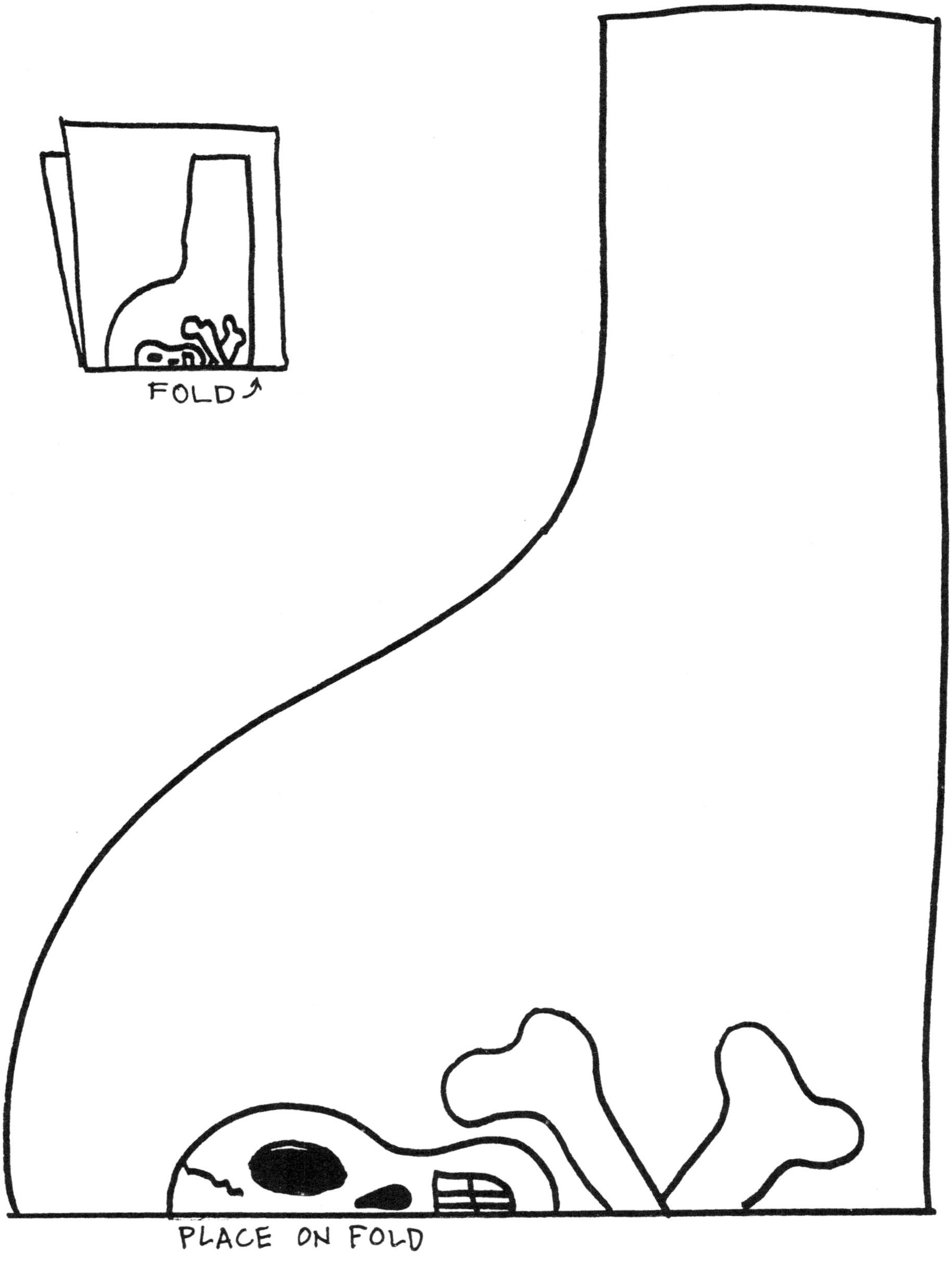

Fig. 11.6.

7. Make "Jolly Roger" flags. Give each child a large (12" x 18") piece of black construction paper and scraps of white and red construction paper. Explain that not all Jolly Rogers were exactly alike. Some had a skull and crossbones, and some were decorated with skeletons or pirates or an arm holding a cutlass. Ask each child to design his or her own Jolly Roger. Shirley and her pirate crew sport a Jolly Roger in *Come Away from the Water, Shirley* by John Burningham.
(Primary)

8. Explain that pirates were actually a rather democratic lot who together decided on the "articles" or rules to govern themselves. These covered things such as electing a captain, distributing the booty, punishments for crimes such as stealing from a fellow pirate, the procedure for taking on new members, and what course to set for the next raid. If the captain was unjust or one of the crew was disobedient, swift action was taken. Read Pat Hutchins's *One-Eyed Jake*, about a pirate captain who never heard of pirate articles. Then let your group come up with their own list of rules.
(Preschool, primary, intermediate)

9. Pirates' favorite booty was coins, because they could be equally divided among the crew and melted down easily. Have the kids do some research on Spanish coins of the sixteenth and seventeenth centuries. Then have them make their own coins from yellow construction paper. Children should either copy the engraving on these old coins or come up with their own insignia. They also can make treasure chests from cardboard boxes to hold their "pieces of eight." Share the book *Captain Teachum's Buried Treasure* by Korky Paul and Peter Cart. Older children might enjoy reading Sid Fleischman's *The Ghost in the Noonday Sun* and Robert Louis Stevenson's *Treasure Island*.
(Primary, intermediate)

10. Lead your pirate band in some games. Read Tony Ross's *The Treasure of Cozy Cove*, and play "Pirates' Treasure." Put some foil-covered chocolate coins in a pouch. Choose one player to be the pirate. He or she must leave the room, and the other players hide the treasure. The pirate then returns and begins searching for the treasure. While the pirate is looking, the other players sing a sea song, such as "What Shall We Do with the Drunken Sailor." They sing louder as the pirate gets nearer the treasure and softer as he or she moves away from it. Set a time limit for the search. If the pirate finds the treasure within the time limit, he or she can keep the candy. If not, choose a new pirate. Repeat until everyone has had a chance to be the pirate.

Another enjoyable game is "The Pirate Captain's Treasure." Choose a player to be the pirate captain. This pirate captain stands at one end of the room facing the wall, with the treasure behind him or her. The other pirates creep toward the captain on tiptoe from the opposite end of the room. If the captain looks around the pirates must freeze. If they are seen moving they must go back to the wall and start again. When close enough to the treasure, the pirates must grab it and run back to the start. If the captain catches them, a new game begins and the thief becomes the new captain.
(Primary)

11. If you are working with preschoolers, let the children pretend to find buried treasure. Hide a number of large, gold construction-paper coins around the room for them to find.
(Preschool)

12. Let the group make paper-bag pirates using the pattern in figure 11.7. Let the children color their pirates. The pirate's head should be glued to the bottom flap of a small lunch-size paper bag. The body parts are glued on the side of the bag under the flap. When the child inserts a hand, he or she can move the pirate's head by moving his or her fingers up and down.
(Preschool, primary)

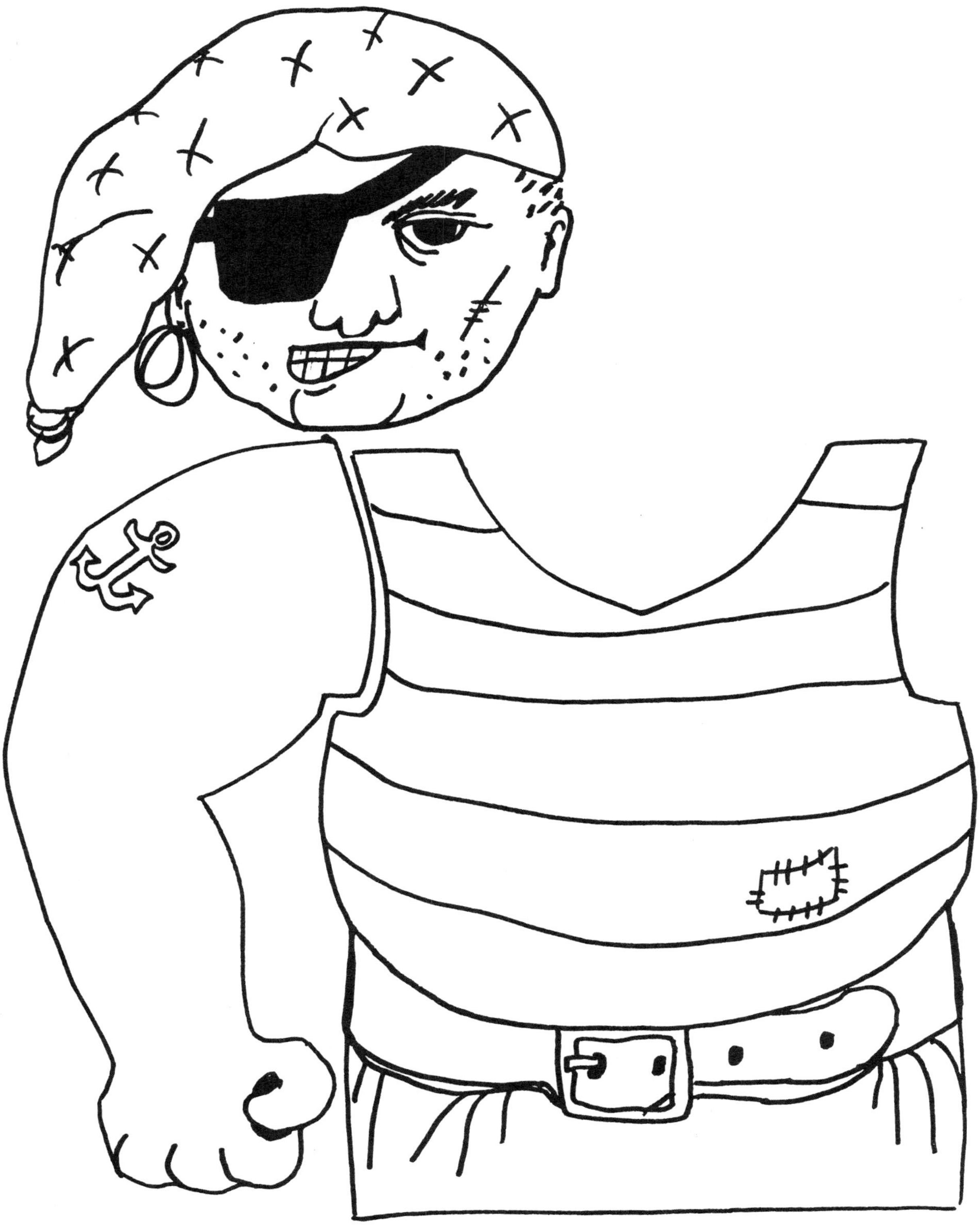

Fig. 11.7.

(Fig. 11.7 continues on page 260.)

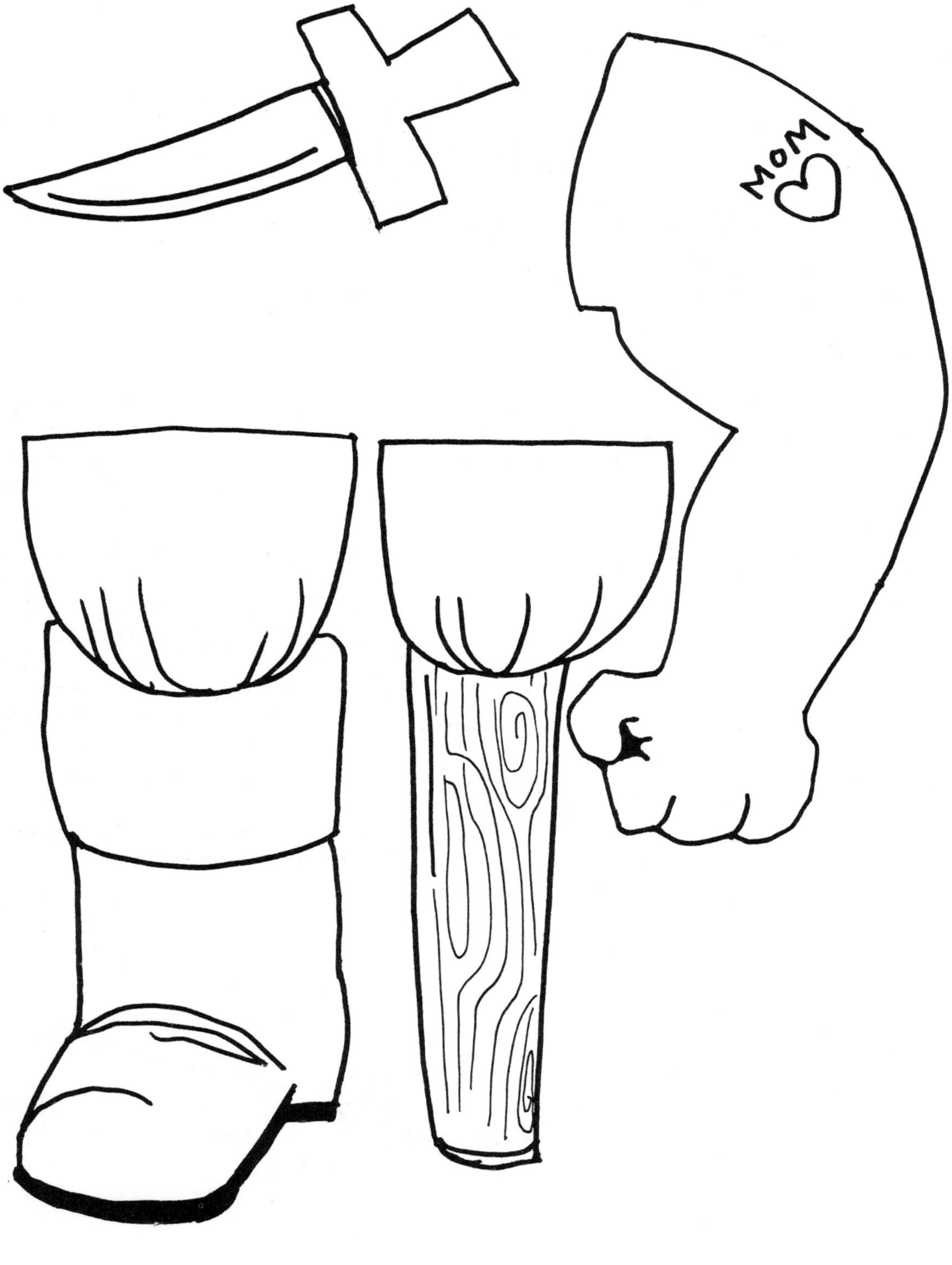

Fig. 11.7 – *Continued*

AROUND THE WORLD

If Columbus's exploits opened a world for discovery, it was Ferdinand Magellan's voyage that began to truly define what the world was like. Magellan was a Portuguese navigator who, having quarreled with King Manuel of Portugal, offered his services and his plan of sailing around the world to Spain. When King Charles approved the plan, Magellan set sail from Seville on September 20, 1519, with five ships and about 270 men.

They sailed first across the Atlantic to the coast of Brazil and then down the coast of South America, searching for a passage through to the Indies. Magellan believed that if he could get past this landmass blocking his way, he would find the Indies only a short sail beyond.

He had to battle storms and mutinies, but he finally found the passage he was searching for on October 21, 1520, when he entered what was later to be known as the Strait of Magellan. It was over a month before the fleet emerged into the Pacific, which they called peaceful because it provided such a contrast to the turbulent passage they had just sailed through.

However, the worst of the trip was yet to come. Unknown to Magellan and his men, the Spice Islands they sought were three months away. By the time they made landfall in the Marianas in March 1521, the men had been reduced to eating rats and the leather from the rigging, and scores had died. Magellan himself never completed the historic voyage. Having gotten embroiled in local politics on one of the Mariana islands, he was killed in April 1521.

Upon Magellan's death, Juan Sebastian del Cano took over as captain and led the only surviving ship, the *Victoria*, on to the Indies. After trading everything they owned, including the shirts off their backs, the crew started home. Their homeward passage was a repeat of the nightmare of the Pacific crossing, with many starving on the way. The *Victoria* finally reached Seville on September 8, 1522, three years after the fleet had set out. Only one ship and seventeen men remained, but they had completed the first circumnavigation of the globe.

This exploit was not to be repeated until Sir Francis Drake sailed around the world for England, starting in 1577. He returned three years later, after raiding Spanish ports in South America, claiming part of California, and trading successfully with local rulers in the Spice Islands. One of his five ships, the *Golden Hind*, remained.

Yet so valuable was the trade with the East that both voyages, despite the shocking losses, more than made up the cost of sending them.

Book List

Bitossi, Sergio. *Ferdinand Magellan*. Silver Burdett, 1982. (Gr. 4-6)
One of the many biographies of this great explorer.

Blackwood, Alan. *Ferdinand Magellan*. Bookwright, 1986. (Gr. 4-6)
This version of Magellan's biography has many illustrations.

Brewster, Scott. *Ferdinand Magellan*. Silver Burdett, 1990. (Gr. 5-up)
A biography of the explorer, for older readers.

Brownlee, W. D. *The First Ships Round the World*. Cambridge University Press, 1974. (Gr. 4-up)
In addition to describing Magellan's historic voyage, Brownlee covers much information on ships and sailing at that time, and includes a number of diagrams.

Coote, Roger. *First Voyage around the World*. Bookwright, 1990. (Gr. 3-6)
Another general biography of Magellan.

Gerrard, Roy. *Sir Francis Drake: His Daring Deeds*. Farrar, Straus & Giroux, 1988. (K-3)
A history of Sir Francis Drake in verse, with pictures.

Goodnough, David. *Francis Drake*. Troll, 1979. (Gr. 3-6)
A biography of Francis Drake for younger readers.

Hargrove, Jim. *Ferdinand Magellan*. Children's Press, 1990. (Gr. 3-up)
An excellent biography of the Portuguese navigator who became the first to circumnavigate the globe.

Harley, Ruth. *Ferdinand Magellan*. Troll, 1979. (Gr. 3-5)
For younger readers, this is a serviceable, if uninspired, account of Magellan's voyage.

Hook, Jason. *Sir Francis Drake*. Bookwright, 1988. (Gr. 3-6)
Biography of the second man to circumnavigate the globe.

Humble, Richard. *The Voyage of Magellan*. Franklin Watts, 1988. (Gr. 4-up)
This entry on Magellan is part of a series on voyages of exploration that brings these exploits to life.

Jonas, Ann. *Round Trip*. Greenwillow, 1983. (PreK-2)
Black-and-white illustrations and text record the sights on a day trip to the city and back home again to the country in this picture book.

Quin-Harkin, Janet. *Peter Penny's Dance*. Dial, 1976. (PreK-2)
Peter Penny sets out to win a bride by dancing around the world.

Rockwell, Thomas. *How to Eat Fried Worms*. Franklin Watts, 1973. (Gr. 3-up)
Billy wants a minibike so badly that he is willing to do almost anything to get it.

Stefoff, Rebecca. *Ferdinand Magellan and the Discovery of the World Ocean*. Chelsea House, 1990. (Gr. 5-up)
A biography for older readers.

Sugden, John. *Sir Francis Drake*. Henry Holt, 1990. (Gr. 5-up)
Another look at the second man to circumnavigate the globe.

Related Activities

1. Magellan started out with high hopes for this voyage from which he would never return. Share the following song to demonstrate how he must have felt.

A-Sailing We Will Go
(sung to "A-Hunting We Will Go")

A-sailing we will go, a-sailing we will go,
We're sailing off around the world!
A-sailing we will go!

(Preschool, primary)

2. In addition to other problems, Magellan faced several attempted mutinies during his voyage when the captains of the other ships decided they had had enough and wanted to go home. At one point, to regain control of the fleet, he abandoned one of the captains on a desolate stretch of the South American coast.

To emphasize this action, play the game "Man Overboard." The players sit in a circle, or in two lines if you are playing two teams against each other. Have one player be the one who calls the moves, as Magellan. Magellan gives a command such as, "On deck!" Everyone jumps up. Magellan says, "Scrub the decks!" Everyone pretends to scrub the deck. Magellan cries, "Hoist the sails!" Everyone pretends to hoist the sails. "Man the helm!" Magellan orders. Everyone pretends to steer the helm. Magellan yells, "Climb the rigging!" Everyone pretends to climb the ropes. The slowest person to react each time is out. Magellan points to him or her and calls, "Man overboard!" and the player falls out of line. The winner is the last person left "on board" or the last team to have any members left.
(Primary)

3. Magellan's voyage was an incredible test of endurance for the men who survived it. After they entered the Pacific Ocean from the Strait of Magellan, more than three months passed before the fleet reached land again. During this time they were unable to obtain fresh food and water and were slowly starving. At one point they lived off the rats on board, and when the rats were all gone, they ate sawdust and the leather from the ship's rigging. Ask your group to try to picture what this experience must have been like. Get suggestions for recipes for rats that would make them seem edible. You might find ideas in Thomas Rockwell's *How to Eat Fried Worms*, in which the main character eats worms to win a bet. Read aloud some of the ways he has his worms prepared. To help children imagine a meal of leather and sawdust, pass out pieces of beef jerky and handfuls of crumbled soda crackers. This would probably have been a feast to Magellan and his crew!

For a more positive way to emphasize that Magellan and his men were reduced to eating parts of their ships, have a ship lunch and serve egg ships, tuna boats, and celery canoes. To make egg ships, peel hard-boiled eggs and cut them in half lengthwise to resemble ships. Make a sail for each ship by cutting a small square of paper. Poke a toothpick through the top and bottom of the sail, and insert the mast into the egg.

For tuna boats, stuff hot-dog rolls with tuna salad. Decorate the boats with sails. Make celery canoes from pieces of celery filled with cream cheese or peanut butter, and insert another sail. Bon appetit!
(Primary, intermediate)

4. Ask the children to pretend they are crew members on Magellan's voyage, and tell them to write letters to family back in Spain describing their experiences firsthand in the hope that somehow the letters will get home. Let children make envelope puppets of Magellan's battered crew, as shown in figure 11.8. They should each seal an envelope and then cut it in half. This creates a pocket for inserting the hand. The sailors can be drawn on construction paper, colored, and cut out. To make them more authentic, the children can add false limbs from toothpicks or tin foil, bits of yarn for beards, fabric scraps, etc.
(Primary, intermediate)

Fig. 11.8.

5. To emphasize the extent to which Magellan and his fleet were traveling blind, with no idea of what was next, have the children make reverse silhouette pictures. They can use black construction paper for the background. They should draw, decorate, and cut out ships like those Magellan sailed. Glue the ships to the black backgrounds. Tear strips of dark blue construction paper to make waves, and glue the "waves" to the backgrounds overlapping the ships. Tear cloud shapes from white construction paper or tissue paper, or use cotton balls glued in place.
(Primary)

6. By the time Magellan's fleet reached the Marianas, the men were desperate to find land. Have the children make sailors searching for land from the crow's nest, as shown in figure 11.9. For each crow's nest, use one egg carton cup and insert a popsicle stick into the bottom to represent the mast. Cut the upper half of a sailor from paper, small enough to be glued into the egg cup. The sailor's arm can be attached with a brad so that he can wave on sighting land.
(Primary)

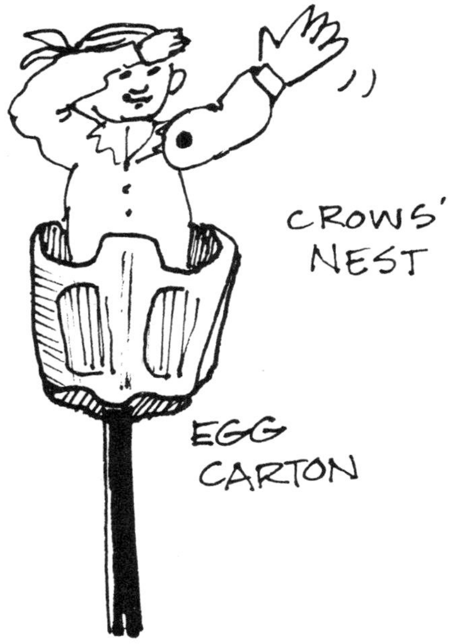

Fig. 11.9.

7. Imagine the excitement on board when land was finally sighted. Many sailors fell to their knees and sang hymns. Let your group sing the following song.

We Went Sailing
(sung to the tune of "She'll Be Coming 'Round the Mountain")

We went sailing on the ocean in our ships,
We went sailing on the ocean in our ships,
We went sailing on the ocean, we went sailing on the ocean,
We went sailing on the ocean in our ships.

Additional verses:

Oh, the stars were there to guide us in our ships...

Oh, the voyage was long and weary in our ships...

Oh, the seaweed floated round us in our ships...

Oh, the food and water rotted in our ships...

Oh, we wanted to sail back home in our ships...

Oh, the passage was well hidden from our ships...

Oh, the strait was long and narrow for our ships...

Oh, the ocean, it was endless in our ships...

Oh, we finally found the Indies in our ships...

Oh, we lost the gallant leader of our ships...

Oh, we finally made it back home in one ship.

(Primary)

8. Make flipbooks of Magellan's voyage. To make a flipbook, each child needs about two dozen index cards, stapled together on the left side. Use the top page for the title. On the last page, make a picture of the *Victoria* finally reaching port in Spain. Working from back to front, repeat the drawing, but move the ship a little bit to the left on each page. Add things to each scene that Magellan might have seen. For example, when he left Spain, the *Victoria* was accompanied by four other ships. Draw these ships in, and then at appropriate points drop them from the scene one at a time. When the children "flip" through their books, the ships will appear to be sailing.
(Primary, intermediate)

9. Introduce Sir Francis Drake by reading aloud Roy Gerrard's version of Drake's life. As a result of Drake's exploits, he was knighted by Queen Elizabeth of England. The children can make silver medallions to symbolize Drake's knighthood as shown in figure 11.10. Then let them create and act out a knighting ceremony.
(Primary, intermediate)

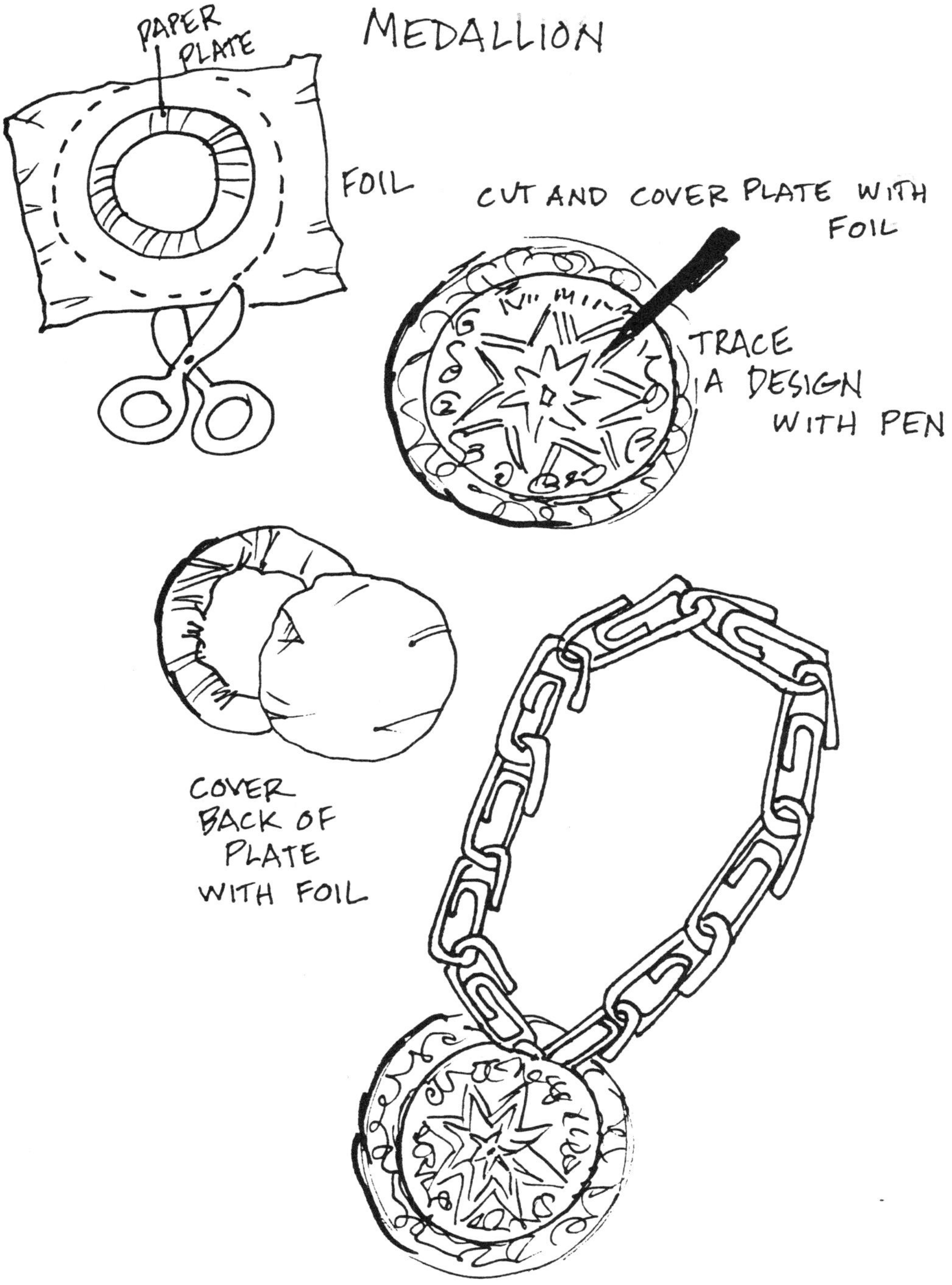

Fig. 11.10.

10. Describe for children all the places Drake went during his circumnavigation of the Earth. Then they can make ships with changing views of these different scenes. Tell them to color the ship picture shown in figure 11.11. They should cut out and remove the inside of the mainsail as indicated. Next, they should cut out the wheel in figure 11.12 and draw a scene Drake might have seen in each section.

(Text continues on page 270.)

Fig. 11.11.

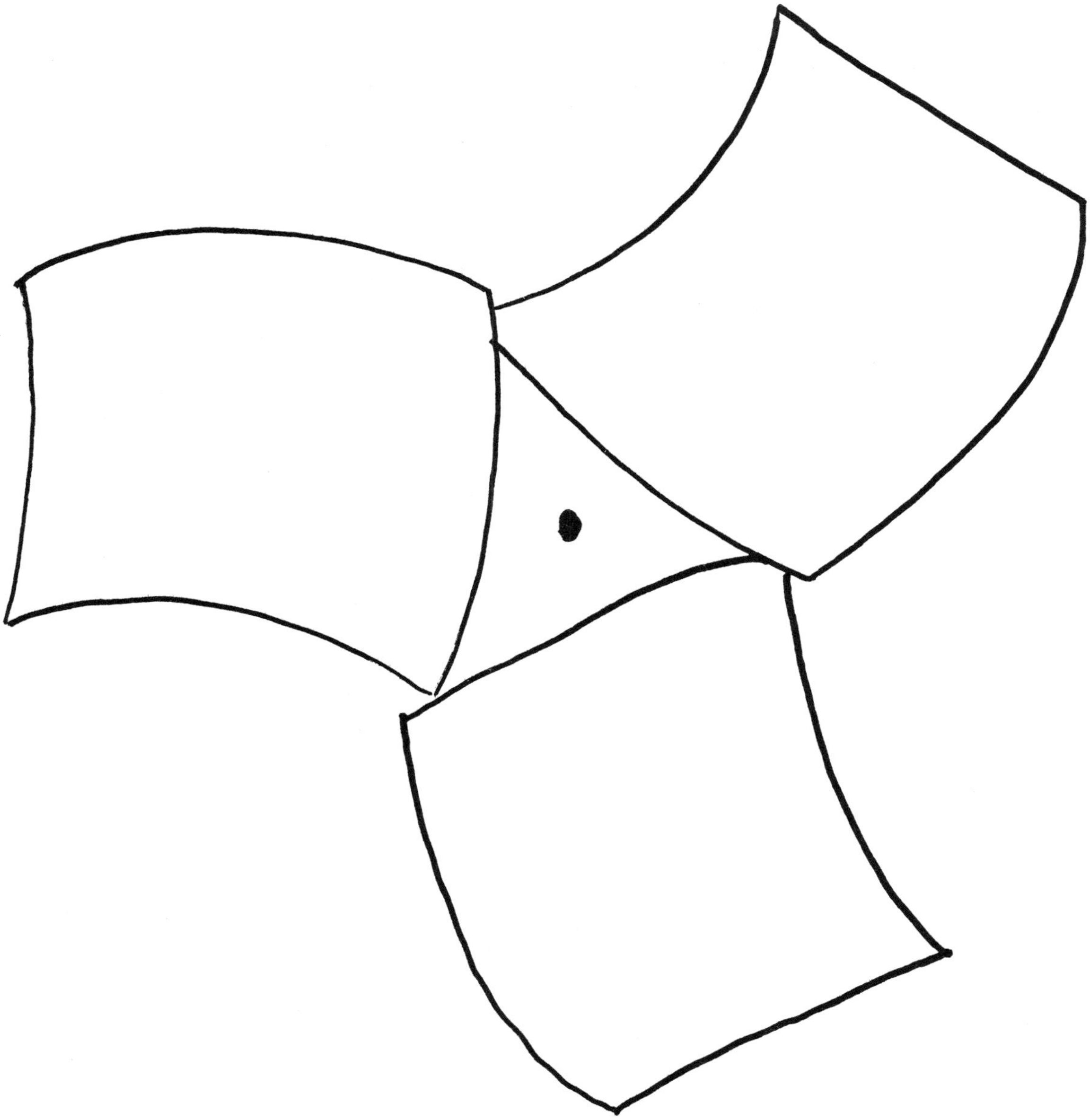

Fig. 11.12.

Fasten the wheel behind the ship with a paper brad pushed through the dot on the ship and on the wheel. Children can now turn the wheel from behind the ship to create different views. (Primary)

11. Read Ann Jonas's book *Round Trip*, about a family trip "there and back again." Then play the game "Around the World." Make a list of about fifteen destinations, such as the Canary Islands, Hispaniola, Brazil, the Spice Islands, India, Africa, China, Japan, the Azores, Madeira, the Cape Verde Islands, Jamaica, Mexico, Cuba, and San Salvador. Write each name on a separate piece of paper and tape it up somewhere in the area (this game is more fun in a large area or a long hallway). Have a spot that is labeled "Home Port." Each player gets a list containing the names of these places, but each list is written in a different order. The children start from "Home Port" and have to run to each place according to the order of their list. When they go to each place, they tick that name off. The first child to complete the list and get back to "Home Port" wins. (Primary, intermediate)

12. To represent both Magellan's and Drake's voyages, make "Around the World" mobiles. Each child should make about half a dozen ships to hang from the mobile. Sails can be drawn and cut from white paper, and designs can be added if desired. Hulls can be cut from brown paper. The hulls and sails are taped together. Next, the frame for the mobile should be made. Give each child a large square of posterboard. The children should draw a spiral circle on the posterboard and cut the spirals out. With the spiral hanging down, the ships should be attached at various points, as shown in figure 11.13. The mobiles will turn around in the wind and represent the circumnavigation of the globe. (Primary, intermediate)

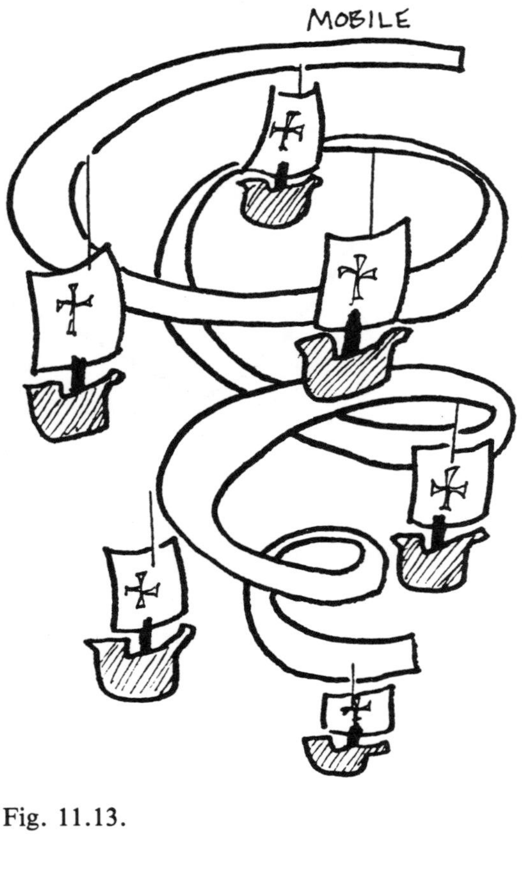

Fig. 11.13.

PASSAGE TO THE INDIES

Columbus set out to reach the Indies. That was his goal, and even though he found much of value in the Caribbean, he continued to search for a passage he was sure would lead him to the marvelous lands of the East. Almost every explorer after Columbus was searching for the same thing—the elusive passage to the Indies. It is ironic to contemplate that most of these explorers were not looking for what they found and never found what they were looking for. Though two new continents were discovered, and a new way of life was created for both the New World and the Old, all the voyages of discovery were, in this respect, a failure.

After Columbus, the lure of the East remained strong. In 1497, John Cabot crossed the Atlantic for England to search for the Indies. He tried again in 1498 but never returned. However, his voyages were the basis of the English claims to land in the New World. As we have seen, in 1498 Vasco da Gama managed to reach the Indies by sailing south and east around Africa. In 1508, Sebastian Cabot explored parts of Canada for England while searching for a route to the Indies. Giovanni da Verrazano was an Italian who explored the coast of North America for France between 1524 and 1528 while looking for a way to the East. In the 1570s, Sir Martin Frobisher, an Englishman, searched for a Northwest Passage in Canada. John Davis was another Englishman searching for the passage after 1585. In 1622, William Baffin, an Englishman, searched for the Northwest Passage and discovered Baffin Bay and Baffin Island, which were named for him.

Henry Hudson searched for both a Northwest and a Northeast Passage and found Hudson Bay instead. In 1611, he was left there to die by his crew, who mutinied against him. The Northwest Passage was not finally found until 1847, by the British explorer Sir John Franklin, who died in the process. It never became commercially significant. It was not until 1914, with the completion of the Panama Canal, that an ocean passage from Europe to the Indies was finally realized.

Book List

Cole, William. *The Sea, Ships and Sailors*. Viking, 1967. (Gr. 3-up)
This collection of poetry includes "Meditations of a Mariner" by Wallace Irwin.

Denton, Terry. *Home Is the Sailor*. Houghton Mifflin, 1988. (PreK-2)
A young boy and his penguin friend set sail to find cooler waters and meet a stranded old sailor in search of the land of the midnight sun.

Ginsburg, Mirra. *Four Brave Sailors*. Greenwillow, 1987. (PreK)
The sailors in this book are afraid of only the cat.

Glazer, Tom. *Do Your Ears Hang Low?* Doubleday, 1980. (All ages)
This collection of songs includes "The Long-Legged Sailor" and "Michael, Row the Boat Ashore."

Goodnough, David. *John Cabot and Son*. Troll, 1979. (Gr. 2-4)
A biography of these explorers for younger readers.

Harley, Ruth. *Henry Hudson*. Troll, 1979. (Gr. 2-4)
A brief look at the explorations of Henry Hudson.

Joseph, Joan. *Henry Hudson*. Franklin Watts, 1974. (Gr. 4-up)
This biography of Hudson is for older readers.

Sendak, Maurice. *Hector Protector and As I Went over the Water*. Harper & Row, 1965. (PreK-K)
Two nursery rhymes with pictures.

Spier, Peter. *Hurrah, We're Outward Bound!* Doubleday, 1968. (PreK-2)
A book of seafaring nursery rhymes.

Syme, Ronald. *John Cabot and His Son Sebastian*. Morrow, 1972. (Gr. 3-6)
A standard biography of the Cabots.

______. *Verrazano: Explorer of the Atlantic Coast*. Morrow, 1973. (Gr. 3-6)
Biography of the explorer who now has a bridge in New York City named for him.

Tashjian, Virginia. *Juba This and Juba That*. Little, Brown, 1969. (PreK-4)
This collection of songs and rhymes includes the song "My Bonnie Lies over the Ocean."

Vincent, Jean Anne, comp. *Patriotic Poems America Loves*. Doubleday, 1968. (Gr. 4-up)
Includes the poem "Henry Hudson's Quest" by Burton Egbert Stevenson.

Related Activities

1. John Cabot was actually an Italian like Columbus, although he sailed for England. He seems to have come up with the same idea of sailing west to reach the East and must have been very disappointed when Columbus apparently succeeded. However, Cabot still thought there was a chance for him to the north, to make a claim on parts of the East not found by Columbus. Therefore, in 1497, with the backing of the merchants of Bristol, he set out on a northerly route and explored the Canadian coast. In some ways, his feat was even more amazing than Columbus's. He took only one ship, so if anything had happened, he had no backup. His ship was the tiny *Matthew*, with only about twenty men as crew.

Share some of the biographies of Cabot with the group. Then, to represent Cabot's daring in braving the Atlantic with so small a force, the children can make little ships from egg-carton cups. Each child needs one cup, which is the hull of the ship. Paint the cup brown. Cut sails and flags from white paper to decorate. Using them like straight pins, insert toothpicks through the sails and flags as the masts. Poke the end of the toothpicks into the bottom of the egg-carton cups and hold them with a drop of glue.
(Primary, intermediate)

2. The early searchers for the Northwest Passage were convinced that if they could just get past the landmass of the Americas, which they guessed was much smaller than it is, they would find the Indies close by. Obviously, they had not yet worked out the puzzle of the world's geography. Share the book *Home Is the Sailor* by Terry Denton, about another sailor's search. Have the children make the Americas into a puzzle that they can put together. Give each child a copy of a map that includes North and South America. Ask them to color the maps, inserting as much detail as you choose. They should then glue their maps to pieces of cardboard for a stiff backing and cut the maps into odd-shaped puzzle pieces. They can use the puzzles as a game to help them learn the geography of the Americas.
(Primary)

3. After Columbus opened the way, a number of countries began to send out ships to the New World, hoping a grab a "piece of Spain's pie." Ask the children in your group to each pick a post-Columbian explorer to research.

Give the children copies of the ship pattern in figure 11.14 to trace onto posterboard. They can decorate the sails with the insignia of the country their explorer represents. Then they should cut out their ships and thread strings through the string hole. If they tie one end of the string to a chair and hold the other, they can race their ships to the New World.
(Primary)

4. Each voyager hoped he would be the one to find the elusive passage to the Indies. Share the books *Hector Protector and As I Went over the Water* by Maurice Sendak and *Hurrah, We're Outward Bound!* by Peter Spier. Then play the game "Find the Passage." Make a map by drawing a large landmass with coves and inlets, and somewhere include a very small passageway through the landmass. Label the passage the "Northwest Passage." Tape the map on a wall and give each child a different colored marker. For each child's turn, blindfold him or her, spin him or her around, and point him or her toward the map. When everyone has had a turn, the child whose mark is closest to the Northwest Passage is the winner.
(Primary, intermediate)

5. Many of the common seamen on these voyages must have found it extremely frustrating to search for a passage that was not there. We know that there were a few mutinies, such as the one that left Henry Hudson floating in Hudson Bay. The children can pretend to be these sailors and make sailor masks from paper plates, as shown in figure 11.15. Cut the scarf and beard from paper and glue them onto the paper plate. Share the poem "Meditations of a Mariner" by Wallace Irving, from William Cole's *The Sea, Ships and Sailors*. For younger children, read Mirra Ginsburg's *Four Brave Sailors*. Have a sailor's sing-along, using the songs below. You can also use "The Long-Legged Sailor" and "Michael, Row the Boat Ashore," from Tom Glazer's *Do Your Ears Hang Low?* and "My Bonnie Lies over the Ocean," from Virginia Tashjian's *Juba This and Juba That*.

Ships Are Sailing
(sung to the tune of "Frere Jacques")

Ships are sailing, ships are sailing,
On the sea, on the sea,
Off to find a passage to lead us to the Indies!
Come with me, come with me!

A Sailor Went to Sea, Sea, Sea
(sung to traditional tune)

A sailor went to sea, sea, sea,
To see what he could see, see, see,
But all that he could see, see, see,
Was the bottom of the deep, blue sea.

(Preschool, primary)

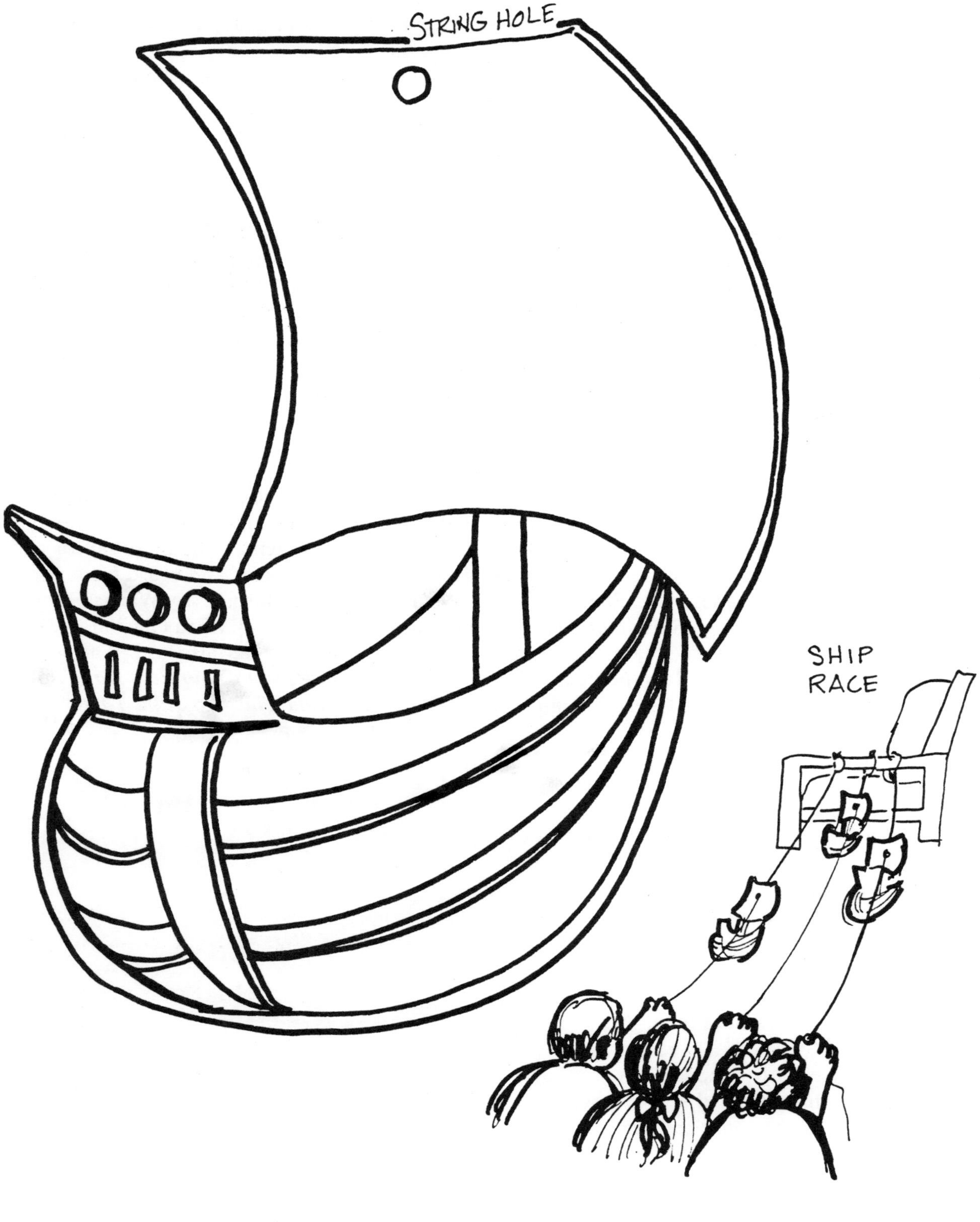

Fig. 11.14.

Fig. 11.15.

6. Henry Hudson was an explorer who sailed twice to try to find the Northwest Passage. Imagine Hudson on his ship, peering out into the fog. Share the biographies about him. Read the poem "Henry Hudson's Quest' by Burton Egbert Stevenson, from *Patriotic Poems America Loves* compiled by Jean Anne Vincent, which reveals how frustrating many explorers found the American landmass. The refrain is "God's crypt is sealed! 'Twill stand revealed in His own good time." The children can make spyglasses, to pretend they are Hudson searching for the passage, by inserting a small cardboard tube into a larger one.
(Primary, intermediate)

12

Where Do We Go from Here?

Throughout this book, we have looked at voyages of discovery leading to the New World. Once the route was charted, permanent colonies began to be established. Ships still plied the Atlantic, but their job had become that of delivering goods rather than carrying searchers. From this point on, most of the exploration of the Americas took place over land. The great age of voyages of discovery was almost over. There was still Captain James Cook's Pacific voyages to come, in which he opened the sea lanes to Australia and the Pacific islands and proved that there was no great southern continent, as people had believed for centuries.

After Captain Cook, the basic outlines of our world were known. Further exploration was undertaken to map the interiors of the great continents discovered by Europeans. By the end of the nineteenth century the interior of North America was mapped. Australia was explored from the sixteenth to the nineteenth centuries. By the end of the 1800s, men such as David Livingstone had covered the African interior. The next goal for exploration became the poles. In 1909, Robert Peary and Matthew Henson reached the North Pole, and in 1911, the South Pole was reached by Roald Amundsen.

Even though it appeared the whole world was known, people were still looking for challenges. In 1953, Sir Edmund Hillary and Tenzing Norgay scaled the heights of Mount Everest. Jacques Cousteau and others have searched for the secrets beneath the oceans.

We began our "voyage to discovery" by looking at the spirit of exploration, with its qualities of imagination, curiosity, and ambition. In the sections below, we end with the same theme but enlarge our vision to include the vast frontier before us. Bon voyage!

SPACE TRAVEL

The next challenge has been called the "final frontier," but so far we have taken only a tiny step into the unknown reaches of space. In 1969, Neil Armstrong and Buzz Aldrin became the first men to explore the moon. The vast universe still stands as a challenge to our inquisitiveness. In the meantime, we work to perfect vehicles for getting around in space, such as the space shuttles, and send out unmanned probes to "scout the terrain." Perhaps one day, some of your students will go on voyages of discovery to New Worlds like Columbus did.

Book List

Ames, Lee J. *Draw 50 Airplanes, Aircraft and Spacecraft*. Doubleday, 1977. (Gr. 3-up)
Spacecraft are included in these vehicles to draw.

Asch, Frank. *Mooncake*. Prentice Hall, 1983. (PreK)
When Little Bear travels to the moon, he thinks it is delicious.

Barton, Byron. *I Want to Be an Astronaut*. Crowell, 1988. (Gr. 2-4)
In this picture book, a child wants to go to outer space and describes all the things astronauts do.

Blocksma, Mary. *Easy-to-Make Spaceships That Really Fly*. Prentice Hall, 1983. (Gr. 2-6)
Great ideas for making flying spaceships. Also use Blocksma's book *Space-Crafting* (1986).

Bolognese, Don. *Drawing Spaceships and Other Spacecraft*. Franklin Watts, 1982. (Gr. 3-up)
A drawing instruction book on spacecraft.

Cole, Ann, Carolyn Haas, Eiizabeth Heller, and Betty Weinberger. *A Pumpkin in a Pear Tree: Creative Ideas for 12 Months of Holiday Fun*. Little, Brown, 1976.
Among the many holidays included in this collection of activities is Moon Day.

Demarest, Chris. *The Lunatic Adventures of Kitman and Willy*. Simon & Schuster, 1988. (PreK-2)
When Kitman and Willy take off for space and dislodge the moon and stars, they have to devise a way of putting them back.

Hall, Carol. *I Been There*. Doubleday, 1977. (K-3)
The boy in this story takes off on a voyage of discovery to the moon—in his imagination.

Keats, Ezra Jack. *Regards to the Man in the Moon*. Macmillan, 1985. (PreK-2)
Neighborhood children use junk to spur their imaginations for a voyage to the moon.

MacDonald, Suse. *Space Spinners*. Dial, 1991. (PreK-2)
Two spiders climb aboard the space shuttle to be the first in space.

Murphy, Jill. *What Next, Baby Bear?* Dial, 1983. (PreK-2)
Baby Bear takes a quick trip to the moon while his mother runs his bath.

Rey, H. A. *Curious George Gets a Medal*. Houghton Mifflin, 1957. (PreK-2)
In the end of this story, George takes off into space.

Smythe, Malcolm. *Build Your Own Space Station*. Franklin Watts, 1985. (Gr. 1-6)
Included are ideas for spaceships, space stations, and space vehicles.

Williams, J. Alan. *Interplanetary Toy Book*. Macmillan, 1985. (Gr. 3-up)
Crafts and other activities about space travel.

Related Activities

1. Introduce the idea of space travel to your group with the books *Mooncake* by Frank Asch, *The Lunatic Adventures of Kitman and Willy* by Chris Demarest, *Space Spinners* by Suse MacDonald, and *Curious George Gets a Medal* by H. A. Rey. Then let the children make rockets. If you are working with young children, give them paper-towel tubes, paper scraps, stickers, sequins, and markers. Tell them to make their own rockets like the one shown in figure 12.1.

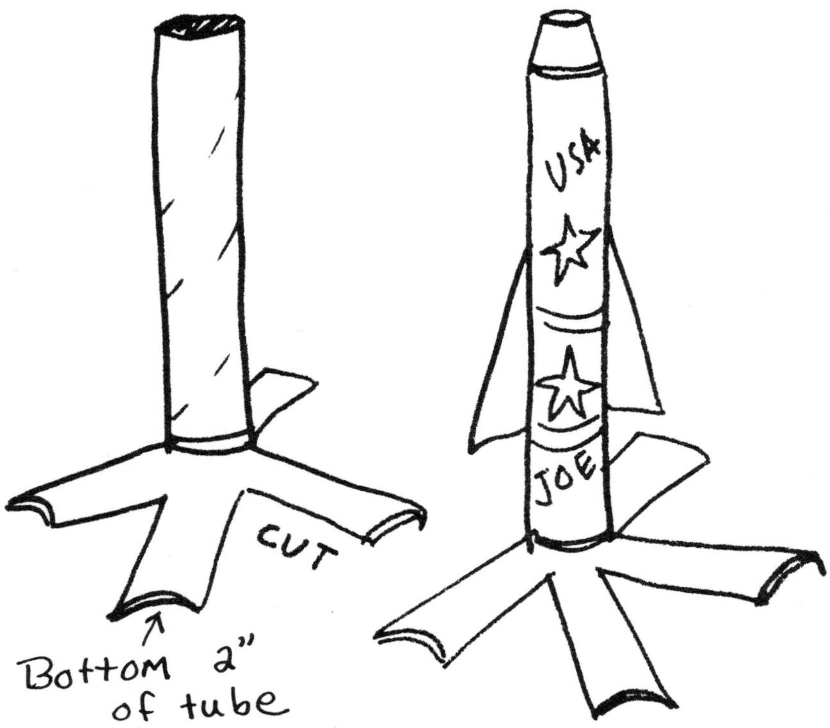

Fig. 12.1.

Older children would enjoy designing more elaborate rockets. They can use the books by Lee Ames, Mary Blocksma, Don Bolognese, and J. Alan Williams to make either detailed drawings or actual rockets from odds and ends.
(Preschool, primary, intermediate)

2. Older children will enjoy making space stations. Show them the ideas from the book by Malcolm Smythe and pictures from books about future space colonies. Then ask them to make a large model similar to the space station in figure 12.2. They could use boxes, paper bags, and other at-hand materials.
(Primary, intermediate)

Fig. 12.2.

3. Set the stage for enacting a space trip. Use a large appliance box to make a rocket big enough for the children to sit in. Decorate the outside to look like a spaceship as shown in figure 12.3. On the inside, create an instrument panel, with markers, empty thread spools, jelly jar lids, and other odds and ends that can be made to look like controls. Make a mobile of the planets to hang above the ship. Older children can make the spaceship themselves. When the kids finish the spaceship, read Carol Hall's *I Been There*, Ezra Jack Keats's *Regards to the Man in the Moon*, and Jill Murphy's *What Next, Baby Bear?*
(Preschool, primary, intermediate)

Fig. 12.3.

4. Have the children dress up like astronauts by making space helmets from large grocery bags (see fig. 12.4). They should put the bags over their heads to check where their eyes are. They can make a light pencil mark on the spot and then cut a square out of the bag at that point. They can decorate the bags using silver paint, tin foil, pipe cleaners, glitter, sequins, buttons, and anything else that makes the bags look authentic. Read Byron Barton's *I Want to Be an Astronaut*.
(Preschool, primary)

Fig. 12.4.

5. Take pictures of your astronauts with a camera, and make a bulletin board using these pictures. Put up a large piece of newsprint cut into a rocket shape. Cover it with astronaut pictures so that they appear to be looking out the windows of the rocket, as shown in figure 12.5.
(Preschool, primary)

6. Let the children play some space games. If you have room, put a lot of cushions and sheets over the floor, give each child a flashlight, turn out the lights, and let children pretend they are walking on the moon.

Play musical chairs, but instead of having the children find a chair when the music stops, have them find a star or planet taped to the floor. Other ideas for games are provided in Ann Cole's *A Pumpkin in a Pear Tree*, listed with ideas for Moon Day.
(Preschool, primary)

7. Share a snack with your astronauts. If you can get some freeze-dried food, let them see what it is like. You can also serve sugar cookies cut into star, crescent, and rocket shapes. Give each child a cup of frosting, sprinkles, and redhots to decorate the cookies.
(Preschool, primary, intermediate)

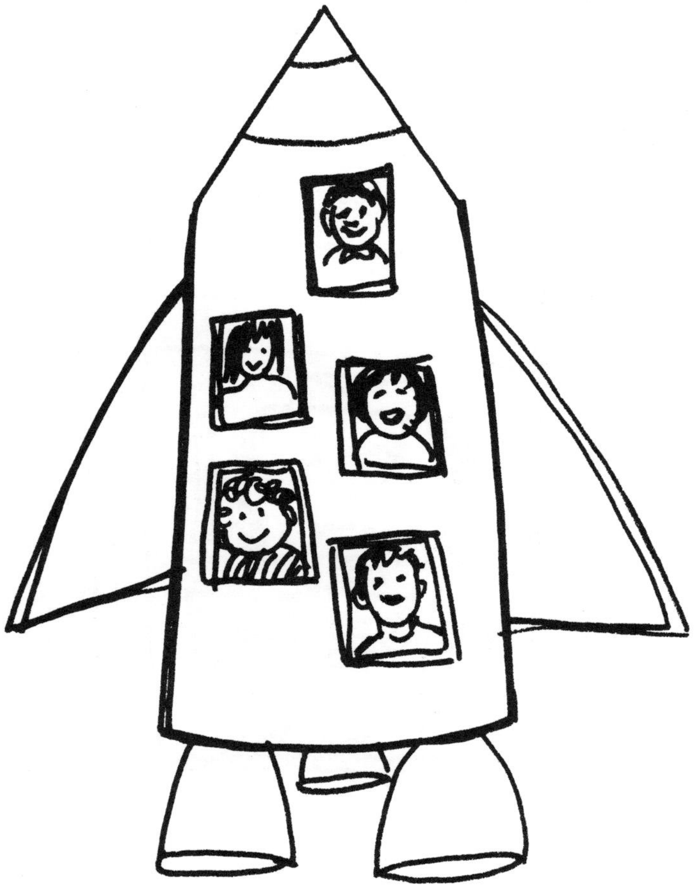

Fig. 12.5.

LIFE FROM OUTER SPACE

Though we are looking at space travel from a perspective of lighthearted adventure in this chapter, there is also a serious side to consider. When we introduce children to the topics of astronomy and space travel, we should also let them know about the possibility of other life in the universe. In the past, "alien" life has all too often been presented in the form of grotesque and hostile creatures. This is the same one-sided attitude that blinded European explorers to the value of the cultures they encountered.

We need to introduce the idea that other life forms out in the universe are as valuable as our own. We can learn to encounter the unknown, not with fear and prejudice, but with awe and curiosity.

Book List

Bradman, Tony. *It Came from Outer Space*. Dial, 1992. (PreK-2)
A twist on the theme of life from outer space, this picture book does not reveal until the end that the alien is a human.

Carey, Valerie. *Harriet and William and the Terrible Creature*. Dutton, 1985. (PreK-2)
While her brother gardens, Harriet takes off on a space adventure.

French, Fiona. *Future Story*. Oxford University Press, 1983. (Gr. 1-4)
A group of astronauts in space are endangered when they respond to a cry for help from the crystalized world of Narvis.

Kitamura, Satoshi. *UFO Diary*. Farrar, Straus & Giroux, 1989. (PreK-2)
An account of the travels of an unidentified flying object (UFO).

Marshall, Edward. *Space Case*. Dial, 1980. (PreK-3)
An alien visits Earth on Halloween, the one night he will not be noticed.

Pryor, Bonnie. *Mr. Munday and the Space Creature*. Simon & Schuster, 1989. (PreK-2)
Mr. Munday, the mailman, trades places with a spaceman.

Ungerer, Tomi. *Moon Man*. Harper & Row, 1967. (K-3)
The man-in-the-moon comes to Earth.

Wiesner, David. *Tuesday*. Clarion, 1991. (K-5)
In this story of the unexpected, frogs rise on their lily pads and fly through the air. What could be next? Pigs!

Willis, Jeanne. *Earthlets: As Explained by Professor Xargle*. Dutton, 1989. (K-3)
A humorous look at how aliens might see us. You can also use *Earth Hounds* (1988) and *Earth Tigerlets* (1990).

Related Activities

1. Have the children think about what life might be like on other planets, and read the books *Harriet and William and the Terrible Creature* by Valerie Carey, *Future Story* by Fiona French, and *UFO Diary* by Satoshi Kitamura. Have the children either draw pictures of creatures from another planet or make sculptures from odds and ends. Remind them that a creature's structure is dependent on its environment. For example, human beings are a product of the environment of Earth. If we came from Mars, we would not be equipped to breathe oxygen. Ask children to write a description of how their creature eats, breathes, thinks, etc., and how it reflects its home environment. (Preschool, primary, intermediate)

2. Read the books by Jeanne Willis, and then suggest other items that these aliens could examine. Instead of babies, dogs, and cats, ask children to describe elephants, buses, and elevators to a class of aliens who have never seen these things before. Have children write a paragraph or two of description for each item.
(Primary, intermediate)

3. If aliens come to visit us, they will not know any of our languages. Ask the children how we will communicate with them. Have children devise a pantomime to communicate the most important things they think an alien should know when first landing on Earth.
(Primary, intermediate)

4. Ask your group to imagine themselves as aliens arriving on Earth and to describe what they see and what happens to them. Share the book *Moon Man* by Tomi Ungerer.
(Preschool, primary, intermediate)

5. Reverse the activity above, and have the children imagine that they meet an alien. How would they feel and what would they do? Read Tony Bradman's *It Came from Outer Space* and Edward Marshall's *Space Case*.
(Preschool, primary, intermediate)

6. Read aloud *Mr. Munday and the Space Creature* by Bonnie Pryor. Then ask the children to imagine trading places with an alien for a day. They should pretend that somehow they have managed to disguise themselves so that no one knows they are not a "local." Ask children to describe everyday situations that are foreign to them and how they would handle these situations.
(Primary, intermediate)

7. Most children are aware that we have sent messages into space, both aboard unmanned flights and with radio signals. Ask the children to create a care package they would like to send into space to let others know about what we humans are like. What would be of great enough significance to be included?
(Primary, intermediate)

8. To emphasize the importance of imagination for future discovery, read *Tuesday* by David Wiesner. Then put a lot of random objects in a pillowcase. Put in as many items as you have children. Your objects could include things such as a shoe, the lid to a pot, a carrot, etc. Have the children each draw one item, and tell them to imagine that the object is alive and in their care. How will they take care of it? What are its needs?
(Primary, intermediate)

Afterword

With Columbus's arrival in the New World, a whole new era in human history began. No longer would the Americas and Europe be able to continue as separate entities. From this point on, their futures were bound together. Columbus's voyages unleashed forces that would change the Americas forever. In his wake would come a vast horde of searchers—first the conquistadors and explorers searching for gold and glory and, later, pilgrims and colonizers searching for religious and political freedom. To some extent, this latter search is still continuing. The United States of America still is eagerly sought by many people whose own countries cannot or will not offer them what they need.

The history of the United States is as complex as its beginnings. Invaded by people driven by greed and ambition, the country has nonetheless become a haven for many in search of a better life. Even though it offers valued freedom to some, the United States has enslaved, destroyed, and downtrodden others. Some immigrants have flourished; some, such as the unwilling African slaves, are just beginning to have the opportunity to enjoy their full share of the country's riches.

The history of exploration parallels the qualities of the human beings who forged it. There are moments of glory and moments of shame, just as in the people who made history there were acts of great daring and courage and acts of incredible cruelty and shortsightedness. At this point, we can only look back, try to understand, and, it is hoped, learn how to combine the best of our drive for progress with the best of our past.

A Chronology of Explorers

Listed below are some of the major explorers in history, from the earliest known through those who landed on the moon in 1969.

c.450 B.C.E.—Hanno. A Carthaginian who explored the northwest coast of Africa.

356-323 B.C.E.—Alexander the Great. The King of Macedonia who conquered the Persian empire, which extended to India.

320 B.C.E.—Pytheas. A Greek who sailed from the Mediterranean up the coast of Europe to Britain and beyond.

484-577 C.E.—Saint Brendan. An Irish abbot and missionary who crossed the Atlantic with seventeen other monks and reached America, according to legend.

c.950-c.1000—Eric the Red. A Viking from Iceland who discovered Greenland in 981. He established a settlement there that survived until the fifteenth century.

c.1000-?—Bjarni Herjolfson. A Viking who may have been the first European to sight North America after being blown off course while traveling from Iceland to Greenland. He did not land.

c.970-c.1020—Leif Ericson. A Viking who may have been the first European to land in North America around 1000. He followed the directions from Bjarni Herjolfson.

c.970-c.1010—Thorfinn Karlsefni. A Viking who followed Leif Ericson to America to establish a settlement around 1005. His group was eventually driven out by native Indians, and he returned to Iceland.

1180-1252—Giovanni da Pian del Carpini. An Italian friar who was sent by Pope Innocent IV as a missionary to the kingdom of the Mongol Khan between 1245 and 1247.

1254-1324—Marco Polo. A Venetian trader who, with his father and uncle, was one of the first Europeans to explore central Asia and China. He spent seventeen years in the service of Kublai Khan, the Mongol emperor of China. On returning to Venice in 1296, he was captured by the Genoese. During his imprisonment he dictated the account of his journeys that became Europe's image of the Orient for 300 years.

1304-1377—Ibn Battuta. An Arab who traveled extensively through North and East Africa, the Middle East, Southeast Asia, and China in the Middle Ages. He compiled an account of his travels.

1394-1460—Henry the Navigator. A Portuguese prince who sponsored many voyages down the coast of Africa. He established a school of navigation that gathered seafaring and exploration knowledge.

1441-1493—Martín Alonso Pinzón. The Spanish seaman who commanded the *Pinta* on Columbus's first voyage to the West Indies. He explored the Caribbean islands with Columbus.

1450-1500—Bartolomeu Dias. A Portuguese seaman who was the first to sail around the southern tip of Africa in 1488 and discover the Cape of Good Hope.

1451-1498—John Cabot. An Italian who crossed the Atlantic for England in 1497 and explored the Canadian coast. His explorations became the basis of English claims in the New World. He believed he had reached the Orient and went on a second voyage in 1498, from which he never returned.

1451-1506—Christopher Columbus. An Italian who discovered the Americas for Spain. Columbus was seeking a way to reach the East by sailing west. He never realized he had found a new world, but his voyage marked the beginning of a lasting relationship between the New World and the Old.

1451-1512—Amerigo Vespucci. An Italian explorer and navigator who first charted the Western Hemisphere and claimed it as a separate continent from that of the Far East. In 1507, the German cartographer Martin Waldseemüller put Amerigo's name on the new continent, calling it America.

1460-1521—Juan Ponce de León. A Spanish explorer who discovered Florida while searching for the Fountain of Youth. He also explored the Florida Keys and part of Florida's west coast. Earlier he had accompanied Columbus on his second voyage.

1460-1523—Vincente Yañez Pinzón. A Spaniard who sailed with Columbus on his first voyage and later explored the coasts of Brazil and Central America.

c.1460-1524—Vasco da Gama. A Portuguese navigator who was the first to sail around Africa to India, 1497 to 1498. He followed Dias's route, and his voyage established Portuguese trade in India.

1465-?—Alonso de Ojeda. A Spanish explorer who sailed with Columbus but rebelled against his leadership of the colony on Hispaniola. Later led his own expedition to South America with Amerigo Vespucci.

1468-1520—Pedro Álvares Cabral. A Portuguese navigator who found Brazil accidentally by sailing west while on an expedition to India around the Cape of Good Hope in 1500. He claimed Brazil for Portugal.

1474-1557—Sebastian Cabot. The son of John Cabot who explored Canada for England in 1508 and the coast of South America for Spain in 1526. In 1553 he searched with Sir Hugh Willoughby and Richard Chancellor for the Northwest Passage to open trade with Russia.

1475-1519—Vasco Núñez de Balboa. A Spanish conqueror who, in 1513, was the first European to see the Pacific Ocean. He founded a colony on the isthmus of Panama. In 1519 he was falsely executed for treason.

1475-1541—Francisco Pizarro. The Spanish conqueror of Peru who went to Hispaniola with Cortes and to Panama with Balboa in 1513. In 1532 he led an expedition to the Inca empire in Peru. He kidnapped the Inca ruler Atahualpa, held him for ransom, and eventually killed him. The Spanish subsequently plundered the Inca empire.

1476-1525—Juan Sebastian del Cano. A Spanish navigator who took command of the first round-the-world voyage after the death of Ferdinand Magellan. He returned to Spain in 1522.

1480-1521—Ferdinand Magellan. A Portuguese navigator who led the first round-the-world voyage for Spain in 1519. He set out with five ships but was killed in the Phillipines. Only one ship with eighteen survivors completed the trip.

1485-1528—Giovanni da Verrazano. An Italian navigator who sailed for France up the east coast of North America to Maine. He discovered New York and Narragansett Bay.

1485-1541—Pedro de Alvarado. A Spaniard who accompanied Cortés during the conquest of Mexico. After conquering much of Central America, he became governor of Guatemala in 1524. He died while searching for the legendary Seven Cities of Cibola.

1485-1547—Hernando Cortés. The Spaniard who conquered the Aztec empire in 1521. He had previously explored the coast of Mexico and later explored parts of Honduras and Baja California.

1490-1557—Alvar Núñez Cabeza de Vaca. A Spanish explorer who sailed to Florida with Panfilo de Narvaez in 1527-1528. The expedition was shipwrecked off the coast of Texas. Cabeza de Vaca survived and wandered the American Southwest until 1536. His stories became the basis for the legend of the Seven Cities of Cibola.

1491-1557—Jacques Cartier. A Frenchman who discovered and explored the St. Lawrence River and its gulf. He explored eastern Canada in three voyages from 1534 to 1542. He claimed the Gaspé Peninsula for France.

c.1500-?—Dirk Hartog. A Dutchman who was possibly the first European to set foot in Australia.

1500-1542—Hernando De Soto. A Spanish explorer who explored the southeastern part of the United States and is credited with the discovery of the Mississippi River.

c.1500-1546—Francisco de Orellana. A Spaniard who explored the Amazon area of South America.

1500-1554—Hugh Willoughby. An Englishman who tried to find the Northwest Passage.

1510-1554—Francisco Vásquez de Coronado. A Spaniard who explored the southwestern United States north of the Rio Grande in search of the Seven Golden Cities of Cibola in 1540.

?-1584—Timofeyevich Yermak. A Cossack commander who explored and conquered Siberia.

c.1539-1594—Sir Martin Frobisher. An Englishman who discovered Frobisher Bay in Baffin Island in 1576. He searched unsuccessfully for a northwest passage around Canada. In 1578, he sailed up a body of water he named the "Mistaken Strait" that became known as the Hudson Strait.

1541-1596—Sir Francis Drake. The first Englishman to lead a round-the-world expedition for England in 1577 to 1580.

1550-1597—Willem Barents. A Dutchman who explored the Arctic between 1594 and 1596 in search of a northeast passage. The Barents Sea is named for him.

1550-1605—John Davis. An Englishman who explored the Arctic while attempting to find the Northwest Passage. He explored the Davis Strait.

1552-1616—Richard Hakluyt. An English geographer who promoted overseas explorations and the colonization of North America with his geographical writing.

?-1611—Henry Hudson. An English navigator who sought both the Northwest and Northeast Passages for England and for the Dutch. He sailed up the Hudson River to Albany and established the Dutch claim to the area. On his fourth voyage to Hudson Bay in 1611 his crew mutinied and set him adrift.

c.1570-?—Willem Jansz. A Dutch seaman who was the first known European to sight Australia.

1570-1635—Samuel de Champlain. A French explorer of Canada who founded Quebec and is called the Father of New France. He discovered the Ottawa River and Lakes Champlain, Ontario, and Huron. He traveled to North America twelve times between 1603 and 1633 searching for the Northwest Passage.

?-c.1625—Luis Vaez de Torres. A Spanish explorer who, in 1606, was the first to sail through the Torres Strait that separates Australia from New Guinea.

1584-1622—William Baffin. An Englishman who explored the Arctic looking for the Northwest Passage. Baffin Bay and Baffin Island are named for him.

1603-1659—Abel Janszoon Tasman. A Dutchman who discovered Tasmania, New Zealand, Tonga, and the Fiji Islands.

1637-1675—Jacques Marquette. A French missionary who explored the Great Lakes area and the Mississippi Valley with Louis Joliet.

1640-1710—Pierre Esprit Radisson. A French fur trader who explored Canada's Hudson Bay area and helped the British establish the fur trade and the Hudson Bay Company. He discovered the source of the Mississippi and was one of the first Europeans in Nebraska and the Dakotas.

1643-1687—René Robert Cavalier, sieur de La Salle. A Frenchman who explored North America from New France (for the Comte de Frontenac between 1672 and 1682) to Louisiana. He also discovered the lower Mississippi River.

1645-1700—Louis Joliet. A French-Canadian who explored the Mississippi River Valley with Father Jacques Marquette in 1673. He later explored and mapped the lower Saint Lawrence River, Labrador, and the Hudson Bay area.

1652-1715—William Dampier. An Englishman who explored the coasts of northwestern Australia.

1681-1741—Vitus Jonassen Bering. A Dane who explored the Bering Strait for Russia. He is credited with being the first to discover Alaska. He mapped much of the Siberian coast.

1728-1779—James Cook. An English navigator who explored the Pacific Ocean. He is considered to be the greatest explorer of the eighteenth century: was the first to survey the coast of Canada; went to Tahiti in search of the alledged great southern continent; proved that New Zealand consisted of two islands; and searched for the Northwest Passage from the Pacific side. He was killed in Hawaii in 1779.

1728-1795—Samuel Wallis. An English navigator who discovered the Wallis Islands in the southwestern Pacific Ocean in 1767.

1729-1811—Louis Antoine de Bougainville. The first Frenchman to sail around the world from 1766 to 1769.

1734—1820—Daniel Boone. An American frontiersman who explored the Kentucky region in the 1770s. He charted the Wilderness Road.

1745-1792—Samuel Hearne. An English fur trader and explorer in Canada who became the first European to reach the Arctic by traveling overland.

1750-1803—Nicolas Baudin. A Frenchman who explored the coast of southern Australia.

1755-1806—Robert Gray. An American navigator who established the U.S. claim to the Oregon Territory when he sailed into the mouth of the Columbia River in 1792. He was also the first seaman to carry the U.S. flag around the world.

1757-1798—George Vancouver. An Englishman who surveyed the west coast of North America from San Francisco to British Columbia. He explored the Pacific Northwest while searching for the Northwest Passage. Vancouver Island is named for him.

1763-c.1803—George Bass. A Briton who explored the coasts of southeast Australia and Tasmania.

1764-1820—Sir Alexander Mackenzie. A Scottish-born Canadian fur trader who explored northwest Canada by following the Mackenzie River to the Arctic Ocean. He reached the Pacific and became the first European to cross the North American continent.

1769-1859—Alexander von Humboldt. A German scientist whose interest in exploration led him to join an expedition to travel through South America from 1799 to 1804. He studied the flora, fauna, climate, and geology of Colombia, Ecuador, Mexico, and Peru. He also explored the Ural Mountains and Siberia.

1770-1838—William Clark. The first American to lead an expedition to the land between the Mississippi River and the Pacific Ocean with Meriwether Lewis between 1804 and 1806.

1771-1806—Mungo Park. A Scot who explored the Niger region and the River Niger in West Africa.

1774-1809—Meriwether Lewis. An American who explored the western United States with William Clark from 1804 to 1806.

1774-1814—Matthew Flinders. A British navigator who, in 1803, was the first European to circumnavigate Australia, mapping the coastlines.

1778-1852—Fabian Gottlieb von Bellingshausen. A Russian naval officer and scientist who, from 1819 to 1821, was the first to circumnavigate Antarctica.

1779-1813—Zebulon Montgomery Pike. An American who explored the West from the sources of the Mississippi to the headwaters of the Arkansas. He tried to scale Pike's Peak in central Colorado.

1786-1847—Sir John Franklin. A British explorer of the Arctic who discovered the Northwest Passage in 1847. The expedition disappeared during the trip. A cairn was later found containing the news of his discovery and his death.

1787-1834—James Weddell. A British navigator who charted the Weddell Sea, which lies southeast of South America within the Antarctic Circle.

1788-1827—Hugh Clapperton. A Scot who explored northern Nigeria. In 1822, he went on an expedition to Lake Chad. In 1825 he searched for the mouth of the Niger River but died before his quest was completed.

1788-1881—Sacajewea. A Shoshoni woman who served as interpreter and guide for the Lewis and Clark expedition from 1804 to 1806.

1790-1842—Jules Sebastian Cesar Dumont d'Urville. A French navigator and explorer of the Antarctic who discovered the statue of the Venus de Milo while charting the Mediterranean in 1820.

1790-1855—Sir William Edward Parry. A British explorer of the Arctic who tried to find the Northwest Passage with Sir John Ross's expedition. He discovered Barrow Strait and Prince Regent Island. In 1827 he tried to reach the North Pole and went further than anyone before him.

1793-1826—Alexander Laing. A Scot who was the first European to see the African city of Timbuktu.

1795-1869—Charles Sturt. A British soldier and colonial administrator who explored southeastern and central Australia between 1828 and 1844. He is called the father of Australian exploration.

1797-1873—Hamilton Hume. An Australian who explored southeastern Australia.

1799-1839—Rene Auguste Caille. A Frenchman who explored the Sahara.

1800-1862—Sir James Clark Ross. A British naval officer and explorer who discovered the north magnetic pole on July 1, 1831, on an expedition to the Arctic led by his uncle Sir John Ross. He also discovered the Ross Sea and the Victoria Land region and named Mount Erebus in Antarctica.

1803-1834—Richard Lander. A Briton who explored the River Niger with his brother John.

1804-1881—James Bridger. An American mountain man who explored the upper Missouri River and the Great Salt Lake area.

1813-1848—Ludwig Leichhardt. A German who explored northern Australia.

1813-1873—David Livingstone. A Scottish missionary who explored the interior of Africa. In 1849 he crossed the Kalahari Desert to Lake Ngami. Between 1853 and 1856 he explored central Africa and discovered Victoria Falls. He became the first European to cross the African continent from east to west. From 1866 to 1877 he searched for the sources of the Nile and Congo Rivers.

1813-1890—John Charles Fremont. An American explorer who surveyed the Oregon Trail in 1842. He was popularly known as the Pathfinder.

1815-1866—John McDouall Stuart. A Scot who went with Sturt's expedition to central Australia in 1844. In 1862, he crossed Australia from south to north.

1820-1861—Robert O'Hara Burke. An Irishman who crossed Australia from south to north with William Wills in 1860.

1821-1865—Heinrich Barth. A German explorer of northern and central Africa.

1821-1890—Richard F. Burton. A Briton who explored East Africa and discovered the great central African lakes. He was the first European to view Lake Tanganyika.

1821-1893—Sir Samuel White Baker. A Briton who explored the Nile and helped determine its source. He discovered Lake Albert in 1864.

1827-1864—John H. Speke. A Briton who discovered Lake Victoria. In 1850 he joined Sir Richard Burton's expedition. He left Burton and was the first to reach the source of the Nile.

1827-1892—James Grant. A Scot who explored the Nile with Speke.

1832-1901—Nils Nordenskjold. A Swede who was the first man to sail through the Northeast Passage.

1833-1905—Ferdinand von Richthofen. A German geologist and geographer who compiled the first survey of China between 1868 and 1872.

1841-1904—Henry Morton Stanley. An American journalist who explored the River Zaire in Africa. In 1871 he met Dr. Livingstone in Tanzania. He circumnavigated Lakes Tanganyika and Victoria and traced the Congo to its mouth.

1844-1894—Verney Lovett Cameron. An English explorer who went to Africa to meet with David Livingstone in 1873. Livingstone had died, so Cameron continued his journey across Africa from coast to coast.

1856-1920—Robert Edwin Peary. An American Arctic explorer who claimed to be the first man to reach the North Pole with Matthew Henson in 1909.

1861-1930—Fridtjof Nansen. A Norwegian who explored the Arctic.

1862-1943—Sir Aurel Stein. The Hungarian-born British geologist and archeologist who explored ancient caravan routes in central Asia. He discovered the Cave of the Thousand Buddhas at Tun-Huang that contained ancient Buddhist art and manuscripts.

1863-1942—Sir Francis Edward Younghusband. A British explorer and military officer who explored northern India, Tibet, and China. He opened trade with Tibet.

1866-1955—Matthew Alex Henson. An American explorer who went in search of the North Pole with Peary in 1909.

1868-1912—Robert Falcon Scott. A British naval officer who explored the Ross Sea in Antarctica. He led the second expedition to the South Pole in 1912, one month after Amundsen. He died on the return trip.

1872-1928—Roald Amundsen. A Norwegian who led the first expedition to the South Pole in 1911. He also discovered the Northwest Passage through the Arctic Ocean above North America between 1903 and 1906.

1874-1922—Sir Ernest Henry Shackleton. An Englishman who led an expedition in 1907 to Antarctica that discovered the south magnetic pole and reached the summit of Mount Erebus.

1882-1958—Sir Douglas Mawson. An Englishman who accompanied Shackleton's 1907 Antarctic expedition to climb Mount Erebus and locate the south magnetic pole. He explored and mapped parts of Antarctica.

1888-1957—Richard Evelyn Byrd. An American pilot who was the first man to fly over the North Pole in 1926 and the South Pole in 1929. He led expeditions to the South Pole between 1933 and 1947.

1908- —Sir Vivian Fuchs. An Englishman who led the twelve-man Commonwealth Trans-Arctic Expedition on the first land crossing of Antarctica in 1957.

1910- —Jacques-Yves Cousteau. A French undersea explorer who developed the aqualung. He has both written about and filmed many of his explorations.

1914- —Thor Heyerdahl. A Norwegian explorer who has studied how early civilizations may have traveled across the oceans. In 1947 on the Kon Tiki expedition he sailed a balsa wood raft from Peru to the Pacific Islands. In 1969 on the Ra expedition he crossed the Atlantic in a reed boat.

1914- —Tenzing Norgay. A Nepalese mountaineer who acted as guide for Sir Edmund Hillary and became one of the first men to reach the summit of Mount Everest in the Himalayas.

1919- —Sir Edmund Hillary. A New Zealand mountaineer and explorer who was the first to reach the summit of Mount Everest in the Himalayas in 1953 with Tenzing Norgay.

1921- —John H. Glenn, Jr. An American astronaut who became the first man to orbit the earth in the *Friendship 7* space capsule in 1962. His flight lasted almost five hours and circled the earth three times. In 1957, he became the first man to fly faster than the speed of sound.

1923- —Alan B. Shepard, Jr. The first American launched into space in 1961 aboard the *Freedom 7* space capsule. He was in space for fifteen minutes. He later became the fifth man to walk on the moon during the *Apollo 14* mission to the moon. He spent thirty-three hours on the moon.

1930- —Edwin Eugene (Buzz) Aldrin, Jr. An American astronaut who was the second man to walk on the moon during the *Apollo 11* lunar landing mission in 1969. He had also walked in space for five and a half hours as part of the *Gemini 12* mission.

1930- —Neil A. Armstrong. An American astronaut who was the first man to walk on the moon during the *Apollo 11* flight in 1969.

1930- —Michael Collins. An American astronaut who piloted *Gemini 10* and flew with *Apollo 11*, the first manned lunar landing mission.

1934-1968—Yuri Gagarin. A Russian cosmonaut who was the first man in space in 1961. He circled the earth once aboard the *Vostok 1* spacecraft.

1934- —Walter (Wally) Herbert. A Briton who led the first Trans-Arctic expedition.

Resource Bibliography

CHRISTOPHER COLUMBUS

Adler, David A. *A Picture Book of Christopher Columbus*. Holiday House, 1991.

Anderson, Joan. *Christopher Columbus: From Vision to Voyage*. Dial, 1991.

Baker, James W. *Columbus Day Magic*. Lerner, 1990.

Bourne, Russell. *Big Golden Book of Columbus and Other Adventurers*. Golden, 1990.

Brenner, Barbara. *If You Were There in 1492*. Bradbury, 1991.

Columbus, Christopher. *The Log of Christopher Columbus*. International Marine, 1987.

______. *The Log of Christopher Columbus's First Voyage to America in the Year 1492 as Copied Out in Brief by Bartholomew Las Casas*. Linnet, 1989.

Copeland, Peter F. *Columbus Discovers America Coloring Book*. Dover, 1988.

Dalghiesh, Alice. *The Columbus Story*. Scribner's, 1955.

D'Aulaire, Ingri, and Edgar Parin D'Aulaire. *Columbus*. Doubleday, 1955.

de Kay, James T. *Meet Christopher Columbus*. Random House, 1968.

Dodge, Stephen C. *Christopher Columbus and the First Voyages to the New World*. Chelsea House, 1991.

Dolan, Sean J. *Christopher Columbus: The Intrepid Mariner*. Fawcett Columbine, 1989.

Dor-Ner, Zvi. *Columbus and the Age of Discovery*. Morrow, 1991.

Dyson, John. *Columbus: For Gold, God, and Glory*. Simon & Schuster, 1991.

First Voyage to America: From the Log of the "Santa Maria." Dover, 1991.

Foster, Genevieve. *The World of Columbus and Sons*. Scribner's, 1965.

______. *Year of Columbus: 1492*. Scribner's, 1969.

Fradin, Dennis. *Columbus Day*. Enslow, 1990.

______. *The Niña, the Pinta, and the Santa Maria*. Franklin Watts, 1991.

Fritz, Jean. *The Great Adventure of Christopher Columbus*. Grosset & Dunlap, 1992.

______. *Where Do You Think You're Going, Christopher Columbus?* Putnam, 1980.

Giardini, Cesare. *The Life and Times of Columbus*. Curtis, 1967.

Gibbons, Gail. *Things to Make and Do for Columbus Day*. Franklin Watts, 1977.

Granzotto, Gianni. *Christopher Columbus: The Dream and the Obsession*. Doubleday, 1985.

Greene, Carol. *Christopher Columbus, A Great Explorer*. Children's Press, 1989.

Haskins, Jim. *Christopher Columbus: Admiral of the Open Sea*. Scholastic, 1988.

Heimann, Susan. *Christopher Columbus*. Franklin Watts, 1973.

Hills, Ken. *The Voyages of Columbus*. Random House, 1991.

Humble, Richard. *The Voyages of Columbus*. Franklin Watts, 1991.

Kent, Zachary. *Christopher Columbus: Expeditions to the New World*. Children's Press, 1991.

Krensky, Stephen. *Christopher Columbus*. Random House, 1991.

Lawson, Robert. *I Discover Columbus*. Viking, 1941.

Levinson, Nancy Smiler. *Christopher Columbus: Voyage to the Unknown*. Lodestar, 1990.

Liestman, Vicki. *Columbus Day*. Carolrhoda, 1991.

Lillegard, Dee. *My First Columbus Day Book*. Children's Press, 1987.

Litowinsky, Olga. *The High Voyage: The Final Crossing of Christopher Columbus*. Viking, 1977.

Lowe, Steve. *The Log of Christopher Columbus*. Philomel, 1992.

Marx, Robert F. *Following Columbus: The Voyage of the Nina II*. World, 1964.

Marzollo, Jean. *In 1492*. Scholastic, 1991.

Matthews, Rupert. *The Voyage of Columbus*. Bookwright, 1989.

Meltzer, Milton. *Columbus and the World around Him*. Franklin Watts, 1990.

Meredith, Robert, and E. Brooks Smith, eds. *The Quest of Columbus*. Little, Brown, 1966.

Monchieri, Lino. *Christopher Columbus*. Silver Burdett, 1985.

Morison, Samuel Eliot. *Admiral of the Ocean Sea: A Life of Christopher Columbus*. Little, Brown, 1942.

Morison, Samuel Eliot, and Mauricio Obregon. *The Caribbean as Columbus Saw It*. Little, Brown, 1964.

Nebenzahl, Kenneth. *Atlas of Columbus and the Great Discoveries*. Rand McNally, 1990.

Osborne, Mary Pope. *The Story of Christopher Columbus: Admiral of the Open Sea*. Dell, 1987.

Parker, Margot. *What Is Columbus Day?* Children's Press, 1985.

Pelta, Kathy. *Discovering Christopher Columbus: How History Is Invented*. Lerner, 1991.

Postgate, Oliver, and Naomi Linnell. *Columbus: The Triumphant Failure*. Franklin Watts, 1992.

Roop, Peter, and Connie Roop, eds. *I, Columbus: My Journal—1492-3*. Walker, 1990.

Sanderlin, George. *Across the Ocean Sea: A Journal of Columbus's Voyage*. Harper, 1966.

Showers, Paul. *Columbus Day*. Crowell, 1965.

Sis, Peter. *Follow the Dream: The Story of Christopher Columbus*. Knopf, 1991.

Soule, Gardner. *Christopher Columbus on the Green Sea of Darkness*. Franklin Watts, 1988.

Syme, Ronald. *Columbus: Finder of the New World*. Morrow, 1952.

Ventura, Piero. *Christopher Columbus*. Random House, 1978.

Weil, Lisl. *I, Christopher Columbus*. Atheneum, 1983.

West, Delno, and Jean M. West. *Christopher Columbus: The Great Adventure and How We Know about It*. Atheneum, 1991.

Young, Robert. *Christopher Columbus and His Voyage to America*. Silver Burdett, 1990.

Yue, Charlotte, and David Yue. *Christopher Columbus*. Houghton Mifflin, 1992.

GENERAL NONFICTION

Abels, Harriette. *The Loch Ness Monster*. Crestwood House, 1987.

______. *The Lost City of Atlantis*. Crestwood House, 1987.

Adkins, Jan. *The Craft of Sail: A Primer of Sailing*. Walker, 1973.

______. *Wooden Ship*. Houghton Mifflin, 1978.

Aliki. *Corn Is Maize: The Gift of the Indians*. Crowell, 1976.

______. *Wild and Woolly Mammoths*. Crowell, 1977.

Alper, Ann Fitzpatrick. *Forgotten Voyager: The Story of Amerigo Vespucci*. Carolrhoda, 1991.

Ames, Lee J. *Draw 50 Airplanes, Aircraft and Spacecraft*. Doubleday, 1977.

______. *Draw 50 Boats, Ships, Trucks, & Trains*. Doubleday, 1976.

______. *Draw 50 Sharks, Whales, and Other Sea Creatures*. Doubleday, 1989.

Anderson, Joan. *A Williamsburg Household*. Ticknor & Fields, 1988.

Armour, Richard. *Strange Monsters of the Sea*. McGraw-Hill, 1979.

Arnold, Caroline. *Llama*. Morrow, 1988.

______. *Maps and Globes*. Franklin Watts, 1984.

Ash, Maureen. *Alexander the Great: Ancient Empire Builder*. Children's Press, 1991.

______. *Vasco Núñez de Balboa*. Children's Press, 1990.

Asimov, Isaac. *The Shaping of North America*. Houghton Mifflin, 1973.

Atkinson, Ian. *The Viking Ships*. Lerner, 1979.

Baity, Elizabeth Chesley. *Americans before Columbus*. Viking, 1961.

Baker, Nina Brown. *Amerigo Vespucci*. Knopf, 1959.

Baker, Olaf. *Where the Buffalos Begin*. Frederick Warne, 1981.

Barden, Renardo. *The Discovery of America*. Greenhaven Press, 1989.

Barrett, Norman. *Sailing*. Franklin Watts, 1988.

Bateman, Penny. *Aztecs and Incas*. Franklin Watts, 1988.

Batherman, Muriel. *Before Columbus*. Houghton Mifflin, 1981.

Baylor, Byrd. *Before You Came This Way*. Dutton, 1969.

Beck, Barbara L. *The Ancient Maya*. Franklin Watts, 1983.

______. *The Aztecs*. Franklin Watts, 1983.

______. *The Incas*. Franklin Watts, 1983.

Bell, Neill. *The Book of Where or How to Be Naturally Geographic*. Little, Brown, 1982.

Bender, Lionel. *Invention*. Knopf, 1991.

Bendick, Jeanne. *The Mystery of the Loch Ness Monster*. McGraw-Hill, 1976.

Berenstain, Michael. *The Ship Book*. David McKay, 1978.

Berger, Josef. *Discoverers of the New World*. American Heritage, 1960.

Bernstein, Bonnie, and Leigh Blair. *Native American Crafts Workshop*. Fearon, 1982.

Beyer, Don E. *The Totem Pole Indians of the Northwest*. Franklin Watts, 1989.

Bierhorst, John, ed. *The Hungry Woman: Myths and Legends of the Aztecs*. Morrow, 1984.

______. *The Monkey's Haircut and Other Stories Told by the Maya*. Morrow, 1986.

______. *The Mythology of Mexico and Central America*. Morrow, 1990.

______. *The Naked Bear: Folktales of the Iroquois*. Morrow, 1987.

______. *The Whistling Skeleton: American Indian Tales of the Supernatural*. Macmillan, 1982.

Bierhorst, John, and Henry Schodcraft, eds. *Ring in the Prairie*. Dial, 1978.

Bitossi, Sergio. *Ferdinand Magellan*. Silver Burdett, 1982.

Blackwood, Alan. *Age of Exploration*. Bookwright, 1989.

______. *Ferdinand Magellan*. Bookwright, 1986.

Blocksma, Mary. *Easy-to-Make Spaceships That Really Fly*. Prentice Hall, 1983.

______. *Easy-to-Make Water Toys That Really Float*. Prentice Hall, 1985.

Blood, Charles L. *American Indian Games and Crafts*. Franklin Watts, 1981.

Bolognese, Don. *Drawing Spaceships and Other Spacecraft*. Franklin Watts, 1982.

Bottomley, Jim. *Paper Projects for Creative Kids of All Ages*. Little, Brown, 1983.

Bowman, John S. *The Quest for Atlantis*. Doubleday, 1971.

Brand, Oscar. *Singing Holidays*. Knopf, 1957.

Branley, Franklyn M. *The Big Dipper*. Crowell, 1990.

______. *Eclipse: Darkness in Daytime*. Crowell, 1988.

______. *North, South, East, and West*. Crowell, 1966.

Brewster, Scott. *Ferdinand Magellan*. Silver Burdett, 1990.

Brewton, John E., comp. *Gaily We Parade*. Macmillan, 1940.

Brown, Laurene Krasny, and Marc Brown. *Visiting the Art Museum*. Dutton, 1986.

Brownlee, W. D. *The First Ships around the World*. Lerner, 1977.

Bruchac, Joseph. *Iroquois Stories: Heroes and Heroines, Monsters and Magic*. Crossing Press, 1985.

Buehr, Walter. *The Portuguese Explorers*. Putnam, 1966.

______. *Sea Monsters*. Norton, 1966.

Burch, Joanne. *Isabella of Castille: Queen on Horseback*. Franklin Watts, 1991.

Burleigh, Robert. *Flight*. Philomel, 1991.

Caney, Steven. *Steven Caney's Invention Book*. Workman, 1985.

Cardini, Franco. *Europe, 1492*. Facts on File, 1989.

Carey, Helen H. *How to Use Maps and Globes*. Franklin Watts, 1983.

Carson, Robert. *Hernando de Soto: Expedition to the Mississippi*. Children's Press, 1991.

Carter, Alden R. *The Shoshoni*. Franklin Watts, 1989.

Cartwright, Sally. *What's in a Map?* Coward, McCann & Geoghegan, 1978.

Caselli, Giovanni. *A Florentine Merchant*. Peter Bedrick, 1986.

______. *A German Printer*. Peter Bedrick, 1986.

Ceserani, Gian Paolo. *Marco Polo*. Putnam, 1982.

Chadefaud, Catherine. *First Empires*. Silver Burdett, 1988.

Chant, Christopher. *Sailing Ships*. Marshall Cavendish, 1989.

Charlip, Remy, and Mary Beth Miller. *Handtalk*. Macmillan, 1974.

Chubb, Thomas Caldecot. *Prince Henry the Navigator and the Highways of the Sea*. Viking, 1970.

Clarke, Helen. *Vikings*. Gloucester Press, 1979.

Cobb, Vicki. *This Place Is Cold*. Walker, 1989.

______. *This Place Is High*. Walker, 1989.

Cohen, Daniel. *Hiram Bingham and the Dream of Gold*. M. Evans & Company, 1984.

Coldrey, Jennifer, and David Shale. *The World of the Jellyfish*. Gareth Stevens, 1987.

Cole, Ann, Carolyn Haas, Elizabeth Heller, and Betty Weinberger. *A Pumpkin in a Pear Tree: Creative Ideas for 12 Months of Holiday Fun*. Little, Brown, 1976.

Cole, Joanna. *Hungry, Hungry Sharks*. Random House, 1986.

Cole, William. *The Sea, Ships and Sailors: Poems, Songs and Shanties*. Viking, 1967.

Collins, James L. *Exploring the American West*. Franklin Watts, 1989.

Comins, Jeremy. *Eskimo Crafts and Their Cultural Background*. Lothrop, Lee & Shepard, 1975.

Connolly, James E. *Why the Possum's Tail Is Bare: And Other North American Indian Nature Tales*. Stemmer, 1985.

Connolly, Peter. *The Legend of Odysseus*. Oxford University Press, 1986.

Cooke, Jean. *Archaeology*. Warwick Press, 1981.

Coote, Roger. *First Voyage around the World*. Bookwright, 1990.

Cosman, Madeleine Pelner. *Medieval Holidays and Festivals*. Scribner's, 1981.

Crosher, Judith. *The Aztecs*. Macdonald Education, 1976.

Cunningham, Maggi. *The Cherokee Tale-Teller*. Dillon, 1978.

Curtis, Edward S. *The Girl Who Married a Ghost and Other Tales from the North American Indian*. Four Winds Press, 1978.

D'Amato, Janet, and Alex D'Amato. *Indian Crafts*. Sayre, 1968.

Darling, Kathy. *Manatee on Location*. Lothrop, Lee & Shepard, 1991.

D'Aulaire, Ingri, and Edgar Parin D'Aulaire. *Leif the Lucky*. Doubleday, 1941.

Davies, Penelope. *Growing Up in the Middle Ages*. Wayland Books, 1972.

DeArmond, Dale. *The Boy Who Found the Light*. Little, Brown, 1990.

Demi. *The Adventures of Marco Polo*. Holt, Rinehart & Winston, 1982.

______. *Chingis Khan*. Holt, Rinehart & Winston, 1991.

de Wit, Dorothy, ed. *The Talking Stone: An Anthology of Native American Tales and Legends*. Greenwillow, 1979.

Dingwall, Laima. *Bison*. Grolier, 1986.

Doherty, Craig A., and Katherine M. Doherty. *The Iroquois*. Franklin Watts, 1989.

______. *The Apaches and Navajos*. Franklin Watts, 1969.

Donnelly, Judy. *All around the World*. Grosset & Dunlap, 1991.

Dyment, John. *Meet the Men Who Sailed the Seas*. Random House, 1966.

Edelman, Lynn. *Kings, Queens, Knights, and Jesters: Making Medieval Costumes*. Harper & Row, 1978.

Elting, Mary. *If You Lived in the Days of the Wild Mammoth Hunters*. Four Winds Press, 1968.

Endacott, Geoff. *Discovery and Invention*. Viking, 1991.

Evitts, William. *Captive Bodies, Free Spirits: The Story of Southern Slavery*. Messner, 1985.

The Explorer World Atlas. Rand McNally, 1991.

Fernandez-Armesto, Felipe, ed. *The Times Atlas of World Exploration*. HarperCollins, 1991.

Fichter, George S. *How the Plains Indians Lived*. Morrow, 1962.

Field, Edward. *Eskimo Songs and Stories*. Delacorte, 1973.

Fine, John Christopher. *Sunken Ships and Treasure*. Macmillan, 1986.

Finger, Charles J. *Tales from Silver Lands*. Doubleday, 1924.

Finkelstein, Norman H. *The Other 1492: Jewish Settlement in the New World*. Scribner's, 1989.

Fisher, Leonard Everett. *Prince Henry the Navigator*. Macmillan, 1990.

Fradin, Dennis. *Archaeology*. Children's Press, 1983.

______. *The Cheyenne*. Children's Press, 1988.

______. *Explorers*. Children's Press, 1984.

______. *The Shoshoni*. Children's Press, 1989.

Frame, Paul. *Drawing Sharks, Whales, Dolphins and Seals*. Franklin Watts, 1983.

Freedman, Russell. *Farm Babies*. Holiday House, 1988.

Fritz, Jean. *Brendan the Navigator: A History Mystery about the Discovery of America*. Coward, McCann & Geoghegan, 1979.

______. *The Man Who Loved Books*. Putnam, 1981.

Gemming, Elizabeth. *Lost City in the Clouds: The Discovery of Machu Picchu*. Coward, McCann & Geoghegan, 1980.

Gemmings, Sara. *The Atocha Treasure*. Rourke, 1988.

Gerrard, Roy. *Sir Frances Drake: His Daring Deeds*. Farrar, Straus & Giroux, 1988.

Gibb, Christopher. *A Viking Sailor*. Rourke, 1986.

Gifford, Douglas. *Warriors, Gods and Spirits from Central and South America*. Schoeken Books, 1983.

Gilbreath, Alice. *Fun with Weaving*. Morrow, 1976.

Glazer, Tom. *Do Your Ears Hang Low?* Doubleday, 1980.

______. *Eye Winker, Tom Tinker, Chin Chopper*. Doubleday, 1973.

Glubok, Shirley. *The Art of the North American Indians*. Harper & Row, 1964.

______. *The Art of the Northwest Coast Indians*. Macmillan, 1975.

______. *The Art of the Plains Indians*. Macmillan, 1975.

______. *The Art of the Woodland Indians*. Macmillan, 1976.

Goldsmith-Carter, George. *Sailing Ships and Sailing Craft*. Grosset & Dunlap, 1970.

Goodnough, David. *Francis Drake*. Troll, 1979.

______. *John Cabot and Son*. Troll, 1979.

Gorsline, Marie, and Douglas Gorsline. *North American Indians*. Random House, 1978.

Grant, Neil. *The Discoverers*. Marshall Cavendish, 1979.

______. *The Explorers*. Silver Burdett, 1979.

Graves, Charles Parlin. *Marco Polo*. Chelsea Juniors, 1991.

Greene, Carol. *Marco Polo, Voyager to the Orient*. Children's Press, 1987.

Gustafson, Anita. *Monster Rolling Skull and Other Native American Tales*. Harper & Row, 1980.

Hahn, Elizabeth. *The Inuit*. Rourke, 1990.

Hamilton, Virginia. *In the Beginning: Creation Stories from around the World*. Harcourt Brace Jovanovich, 1988.

______. *The Dark Way: Stories from the Spirit World*. Harcourt Brace Jovanovich, 1990.

Hargrove, Jim. *Ferdinand Magellan*. Children's Press, 1990.

Harley, Ruth. *Ferdinand Magellan*. Troll, 1979.

______. *Henry Hudson*. Troll, 1979.

Harris, Christie. *Mouse Woman and the Vanished Princesses*. Atheneum, 1976.

Harris, Nathaniel. *Montezuma and the Aztecs*. Bookwright, 1986.

Hart, Jane. *Singing Bee! A Collection of Favorite Children's Songs*. Lothrop, Lee & Shepard, 1982.

Haskins, Jim. *Against All Opposition: Black Explorers in America*. Walker, 1992.

Hautzig, Esther. *At Home: A Visit in Four Languages*. Macmillan, 1968.

Hellman, Hal. *Navigation: Land, Sea & Sky*. Prentice Hall, 1966.

Herda, D. J. *Model Boats and Ships*. Franklin Watts, 1982.

Hillerman, Tony, ed. *The Boy Who Made a Dragonfly: A Zuni Myth*. Harper & Row, 1972.

Hirsch, S. Carl. *On Course! Navigating in Sea, Air, and Space*. Viking, 1967.

Hofsinde, Robert. *Indian Costumes*. Morrow, 1968.

______. *Indian Sign Language*. Morrow, 1956.

Hook, Jason. *Sir Francis Drake*. Bookwright, 1988.

Houston, James. *Kiviok's Magic Journey*. Atheneum, 1974.

______. *Songs of the Dream People*. Atheneum, 1972.

Humble, Richard. *The Age of Leif Eriksson*. Franklin Watts, 1989.

______. *Ships: Sailors and the Sea*. Franklin Watts, 1991.

______. *The Travels of Marco Polo*. Franklin Watts, 1990.

______. *The Voyage of Magellan*. Franklin Watts, 1988.

Hunter, Nigel. *Expedition of Cortés*. Bookwright, 1990.

Ipcar, Dahlov. *Horses of Long Ago*. Doubleday, 1965.

Irwin, Constance. *Strange Footprints on the Land: Vikings in America*. Harper & Row, 1980.

Jacobs, Francine. *The Tainos: The People Who Welcomed Columbus*. Putnam, 1992.

Jacobs, W. J. *Prince Henry the Navigator*. Franklin Watts, 1973.

Jacobson, Daniel. *Indians of North America*. Franklin Watts, 1983.

Jensen, Malcolm C. *Francisco Coronado*. Franklin Watts, 1974.

______. *Leif Erikson the Lucky*. Franklin Watts, 1979.

Johnson, Sylvia. *Coral Reefs*. Lerner, 1984.

Jones, Hettie. *Longhouse Winter*. Holt, Rinehart and Winston, 1972.

Joseph, Joan. *Henry Hudson*. Franklin Watts, 1974.

Jurmain, Suzanne. *Once upon a Horse: A History of Horses and How They Shaped Our History*. Lothrop, Lee & Shepard, 1989.

Karen, Ruth. *Song of the Quail: The Wondrous World of the Maya*. Four Winds Press, 1972.

______. *Kingdom of the Sun*. Four Winds Press, 1975.

Kelly, Karin. *Weaving*. Lerner, 1973.

Kemp, Peter. *The History of Ships*. Orbis, 1978.

Kemp, Peter, ed. *Encyclopedia of Ships and Seafaring*. Crown, 1980.

Knight, David. *Vasco da Gama*. Troll, 1979.

Knowlton, Jack. *Maps and Globes*. Harper & Row, 1985.

Kramer, Ann, and Simon Adams. *Exploration and Empire*. Warwick Press, 1990.

Krensky, Stephen. *Conqueror and Hero: The Search for Alexander*. Little, Brown, 1981.

______. *Who Really Discovered America?* Hastings House, 1987.

Landstrom, Bjorn. *Sailing Ships*. Doubleday, 1969.

LaPlaca, Michael. *How to Draw Boats, Trains and Planes*. Watermill Press, 1982.

Lasker, Joe. *Alexander the Great*. Viking, 1983.

______. *Merry Ever After*. Viking, 1976.

______. *Tournament of Knights*. Harper & Row, 1986.

Lasky, Kathryn. *Tall Ships*. Scribner's, 1978.

______. *The Weaver's Gift*. Frederick Warne, 1980.

Landau, Elaine. *The Sioux*. Franklin Watts, 1989.

Lauber, Patricia. *How We Learned the Earth Is Round*. Crowell, 1990.

______. *An Octopus Is Amazing*. Crowell, 1991.

______. *Snakes Are Hunters*. Crowell, 1988.

______. *Who Discovered America?* Random House, 1970.

Lee, Martin. *The Seminoles*. Franklin Watts, 1989.

Lehner, Ernst, and Johanna Lehner. *How They Saw the New World: A Most Revealing and Wonderful Collection of over 200 Rare Woodcuts and Engravings of Olde Maps, the Natives, Plants, Views, Towns and Curious Animals of the Newly Discovered Land*. Tudor Publishing, 1966.

Leon, George deLucenay. *Explorers of the Americas before Columbus*. Franklin Watts, 1989.

Lepthien, Emilie U. *Buffalo*. Children's Press, 1989.

______. *The Cherokee*. Children's Press, 1985.

Lester, Julius. *To Be a Slave*. Dial, 1968.

Let's Discover Ships and Boats. Raintree, 1981.

Lingelbach, Jenepher. *Hands-On Nature: Information and Activities for Exploring the Environment with Children*. Vermont Institute of Natural Science, 1986.

Lippman, Peter. *Busy Boats*. Random House, 1977.

Liptak, Karen. *North American Indian Sign Language*. Franklin Watts, 1990.

Livingston, Myra Cohn. *Celebrations*. Holiday House, 1985.

Livingston, Myra Cohn, ed. *O Frabjous Day*. Atheneum, 1977.

Luling, Virginia. *Indians of the North American Plains*. Silver Burdett, 1979.

Lye, Kenneth. *Explorers*. Silver Burdett, 1983.

Lyons, George. *Pacific Coast Indians of North America*. Messner, 1983.

Macdonald, Fiona. *The Middle Ages*. Silver Burdett, 1984.

McCall, Edith. *Pirates and Privateers*. Children's Press, 1980.

McCormack, Alan J. *Inventors Workshop*. Pitman Learning, 1981.

McFall, Christie. *Maps Mean Adventure*. Dodd, Mead, 1972.

McIntyre, Loren. *The Incredible Incas and Their Timeless Land*. National Geographic Society, 1975.

McKissack, Patricia. *The Apache*. Children's Press, 1984.

______. *Aztec Indians*. Children's Press, 1985.

______. *The Inca*. Children's Press, 1985.

______. *The Maya*. Children's Press, 1985.

McMullan, David. *Atlantis: The Missing Continent*. Raintree, 1977.

Maestro, Betsy, and Giulio Maestro. *The Discovery of the Americas*. Lothrop, Lee & Shepard, 1991.

Magnuson, Magnus. *Viking Expansion Westward*. Henry Z. Walck, 1973.

Mango, Karin N. *Mapmaking*. Messner, 1984.

Marrin, Albert. *The Sea Rovers: Pirates, Privateers, and Buccaneers*. Atheneum, 1988.

Martell, Hazel. *The Vikings*. Warwick Press, 1986.

Martin, Frances Gardiner. *Raven-Who-Sets-Things-Right: Indian Tales of the Northwest Coast*. Harper & Row, 1975.

Martini, Teri. *Indians*. Children's Press, 1982.

Masselman, George. *The Atlantic: Sea of Darkness*. McGraw-Hill, 1969.

Matthews, Rupert. *Explorers*. Knopf, 1991.

______. *Viking Explorers*. Bookwright, 1991.

May, Julian. *Before the Indians*. Holiday House, 1969.

May, Robin. *A Plains Indian Warrior*. Rourke, 1988.

______. *Plains Indians of North America*. Rourke, 1987.

Mayo, Gretchen Will. *Earthmaker's Tales: North American Indian Stories about Earth Happenings*. Walker, 1989.

______. *Star Tales: North American Indian Stories about the Stars*. Walker, 1987.

Meltzer, Milton. *All Times, All Peoples*. Harper & Row, 1980.

Menton, Theodore. *The Illuminated Alphabet*. Dover Publications, 1971.

Merriman, Nick. *Early Humans*. Knopf, 1989.

Metayer, Maurice. *Tales from the Igloo*. St. Martin's Press, 1972.

Meyer, Carolyn, and Charles Gallencamp. *The Mystery of the Ancient Maya*. Atheneum, 1985.

Milord, Susan. *The Kids' Nature Book*. Williamson, 1989.

Miquel, Pierre. *The Age of Discovery*. Silver Burdett, 1980.

Mitgutsch, Ali. *From Cacao Bean to Chocolate*. Carolrhoda, 1981.

Monroe, Jean Guard, and Ray A. Williamson. *They Dance in the Sky*. Houghton Mifflin, 1987.

Moore, Patrick, and Henry Brinton. *Exploring Maps*. Hawthorn Books, 1967.

Morgan, Gwyneth. *Life in a Medieval Village*. Lerner, 1982.

Morrison, Marion. *An Inca Farmer*. Rourke, 1988.

Murphy, Barbara Beasley, and Norman Baker. *Thor Heyerdahl and the Reed Boat Ra*. Lippincott, 1974.

Murphy, Jim. *Weird and Wacky Inventions*. Crown, 1978.

Neal, Harry Edward. *Before Columbus: Who Discovered America?* Messner, 1981.

Nevins, Ann. *Super Stitches: A Book of Superstitions*. Holiday House, 1983.

Nougier, Louis-Rene. *The Days of the Mayas, Aztecs and Incas*. Silver Burdett, 1985.

Oakley, Ruth. *The North American Indians: In the Beginning*. Marshall Cavendish, 1991.

O'Bryne-Pelham, Fran, and Bernadette Balcer. *The Search for the Atocha Treasure*. Dillon, 1989.

Odijk, Pamela. *The Aztecs*. Silver Burdett, 1989.

______. *The Incas*. Silver Burdett, 1989.

______. *The Mayas*. Silver Burdett, 1989.

______. *The Phoenicians*. Silver Burdett, 1989.

Osinski, Alice. *The Eskimo*. Children's Press, 1985.

______. *The Navajo*. Children's Press, 1987.

______. *The Nez Perce*. Children's Press, 1988.

______. *The Sioux*. Children's Press, 1984.

Overbeck, Cynthia. *The Fish Book*. Lerner, 1978.

Patent, Dorothy Hinshaw. *Buffalo: The American Bison Today*. Clarion, 1986.

Perl, Lila. *Don't Sing before Breakfast, Don't Sleep in the Moonlight: Everyday Superstitions and How They Began*. Ticknor & Fields, 1988.

Pickering, Robert B. *I Can Be an Archaeologist*. Children's Press, 1987.

Pollard, Michael. *Finding the Way*. Schoolhouse Press, 1986.

Polo, Marco. *The Travels of Marco Polo, the Venetian*. Doubleday, 1948.

Poole, Frederick King. *Early Exploration of North America*. Franklin Watts, 1989.

Porell, Bruce. *Digging the Past: Archaeology in Your Own Backyard*. Addison-Wesley, 1979.

Powell, Anton. *Renaissance Italy*. Warwick Press, 1979.

Price, Christine. *Made in the Middle Ages*. Dutton, 1961.

Purdy, Susan, and Cass R. Sandak. *The Aztecs*. Silver Burdett, 1989.

______. *Eskimos*. Franklin Watts, 1982.

______. *North American Indians*. Franklin Watts, 1982.

Quackenbush, Robert. *Holiday Song Book*. Lothrop, Lee & Shepard, 1977.

Rabinowich, Ellen. *The Loch Ness Monster*. Franklin Watts, 1979.

Redleaf, Rhoda. *Open the Door, Let's Explore: Neighborhood Field Trips for Young Children*. Toys 'n Things Press, 1983.

Richardson, I. M. *Odysseus and the Cyclops*. Troll, 1984.

Roberts, David. *Lost City of the Incas*. Rand McNally, 1977.

Robinson, Gail. *Raven the Trickster*. Atheneum, 1982.

Ross, Stewart. *A Crusading Knight*. Rourke, 1986.

Roth, Susan. *Marco Polo: His Notebook*. Doubleday, 1990.

Rubenstone, Jessie. *Weaving for Beginners*. Lippincott, 1975.

Rugoff, Milton. *Marco Polo's Adventures in China*. American Heritage, 1964.

Rutland, J. P. *The Amazing Fact Book of Ships and Boats*. Creative Education, 1979.

Rutland, Jonathan. *Ships*. Warwick Press, 1975.

Ryan, Peter. *Explorers and Mapmakers*. Dutton, 1989.

San Souci, Robert D. *The Loch Ness Monster*. Greenhaven Press, 1989.

Scarry, Huck. *Looking into the Middle Ages*. Harper & Row, 1985.

Schaffler, Robert Haven, ed. *Days We Celebrate*. Dodd, Mead, 1940.

Schere, Monroe. *The Story of Maps*. Prentice Hall, 1969.

Schiller, Barbara. *The Vinlanders' Saga*. Holt, Rinehart & Winston, 1966.

Schoolcraft, Henry R. *Legends of the American Indians*. Crescent, 1980.

Schwartz, Alvin. *Gold and Silver, Silver and Gold: Tales of Hidden Treasure*. Farrar, Straus & Giroux, 1988.

Scott, Geoffrey. *Egyptian Boats*. Carolrhoda, 1981.

Scott, Jack Denton. *The Return of the Buffalo*. Putnam, 1976.

Sechrist, Elizabeth. *Poems for Red Letter Days*. Macrae Smith, 1951.

Seixas, Judith. *Tobacco: What It Is, What It Does*. Greenwillow, 1981.

Selsam, Millicent E., and Joyce Hunt. *A First Look at Sharks*. Walker, 1979.

Sewall, Marcia. *People of the Breaking Day*. Atheneum, 1990.

Seymour, Simon. *Volcanoes*. Morrow, 1988.

Shaffer, Carolyn, and Erica Fielder. *City Safari: A Sierra Club Explorer's Guide to Urban Adventures for Grownups and Kids*. Sierra Club, 1987.

Siegel, Alice, and Margo McLoone. *The Herb and Spice Book for Kids*. Holt, Rinehart & Winston, 1978.

Siegel, Beatrice. *Indians of the Woodlands before and after the Pilgrims*. Walker, 1972.

Silverstein, Shel. *A Light in the Attic*. Harper & Row, 1974.

______. *Where the Sidewalk Ends*. Harper & Row, 1974.

Simon, Charnan. *Explorers of the Ancient World*. Children's Press, 1990.

______. *Leif Eriksson and the Vikings: The Norse Discovery of America*. Children's Press, 1991.

Singer, Marilyn. *Exotic Birds*. Doubleday, 1990.

Slocombe, Lorna. *Sailing Basics*. Prentice Hall, 1982.

Smith, J. H. Greg. *Eskimos: The Inuit of the Arctic*. Rourke, 1987.

Smythe, Malcolm. *Build Your Own Space Station*. Franklin Watts, 1985.

Snyder, Gerald. *Is There a Loch Ness Monster?* Messner, 1977.

Soloff-Levy, Barbara. *How to Draw Sea Creatures*. Watermill, 1987.

Stangl, Jean. *Paper Stories*. Fearon, 1984.

Steele, Anne. *An Aztec Warrior*. Rourke, 1988.

Steele, William O. *Talking Bones: Secrets of Indian Burial Mounds*. Harper & Row, 1978.

Stefoff, Rebecca. *Ferdinand Magellan and the Discovery of the World Ocean*. Chelsea House, 1990.

______. *Marco Polo*. Chelsea House, 1990.

Stein, R. Conrad. *Hernando Cortés: Conqueror of Mexico*. Children's Press, 1991.

Steltzer, Ulli. *Building an Igloo*. Meadow House, 1981.

Sterling, Thomas. *Exploration of Africa*. American Heritage, 1963.

Storr, Catherine. *Odysseus and the Enchanters*. Raintree, 1985.

Stuart, George E., and Gene S. Stuart. *The Mysterious Maya*. National Geographic Society, 1975.

Sugden, John. *Sir Francis Drake*. Henry Holt, 1990.

Sweeney, James R. *Sea Monsters*. David McKay, 1977.

Syme, Ronald. *Amerigo Vespucci: Scientist and Sailor*. Morrow, 1969.

______. *John Cabot and His Son Sebastian*. Morrow, 1972.

______. *Vasco da Gama: Sailor toward the Sunrise*. Morrow, 1959.

______. *Verrazano: Explorer of the Atlantic Coast*. Morrow, 1973.

Tamarin, Alfred, and Shirley Glubok. *Ancient Indians of the Southwest*. Doubleday, 1975.

Tashjian, Virginia. *Juba This and Juba That*. Little, Brown, 1969.

______. *With a Deep Sea Smile*. Little, Brown, 1974.

Taylor, Barbara. *Be an Inventor*. Harcourt Brace Jovanovich, 1987.

Tayntor, Elizabeth, Paul Erickson, and Les Kaufman. *Dive to the Coral Reefs*. Crown, 1986.

Thurman-Veith, Jan. *Natural Wonders*. Monday Morning Press, 1986.

Tinling, Marion. *Women into the Unknown: A Sourcebook on Women Explorers and Travelers*. Greenwood Press, 1984.

Tomchek, Ann Heinrichs. *The Hopi*. Children's Press, 1987.

Tunis, Edwin. *Indians*. Crowell, 1979.

______. *Oars, Sails and Steam*. World, 1952.

Turner, Geoffrey. *Indians of North America*. Sterling, 1992.

Unstead, R. J. *From Cavemen to Vikings*. Adam and Charles Black, 1982.

Vandervoort, Thomas J. *Sailing Is for Me*. Lerner, 1981.

Ventura, Piero. *1492 The Year of the New World*. Putnam, 1992.

______. *Man and the Horse*. Putnam, 1980.

______. *Venice: Birth of a City*. Putnam, 1987.

Villiers, Alan. *The New Mayflower*. Scribner's, 1958.

Vincent, Jean Anne, comp. *Patriotic Poems America Loves*. Doubleday, 1968.

Ward, Ralph T. *Ships through History*. Bobbs-Merrill, 1973.

Watson, Jane Werner. *The First Americans: Tribes of North America*. Pantheon, 1980.

Watson, Lucilla. *An Ice Age Hunter*. Rourke, 1987.

Weil, Lisl. *Let's Go to the Museum*. Holiday House, 1989.

Weiss, Harvey. *How to Be an Inventor*. Crowell, 1980.

______. *Maps: Getting from Here to There*. Houghton Mifflin, 1991.

______. *Sailing Small Boats*. Young Scott, 1967.

______. *Ship Models and How to Build Them*. Crowell, 1973.

Wharton, Anthony. *Discovering Sea Birds*. Franklin Watts, 1987.

Wheeler, M. J. *First Came the Indians*. Macmillan, 1983.

Whitman, Sylvia. *Hernando de Soto and the Explorers of the American South*. Chelsea House, 1991.

Williams, Garth. *Baby Farm Animals*. Western, 1983.

Williams, J. Alan. *Interplanetary Toy Book*. Macmillan, 1985.

Williams, Jay. *Life in the Middle Ages*. Random House, 1966.

Windrow, Martin. *The Invaders*. Marshall Cavendish, 1979.

Wiseman, Ann. *Making Things, Book II*. Little, Brown, 1975.

Wolfson, Evelyn. *From Abenaki to Zuni: A Dictionary of Native American Tribes*. Walker, 1988.

______. *Growing Up Indian*. Walker, 1986.

Wood, Marion. *Ancient American*. Facts on File, 1990.

______. *Spirits, Heroes and Hunters from North American Indian Mythology*. Schocken Books, 1982.

Wulffson, Don L. *The Invention of Ordinary Things*. Lothrop, Lee & Shepard, 1981.

Wurmfeld, Hope Herman. *Boatbuilder*. Macmillan, 1988.

Yates, Elizabeth. *Amos Fortune: Free Man*. Dutton, 1967.

Yue, Charlotte. *The Tipi: A Center of Native American Life*. Knopf, 1984.

Yue, Charlotte, and David Yue. *The Igloo*. Houghton Mifflin, 1988.

______. *The Pueblo*. Houghton Mifflin, 1986.

PICTURE BOOKS

Aesop. *The Goose That Laid the Golden Egg*. Andre Deutsch, 1986.

Aitken, Amy. *Kate and Mona in the Jungle*. Bradbury, 1981.

Aliki. *A Medieval Feast*. Crowell, 1983.

Allen, Pamela. *The Hidden Treasure*. Putnam, 1989.

______. *I Wish I Had a Pirate Suit*. Viking, 1990.

______. *Who Sank the Boat?* Coward, McCann & Geoghegan, 1983.

Anderson, Joan. *Harry's Helicopter*. Morrow, 1990.

Anderson, Lonzo. *The Day the Hurricane Happened*. Scribner's, 1974.

Anholt, Catherine. *When I Was a Baby*. Little, Brown, 1989.

Anno, Mitsumasa. *Anno's Italy*. Collins World, 1978.

______. *Anno's Journey*. Collins World, 1977.

______. *Anno's Medieval World*. Philomel, 1979.

______. *Anno's U.S.A.* Putnam, 1983.

Ardizzone, Edward. *Little Tim and the Brave Sea Captain*. Henry Z. Walck, 1955.

______. *Ship's Cook Ginger*. Macmillan, 1977.

Asch, Frank. *Mooncake*. Prentice Hall, 1983.

Ata, Te. *Baby Rattlesnake*. Children's Book Press, 1989.

Balian, Lorna. *The Aminal*. Abingdon, 1972.

Baker, Leslie. *Third-Story Cat*. Little, Brown, 1987.

Ballard, Robin. *Cat and Alex and the Magic Flying Carpet*. HarperCollins, 1991.

Barbour, Karen. *Little Nino's Pizzeria*. Harcourt Brace Jovanovich, 1987.

Barrett, Judi. *Cloudy with a Chance of Meatballs*. Atheneum, 1978.

Barton, Byron. *Boats*. Crowell, 1986.

______. *I Want to Be an Astronaut*. Crowell, 1988.

Baum, Louis. *JuJu and the Pirate*. Peter Bedrick, 1983.

Benchley, Nathaniel. *Snorri and the Strangers*. Harper & Row, 1976.

Benjamin, Alan. *A Change of Plans*. Four Winds Press, 1982.

______. *Ribtickle Town*. Four Winds Press, 1983.

Blos, Joan. *Martin's Hats*. Morrow, 1984.

Bodsworth, Nan. *A Nice Walk in the Jungle*. Viking, 1990.

Bradman, Tony. *It Came from Outer Space*. Dial, 1992.

Brandenberg, Franz. *Otto Is Different*. Greenwillow, 1985.

Brown, Marc. *The True Francine*. Little, Brown, 1981.

Buckingham, Simon. *Alec and His Flying Bed*. Lothrop, Lee & Shepard, 1990.

Burnett, Carol. *What I Want to Be When I Grow Up*. Simon & Schuster, 1975.

Burningham, John. *Come Away from the Water, Shirley*. Crowell, 1977.

______. *John Patrick Norman McHennessey—The Boy Who Was Always Late*. Crown, 1987.

______. *Mr. Gumpy's Outing*. Henry Holt, 1970.

______. *Time to Get Out of the Water, Shirley*. Crowell, 1978.

______. *Where's Julius?* Crown, 1986.

Carey, Valerie. *Harriet and William and the Terrible Creature*. Dutton, 1985.

Carle, Eric. *Rooster's Off to See the World*. Picture Book Studio, 1972.

Carlson, Nancy. *Loudmouth George and the New Neighbors*. Carolrhoda, 1983.

Carrick, Carol. *Octopus*. Clarion, 1978.

Carrick, Donald. *Harald and the Giant Knight*. Houghton Mifflin, 1982.

Cleaver, Elizabeth. *The Enchanted Caribou*. Macmillan, 1985.

Clements, Andrew. *Big Al*. Picture Book Studio, 1988.

Cohen, Caron Lee. *Whiffle Squeek*. Dodd, Mead, 1987.

Cole, Joanna. *The Magic School Bus Lost in the Solar System*. Scholastic, 1990.

Collington, Peter. *The Angel and the Soldier Boy*. Knopf, 1987.

Cooper, Susan. *The Silver Cow*. Macmillan, 1983.

Crews, Donald. *Harbor*. Greenwillow, 1982.

______. *Parade*. Greenwillow, 1983.

Dalmais, Anne-Marie. *The Elephant's Airplane and Other Machines*. Golden, 1984.

Davis, Maggie S. *The Best Way to Ripton*. Holiday House, 1982.

Day, Edward. *John Tabor's Ride*. Knopf, 1987.

DeArmond, Dale. *Berry Woman's Children*. Greenwillow, 1985.

Demarest, Chris. *The Lunatic Adventures of Kitman and Willy*. Simon & Schuster, 1988.

Demi. *Find Demi's Sea Creatures*. Grosset & Dunlap, 1991.

Denton, Terry. *Home Is the Sailor*. Houghton Mifflin, 1988.

dePaola, Tomie. *Bill and Pete*. Putnam, 1978.

______. *Charlie Needs a Cloak*. Prentice Hall, 1973.

______. *The Clown of God*. Harcourt Brace Jovanovich, 1978.

______. *The Knight and the Dragon*. Putnam, 1980.

______. *The Popcorn Book*. Holiday House, 1978.

Dewey, Ariane. *Lafitte the Pirate*. Greenwillow, 1985.

______. *The Thunder God's Son*. Greenwillow, 1981.

Domanska, Janina. *I Saw a Ship A-Sailing*. Macmillan, 1972.

Dragonwagon, Cresent. *Coconut*. Harper & Row, 1984.

Drescher, Henrik. *Simon's Book*. Lothrop, Lee & Shepard, 1983.

Dupasquier, Philippe. *Dear Daddy....* Bradbury, 1985.

______. *Jack at Sea*. Prentice Hall, 1987.

Dutton, Cheryl. *Not in Here, Dad*. Barron's, 1989.

Dyke, John. *Pigwig and the Pirates*. Methuen, 1977.

Ekker, Ernst A. *What Is beyond the Hill?* Lippincott, 1985.

Esbensen, Barbara Juster. *The Star Maiden: An Ojibway Tale*. Little, Brown, 1988.

Faulkner, Matt. *The Amazing Voyage of Jackie Grace*. Scholastic, 1987.

Felix, Monique. *The Further Adventures of the Little Mouse Trapped in a Book*. Green Tiger Press, 1983.

Fischetto, Laura. *All Pigs on Deck*. Delacorte, 1991.

Fisher, Leonard Everett. *Prince Henry the Navigator*. Macmillan, 1990.

______. *Pyramid of the Sun, Pyramid of the Moon*. Macmillan, 1988.

______. *Sailboat Lost*. Macmillan, 1991.

Flack, Marjorie. *Angus and the Cat*. Doubleday, 1931.

Florian, Douglas. *People Working*. Crowell, 1983.

Foreman, Michael. *Land of Dreams*. Holt, Rinehart & Winston, 1982.

______. *Panda's Puzzle and His Voyage of Discovery*. Bradbury, 1977.

Fradon, Dana. *Sir Dana: A Knight, as Told by His Trusty Armor*. Dutton, 1988.

Freeman, Don. *Come Again, Pelican*. Viking, 1961.

French, Fiona. *Future Story*. Oxford University Press, 1983.

Freschet, Berniece. *Bernard Sees the World*. Scribner's, 1976.

Friedman, Ina R. *How My Parents Learned to Eat*. Houghton Mifflin, 1984.

Fritz, Jean. *The Good Giants and the Bad Pukwudgies*. Putnam, 1982.

Gackenbach, Dick. *Dog for a Day*. Clarion, 1987.

Gay, Michel. *Little Boat*. Macmillan, 1985.

Geisert, Arthur. *The Ark*. Houghton Mifflin, 1988.

Gerrard, Roy. *Mik's Mammoth*. Farrar, Straus & Giroux, 1990.

______. *Sir Cedric*. Farrar, Straus & Giroux, 1984.

______. *Sir Cedric Rides Again*. Farrar, Straus & Giroux, 1986.

Gibbons, Gail. *The Boat Book*. Holiday House, 1983.

______. *Sunken Treasure*. Crowell, 1988.

Ginsburg, Mirra. *Four Brave Sailors*. Greenwillow, 1987.

______. *The Proud Maiden, Tungak, and the Sun: How Moon Came to Live in the Sky*. Macmillan, 1974.

Goble, Paul. *Buffalo Woman*. Bradbury, 1984.

______. *Iktomi and the Boulder: A Plains Indian Story*. Franklin Watts, 1988.

Goodall, John S. *Paddy under Water*. Atheneum, 1984.

______. *The Story of a Farm*. Macmillan, 1989.

______. *The Story of an English Village*. Atheneum, 1979.

Graham, Thomas. *Mr. Bear's Boat*. Dutton, 1988.

Gramatky, Hardie. *Little Toot*. Putnam, 1939.

Grimm, Jacob, and Wilhelm K. Grimm. *The Fisherman and His Wife*. Picture Book Studio, 1988.

Haas, Irene. *The Maggie B*. Atheneum, 1975.

Haley, Gail E. *Sea Tale*. Dutton, 1990.

Hall, Carol. *I Been There*. Doubleday, 1977.

______. *Super-Vroomer!* Doubleday, 1978.

Handford, Martin. *Find Waldo Now*. Little, Brown, 1988.

Hartman, Gail. *As the Crow Flies: A First Book of Maps*. Bradbury, 1991.

Haus, Felice. *Beep! Beep! I'm a Jeep!* Random, 1986.

Havill, Juanita. *Jamaica's Find*. Houghton Mifflin, 1986.

Hayes, Geoffrey. *The Secret of Foghorn Island*. Random House, 1988.

Heine, Helme. *The Pearl*. Atheneum, 1985.

Helldorfer, M. C. *The Mapmaker's Daughter*. Bradbury, 1991.

Heller, Nicholas. *The Adventure at Sea*. Greenwillow, 1988.

Heller, Ruth. *How to Hide an Octopus and Other Sea Creatures*. Grosset & Dunlap, 1985.

Hewitt, Garnet. *Ytek and the Arctic Orchard*. Vanguard, 1981.

Hewitt, Kathryn. *King Midas and the Golden Touch*. Harcourt Brace Jovanovich, 1987.

Heyer, Marilee. *The Weaving of a Dream: A Chinese Folktale*. Viking, 1986.

Hinojosa, Francisco. *The Old Lady Who Ate People: Frightening Stories*. Little, Brown, 1984.

Hoban, Russell. *How Tom Beat Captain Najork and His Hired Sportsmen*. Atheneum, 1974.

Hoopes, Lyn Littlefield. *Half-a-Button*. Harper & Row, 1989.

Hutchins, Pat. *King Henry's Palace*. Greenwillow, 1983.

______. *One-Eyed Jake*. Greenwillow, 1979.

James, Simon. *My Friend the Whale*. Bantam, 1991.

Johnson, Jane. *Today I Thought I'd Run Away*. Dutton, 1985.

Jonas, Ann. *Now We Can Go*. Greenwillow, 1986.

______. *Round Trip*. Greenwillow, 1983.

______. *The Trek*. Greenwillow, 1985.

Kalan, Robert. *Blue Sea*. Greenwillow, 1979.

Kandoian, Ellen. *Is Anybody Up?* Putnam, 1989.

______. *Under the Sun*. Dodd, Mead, 1987.

Keats, Ezra Jack. *My Dog Is Lost*. Crowell, 1960.

______. *Regards to the Man in the Moon*. Macmillan, 1985.

______. *The Trip*. Greenwillow, 1978.

Kellogg, Steven. *The Island of the Skog*. Dial, 1973.

______. *The Mysterious Tadpole*. Dial, 1977.

Khalsa, Dayal Kaur. *How Pizza Came to Queens*. Crown, 1989.

Kipling, Rudyard. *The Elephant's Child*. Harcourt Brace Jovanovich, 1983.

Kitamura, Satoshi. *UFO Diary*. Farrar, Straus & Giroux, 1989.

Koehler, Phoebe. *The Day We Met You*. Bradbury, 1990.

Kraus, Robert. *The Gondolier of Venice*. Dutton, 1976.

______. *Herman the Helper*. Prentice Hall, 1974.

Lasker, Joe. *Tales of a Seadog Family*. Viking, 1974.

Lattimore, Deborah. *The Flame of Peace: A Tale of the Aztecs*. HarperCollins, 1987.

______. *The Sailor Who Captured the Sea: A Story of the Book of Kells*. HarperCollins, 1991.

Lecher, Doris. *Angelita's Magic Yarn*. Farrar, Straus & Giroux, 1992.

Lennon, John. *Imagine*. Birch Lane Press, 1990.

Lenski, Lois. *The Little Sail Boat*. Henry Z. Walck, 1937.

Lessac, Frane. *My Little Island*. Lippincott, 1984.

Lewis, Thomas. *Hill of Fire*. Harper & Row, 1971.

Lillegard, Dee. *Sitting in My Box*. Dutton, 1989.

Lindgren, Barbro. *Wild Baby Goes to Sea*. Greenwillow, 1982.

Lionni, Leo. *Fish Is Fish*. Pantheon, 1970.

______. *I Want to Stay Here! I Want to Go There!* Pantheon, 1977.

______. *Matthew's Dream*. Knopf, 1991.

______. *Nicholas, Where Have You Been?* Knopf, 1987.

______. *Swimmy*. Pantheon, 1963.

Lippman, Peter. *Busy Boats*. Random House, 1977.

Locker, Thomas. *Sailing with the Wind*. Dial, 1986.

Lund, Doris Herold. *Did You Ever Dream?* Parents Magazine Press, 1969.

McCarthy, Patricia. *Ocean Parade*. Dial, 1990.

McDermott, Gerald. *Arrow to the Sun: A Pueblo Indian Tale*. Viking, 1974.

______. *Papagayo the Mischief Maker*. Windmill Books, 1980.

MacDonald, Golden. *The Little Island*. Doubleday, 1946.

MacDonald, Suse. *Space Spinners*. Dial, 1991.

McGovern, Ann. *Nicholas Bentley Stoningpot III*. Holiday House, 1982.

McLerran, Alice. *Roxaboxen*. Lothrop, Lee & Shepard, 1991.

McNaughton, Colin. *Anton B. Stanton and the Pirates*. Doubleday, 1979.

______. *Jolly Roger and the Pirates of Abdul the Skinhead*. Simon & Schuster, 1988.

McPhail, David. *Andrew's Bath*. Little, Brown, 1984.

______. *Dream Child*. Dutton, 1985.

Maestro, Betsy. *Big City Port*. Four Winds Press, 1983.

Maestro, Betsy, and Giulio Maestro. *Ferryboat*. Crowell, 1986.

Mahy, Margaret. *The Man Whose Mother Was a Pirate*. Viking, 1986.

Manson, Christopher. *Two Travelers*. Holt, Rinehart & Winston, 1990.

Marshak, Susan. *I Am the Ocean*. Arcade, 1991.

Marshall, Edward. *Space Case*. Dial, 1980.

Marshall, James. *George and Martha Round and Round*. Houghton Mifflin, 1988.

Martin, Rafe. *Will's Mammoth*. Putnam, 1989.

Matsuoka, Kyoko. *There's a Hippo in My Bath!* Doubleday, 1982.

Meyers, Bernice. *The Extraordinary Invention*. Macmillan, 1984.

Mobley, Jane. *The Star Husband*. Doubleday, 1977.

Moerbeek, Kees. *Six Brave Explorers*. Price Stern Sloan, 1988.

______. *When the Wild Pirates Go Sailing*. Price Stern Sloan, 1988.

Morris, Ann. *Bread, Bread, Bread*. Lothrop, Lee & Shepard, 1989.

Moses, Amy. *I Am an Explorer*. Children's Press, 1990.

Murphy, Jill. *What Next, Baby Bear?* Dial, 1983.

Neuhaus, David. *His Finest Hour*. Viking, 1984.

Newsham, Ian, and Wendy Newsham. *Lost in the Jungle*. Kaye & Ward, 1987.

Noble, Trinka Hakes. *Hansy's Mermaid*. Dial, 1983.

Nolan, Dennis. *Wizard McBean and His Flying Machine*. Prentice Hall, 1979.

Oakley, Graham. *The Diary of a Church Mouse*. Atheneum, 1987.

Obrist, Jurg. *The Miser Who Wanted the Sun*. Atheneum, 1984.

Otsuka, Yuzo. *Suho and the White Horse*. Viking, 1981.

Pallotta, Jerry. *Ocean Alphabet Book*. Charlesbridge, 1986.

Paterson, Diane. *The Bathtub Ocean*. Dial, 1973.

Patz, Nancy. *Gina Farina and the Prince of Mintz*. Harcourt Brace Jovanovich, 1986.

Paul, Korky, and Peter Cart. *Captain Teachum's Buried Treasure*. Oxford University Press, 1989.

Peet, Bill. *Chester the Worldly Pig*. Houghton Mifflin, 1978.

______. *Cowardly Clyde*. Houghton Mifflin, 1979.

______. *Cyrus the Unsinkable Sea Serpent*. Houghton Mifflin, 1975.

______. *How Droofus the Dragon Lost His Head*. Houghton Mifflin, 1971.

Peppe, Rodney. *The Kettleship Pirates*. Lothrop, Lee & Shepard, 1983.

Pfanner, Louise. *Louise Builds a Boat*. Orchard, 1989.

Pinkwater, Daniel. *The Big Orange Splot*. Hastings House, 1977.

______. *Guys from Space*. Macmillan, 1989.

Politi, Leo. *Three Stalks of Corn*. Scribner's, 1976.

Pomerantz, Charlotte. *Flap Your Wings and Try*. Greenwillow, 1989.

Pryor, Bonnie. *Mr. Munday and the Space Creatures*. Simon & Schuster, 1989.

Quin-Harkin, Janet. *Peter Penny's Dance*. Dial, 1976.

Rand, Gloria. *Salty Dog*. Holt, Rinehart & Winston, 1989.

______. *Salty Sails North*. Holt, Rinehart & Winston, 1990.

Rey, H. A. *Curious George*. Houghton Mifflin, 1941.

______. *Curious George Gets a Medal*. Houghton Mifflin, 1957.

______. *Curious George Rides a Bike*. Houghton Mifflin, 1952.

______. *Curious George Takes a Job*. Houghton Mifflin, 1947.

Robbins, Ken. *Boats*. Scholastic, 1989.

Roche, P. K. *Webster and Arnold and the Giant Box*. Dial, 1980.

Rockwell, Anne. *Boats*. Dutton, 1982.

Rohmer, Harriet, and Jesus Guerrero Rea. *Atariba and Niguayona*. Children's Book Press, 1988.

______. *The Legend of Food Mountain*. Children's Book Press, 1982.

Ross, Katherine. *Bear Island*. Random House, 1987.

Ross, Tony. *The Boy Who Cried Wolf*. Dial, 1985.

______. *The Treasures of Cozy Cove*. Farrar, Straus & Giroux, 1989.

Roth, Susan L. *Kanahena*. St. Martin's Press, 1988.

______. *The Story of Light*. Morrow, 1990.

Ryder, Joanne. *Winter Whale*. Morrow, 1991.

San Souci, Robert D. *The Legend of Scarface: A Blackfeet Indian Tale*. Doubleday, 1978.

Scieszka, Jon. *The True Story of the Three Little Pigs by A. Wolf*. Viking Kestrel, 1989.

Sendak, Maurice. *Hector Protector and As I Went over the Water*. Harper & Row, 1965.

______. *Outside Over There*. Harper & Row, 1981.

______. *Where the Wild Things Are*. Harper & Row, 1963.

Seuss, Dr. *I Had Trouble in Getting to Solla Sollew*. Random House, 1965.

______. *Yertle the Turtle and Other Stories*. Random House, 1958.

Seymour, Peter. *What's in the Deep Blue Sea?* Henry Holt, 1990.

______. *What's in the Jungle?* Henry Holt, 1988.

Sharmat, Marjorie Weinman. *Gila Monsters Meet You at the Airport*. Macmillan, 1980.

Shaw, Nancy. *Sheep on a Ship*. Houghton Mifflin, 1989.

Shecter, Ben. *If I Had a Ship*. Doubleday, 1970.

Sheldon, Dyan. *Whale's Song*. Dial, 1991.

Shetterly, Susan Hand. *The Dwarf-Wizard of Uxmal*. Atheneum, 1990.

Shulevitz, Uri. *The Treasure*. Farrar, Straus & Giroux, 1979.

Siberell, Anne. *Whale in the Sky*. Dutton, 1982.

Sleator, William. *The Angry Moon*. Little, Brown, 1970.

Smith, Barry. *The First Voyage of Christopher Columbus*. Viking, 1992.

Smith, Jim. *Nimbus the Explorer*. Little, Brown, 1981.

Smith, Roger. *Empty Island*. Crocodile, 1991.

Smyth, Gwenda. *A Pet for Mrs. Arbuckle*. Crown, 1981.

Spier, Peter. *Hurrah, We're Outward Bound!* Doubleday, 1968.

______. *People*. Doubleday, 1980.

Stadler, John. *Gorman and the Treasure Chest*. Bradbury, 1984.

Steig, William. *Amos and Boris*. Farrar, Straus & Giroux, 1971.

______. *The Zabajaba Jungle*. Farrar, Straus & Giroux, 1991.

Stevenson, James. *"Could Be Worse!"* Greenwillow, 1977.

Stevenson, Robert Louis. *Block City*. Dutton, 1988.

Tafuri, Nancy. *Junglewalk*. Greenwillow, 1988.

Taylor, Mark. *The Case of the Purloined Compass*. Atheneum, 1985.

______. *Henry Explores the Jungle*. Atheneum, 1968.

______. *Henry Explores the Mountains*. Atheneum, 1975.

______. *Henry the Castaway*. Atheneum, 1972.

______. *Henry the Explorer*. Little, Brown, 1966.

Testa, Fulvio. *If You Take a Pencil*. Dial, 1982.

Thaler, Mike. *How Far Will a Rubber Band Stretch?* Parents Magazine Press, 1974.

Titherington, Jeanne. *Where Are You Going, Emma?* Greenwillow, 1988.

Tobias, Tobi. *The Quitting Deal*. Viking, 1975.

Tompert, Ann. *Charlotte and Charles*. Crown, 1979.

______. *Little Fox Goes to the End of the World*. Crown, 1976.

Trez, Denise. *The Little Knight's Dragon*. Collins World, 1963.

Udry, Janice May. *Let's Be Enemies*. Harper & Row, 1961.

Ungerer, Tomi. *Moon Man*. Harper & Row, 1967.

Van Allsburg, Chris. *Ben's Dream*. Houghton Mifflin, 1982.

______. *The Mysteries of Harris Burdick*. Houghton Mifflin, 1984.

______. *The Wreck of the Zephyr*. Houghton Mifflin, 1983.

______. *The Wretched Stone*. Houghton Mifflin, 1991.

Vidal, Beatriz. *The Legend of El Dorado*. Knopf, 1991.

Wahl, Jan. *The Clumpets Go Sailing*. Parents Magazine Press, 1975.

Wade, Alan. *I'm Flying*. Knopf, 1990.

Walsh, Jill Paton. *Lost and Found*. Andre Deutsch, 1984.

Watanabe, Shigeo. *I Can Take a Walk*. Putnam, 1984.

Waters, Tony. *The Sailor's Bride*. Doubleday, 1991.

Weil, Lisl. *Pandora's Box*. Atheneum, 1986.

Weller, Frances Ward. *I Wonder If I'll See a Whale*. Philomel, 1991.

West, Colin. *Have You Seen the Crocodile?* Lippincott, 1986.

Westwood, Jennifer. *Going to Squintum's*. Dial, 1985.

Where in the World Is Geo? Barrons, 1991.

Wiesner, David. *Free Fall*. Lothrop, Lee & Shepard, 1988.

______. *Hurricane*. Clarion, 1990.

______. *Tuesday*. Clarion, 1991.

Wildsmith, Brian. *Pelican*. Pantheon, 1982.

Williams, Vera B. *Stringbean's Trip to the Shining Sea*. Greenwillow, 1988.

______. *Three Days on a River in a Red Canoe*. Greenwillow, 1981.

Willis, Jeanne. *Earthlets: As Explained by Professor Xargle*. Dutton, 1989.

Wilson, Sarah. *Beware the Dragons!* Harper & Row, 1985.

______. *Muskrat, Muskrat, Eat Your Peas*. Simon & Schuster, 1989.

Winter, Jeannette. *Follow the Drinking Gourd*. Knopf, 1988.

Wood, Audrey. *King Bidgood's in the Bathtub*. Harcourt Brace Jovanovich, 1985.

Woychuk, Denis. *Pirates!* Lothrop, Lee & Shepard, 1992.

Yolen, Jane. *Encounter*. Harcourt Brace Jovanovich, 1992.

Yorinks, Arthur. *Company's Coming*. Crown, 1988.

______. *Hey, Al*. Farrar, Straus and Giroux, 1986.

Young, Ruth. *Daisy's Taxi*. Orchard, 1991.

Zemach, Harve. *The Judge*. Farrar, Straus & Giroux, 1969.

______. *Salt*. Follett, 1965.

GENERAL FICTION

Avi. *Something Upstairs: A Tale of Ghosts*. Franklin Watts, 1988.

Babbitt, Natalie. *Tuck Everlasting*. Farrar, Straus & Giroux, 1975.

Bellairs, John. *The Treasure of Alpheus Winterborn*. Harcourt Brace Jovanovich, 1985.

Bulla, Clyde Robert. *The Sword in the Tree*. Lothrop, Lee & Shepard, 1958.

Chaucer, Geoffrey. *Canterbury Tales*. Lothrop, Lee & Shepard, 1988.

Christopher, John. *Empty World*. Dutton, 1978.

Clark, Ann Nolan. *Secret of the Andes*. Viking, 1952.

Conrad, Pam. *Pedro's Journal: A Voyage with Christopher Columbus—August 3, 1492-February 14, 1493*. St. Martin's Press, 1991.

Davis, Gibbs. *Fishman and Charlie*. Houghton Mifflin, 1983.

Defoe, Daniel. *Robinson Crusoe*. Putnam, 1963.

Dyson, John. *Westward with Columbus*. Scholastic, 1991.

Fisher, Leonard Everett. *Jason & the Golden Fleece*. Holiday House, 1990.

Fleischman, Sid. *The Ghost in the Noonday Sun*. Greenwillow, 1965.

Forman, Michael. *The Boy Who Sailed with Columbus*. Arcade, 1992.

Giff, Patricia Reilly. *Snaggle Doodles*. Delacorte, 1985.

Gray, Elizabeth Janet. *Adam of the Road*. Viking, 1942.

Hamilton, Virginia. *The House of Dies Drear*. Macmillan, 1968.

Houston, James. *Kiviok's Magic Journey*. Atheneum, 1973.

Honness, Elizabeth. *The Mystery of the Maya Jade*. Lippincott, 1971.

James, Carolyn. *Digging Up the Past: The Story of an Archaeological Adventure*. Franklin Watts, 1990.

Johnson, Charles. *Pieces of Eight*. Discovery, 1989.

Lane, Carolyn. *Ghost Island*. Houghton Mifflin, 1985.

McGraw, Eloise. *The Money Room*. Macmillan, 1981.

Martin, Susan. *I Sailed with Columbus: The Adventures of a Ship's Boy*. Overlook Press, 1991.

Moeri, Louise. *Journey to the Treasure*. Scholastic, 1985.

Naden, C. J. *Jason and the Golden Fleece*. Troll, 1980.

Osborne, Chester. *The Memory String*. Macmillan, 1984.

Pierce, Tamora. *Alanna: The First Adventure*. Macmillan, 1983.

Pyle, Howard. *Men of Iron*. Harper Brothers, 1930.

Rockwell, Thomas. *How to Eat Fried Worms*. Franklin Watts, 1973.

Schlein, Miriam. *I Sailed with Columbus*. HarperCollins, 1991.

Sherlock, Philip M. *The Iguana's Tale*. Crowell, 1969.

Shub, Elizabeth. *Cutlass in the Snow*. Greenwillow, 1986.

Skurzynski, Gloria. *Minstrel in the Tower*. Random House, 1988.

Sloat, Teri. *Eye of the Needle*. Dutton, 1990.

Smucker, Barbara. *Runaway to Freedom*. Harper & Row, 1971.

Steig, William. *Abel's Island*. Farrar, Straus & Giroux, 1978.

Stevenson, Robert Louis. *Treasure Island*. Macmillan, 1981.

Weil, Lisl. *Pandora's Box*. Atheneum, 1986.

Wyss, Johann D. *Swiss Family Robinson*. Putnam, 1949.

Zitger, Cary B. *The Moon of Falling Leaves: The Great Buffalo Hunt*. Franklin Watts, 1988.

Index

About the Author

Diane Ramsay has been a librarian since 1978 and currently serves as the children's librarian of the Worcester, Massachusetts, Public Library, Greendale Branch. In addition, she is a storyteller and presenter of children's puppet programs in schools and libraries and has written for *Learning, Cobblestone Magazine, The Friend*, and *Public Libraries*. Diane Ramsay is married to a fellow librarian, and they have three children.